Twins in African and Diaspora Cultures

Twins
in African and Diaspora Cultures

DOUBLE TROUBLE, TWICE BLESSED

EDITED BY PHILIP M. PEEK

Indiana University Press

BLOOMINGTON AND INDIANAPOLIS

This book is a publication of

Indiana University Press
601 North Morton Street
Bloomington, Indiana 47404-3797 USA
www.iupress.indiana.edu

Telephone orders   800-842-6796
Fax orders   812-855-7931
Orders by e-mail   iuporder@indiana.edu

Manufactured in the United States of
America

1 2 3 4 5 16 15 14 13 12 11

LIBRARY IN CONGRESS CATALOGING-
IN-PUBLICATION DATA

Twins in African and diaspora cultures :
double trouble, twice blessed / edited by
Philip M. Peek.
    p.   cm.
  Includes bibliographical references and
index.
  ISBN 978-0-253-35624-6 (hardcover : alk.
paper)
  ISBN 978-0-253-22307-4 (pbk. : alk. paper)
  1. Twins—Social aspects—Africa. 2.
Twins—Africa—Religious aspects. 3.
Twins in art. 4. African diaspora. I. Peek,
Philip M.
  GN236.5.T85   2011
  306.875096—dc23   2011017162

Contents

Acknowledgments

I am extremely grateful for the aid of a Visiting Research Fellowship at the Sainsbury Research Unit, Sainsbury Centre for Visual Arts, University of East Anglia, in spring 2003, which permitted me to initiate this project on twins in Africa. My sincerest thanks also to colleagues who participated in a panel on twins in African arts at the Thirteenth Annual Symposium on African Arts, 2004, and contributed to a special issue on twins in *African Arts* 41:1 (2008). These events are the foundation on which the current volume is built. Finally, my sincerest thanks to readers and editors, especially Dee Mortensen and Emma Young at Indiana University Press, for invaluable aid, and to my wife, Pat, for her always patient proofreading.

Twins in African and Diaspora Cultures

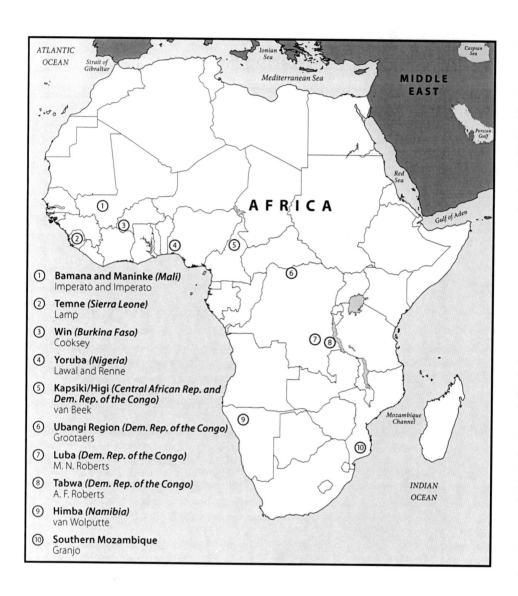

ATLANTIC
OCEAN
Strait of Gibraltar
Ionian Sea
Caspian Sea
Mediterranean Sea
MIDDLE EAST
Persian Gulf
Red Sea
Gulf of Aden

A F R I C A

① Bamana and Maninke *(Mali)*
Imperato and Imperato

② Temne *(Sierra Leone)*
Lamp

③ Win *(Burkina Faso)*
Cooksey

④ Yoruba *(Nigeria)*
Lawal and Renne

⑤ Kapsiki/Higi *(Central African Rep. and Dem. Rep. of the Congo)*
van Beek

⑥ Ubangi Region *(Dem. Rep. of the Congo)*
Grootaers

⑦ Luba *(Dem. Rep. of the Congo)*
M. N. Roberts

⑧ Tabwa *(Dem. Rep. of the Congo)*
A. F. Roberts

⑨ Himba *(Namibia)*
van Wolputte

⑩ Southern Mozambique
Granjo

Mozambique Channel

INDIAN OCEAN

CHAPTER ONE

Introduction

Beginning to Rethink Twins

PHILIP M. PEEK

... there was no doubt about the fate of twins (*ejima*) under old Igbo law and custom; it was incumbent that they should be destroyed without delay. At the same time, reproaches were heaped upon the stricken mother for being the author of such a forbidden issue. (Basden [1938] 1966: 181)

Give us births, give us male and female, let us deliver two by two, that we may always hold twin ceremonies here. (Whyte 1997: 55)

How could any phenomenon generate such diametrically opposed responses? How could one society, such as the Igbo of eastern Nigeria, revile twins so much as to kill them and shun the mother, while another society, like the Nyoro of Uganda, rejoices with songs and prayers for more twins? Even if the Igbo did not literally kill twins, clearly twins were in no way desired. There are few events in the lives of African peoples which cause reactions as intense and dramatically different as the birth of twins does.[1]

Although for some African peoples cultural practices surrounding twins have changed, for most the power of twins and twin imagery has not diminished. By way of introduction to this unique collection of essays on the ways that twins are thought of and treated in a variety of African and African American cultures, we need first to establish twins' biological foundations, then briefly review the ethnographic record and evidence from popular culture as well as the volume's essays. Before concluding, we will reflect comparatively on some issues that touch twins from other parts of the world. Previously, study of twins in Africa has focused on the problems they seem to cause for their parents and communities, but a closer examination of beliefs and practices throughout Africa and the African Diaspora demonstrates that in many cultures there is an acceptance of twins which is embedded in larger worldviews and epistemologies often based on complementary dualities. This provides a far more positive and enriching perspective on twins, a perspective that the scholars in this volume will develop. We can no longer assume twins are only causes of antagonisms and conflicts, because they can also stand for ideals of harmony and interdependence.

Fertility and Fatality

The ethnographic record about twins in Africa begins with horrifying accounts of infanticide. Some observers offered "rational" explanations to avoid the conclusion that the people they observed were simply heartless savages.[2] The literature on twins has been so full of infanticide accounts that several scholars have studied that aspect alone from various perspectives (see, e.g., Ball and Hill 1996; Granzberg 1973; Leis 1965; Onimhawo 1996–1997). Some early studies assure us that the abnormality—usually interpreted by subjects as animality—of multiple births was considered so horrible that even the mother had to be killed. Accounts of the difficulties of nursing, feeding, and raising twins abound—and it is certainly possible that some Africans did resolve these problems via infanticide.

Speculation rather than statistics characterized these earlier accounts of twin births in Africa. Contemporary birth records clearly testify to the high number of twins throughout Africa in comparison to other parts of the world. While there are actually various types of twin births, our discussion will focus on the most common: monozygotic or "identical" (two children born from one egg) and dizygotic or "fraternal" (two children born from two eggs fertilized at the same time). A distinction between kinds of twins based on physical appearance is paramount for popular Western thinking about twins, but, intriguingly, is not emphasized or even noticed by most African peoples. In Africa, the criterion for twinness is not superficial similarity but the shared womb experience.

Birth statistics for twins, especially from Africa, are notoriously unreliable due to erratic reporting (the result of economic and cultural factors). Imperato and Imperato (chapter 2) provide a good summary of figures for West Africa. Generally speaking, Africa has the highest rates of twinning in the world, and West Africa is the most prolific area, with approximately 20 twins per 1,000 births. The Yoruba of western Nigeria have had the world's highest rates, with estimates ranging from 25 to 45 per 1,000 births (Pison 1992; Imperato and Imperato, chapter 2). Contemporary

FIGURE 1.1. Young mother with her twin girls, born August 11, 2006, Tomote family in Jebedaga, a Bozo village near Mopti, Mali; July, 2007. *Photo: Philip M. Peek.*

rates of twinning worldwide are increasing, with the United States now topping the list, having moved from 10.5 twins per thousand births to 28.8 in recent years—due primarily to use of fertility enhancements, in vitro fertilization, and more older mothers.[3]

Pison (1992: 264) offers an excellent map of the distribution of those African cultures that accept twins favorably and those that have traditionally considered them an abomination. Decades earlier, Talbot (1926, vol. 2: 721) surveyed the treatment of twins in southern Nigeria. Both scholars attempted to visually depict the responses to twins and show how neighboring peoples may have absolutely opposite responses. For sub-Saharan Africa, Pison identifies approximately forty-one cultures that accept twins, twenty-six that condemn them, and some forty-five that display mixed responses (1992: 264). Another regional survey is Seligman's (1932) for the Sudan; for Central Africa, Grootaers' charts (chapter 9) demonstrate great diversity among neighboring peoples. It appears that in previous research those cultures which viewed twins ambiguously were considered to despise them, but if we instead accept their middle position, then the acceptance rate of twins is actually greater than previous studies indicated. Complicating matters even among the "pro" and "con" cultures, practices may vary among villages of the same ethnic group.

There are myriad reasons for twins' significance, beyond the obvious demonstration they provide of fertility and abundance. For the Kedjom of the Cameroon Grasslands and the Hausa of northern Nigeria, twins are "children of God" (Diduk 2001; Masquelier 2001), while the Luba associate twins with kings (M. Roberts, chapter 12; see also Adler 1973), and the Nuer equate twins with birds and spirituality (Evans-Pritchard 1936). At the opposite end of the continuum one finds that twins were once abhorred among the Yoruba (see Lawal, chapter 4) and the Igbo, as well as throughout Southern Africa, where twins were abandoned (Schapera 1927). According to Beidelman, among the Kaguru, the perceived abnormality of twins in the past led to their being killed (1963: 55). But most typical are cultures in which twins are both loved and feared due to their extraordinary powers— these include the Mossi (Dugast 1996) and the people of northern Cameroon (Vincent 2001). Among the Himba (Van Wolputte, chapter 3) and in Mozambique (Granjo, chapter 16) twins are critically linked to rainfall and a fear that they could "dry the land."[4] The Luba consider twins "children of the moon" (M. Roberts, chapter 12). Attitudes of deep ambivalence toward twin sexuality are discussed by Lamp (chapter 10).

Even where twin births are celebrated, they are usually grouped with other uncommon births. The category of "abnormalities" usually includes multiple births, babies born with a caul (membrane over the head) or with teeth, babies appearing feet or buttocks first (breech birth), albinos, or infants with major physical deformities (e.g., Downs Syndrome, hermaphroditism). The precise categories of normal and abnormal, as well as responses to them, vary greatly among cultures. Frequently, basic physical abnormalities are virtually ignored and such children are raised in normal fashion. Abnormalities, it seems, literally are in the eye of the beholder. Imperato and Imperato (chapter 2) describe how albinism and hermaphroditism are understood and treated by the Bamana and Maninka in relation to how twins are viewed; as it turns out, all three share some ontological features in this paradigm. An apt illustration of this flexibility of categorizing physical features is an explanation given for individuals with six digits among some African peoples as well as among Haitians (see Houlberg, chapter 13): extra digits are taken as evidence that the bearer is a twin—the additional digits being remnants of the twin who has been absorbed.

This explanation reflects the global "Vanishing Twin" Syndrome that has been receiving increased attention.[5] Initially, this was limited to reports of a vague feeling that one had a twin somewhere, but recent medical information confirms that at least 4 percent of all births begin as twins. One twin apparently absorbs the other in the womb. Among the Nyoro, there are beliefs about Mukama, "the invisible twin," a twin who is not noticed at birth, is forgotten, and will cause harm to its "real" twin and mother until it is recognized and treated properly (Whyte 1997: 140–144). All of this echoes Micheli's comment about West Africans making "twin photos" (chapter 7) as trying to portray "a missing twin they feel inside themselves."

The causes ascribed to unusual births are dependent on culture, ranging from "gifts of God" to lightning striking the mother. Violations of taboos are often considered to result in various types of abnormal births. The most frequently encountered causes relate to the dangers of eating "double" foods (e.g., two fruits grown together). More recently, diet has also been considered a cause of twins among the Yoruba specifically (see chapter 4, for example).[6] For others, dual births are understood to be evidence of dual fathers, one of whom may be understood to be a spiritual entity (e.g., see Grootaers, chapter 9)—a belief also held in ancient Greece and Rome. In this volume, Imperato and Imperato discuss the correlations

FIGURE 1.2. Two young boys, "identical" twins seeking gifts in Bamako, Mali; August, 2007. *Photo: Philip M. Peek.*

between twins and albinos among the Bamana and Maninka of Mali, while Granjo analyzes contemporary associations between these unusual births and the fates of political prisoners. Recent reports of the killing of albino people in East Africa, allegedly for medicines, remind us of the real need to learn more about traditional beliefs surrounding albinos.[7]

Altogether, it is clear that however they are explained, whether they are abhorred or desired, the unique biological nature of twins has always defined them as a special category in some way.

Traditional Approaches to Twins in Africa

There is little dispute that sensationalism characterized early observations by outsiders about practices surrounding twin births in Africa. While it is clear that twins are fragile beings—and increasingly at danger given the high infant mortality rates in Africa—it is noteworthy that this issue is seldom the initial observation Africans themselves will make about twin births. In fact, African traditions are far more likely to cite the wonder and spirituality of twins and/or the fertility of the parents, especially of the mother. Because twins embody extreme potentiality, there is usually apprehension as to which direction this power will take. Therefore, many communities have ritual responses which serve to control the situation. One cannot, however, assume that these demonstrate negative reactions to twins.

Surely one must be cautious in making generalizations. Nevertheless, most previous scholarship has indeed generalized and usually portrayed twins as a biological and/or social problem which needed to be solved. As we hope to demonstrate in this collection of essays, twins are exceptional not solely because of the problems they present but more for the solution they represent. Twins and twinning, along with dualities of many types, are fundamental for many African societies; their importance is demonstrated by their continued veneration in the Americas among communities of African heritage. Yet, this perspective has been absent from previous scholarly studies of twins.

There have been several basic anthropological approaches to the study of twins which we might broadly characterize as being symbolic, stemming from Evans-Pritchard's research; structural-functionalist, epitomized by Turner's writings; or in the vein of Levi Strauss' structuralism. Turner's approach seems to be most frequently applied, as seen in several of our contributors' essays (e.g., A. Roberts, chapter 11), but this volume as a whole takes no specific theoretical orientation; rather, aspects of all three approaches as well as straightforward ethnographic description are employed. As opposed to an either/or stance, a more productive orientation for twin studies here emerges, one which does not deny the problematic aspects of twins but does emphasize the positive dimensions. Van Wolputte develops this basic point in his insightful discussion of intertwinement and a matrix model of simultaneous factors (chapter 3). Ultimately, with such a flexible orientation we will gain a better understanding of twins in African cultures.

The first major statement about the ideologies surrounding twins in Africa is Evans-Pritchard's writings based on research among the Nuer of the Sudan in the 1930s. They consider twins to be two physical beings but with one personality—a concept found widely throughout Africa. The Nuer also assert that "twins are birds" in that they share, symbolically, a similar relationship with "Spirit" (Evans-Pritchard 1967: 80–81).[8] When analyzing Evans-Pritchard and the Nuer, many make this assertion more of a puzzle than is necessary, as Evans-Pritchard himself has said (see Littleton 1949). There are indeed several ways by which the association of birds and twins can "make sense." However, by their very nature, twins are ambiguous, as are snakes and other reptilian creatures frequently used to symbolize anomalies including twins (many of this volume's contributors demonstrate this point). More important is the Nuer belief that "twins form the closest possible human relationship" (Evans-Pritchard 1936: 234)—a perspective that is central to this introduction and several of the essays gathered here.

Most recent studies of twinship in Africa begin either with Evans-Pritchard's "puzzle" or Turner's discussion of the social-structural stress twins create for the Ndembu of Zambia. Turner's argument is in debt to Schapera's earlier work on Southern African peoples, which was the first to identify the social-structural problem about twins in that their "social personalities will . . . be identical" (1927: 135). Turner later rephrased this issue of two beings occupying one social position: ". . . twinship presents the paradoxes that what is physically double is structurally single and what is mystically one is empirically two" (1977: 45). Do two become one or does one become two? Thus, for Turner when twins come into this world at the "same" time and perhaps sharing the same soul, they disrupt carefully wrought social systems based on one entity in one position. The Ndembu respond to this ambiguous and potentially threatening situation with a number of rituals for which Turner (1977) provides detailed symbolic analyses.

Many have found Turner's model the most appropriate. In a survey of the study of twins in Africa, Renne and Bastian (2001) and their collaborators build on Turner's observations by adding several important qualifications focusing on contextualization, both historically and culturally, of any study of twins. While they share an "awareness of dissonance," they urge caution in using outside analytical models. In the present anthology, we find further comment on Turner in Van Beek's and A. Robert's chapters (8 and 11), while Grootaers' (chapter 9) provides a review of Evans-Pritchard's work.

One aspect of the social-structural problem which Turner highlights is rather readily dealt with in most African cultures by giving twins different names that forever distinguish the older from the younger, thereby settling one of the most critical issues, that of inheritance. For the Yoruba, "Taiwo," the junior is the one born first, while "Kehinde," the senior, follows (see Lawal, chapter 4). Nangendo (1996) and A. Roberts (chapter 11) provide other examples of naming traditions for twins. Nevertheless, debates over twins and "traditional" practices continue; McClendon (1997) describes a court case concerning a twin's attempt to inherit his deceased twin's property because "twins count as one person." Clearly, some conflicts about twins continue in contemporary contexts (see also Renne and Bastian 2001).

A fascinating reflection of the social conflicts generated by twins in some cultures is the association of "obscene" songs with their rituals. The voluntary response to one form of perceived deviance by another as a sort of "rite of reversal" is encountered widely among African peoples (see Peek 1995). Both the Tabwa and Luba (chapters 11 and 12) link such marginal behavior with liminal states as signified by twins.

Southall's essay "Twinship and Symbolic Structure" (1972) provides an excellent review of both Evans-Pritchard and Turner as well as serving as, in its discussion of English and French Africanist scholarship, a transition to the "third" approach to twins, that of Levi-Strauss' structuralism. Despite the apparent applicability of the dialectical oppositions highlighted by Levi-Strauss, there has been relatively little use of his models with regard to twins, although Hammond-Tooke (1992) provides a structural analysis of tales about twins.[9] Luc De Heusch also uses Levi-Strauss in illuminating the symbolism of twins in Central African traditions (1982 and 1985) and in his review of Junod's studies of the Thonga of Southern Africa (1980).

Counter to the social-structural conflict which Turner describes for the Ndembu and to Levi-Strauss' dialectical oppositions, many African cultures delight in anomalies and ambiguities, often framing them in spiritual terms. Kilson describes twins among the Ga of Ghana as "desirable anomalies" and provides details about how they emphasize the "structural and mystical duality of twins" (1973: 172; see also Gufler 1995). Even for those cultures for which twins are a problem, it is more often a spiritual issue than a political issue.

If twins pose such a conundrum, it is curious they do not appear in African dilemma tales, stories which end in a question or "dilemma" to be answered by the audience. Of world culture areas, Africans tell more dilemma tales than any other area and yet do not use twins in this context (see Bascom 1975). There are virtually no stories about possible confusion of identical twins, such a popular device in Western literature from Shakespeare to Mark Twain,[10] although recently Nigerian video dramas have tried to use the motif (see Renne, chapter 15).

While the structuralist models of Turner and of Levi-Strauss seem totally appropriate to analyze twins in African cultures, both emphasize conflict, whether it is social, symbolic, or structural. But there is another, perhaps more valuable path to understanding via nonoppositional dualities. The most dramatic examples of such a model come from West African peoples such as the Dogon and Fon who are very much identified with French Africanist scholarship. Marcel Griaule and others have documented the presence of twins and twinning in virtually all aspects of Dogon life and myth (see Griaule 1960; and Griaule and Dieterlen 1968). While the extent to which Griaule emphasizes twins has been countered by Van Beek (1990) and others, it remains clear that twins are important in Dogon life. We also find much by Mercier (1963), Zahan (1979), and De Heusch (1982), as well as by the scholars in the anthology *Des jumeaux et des autres* (1995) on duality and the importance of twinness in West and Central Africa.

Among the Fon, for example, Mercier writes: "The notion of twin beings . . . expresses the equilibrium maintained between opposites, which is the very nature of the world. The ideal birth is a twin birth" (1963: 219). Further, Zahan contributes: "In other words, one might think that the cultures in which man's original androgyny is considered an ideal state of equilibrium would have a reverential attitude towards twins because, by their ambivalent unity, they represent one of the social manifestations of the original equilibrium of man" (1979: 12). These observations signal a critical shift in the study of twins in Africa that needs to be better understood. Nonoppositional dualities, pairs and couples, symmetries, and "intertwinements" (see Van Wolputte, chapter 3) also serve to characterize twins—a perspective we will now consider.

Part of our theoretical dilemma is that no single analytical approach can account for such a diversity of responses to twins. Our emphasis in this volume will be on those peoples for whom twins are significant, perhaps even good, while still being viewed ambiguously. Considering these essays as a whole, and considering the territory covered, it is also evident that more peoples in Africa find positive associations for twins than negative—a generalization supported by evidence from the Diaspora, where twins are, for example, associated widely with ensuring good health. The older stereotype which guided previous study—that twins were abominations or social anomalies—can no longer be our only framework.

New Perspectives on Twins
Dualism and the Dialogical Impulse in African Expressive Behavior

After reviewing ethnographic data not previously introduced into the discussion of twins, we will turn to the essays gathered in this volume. The centrality for many African peoples of twins and twinning, doubles and dualities, pairs and couples, dyads and dialogics, will become strikingly evident. Whether reflecting opposition or harmony, dualities of all kinds appear in most African societies; but how do they relate to the phenomenon of twins? Nigel Barley offers a revealing anecdote from Cameroon which serves to underscore the variety of possible associations not only of twins but the matter of doubles in general. Barley recalls a discussion with twins: "Having sought the term for 'twins' in a French-English dictionary, they had discovered that they were 'binoculars' and referred to themselves by this term. 'This is my sister, Naomi, patron. We are binoculars'" (1986: 153).

Indeed, one needs both elements for complete functioning, whether the elements be binoculars or twins. In order to see one image more completely, we need two lenses. It is as basic as the ancient wisdom that a coin has two sides. The interplay of dualities can take many forms, but the meaning is in the relationship. Twins are only twins in relation to each other, and it is this interactive relationship that finds expression throughout Africa. Twins must be understood primarily in this context of duality, as several chapters (see 3–6) discuss in detail below. The phenomenon of the dialogic pervades African expressive behavior, especially performance. For example, masqueraders are joined at some point by an elder (male or female) from the audience who will vigorously "challenge" their elaborate dance steps, or provide a move and countermove, or they might be in perfect synchronous movement (see, e.g., chapter 2). There is always a dialogue occurring between the drums and the dancers, the singer and the chorus, even between sound and silence in performance. Yes, this is call and response, but how often has it been noted that call and response literally permeates all of African cultures, not just their music? And how often does this exchange involve mirrored acts or twinning behavior?

In writing about oral traditions and narrative events as responsorial, dialogic performances, Fretz (2004) summarizes the role of the "answerer" or "word catcher" in narrative performances throughout Africa. This is a formal role in which an appointed respondent maintains an affirming dialogue with the storyteller. Along similar lines, we can now more fully understand divination (found in all African societies) as relying on some form of dialogue between diviner and spirit or ancestor, between diviner and client, and within the divinatory contingent (Peek 1991). In addition, diviners and clients will sometimes move into perfectly synchronous movement (much as a masquerader and audience companion do), which reveals another type of "twinning" that serves to enhance the divinatory enterprise (Peek 2005, 2010).

Some divination traditions literally depend upon twins, either of this world or the spirit world, as among the Senufo and Luba. As the Senufo say, "Twins have perfect knowledge of each other" (Suthers 1987). In fact, this is the phrase which first drew me to the study of twins. In her excellent work, Suthers (1987) presents Dijimini Senufo ideas about twins and their association with communication and divination. For the Senufo, twins have "perfect knowledge of each other" due to their intimate contact in their mother's womb, permitting them to communicate without words. Special communication also occurs among the Kapsiki and Win (chapters 6 and 8).[11] Senufo diviners seek out twins in the other world with whom to communicate during their oracular sessions. During divination sessions, which occur in a small "hut for twins," diviners also establish twin-like relations with their clients. I have argued that this "twinning" (physically, psychically, and spiritually between diviner and client, left and right hemispheres of the brain, and diviner and spirits) occurs in other divination systems in many cultures throughout the African continent (Peek 1991, 2004, 2007, 2008). Others, such as Mary Nooter Roberts (chapter 12), reflect similar conclusions.

Communal Self / Multiple Soul / Composite Individual

In addition to these instances of doubling or twinning which occur in expressive behavior and divination, there is an even larger aspect of virtually all African cultures which provides an important context for attitudes toward twins. Although the examples are usually drawn from West African peoples, there is no question that throughout Africa the individual is understood to be constituted of a number of independent elements. These aspects may even have volition of their own. If the individual does not successfully unite these components, he or she will never live a successful life. These are often spiritual elements from the mother's and father's side, a "spirit double" who often stays in the other world, and various characteristics of the individual personality. The Isoko of the Niger Delta seek to unite their *oma* (spirit double), *obo* (personal initiative and hard work), and *ivri* (determination) for a successful life. Similar configurations are found among the Ashanti, Baule, and others throughout West Africa.[12] The Dogon individual consists of *nyama* ("life force") and *kindu kindu* ("conscious shadow"), which, as the double name indicates, denotes a double soul: one male and one female (Griaule 1960; see also Van Beek 1992). Even the Yoruba twins have spirit doubles, as do the Bamana and Maninka and the Win (see, respectively, chapters 4, 2, and 6). This basic paradigm of the complete individual also continues to underpin the concepts of African descendants in the Americas. See, for example, Karen McCarthy Brown's discussion of the "relational web" of spiritual elements that constitute the Haitian individual (1989), and the duality of the individual in Brazil described by Dos Santos and Dos Santos (1973). Angelo Micheli (2009) sent me a funeral announcement of a deceased woman from Lome, Togo, with "her soul (double)" now departed. This relationship was depicted by duplicating the original photograph of the woman in miniature in the upper corner of the photograph amid the stars of the heavens. Her spirit looked exactly the same—she was her twin. Today's reproductive photographic technologies allow vivid representation of cultural beliefs.

There is also the broadly noted tradition of a spirit twin and/or deceased twin seeking to bring the living twin to the spirit world and/or placating the living twin to keep it in this world—another form of completion of the self. In addition, we need to recall the variety of relationships, such as joking relations and formally declared best friends, that establish twin-like connections between people.[13] The Gola of Liberia combine these categories: "Some persons are born with a [spiritual] friend that has joined them in their mother's womb . . . ," usually of the opposite sex (D'Azevedo 1973: 294). Robert Brain writes about twins among the Bangwa of Cameroon: "In Bangwa, the only true equals, and therefore the best friends, are twins, born of one womb, at one time, and sharing the same rank" (1969: 215). This certainly reflects a harmonious vision of twins based on the closeness of one human to another. As Micheli illustrates in chapter 7, on friends dressing as twins for photographs, it appears that if one does not have a twin, one seeks to find one: as he expresses it, "completion of the self implies the presence of one's twin." Individuality is not a solitary existence as in Western tradition, but a uniting of diverse elements. Thus, the birth of twins is, for many, the actualization of that imagined ideal—the self and the other coming forward at once, together.

Cosmological Roots

In addition to the duality of individuals and their spirit doubles, many African cosmologies portray dual creator deities, usually depicted as male and female. It remains an open question whether concepts of individual spirit doubles preceded the belief in dual deities or not. The beliefs and practices of Ancient Egypt provide a critical point of reference on the history of twins and dualities in Africa.[14] It is widely reported that Khnum (God) creates "the human being and its double simultaneously. Every being is created dual . . ." (Lash 1993: 10). In his extensive review of twins in Ancient Egypt, John Baines notes that ". . . Shu and Tefenet, the original pair of creation . . . [were] . . . rendered identical in form . . ." (1985: 473) and were predecessors of the Gemini twins (1985: 475–476). Further, Baines even suggests that Ancient Egyptian concepts of twins were similar to those of the Nuer (1985: 480) who live just to the south.

In Benin the dual/twin Fon creator deities of Mawu and Lisa are but one example of original, mythic twins (Mercier 1963: 219). And ". . . in Winye society all good things must adopt the form of the original twin couple . . ." (Jacob 1990: 83). Perhaps the Dogon, with numerous pairs of Nommo, the ancestral twins, are the classic example (Griaule 1960) (see also, Imperato and Imperato, chapter 2). Berglund (1989: 34) relates the richness of twin imagery among the Zulu to describe the relationship between the sky and the earth: "Yes, they are twins, but they are also husband and wife. We call them twins because we do not know which one is the more important. If we say twins, then we do not say that one is greater than the other. But they are different. It is like humans. The one is this way. The other is another way. But they have their similarities."

It is important to observe that such dual deities can be understood as merged entities (two become one), and/or as androgynous beings who embody both male and female principles, and/or as twins. In *Childhood and Cosmos* (1973), Erny provides a synthesis of West African associations for various dualities, twins, and so on. Pelton (1980: 193, 208) writes at length about the wholeness embodied in twinness. In describing the dualistic patterns of the Fon, Mercier asserts, "The ideal type of every group in the divine world is a pair of twins of opposite sex . . ." (1963: 231) (an association shared by the Yoruba—see chapter 4). Coupling this idea with the Fon's dual deity Mawu/Lisa, we are reminded of Plato's proposal that, originally, all humans were two-sided in various combinations of male and female halves, but Zeus cut all in half. Humans were thus driven to find their other, original half (1989).[15] This "original nature" of conjoined twins could also refer to androgynous beings, which would mesh strikingly well with the worldviews and mythologies of a number of West African peoples, such as the Dogon, as well as with concepts about human twinning in general throughout Africa. Many African diviners strive for such an identity to improve oracular communication (Peek 1991). Thus, the complementarity of male and female pairs as well as the harmony of having both male and female principles within one individual is an ideal. This certainly seems to demonstrate Jung's contention that each of us has elements of the opposite sex within us, the anima and animus.

Equality of Twins?

Numerous cultures demand equal treatment of twins, for example, the Songye of the Congo (Merriam 1974: 211). In fact, in some societies there are dire consequences if the twins are not treated equally. Twins may not simply become angry at the lack of "proper" treatment, but they may intentionally harm their parents. This is the case for the Kapsiki, with the father especially at risk (Van Beek, chapter 8). For the Win, people desire twins of opposite sexes; otherwise, same-sex twins would plot against their same-sexed parent due to jealousy and desire for the other parent (Cooksey, chapter 6). Intriguingly, Evans-Pritchard (1936: 230) reports exactly the same belief among the Nuer far across the continent.

Curiously, a number of peoples who accept twins have traditions which can be interpreted as requiring them to beg or to receive gifts from others, as among the Bamana of Mali, the Yoruba of Nigeria, and in Brazil (see chapters 2, 4, 14). The Bamana say that one will benefit by gifting to twins who gather near the main mosque in Bamako (see figures 2 and 3). Elsewhere, as with the Kapsiki, one risks a twin's wrath if one does not give them something they desire. There may also be a tradition that each twin must receive exactly the same thing or amount. Thereby, the community maintains the unity of twins, whereas Western psychology, while urging general equality, cautions against identical treatment of twins for fear of the loss of individuality. The strength of the African tradition is demonstrated by its presence in the Americas, especially in Lucumí culture in Cuba, where twins are considered to represent "dual equality" (Flores-Pena, chapter 5).

FIGURE 1.3 . Two pairs of twins seeking gifts in Bamako ("identical" boys in front; "fraternal" girls in back), Mali; August, 2007. *Photo: Philip M. Peek.*

"The One Who Follows"

Many cultures from all over Africa cite the importance of the child who follows twins. In some cases, the twin unit actually includes the child who comes next. Among the Lucumí in Cuba, this child is considered a triplet (see chapter 5). The child who follows twins is often considered to have more power than even the twins. Pemberton (2003: 41) notes that "Idowu is the servant of twins" and yet must be served first due to its trickster nature. The significance of this individual is demonstrated by the fact that we find the tradition still strongly followed with cognates of the Yoruba name in Cuba and Haiti, as seen in chapters 5 and 13. Some echoes of this concept appear to be linked to beliefs and practices related to sacred children in Brazilian Candomblé (see chapter 14).

There has not been any comparative discussion of the attributions of power given the child who follows twins. This is especially striking because similar customs are found throughout Africa.[16] In some cases, this power is expressed only as potentiality; in other cases it is thought to be truly dangerous (e.g., among the Uduk of the Sudan [James 1988: 109]). Among the Ga, "the sibling born immediately after a pair of twins is thought to be more powerful than the twins themselves" (Kilson 1973: 175). Other contributors add to our knowledge here about the Tabwa (chapter 11) and the Ubangi area (chapter 9). While the singleton following twins might signal a return to "normal" single births, they still share mystically in their siblings' power.

Twins in Recent Literature and the Arts

There is little doubt that attitudes toward twins continue to be influenced by tradition in Africa and the Diaspora. While this is to be expected in Mali and Brazil, its persistence in London may not be, yet there too, the power of twin imagery remains. Twins are not just arcane traditions but still vital symbols which aid contemporary novelists raised outside of Africa to portray human dilemmas and cultural values. For example, *The Icarus Girl* (2005) by Helen Oyeyemi (discussed more fully in chapter 15) draws on Yoruba twin tradition to capture the intensity of a "living" twin's attraction to and repulsion from her other "deceased" half as it simultaneously portrays a British-Nigerian child's first encounters with her mother's homeland. Two other Nigerian writers have recently published books featuring twin protagonists but use their twinness only to create comparative character studies: Chimamanda Ngozi Adichie, an Igbo of eastern Nigeria, writes of twin sisters in *Half a Yellow Sun* (2006); while Helon Habila portrays twin brothers in *Measuring Time* (2007). Why do Adichie and Habila identify their main characters as twins if they are not going to use the twin motif in some dramatic fashion? It may be, as Van Beek suggests below, these sisters and brothers are meant to portray the two sides of an individual, another aspect of twinning. This analysis might also explain a recent video drama, *Evil Twins,* directed by Chuma Ezenyirioha, in which two brothers are contrasted but, again, nothing is done specifically with the idea of their being twins (see also Renne below).[17] A more successful use of the twin motif is Buchi Emecheta's *Kehinde* (1990), a novel about the struggles of a Nigerian family in London and Lagos. While this work is named after the second-born twin among the Yoruba, Emecheta is Igbo. Although the Igbo abhorred twins, they still honor the tradition of recognizing one's individual *chi*, or personal spirit. Following the points raised earlier about the communal self, it may be that Emecheta draws on that ultimately similar tradition in order to effectively depict the interactions of twins in both worlds.

Actual, not just fictive, twins continue to have an impact in African arts. Elisha Renne (chapter 15) offers further fascinating discussion of both contemporary literature and Nigerian videos that feature twins. In the contemporary visual arts, there is Twins Seven-Seven, an extraordinary artist in various media who has, appropriately, two biographies—one via Ulli Beier (1999), who encouraged him at the beginning of his career, and the other with the aid of a recent friend, Henry Glassie (2010). His name describes his birth seven times (and death six times) as a twin before he survived in this world. Twins Seven-Seven became known internationally for his music and his unique prints, among them a piece titled *The Spirit of Twins* (2007). The Lalijadu Sisters, Kehinde and Taiwo, a famous pair of twin singers who proudly bear their traditional Yoruba twin names, have been successful as world musicians. Their popular album from the 1980s was titled *Double Trouble*—a title which brings to mind Wangechi Mutu's extraordinary work of art *Double Fuse*, which has been described by Thompson: "From her larger *Creature* series, *Double Fuse* features two idealized female figures, menacing twins who tease out the boundaries between balance and disproportion, beauty and deformation" (2008: 281). Twin imagery continues to awe even today.

In fact, twin imagery has been a frequent topic in African art studies of "traditional" arts as well. In terms of the verbal and performing arts, twins are a widespread motif. There are songs for twins sung among the Bamana, Luba, Ngbandi, Tabwa, Temne, and Yoruba, all with examples discussed in this volume. One of the most dramatic of Yoruba masquerades is *Gelede*, in which identical pairs perform. Twin pots play significant roles among the Senufo (Peek 2008) and in the Cameroon (Jeffreys 1947). Such images are found among African descendants in Haiti, Brazil, and Cuba as well. Special shrines full of double imagery dedicated to twins are found in many West African and African American cultures. And as Renne discusses below, twins continue to feature in Yoruba life as figures in advertisements and video dramas. Lawal (2008) and Micheli (2008) have both written on the philosophical and behavioral delights of doubling, from abstract dualities to basic photographs.

An especially famous case of twin imagery is the *ere ibeji*, or small statues carved for departed *ibeji* (twin) among the Yoruba, which have become an iconic African art form (Chemeche 2003; Lawal, chapter 4). Similar twin sculptures are found among other African peoples as well. Corney (1975: 7–10), in discussing twin "effigies," cites Segy that only thirty of the estimated two hundred African peoples who welcomed twins also made carvings of them; however, cultures that make notable twin statues include the Bamana, Fon, Senufo, Temne, Tabwa, and Luba. The representation of male and female couples as a reference to marriage can serve as a metaphor for personal completeness or it can represent the primordial couple and signify fertility, both ancient and contemporary (Cole 1989; LaGamma 2004). Opposite-sexed pairs of bronze figures define the Yoruba Ogboni traditions (Lawal 2008). Such pairs might well *also* represent twins, in accordance with the beliefs noted above that opposite-sex twins embody the perfect human (Peek 2008). There has been virtually no study of Janus-headed or "piggy-back" figures, although such representations surely demonstrate something about "doubling" and possibly twinning.

Because visual imagery of twins is so prominent in Africa and the Americas, as demonstrated in the following essays, it behooves us to consider why. Why are paired "identical" images so important for the Luba and Yoruba? Portraiture, in the sense of exact replication of external physical features, has not been a feature of African arts; far more to the point is the portrayal of internal states of being, of moral values, and so on. Most now accept characterizations like "idealized naturalism" or "stylized realism" as typifying African depictions of the human face and form. Because the shared intimacy of the mother's womb is the defining characteristic of twins, the duplication of carved or costumed forms may be a way by which to symbolize that common experience. Superficial sameness can also symbolize an individual's spirit double. Such observations only serve to highlight the extraordinary nature of Micheli's study of "twin photographs" in which friends strive to appear identical (chapter 7). While the Yoruba *ere ibeji* only portray an idealized "standard" twin, not a portrait of an actual individual, the photograph now gives us an exact replication of a previously "unique" individual, technologically mimicking the appearance of twinness.

Africa in the Americas

Before turning to the essays of this volume, the inclusion of Africa in the Americas must be noted. It is clear that we would not fully understand twins among African descendants in the New World without a background about African twins. Despite distinct histories and cultural patterns, the traditions surrounding twins as "divine children" and healers in Brazil, Cuba, and Haiti show commonalities that are of fundamental importance, as we shall see in more detail below. The acknowledgment of African roots for twins was noted decades ago. Frances and Melville Herskovits wrote of the celebrations for twins and the child who follows in Suriname (1934) and, recalling the behavior of twins in Cameroon, described the capriciousness and jealousy of twins in Haiti (1937; see also Metraux 1972). In addition to Brown's observations noted above and Houlberg's discussion in chapter 13, Maya Deren's description of twins in Haiti echoes many African accounts: "The worship of the Marassa, the Divine Twins, is a celebration of man's twinned nature: half matter, half metaphysical; half mortal, half immortal; half human, half divine" (1970: 38). Robert Farris

Thompson provides an excellent overview of the African roots of twin worship and celebration in the Americas (1993: 250–261).

Breaking New Ground

Rather than portraying twins as a marginal issue, the essays collected here bring twins to the fore by providing important new perspectives. It is critical to appreciate that seldom have studies of twins in Africa focused on the positive aspects of double births and the surrounding cultural matrix. Few have noted the presence of dual creator gods, the power of twins, the desire for doubling one's self through friendships, the fact of the composite individual, and so on. Clearly, concepts of selfhood and agency need to be considered. And once these are taken into account, we realize that for most Africans "more is better" and individuality is built out of communalism. There is abundant evidence from West African peoples, for example, that twins represent the Ideal and that there are various ways individuals aspire to "twinness" (Peek 2005, 2008, 2010). Patterns of behavior and belief concerning twins have changed over the years, but they are still vital and continue to portray the value and desirability of twins, and, even more importantly, twins serve as vehicles for additional concerns within the society. Just as twin births must be viewed in the context of all births; so also must they be viewed in relation to other issues touching on duality, doubles, and complementarities among people in each culture. Clearly, twinness often relates to fundamental cosmology and epistemology of a people.

The two essays in part 1, "Roots," introduce a range of fundamental issues raised by the birth of human twins. By treating origins biologically and culturally in chapter 2, "Twins and Double Beings among the Bamana and Maninka of Mali," Pascal James Imperato and Gavin H. Imperato (father and son, not twins!) introduce an extensive culture area represented by two ethnic groups of the Mande-speaking peoples of West Africa among whom twins hold essential roles in myth and in daily life. They also provide further understanding of the biological issues of twin and other "unusual" human births, specifically albinos and hermaphrodites. These three types of births are considered related by many peoples in Africa. What is or is not an "unusual" birth and how it is responded to is always a culture-specific matter.

Chapter 3, Steven Van Wolputte's "Twins and Intertwinement: Reflections on Ambiguity and Ambivalence in Northwestern Namibia," analyzes the centrality of twins and dualities within a single culture and provides important new perspectives from southern Africa. Both these initial chapters anticipate issues raised in Paulo Granjo's concluding essay about Mozambique and the relationships of albinos, twins, and water. The fundamental nature of duality for the Himba of northwestern Namibia underpins twins' link between worlds and their representation of "consonance," not just opposition or dissonance. Earlier studies of twins in southern Africa placed them in a dialectic frame, but Van Wolputte, as he analyzes doubles throughout Himba life, with twins being the epitome of this perspective, argues for an ultimate unification and consonance.

For a long time the novelty of twin births seems to have been sufficient rationale to explain the enormous variety of associated beliefs and rituals. But it may be that twins are but one, albeit especially dramatic, manifestation of larger cultural complexes based on dualities, doubles, and symmetries. While there is a tendency to think only in terms of oppositions, of dichotomies and dialectics, if we shift perspectives to focus on a dialogic, interactive, supportive, even harmonious model, we have a very different understanding of the symbolism of twins more akin to the image of yin and yang intertwined.

This is the concern of "Doubles and Dualities," our second grouping. Babatunde Lawal's "Sustaining the Oneness in Their Twoness: Poetics of Twin Figures (Ère Ìbejì) among the Yoruba" (chapter 4) discusses *ibejì* in the context of the Yoruba worldview based on *ejiwapo*, "twoness"—an excellent starting point for this section, which situates Africa's best-known complex of twin practices in a larger cultural context of stable, harmonious dualities. Yoruba practices and terminology are found throughout the Americas. This heritage is evident in Ysamur Flores-Pena's essay about twins and the third child in the Lucumí culture of Cuba: "'Son Dos los Jimagüas' ('The Twins Are Two'): Worship of the Sacred Twins in Lucumí Religious Culture" (chapter 5). Himself a priest of the religion and a twin, he stresses the harmony which twins exemplify, while the third child remains problematic, as later chapters elaborate.

Chapter 6, "Twins, Couples, and Doubles and the Negotiation of Spirit-Human Identities among the Win" grows out of Susan Cooksey's research on divination art forms in Burkina Faso. Here, twins are but one manifestation of the larger phenomenon of doubles—the common thread in part 2. The description of spirits' appearance in this world leads to a complex analysis of representation and meaning among the Win. Despite their generally positive outlook on twins, indeed on the complementarity of doubles in general, there is reason for caution. There are echoes of the current problem in the United States and Europe about cloning and copies. C. Angelo Micheli's fascinating investigation of double photographs in chapter 7 provides another example of the importance of twin imagery in West African societies, especially today, and the effectiveness of contemporary media. "Double Portraits: Images of Twinness in West African Studio Photography" testifies to the adaptability and vitality of central cultural concepts, which is another of our themes.

If twins are understood to be a challenge to the biological or social order, they also become a focal point for other issues, especially other perceived anomalies. Equally, twins may be such a powerful image that they are used as a vehicle for various problematic cultural issues. Victor Turner suggested that those aspects of belief which seem most problematic actually serve to crystallize and articulate a society's most cherished principles (1969). Whether as cause or effect, clearly twins are ambiguous and thereby gain attention—if not fear and awe—due to their potentiality. Such ambiguity— truly ambi-valence in its literal sense of "both (or two) meanings"— is often linked to other "stateless" entities such as anomalous creatures. Twins are linked in various cultures throughout Africa to snakes, scorpions, and other creatures with unique identities. Especially from a social-structural perspective, liminality is taken as marginality; but more often the opposite is the case: that which is liminal or "stateless" is in actuality central to the culture.[18] Thus, "The Centrality of Liminality" forms our third unit of essays.

Walter E. A. Van Beek's "Forever Liminal: Twins among the Kapsiki/ Higi of North Cameroon and Northeastern Nigeria," chapter 8, builds on his extensive research in Cameroon. Among the Kapsiki there, twins are always in transition, "forever liminals," eternally between worlds. Given their positive powers, they can enhance anything; but given their potentiality, they are feared as well. In Jan-Lodewijk Grootaers' discussion of the symbolic associations of twins in chapter 9, "Snake, Bush, and Metaphor: Twinship among Ubangians," he helps us understand a relatively little-researched part of Central Africa. Here again the ambiguity of twins is foregrounded through review of their metaphoric expressions (e.g., as snakes) and related practices in the context of culture change. In "Fiction and Forbidden Sexual Fantasy in the Culture of Temne Twins," chapter 10, Frederick John Lamp confronts another area of liminality, of possible marginality and danger: sexual identity and behavior. Lamp notes that parents speak to their twins in contradictions so they will have "separate minds." But it seems that the need to separate twins is not just an intellectual matter; there may also be sexual transgressions given the proximity of twins in the womb, especially for same-sex twins. We also must recall the image for many other West African peoples of the "perfect pair" of twins being opposite-sex. Many levels of ambiguity here!

Allen F. Roberts has discussed duality among the Tabwa elsewhere (1986), but in "Embodied Dilemma: Tabwa Twinship in Thought and Performance," chapter 11, he focuses on twins revealing numerous themes which have been recorded in other parts of Africa. Not only do we have the celebration of twins in carved images and songs but also links to chieftaincy, an association shared with the Luba. Just as twins may represent "reversals" of nature, they are often associated, as for the Tabwa (and Ndembu), with reversals of social propriety marked by the ribald songs sung for them. With regard to cultural placement of twins, the Luba may well epitomize the centrality of the liminal, for accounts of twins fill their history and underpin their divination system; twins are linked to cosmology, diviners, and kingship. As Mary Nooter Roberts reports in chapter 12, "Children of the Moon: Twins in Luba Art and Ontology," twins may continue to be considered ambiguous but as such are at the core of Luba society, past and present, in divination and history. Here, as with the rest of part 3, it is at the margins, near borders that we find core beliefs—what is in, what is out, and what is unclear. Twins often aid in understanding those distinctions—and continue to aid people in New York City today, as Mary Nooter Roberts was surprised to learn.

We find that for many African peoples twins remain powerful images that continue to articulate their concerns. This was made evident by each of the contributions to Renne and Bastian's "Reviewing Twinship in Africa" (2001), each of which showed how different factors—Christian missionaries (Bastian 2001), economics (Diduk 2001), Islamic revisionists (Masquelier 2001), and internal cultural change (Renne 2001)—all played a part in affecting but not eliminating twins' roles in their respective cultures. Further testimony to these concepts' significance is their presence among Africans in the Americas, where they still provide ways by which to comprehend this world. Even more striking are the permutations, elaborations, and creolizations—new arrangements of old ideas which allow the past to speak afresh to the present. Thus, part 4, our last group of chapters, is labeled "Transformations."

The next two chapters clearly demonstrate the phenomenon of syncretism in African American traditions which Herskovits outlined decades ago. No one can doubt any longer the presence of African traditions in the Americas despite the horrors of the Middle Passage and slavery. Marilyn Houlberg combines knowledge about twins among the Yoruba and Fon peoples of West Africa and about Haitian Vodou practitioners in "Two Equals Three: Twins and the Trickster in Haitian Vodou," chapter 13. From her dramatic examples of songs, carvings, paintings, and performances, we can trace the morphing of twins arriving in Haiti from several sources, and see as well the importance of "the one who follows." While twins and their "third" remain significant in the Americas, there have been intriguing developments in related spiritual practices, one of which is discussed by Stefania Capone in chapter 14, "Divine Children: the *Ìbejìs* and the *Erês* in Brazilian Candomblé." Often confused with *ibeji* (the Yoruba twin), the *Erê* (the sacred child) has grown in importance and demonstrates yet further transformations of African traditions in the Americas, especially in the complexities of religious practices and representations. Now the replication of the twin has moved from a carved wooden form to replication in a human through spirit possession.

Elisha P. Renne, who has contributed much to this topic elsewhere (Renne and Bastian 2001) now gives us our chapter 15, "The Ambiguous Ordinariness of Yoruba Twins," wherein she discusses striking examples of the continued power of the twin as a feature in advertisements and videos that persuade contemporary Yoruba—a phenomenon in the United States as well, witness the Doublemint Twins. Finally, Paulo Granjo's chapter 16, "Twins, Albinos, and Vanishing Prisoners: A Mozambican Theory of Political Power," offers sobering reminders of other ways by which traditions about twins and albinos are perpetuated. Here, they provide a startling means by which to understand death and the types of victims of Mozambique's revolution and tragic civil war. Traditional beliefs provide clarity for the ambiguity of "disappeared" relatives. Without a doubt, African and African American cultures continue to change, but the ancient potency of core beliefs and metaphors—such as those about twins—remains.

"Double Thinking" about Twins in Africa and the Diaspora

Clearly twins are never *not* noticed. From cosmologies to daily behavior, twins are marked off, and something, be it good or bad, is made of them. Generalizations are always risky, but periodically we need to consider the forest and compare it to other forests, not just continue to count trees. From what we have reviewed in terms of African and African American cultures, the research of our contributors and others, twins are clearly more important than previously thought. They are not simply abnormalities to be eliminated or elevated—they participate in larger paradigms. Their continued significance in Africa and the Diaspora must not be underestimated. Rather than being exclusively understood as emblems of discord and dissonance, they must also be recognized for their links to harmony and balance.

African twins remain an enigma because they embody ambivalence and ambiguity; but our study of them has developed greatly from simply trying to explain infanticide or obscure symbolism. What enhances the significance of our observations about twins in contemporary African and Diaspora cultures is how different they are when compared to attitudes toward twin topics in Western traditions. Twins are still somewhat of an enigma, but clearly there are more problematic perspectives about them in Europe and the United States than in Africa. A full comparison of beliefs and behaviors in relation to twins cannot be undertaken here; but there are a number of surveys that reveal how much attention is paid around the world to twins.[19]

Contemporary psychology has much to say about twins which may have roots in the deep distrust and fear founders of the psychoanalytic movement had about the alter ego, the "second self," the Doppelganger.[20] Carl Jung took these concerns even further in his descriptions of the Shadow: "So, whatever form it takes, the function of the shadow is to represent the opposite side of the ego and to embody those qualities that one dislikes most in other people" (1964: 173). There is no question that Jung only depicted this "double" as the dark side of the individual, a perspective that Baudrillard more recently seemed to echo in a discussion about clones: "[The double] . . . is an imaginary figure, which, just like the soul, the shadow, the mirror image, haunts the subject like his other . . ." (1994: 95). There is no friendly spirit double here like there is among so many African peoples! And perhaps this explains why Western tradition readily develops the "Evil Twin" motif while Nigerian video dramas are less successful with the concept.

While Africans tend to seek incorporation of spiritual entities, Western patterns remain premised on a logic of either/or—as in the recent film *Avatar*, where one either becomes the avatar or not. Again, we see that the African "communal self" cannot exist in the West. Thus, the linkages of twins so important among many African peoples are limited or even severed in Europe and the United States. There is no custom of seeking to appear identical to others comparable to the West African tradition Angelo Micheli documents (chapter 7). Nor do we find the communal self/ compound individual so common in African cultures in any way accepted in the West, where only single states of consciousness are allowed, and "schizophrenia" is distinctly undesirable.

Not only does Western psychology warn us against multiple states of being, but the extensive literature on twins seems to be more on the "double trouble" rather than the "twice blessed" side. Guides for parents in the United States focus on the difficulties of raising two children simultaneously,

FIGURE 1.4. Sign about twins on the London Underground reflecting the desire for individuality; August, 2003. *Photo: Philip M. Peek.*

and parents are constantly warned against treating twins in the same way. The fear is not simply of jealousy (which is sometimes a factor in African cultures) but of the loss of individuality for each twin (which is never voiced as a concern among Africans). "The problem occurring is that each twin makes no clear distinction between his twin's personality and his own" (Ortmeyer 1970: 126). If this matter of shared personalities is noted among Africans, it is considered desirable. And, as noted earlier, equal treatment is often absolutely required, as among the Kapsiki. In other words, the perspectives of European and African theories of personality are diametrically opposed. Indeed, one's uniqueness, one's individuality is paramount in Western cultures, as illustrated in figure 1.4, showing a pair of twins in the London Underground demanding different clothes.[21]

More philosophical perspectives on twins are raised in important works by Hillel Schwartz, *The Culture of the Copy* (1997), and Jean Baudrillard, *Simulacra and Simulation* (1994), both of which offer critical observations on replications in today's world. We have become a culture of semblance, or at best, resemblance. Reality seems to have slipped away—though it is available on reruns and TiVo! Baudrillard observes (1994: 122): "Today, it is the real that has become the alibi of the model, in a world controlled by the principle of simulation"—a world where the counterfeit, the sham triumphs. The copy or simulacrum is "more real" than the original.

But a twin is not a copy. Even with the technology of cloning available to us, twins are somehow more. They are the "real" thing—they are and are not like each other, but we do know that they are each equally "real." While we can never really see ourselves (mirrors give us only reversals and photographs are never satisfactory), identical twins do see "themselves."

Some of our contributors offer tantalizing observations on both sides of this discourse about replication. The problems posed by reproductions are noticed by the Win also (chapter 6), given their apprehension about spirit manifestations. And in Brazil the *ere*, originally the term for sculpted representations of twins among the Yoruba in Nigeria, have become the divine children of Candomblé worship. Here, the replica has become the original.

Finally, twins provide the ultimate relational event—a twin cannot be a twin without the other. They only exist in relation to the other. Thus, the presence of manifestations of twins in sculptures, photographs, other visual representations, and memories serves to maintain that relationship despite the absence of the other. The seriousness of this relationship is summed up by Schwartz: "The legend of the vanishing twin articulates our profound uneasiness with post-modern confusions of identities and post-industrial confusions of the 'real thing'" (1996: 21). And from the evidence in several of this volume's essays, this existential emptiness is fulfilled for many African peoples by twins and twinning.

The understanding of twins in Africa may represent but one facet of larger paradigms that accord special status to doubles and dualities of all kinds. In fact, a dialogic orientation is very widespread in ritual as well as daily life among many African peoples. We need to better understand the correspondences between each African society's worldview and its attitudes toward twins. Concepts of dualities, of doubles, of dialogics provide very promising avenues to follow; but are the Dogon and Yoruba, for example, truly "dualistic" cultures? Are there others? Other questions emerge from such wide-ranging studies as this. Will we find similar or different patterns of attitudes toward twins in areas not treated in this volume, such as North Africa and Madagascar? [22] It is perhaps obvious, but still important, to emphasize that further investigation must be conducted with twins themselves—as Flores-Pena's work (chapter 5) reminds us.

Twinness seems far more related to symmetry, reconciliation, harmony, and synthesis than to oppositions and conflicts. Also, we should keep in mind the composite nature of selfhood in Africa. For many, the ideal birth is one of opposite-sex twins who are seen as the epitome of human completeness. Perhaps twins do symbolize a more complete self, the physical manifestations of the spirit double that philosophies of multiple selves /

composite individuals and androgynous beings suggest. The reorientation presented here goes counter to much scholarship on twins since Turner. Some go even further; for example, Schoffeleers (1991) links twins with symmetry and social disorder, but associates asymmetry with social harmony in African cultures.

While the birth of twins clearly reveals many of the fears and promises of human reproduction, too often they have been taken to introduce social conflict. Most previous scholarship on twins in Africa has stressed the opposition of twins, the dichotomy they manifest, but not their symbolic and literal harmony of unification. In fact, the majority of the essays collected here demonstrate unification rather than bifurcation, completion over separation, consonance instead of dissonance, positive not negative reactions. This does not deny that there can be apprehension about twins or that they can be used to represent issues of conflict, but it does underscore a more positive view, one which strikingly dominates among Africans in the Americas. In fact, the similarity of ideas about twins in African American traditions proves the tenacity of fundamental African ideas about children.

What is clear from the essays presented here is that twins can no longer simply be understood as a burden, spiritually or physically. Twins may or may not be noticed, feared, emulated, avoided, cherished, or condemned. We now understand more fully how twins provide models for behavior and means by which to understand our world better. We see twins linked to chieftaincy and political authority, to artistic expression in all media, to the spiritual world, and to models of enhanced human interaction and communication. The cumulative impact of these fascinating essays is that twins come to stand for far more than the basic awe of dual birth. Their extra-ordinariness serves to highlight other topics of exceptional nature. The sheer variety of practices surrounding twins in African cultures prevents any tidy generalizations or single theoretical models to guide us; in fact, a variety of approaches is far more fruitful.

Thus, perhaps we end by answering our initial questions: Yes, we are "twice blessed" with twins. In these days of easy replication, instant replay, and Photoshopped reality, all are impressed by the "real" replication of twins. Visual replication may be the counterpart to responsive dialogic performance. There seems to be an aesthetic of sameness that is good. Still, as "good" as the sameness of two "identical" carved images or the eerily "identical" friends shown in twin-style photographs are, these are artificially created. They are not the same as "real" duplication, real twins. It is the immediacy of the womb, not simple external similarity, which

establishes "real" twinness, an intimacy which transcends all other relationships . . . except perhaps that of the successful integration of the individual with their spirit double—which may in fact be the same experience! For the Yoruba and others, the harmony between twins is the same
as the balancing of the two aspects of the self.

NOTES

1. I accept the risks of generalizing about "Africa." Essentially this volume
focuses on sub-Saharan "Black" Africa and its descendants in parts of the Americas. Certainly not all of any human groupings behave identically, but at some
point in our studies culture-specific data needs to be reviewed and compared
more broadly for possible patterns which may educate us further.

2. For early surveys of infanticide accounts, see H. U. Hall (1928); I. Schapera
(1927); and P. A. Talbot (1926); while E. A. Pector (2002) provide more contemporary reviews of the issue.

3. See also Nylander (1975); Schwartz (1996: 386–388); and Mosnro et al.
(2001). Valuable websites include www.twins.co.uk, www.twinsworld.com, www
.twintalk.co.za (from South Africa), and www.twinsindia.com (perhaps the single
best site on twins).

4. In addition to biological aspects of twins, there are also fascinating facts
about twinning in the universe, starting with the Gemini Twins constellation.
"Everywhere they look, astronomers see doubles" (Berman 2001: 13) as they
record more of the universe. Correlations of recent science with traditional beliefs
are most striking. The fact that rainbows occur in pairs (http://eo.ucar.edu/rain-
bows) provides support for the association of "rainbow serpents" and their link to
twins among a number of West and Central African peoples (e.g., Mercier 1963,
Grootaers, chapter 9, and A. Roberts, chapter 11). Ancient associations between
twins, water, and lightning are still accepted in East and Southern Africa (see, e.g.,
Ten Raa 1980 and Granjo, chapter 16, this volume).

5. For further information on the "Vanishing Twins," see Courtney Davis
(2002) and http://vanishingtwin.com.

6. See Newsweek, Nov. 23, 1987, p. 62, and Creinin and Keith (1989). Recently,
there was an account about possible environmental causes of twins in Brazil,
"Mystery of the 'Land of Twins': Something in the Water? Mengele?" (Barrionuevo 2009), which questioned the large number of twins recorded for an area
settled mostly by Germans. This recalled the fanatic Dr. Josef Mengele's horrendous twin research in Nazi concentration camps, because some thought he had
once lived in that area of Brazil.

7. In addition to the reports of killings of albinos in East Africa for medicinal
reasons (New York Times 2008), there are continuing accounts of discrimination
against albinos elsewhere. One of Mozambique's most popular singers, Momade Ali
Faque, an albino, was rescued from a garbage dump when his parents rejected him.

8. Other studies by British social anthropologists among East African peoples provide additional information on symbolic associations of twins; see Beattie (1962); Beidelman (1963); Abrahams (1972); and Buxton (1973).

9. Intriguingly, Levi-Strauss' essay on twins, "Harelips and Twins: The Splitting of a Myth" (1979), is based on an association not found in the African material, although later he cited African traditions about "split" babies (1987). Trickster hares abound in Africa but without the link to twins which Levi-Strauss found in the Americas (see Bascom 1975).

10. From Shakespeare to Lewis Carroll, from the Bobbsey Twins to Mark Twain, many comic and tragic uses of identical twins are found in English literature. One of the most complex embodiments of twinness is Samuel Clemens' creation of his own "twin," Mark Twain, who focused on twins in his fiction and newspaper reporting, as discussed by Susan Gillman in *Dark Twins: Imposture and Identity in Mark Twain's America* (1989).

11. The special empathetic communication abilities of twins are recorded in the U.S. as well. For example, there are the famous twin advice-givers "Dear Abby" (Abigail Van Buren) and "Ann Landers," and Scott and Stephen Petullo, "The Mystic Twins." It is well known that Elvis Aaron Presley maintained frequent and reassuring communication with his stillborn twin Jesse Garon Presley (Guralnick 1994; Marcus 1990).

12. There is an abundance of descriptions of the "communal self" in numerous African cultures, such as among the Kpelle, for whom "two-brained people" have a brain in this and one in the spirit world (Bellman 1975); see Appiah (1992: 98–99) concerning Asante tradition; but there is no development of this phenomenon in relation to twins in the basic works on personhood and the individual in Africa (e.g., La Fontaine 1989; Carrithers et al. 1989; or Jackson and Karp 1990).

13. In addition to the extensive literature on joking relationships and other formalized best-friend relationships, there are even same-sex marriages (e.g., Signorini 1973) which demonstrate the importance of establishing and maintaining close affiliations.

14. In addition to the discussion about how twins were viewed in Ancient Egypt there has been further debate over the representations of Niankhkhnum and Khnumhotep as to whether they were a homosexual couple, just twins, or conjoined twins (Reeder 2000; Wilford 2005). The discussion of twins in Ancient Egypt provides a fascinating link between sub-Saharan Africa and the Mediterranean world.

15. From "The Speech of Aristophanes": "Now, since their natural form had been cut in two, each one longed for its own other half. . . ."; "Love is born into every human being; it calls back the halves of our original nature together; it tries to make one out of two and heal the wound of human nature" (Plato 1989:27).

16. On the child born after twins: Beattie (1962: 1); Evans-Pritchard (1936: 27); Hammond-Tooke (1992: 205); and Turner (1969: 88).

17. It is striking that the "Evil Twin" is so much more fully developed in Western literature and popular culture than in Africa. Such films as Cronenberg's

Dead Ringers and De Palma's *Sisters* readily come to mind, as well as television dramas such as Lynch's *Twin Peaks* and the recent sci-fi twist on the motif used by *Caprica*.

18. The association of diviners, divine kings, and other ritual specialists with a liminal status as they move between worlds is long established (see, e.g., Peek 1991). Proposing a closer link to our topic of twins, Schnepel (1995) provides a cross-cultural study of divine kings as twinned beings.

19. A number of works provide broad surveys of twins in world mythologies and traditions, such as B. Beit-Hallahmi and M. Paluszny, "Twinship in Mythology and Science: Ambivalence, Differentiation and the Magical Bond" (1974); G. Corney, "Mythology and Customs Associated with Twins" (1975); and J. Lash, *Twins and the Double* (1993). The most exuberant recognition of twins are the festivals now held worldwide, with the first begun in Twinsburg, Ohio; see www.twinsdays.org and www.twinsworld.com. And, of course, there is a huge range of references in Wikipedia. Even the Yoruba are reintroducing twin festivals (see Renne, chapter 15).

20. See, e.g., Rank's "The Double" (1979) and Freud's description of "the Uncanny" as "a vision of terror" (1963: 41–42). Although Doppelgangers were ghostly doubles, contemporary "Googlegangers," "others" found when one Googles one's own name on the Internet, seem to be more benign (personal communication, Evan Heimlich, January 9, 2008).

21. All guides for parents of twins in the U.S. are concerned with the loss of individuality of twins; see, e.g., Bryan 1995; Clegg and Woolett 1983; Novotny 1994; and Stewart 2000. Much of contemporary psychologists' fascination with twins relates to the ancient debate about Nature and Nurture as the prime directive for human behavior. The twins' festival in Twinsburg, Ohio, has attracted so many psychologists that extra tents have to be erected for them. Scholars find this a perfect setting to research differences between inherited and learned traits by interviewing twins.

22. For example, would we find, as Micheli wonders (chapter 7), special acknowledgment in North Africa of the Prophet Ali's sons, Hassan and Hussein, who are considered twins throughout West Africa? Does the prominent dialogic perspective which permeates the expressive culture of Madagascar (see Haring 1992) also manifest in positive attitudes toward twins?

WORKS CITED

Abrahams, R. G. 1972. "Spirit, Twins, and Ashes in Labwor, Northern Uganda." In *The Interpretation of Ritual*, ed. J. S. La Fontaine, 115–134. London: Tavistock Publications.

Adichie, Chimamanda Ngozi. 2006. *Half of a Yellow Sun*. New York: Anchor Books.

Adler, Alfred. 1973. "Les Jumeaux sont rois." *Homme* 13 (1–2): 167–192.

Appiah, Kwame Anthony. 1992. *In My Father's House: Africa in the Philosophy of Culture*. New York: Oxford University Press.

Baines, John R. 1985. "Egyptian Twins." *Orientalia* 54: 461–481.

Ball, Helen L., and C. M. Hill. 1996. "Reevaluating 'Twin Infanticide.'" *Current Anthropology* 37 (5): 856–863.

Barley, Nigel. 1986. *Ceremony*. New York: Henry Holt and Co.

Barrionuevo, Alexei. 2009. "Mystery of the 'Land of Twins': Something in the Water? Mengele?" *New York Times*, A11, February 23.

Bascom, William R. 1975. *African Dilemma Tales*. The Hague: Mouton.

Basden, G. T. 1966 [1938]. *Niger Ibos*. London: Frank Cass and Co.

Baudrillard, Jean. 1994 [1981]. *Simulacra and Simulation*. Ann Arbor: University of Michigan Press.

Beattie, J. H. M. 1962. "Twin Ceremonies in Bunyoro." *Journal of the Royal Anthropological Institute* 92 (1): 1–12.

Beidelman, T. O. 1963. "Kaguru Omens." *Anthropological Quarterly* 36 (2): 43–59.

Beier, Ulli, ed. 1999. *A Dreaming Life: An Autobiography of Twins Seven-Seven*. Bayreuth African Studies 52. Bayreuth, Germany: Bayreuth University.

Beit-Hallahmi, Benjamin, and M. Paluszny. 1974. "Twinship in Mythology and Science: Ambivalence, Differentiation, and The Magical Bond." *Comprehensive Psychiatry* 15 (4): 345–353.

Bellman, Beryl L. 1975. *Village of Curers and Assassins—On the Production of Kpelle Cosmological Categories*. The Hague: Mouton.

Berglund, Axel-Ivar. 1989. *Zulu Thought-Patterns and Symbolism*. Bloomington: Indiana University Press.

Berman, Bob. 2001. "Tangled Twins." *Discover*, July 31.

Brain, Robert. 1969. "Friends and Twins in Bangwa." In *Man in Africa*, ed. M. Douglas and P. M. Kaberry, 213–227. London: Tavistock.

Brown, Karen McCarthy. 1989. "Afro-Caribbean Spirituality: A Haitian Case Study." In *Healing and Restoring*, ed. Lawrence Sullivan, 255–285. New York: Macmillan.

Bryan, Elizabeth M. 1995. "The Death of a Twin." *Palliative Medicine* 9 (3): 187–192.

Buxton, Jean. 1973. *Religion and Healing in Mandari*. Oxford: Clarendon Press.

Carrithers, Michael, S. Collins, and S. Lukas, eds. 1989. *The Category of the Person*. Cambridge: Cambridge University Press.

Chemeche, George. 2003. *Ibeji: The Cult of Yoruba Twins*. Milan: 5 Continents.

Clegg, Averil, and A. Woolett. 1983. *Twins: From Conception to Five Years*. New York: Ballantine Books.

Cole, Herbert M. 1989. "Two as One: The Male and Female Couple." In *Icons: Ideals and Power in the Art of Africa*, 52–73. Washington, D.C.: Museum of African Art, Smithsonian Institute Press.

Corney, Gerald. 1975. "Mythology and Customs Associated with Twins." In *Human Multiple Reproduction*, ed. I. MacGillivray, P. P. S. Nylander, and G. Corney, 1–15. London: W. B. Saunders.

Creinin, Mitchell, and L. G. Keith. 1989. "The Yoruba Contribution to Our Understanding of the Twinning Process." *Journal of Reproductive Medicine* 34 (6):
379–387.

Davis, Courtney. 2002. "Vanishing Twin Syndrome." *Discover*, October, 24–25.

D'Azevedo, Warren L. 1974. "Sources of Gola Artistry." In *The Traditional Artist in
African Societies*, ed. W. L. D'Avezedo, 282–349. Bloomington: Indiana University Press.

De Heusch, Luc. 1980. "Heat, Physiology, and Cosmogony." In *Explorations in
African Systems of Thought*, ed. Ivan Karp and Charles S. Bird, 27–43. Bloomington: Indiana University Press.

———. 1982. *The Drunken King or the Origin of the State*, trans. R. Willis. Bloomington: Indiana University Press.

———. 1985. *Sacrifice in Africa: A Structuralist Approach*. Manchester, U.K.: Manchester University Press.

Deren, Maya. 1970 [1953]. *Divine Horsemen: The Living Gods of Haiti*. New York:
McPherson and Co.

Diduk, Susan. 1993. "Twins, Ancestors, and Socio-Economic Change in Kedjo
Society." *Man* (n.s.), 28:3, 551–571.

———. 2001. "Twinship and Juvenile Power: The Ordinariness of the Extraordinary." *Ethnology* 40: 1, 29-43.

Dos Santos, Juana Elbein, and Deoscoredes M. Dos Santos. 1973. "Esu Bara,
Principle of Individual Life in the Nago System." In *La Notion de Personne in
Afrique Noire*, ed. G. Dieterlen, 45–60. Paris: Editions de Centre National de la
Recherche Scientifique, 1973.

Dugast, Stephan. 1996. "Meurtriers, Jumeaux, et Devins: Trois variations sur le
theme du double (Bassar, Togo)." *Destins de meurtriers: Systemes de pensée en
Afrique Noire* 14: 175–209.

Dundy, Elaine. 1985. *Elvis and Gladys*. New York: Macmillan.

Emecheta, Buchi. 1994. *Kehinde*. Long Grove, Ill.: Waveland Press.

Erny, Pierre. 1973. *Childhood and Cosmos*. New York: New Perspectives.

Evans-Pritchard, E. E. 1936. "Customs and Beliefs Relating to Twins among the
Nilotic Nuer." *Uganda Journal* 3: 230–238.

———. *Nuer Religion*. 1956. Oxford: Clarendon Press.

Fretz, Rachel I. 2004. "Dialogic Performances: Call-and-Response in African Nar-
rating." In *African Folklore: An Encyclopedia*, ed. P. M. Peek and K. Yankah,
81–83. New York: Routledge.

Freud, Sigmund. 1963 [1919]. "The Uncanny." In *Studies in Parapsychology*, 19–60.
New York: Collier Books.

Gettleman, Jeffrey. 2008. "Albinos, Long Shunned, Face Deadly Threat in Tanzania." *New York Times*, June 8, A8 and A20.

Gillman, Susan. 1989. *Dark Twin: Imposture and Identity in Mark Twain's America*.
Chicago: University of Chicago Press.

Glassie, Henry. 2010. *Prince Twins Seven-Seven*. Bloomington: Indiana University
Press.

Granzberg, Gary. 1973. "Twin Infanticide: A Cross-cultural Test of a Materialistic Explanation." *Ethos* 1 (4): 405–412.

Griaule, Marcel. 1960. "The Idea of Person among the Dogon." In *Cultures and Societies of Africa*, ed. Simon Ottenberg and Phoebe Ottenberg, 365–371. New York: Random House.

Griaule, Marcel, and Germaine Dieterlen. 1968 [1954]. "The Dogon of the French Sudan." In *African Worlds*, ed. D. Forde, 83–110. London: Oxford University Press.

Gufler, Hermann. 1995. "Yamba Twin Ritual." *Anthropos* 91 (1–3): 33–51.

Guralnick, Peter. 1994. *Last Train to Memphis: The Rise of Elvis Presley*. Boston, Mass.: Little Brown.

Habila, Helon. 2007. *Measuring Time*. New York: Norton.

Hall, H. U. 1928. "Twins in Upper Guinea." *Museum Journal* 19: 403–427.

Hammond-Tooke, W. D. 1992. "Twins, Incest, and Mediators: The Structure of Four Zulu Folk Tales." *Africa* 62 (2): 203–219.

Haring, Lee. 1992. *Verbal Arts of Madagascar: Performance in Historical Perspective*. Philadelphia: University of Pennsylvania Press.

Herskovits, Melville J. 1937. *Life in a Haitian Valley*. New York: Knopf.

Herskovits, Melville J., and Francis S. 1934. *Rebel Destiny: Among the Bush Negroes of Dutch Guiana*. New York: McGraw-Hill.

Jackson, Michael, and Ivan Karp, eds. 1990. *Personhood and Agency: The Experience of Self and Other in African Cultures*. Washington, D.C.: Smithsonian Institution Press.

Jacob, Jean-Pierre. 1990. "Fertility and Social Order among the Winye Gurunsi of Burkina Faso." In *The Creative Communion: African Models of Fertility and the Regeneration of Life*, ed. Anita Jacobson-Widding and Walter Van Beek, 75–92. Uppsala, Sweden: Acta Universitatis Upsaliensis, Uppsala Studies in Cultural Anthropology.

James, Wendy. 1988. *The Listening Ebony: Moral Knowledge, Religion, and Power among the Uduk of Sudan*. Oxford: Clarendon Press.

Jeffreys, M. D. W. 1947. "Notes on Twins: Bamenda." *African Studies* 6: 189–195.

Jung, Carl G., et al. 1964. *Man and His Symbols*. New York: Doubleday.

Junod, Henri. 1962 [1927]. *The Life of a South African Tribe*, 2 vols. New Hyde Park, N.Y.: University Books.

Kilson, Marion. 1975. "Twin Beliefs and Ceremony in Ga Culture." *Journal of Religion in Africa* 5: 171–197.

La Fontaine, J. S. 1985. "Person and Individual: Some Anthropological Reflections." In *The Category of the Person*, ed. Michael Carrithers, S. Collings, and S. Lukes, 123–140. Cambridge: Cambridge University Press.

LaGamma, Alisa. 2004. *Echoing Images: Couples in African Sculpture*. New York: Metropolitan Museum of Art / New Haven: Yale University Press.

Lash, John. 1993. *Twins and the Double*. London: Thames and Hudson.

Lawal, Babatunde. 2008. "Ejiwapo: the Dialectics of Twoness in Yoruba Art and Culture." *African Arts* 41 (1): 24–39.

Leis, Philip E. 1965. "The Nonfunctional Attributes of Twin Infanticide in the Niger Delta." *Anthropological Quarterly* 38 (3): 97–111.

Levi-Strauss, C. 1979. "Harelips and Twins." In *Myth and Meaning*, 25–33. New York: Schocken Books.

———. 1987. "An Anatomical Foreshadowing of Twinship." In *The View from Afar*, trans. Joachim Neugroschel and Phoebe Hoss, 201–209. London, Penguin.

Littlejohn, James. 1970. "Twins, Birds, Etc." *Bijdragen tot de tall-, land- en Volkern-kunde* (n.s.) 91–114.

Marcus, Greil. 1991. *Dead Elvis: A Chronicle of a Cultural Obsession*. New York: Doubleday.

McClendon, Thomas V. 1997. "'A Dangerous Doctrine': Twins, Ethnography, and the Natal Code." *Journal of Legal Pluralism and Unofficial Law* 39: 121–140.

Mercier, Paul. 1963. "The Fon of Dahomey." In *African Worlds*, ed. Daryll Forde, 210–234. London: Oxford University Press.

Merriam, Alan P. 1974. *An African World: The Basongye Village of Lupupa Ngye*. Bloomington: Indiana University Press.

Metraux, Alfred. 1972 [1959]. *Voodoo in Haiti*. New York: Schocken Books.

Micheli, C. Angelo. 2008. "Doubles and Twins: A New Approach to Contemporary Studio Photography in West Africa." *African Arts* 41 (1): 66–85.

Mosnro, A. A., A. N. Agyapong, M. Opoku-Fofie, and S. Deen. 2001. "Twinning Rates in Ghana." *Twin Research* 4: 4, 238–241.

Nangendo, Stevie M. 1996. "Twinship among Babukusu of Bungoma District, Western Kenya: A Misfortune or Blessing?" *MILA* (n.s.) 1: 16–27.

Novotny, Pamela Patrick. 1994. *The Joy of Twins*, rev. ed. New York: Three Rivers Press.

Nylander, P. P. S. 1975. "Frequency of Multiple Births." In *Human Multiple Reproduction*, ed. I. MacGillivray, P. P. S. Nylander, and G. Corney, 87–97. London: W. B. Saunders Co.

Onimhawo, John A. 1996–97. "Euthanasia: A Philosophical-Theological Evaluation of the Traditional Nigerian Experience." *Orita* 28 (1): 106–131.

Ortmeyer, Dale H. 1970. "The We-Self of Identical Twins." *Contemporary Psychoanalysis* 6: 125–142.

Pector, Elizabeth A. 2002. "Twin Death and Mourning Worldwide: A Review of the Literature." *Twin Research* 5 (3): 196–205.

Peek, Philip M. 1991. "African Divination Systems: Non-Normal Modes of Cognition." In *African Divination Systems*, ed. P. M. Peek, 193–212. Bloomington: Indiana University Press.

———. 1995. "The Roles of Sexual Expressions in African Insulting Languages and Verbal Arts. In *Folklore Interpreted: Essays in Honor of Alan Dundes*, ed. Regina Bendix and Rosemary L. Zumwalt, 401–414. New York: Garland Press.

———. 2005. "The Communal Self: Diviners, Twins, and Doubles." Paper presented for "Realities Re-Viewed and Revealed: Divination in Sub-Saharan Africa," conference at the University of Leiden, the Netherlands, July 4–5.

———. 2008. "Couples or Doubles? Representations of Twins in African Arts." *African Arts* 41 (1): 14–23.

———. 2010. "Twinning and 'Perfect Knowledge' in African Systems of Divination." In *Divination: Perspectives for a New Millenium*, ed. P. Curry, 25–38. Farnham, Surrey, U.K.: Ashgate Publishers.

Pelton, Robert D. 1980. *The Trickster in West Africa*. Berkeley: University of California Press.

Pemberton, John, III. 2003. "*Ere Ibeji*: An Affirmation of Life in the Face of Death." In *Ibeji: The Cult of Yoruba Twins*, ed. G. Chemeche, 31–49. Milan: 5 Continents.

Pison, Giles. 1992. "Twins in Sub-Saharan Africa: Frequency, Social Status, and Mortality." In *Mortality and Society in Sub-Saharan Africa*, ed. E. Van de Walle, G. Pison, and M. Sala-Diakanda, 253–278. Oxford: Clarendon Press.

Plato. 1989. "The Speech of Aristophanes." In *Symposium*, trans. A. Nehamas and P. Woodruff, 25–31. Indianapolis, Ind.: Hackett Publishing Co.

Rank, Otto. 1979 [1914]. *The Double*. Translated and edited by H. Tucker, Jr. New York: New American Library,

Reeder, Greg. 2000. "Same-sex Desire, Conjugal Constructs, and the Tomb of Niankhkhnum and Khnumhotep." *World Archaeology* 32 (2): 193–208.

Renne, Elisha P. 2001. "Twinship in an Ekiti Yoruba Town." *Ethnology* 40 (1): 63–78.

Renne, Elisha P., and M. L. Bastian. 2001. "Reviewing Twinship in Africa." *Ethnology* 40 (1): 1–11.

Roberts, Allen F. 1986. "Duality in African Art." *African Arts* 19 (4): 26–35, 86–88.

Schapera, I. 1927. "Customs Relating to Twins in South Africa." *Journal of the African Society* 26: 102, 117–137.

Schnepel, Burkhard. 1994. *Twinned Beings: Kings and Effigies in Southern Sudan, East India, and Renaissance France*. Göteborg, Sweden: Institute for Advanced Studies in Social Anthropology.

Schoffeleers, Matthew. 1991. "Twins and Unilateral Figures in Central and Southern Africa: Symmetry and Asymmetry in the Symbolization of the Sacred." *Journal of Religion in Africa* 31 (4): 345–372.

Schwartz, Hillel. 1997. *The Culture of the Copy: Striking Likenesses, Unreasonable Facsimilies*. New York: Zone Books.

Seligman, C. G., and B. Z. Seligman. 1932. *Pagan Tribes of the Nilotic Sudan*. London: George Routledge and Sons.

Signorini, Italo. 1973. "Agonwole Agyale: The Marriage Between Two Persons of the Same Sex Among the Nzema of Southwestern Ghana." *Journal de la Société des Africanistes* 43 (2): 221–234.

Southall, Aidan. 1972. "Twinship and Symbolic Structure." In *The Interpretation of Ritual*, ed. J. S. La Fontaine, 73–114. London: Tavistock Publications.

Stewart, Elizabeth A. 2000. "Towards the Social Analysis of Twinship." *British Journal of Sociology* 51 (4): 719–737.

Suthers, Ellen Moore. 1987. "Perception, Knowledge, and Divination in Djimini Society, Ivory Coast." Ph.D. dissertation, University of Virginia.

Talbot, P. A. 1926. *The Peoples of Southern Nigeria*, vol. 3: *Ethnology.* London: Oxford University Press.

Ten Raa, Eric. 1980. "Ritual Change: Sandawe Twin-Birth Festivals Before and After Tanzania's Villagization." *Paideuma* 27: 181–195.

Thompson, Barbara. 2008. *Black Womanhood: Images, Icons, and Ideologies of the African Body.* Hanover, N.H.: Hood Museum, Darmouth College / Seattle: University of Washington Press.

Thompson, Robert Farris. 1993. *Face of the Gods: Arts and Altars of Africa and the African Americas.* New York: Museum for African Art / Munich: Prestel.

Turner, Victor. 1977 (1969). "Paradoxes of Twinship in Ndembu Ritual." In *The Ritual Process: Structure and Anti-Structure,* 44–93. Ithaca, N.Y.: Cornell University Press.

Van Beek, Walter. 1991. "Dogon Restudied: A Field Evaluation of the Work of Marcel Griaule." *Current Anthropology* 32 (2): 139–167.

———. 1992. "Becoming Human in Dogon, Mali." In *Coming into Existence: Birth and Metaphors of Birth*, ed. G. Aijmer, 47–70. Göteborg, Sweden: IASSA.

Vincent, Jeanne-Francoise. 2001. "Des enfants pas comme les autres, les jumeaux dans les montagnes Mofu-Diamare (Nord-Cameroun)." *Journal des Africanistes* 72 (1): 105–118.

Whyte, Susan Reynolds. 1997. *Questioning Misfortune.* Cambridge: Cambridge University Press.

Wilford, John Noble. 2005. "A Mystery, Locked in Timeless Embrace." *New York Times*, December 20.

Zahan, Dominique. 1979. *The Religion, Spirituality, and Thought of Traditional Africa*, trans. K. Ezra. Chicago: University of Chicago Press.

Part One

Roots

CHAPTER TWO

Twins and Double Beings among the Bamana and Maninka of Mali

PASCAL JAMES IMPERATO AND GAVIN H. IMPERATO

The Bamana (Bambara) of Mali in West Africa are the largest ethnic group in the country, numbering close to 4.5 million. As such, they occupy a dominant cultural, political, and social position in the life of modern Mali. Although the Bamana and the closely related Maninka (Malinke) have been undergoing conversion to Islam for a very long time, many retain beliefs and practices with origins in *Bamanaya,* a traditional religion and way of life characterized by initiation societies, blood sacrifices, and belief in a complex religion characterized by several deities and a complex legend of creation (Imperato 2001: 6–22).

The Bamana and Maninka conceive of double beings in a broad context. This category includes monozygotic twins (two individuals born together and derived from one egg and one sperm) (*flaniw*), dizygotic twins (two individuals born together and derived from two separate eggs and two separate sperm) (*flaniw*), true and pseudo-hermaphrodites (*tyétémouso-téw*), and albinos (*yéféguéw*). The respective singular forms are *flani, tyé-témousoté,* and *yéfégué.* The plural of Bamana nouns is generally rendered by the addition of a "-w" as a suffix. When the noun is modified, the "-w" is added only to the modifier. There are regional variations of the word for albino, including *yéfégué, yafégé, yépégé, yéfougué,* and *yéfugé.* The word for albinism is *yéfégéya.* Another term used for albino is *founé,* which is also used to denote praise singers, who in Bamana and Maninka society are part of the *nyamankalaw* caste of artisans, bards, and blacksmiths. It is noteworthy that the term *founé* is also used by the Maninka and Khassonke for twins; a female twin is called *founémouso* and a male twin *founétyé.* The fact that a single term is used to describe both twins and albinos is significant, because it demonstrates that both are considered true twins (personal communication, Modibo N'Faly Keita, Kita, Mali, July 24,

2005). The term *gomblé* or *gombolé*, which literally means "red monkey," is used to describe those albinos who have a less severe form of the condition manifested by tan or bronze colored skin and light brown hair.

Triplets (*sabani*) and quadruplets (*nanini*) are extremely rare among the Bamana and Maninka, and are unknown to most. In many areas, they are considered as twins. While monozygotic (identical) twins are recognized as being different from dizygotic (fraternal) ones because of their seemingly identical physical appearance and because they are always of the same sex, they are not viewed differently from their dizygotic counterparts in terms of cultural beliefs and practices. In part, this derives from the often confounding characteristics present in monozygotic twins such as inverse laterality and discordance in a number of traits. The former, sometimes referred to as mirror-image twinning, occurs in 10–15 percent of healthy monozygotic twins. In these mirror-image twins, a number of features are on the opposite sides, such as handedness, nevi (birthmarks), cowlicks, hair whorls, and the first tooth to erupt. Discordance refers to the expression of a minor trait in only one of a twin pair, and occurs in most, if not all, monozygotic twins (Hall 2003: 735–743). In addition, about 10 percent of monozygotic twins are affected by congenital abnormalities and genetic disorders, often obvious at birth. This is two to three times the rate seen in singleton (one baby) pregnancies, where the rate of congenital abnormalities is 2–3 percent (Myrianthopoulos 1975: 1–39). From a certain perspective, monozygotic twins are clones, and as such have poor epigenetic control[1] during development, leading to somatic mutations. As a result, congenital abnormalities are common in these types of twins (Hay and Wehrung 1970: 662–678).

The presence of malformations, disruptions, or deformations due to discordant mutation in one monozygotic twin can alter his or her appearance, and in a rural Bamana or Maninka setting this renders clear identification of "identical" twins impossible. Disruptions such as limb reduction defects and hemifacial microsomia (smallness of one half of the face) greatly alter appearance, as do deformations such as club feet, dislocated hips, and cranial synostosis (premature closure of the sutures of the skull). Also, malformations such as cloacal anomalies, neural-tube defects, and congenital cardiac defects contribute to higher neonatal mortality rates among these twins.

Dizygotic twins are also susceptible to deformities that result from two babies growing in a space meant for one, but they are less susceptible to some of the above genetics-based malformations and disruptions. As a consequence, perinatal mortality rates in rural African settings are higher among monozygotic twins than among their dizygotic counterparts. However, premature birth is a higher risk for both types of twins than for single babies. It has been estimated that only one third of twin pregnancies come to term. Research in a rural Malian setting showed that this results in more infant deaths among twins—whether one or both of a twin pair—based on prematurity alone. Monozygotic twins have a higher mortality rate than dizygotic twins or singletons because 10 percent of them have some type of congenital anomaly (Hall 1996: 202–204).

Many twin pregnancies are lost or else become singleton pregnancies. It is estimated that only one in eight fetuses beginning as a twin goes on to be born as a twin (Boklage 1990: 75–94). These early intrauterine losses, also more common among monozygotic twins due to congenital anomalies, are not generally observed in the absence of advanced radiological imaging. The remaining monozygotic twin, now a singleton, is still vulnerable to developing the congenital anomalies that affected the other fetus. Neonatalogists are well aware that a singleton born with certain anomalies may have started as a monozygotic twin.

Twinning Rates among the Bamana and Maninka and Other Population Groups

In 1968, there were 761 twin births reported among 34,780 live births in fifty-two maternity centers in Mali, representing about one quarter of all live births in Mali. Thus, the rate of twin births was 21.8/1,000 births. Data for maternity centers serving Bamana and Maninka populations showed a rate of 17.9/1,000 births (Keita 1968: 128–131). These Ministry of Health and Social Affairs data did not differentiate between dizygotic and monozygotic twins. However, it can be assumed that the majority of these twins were dizygotic because the rate of monozygotic twin births is fairly constant across different populations at 3.5/1,000 births. In 1990, Dolo, Diall, and Diabate reported a twinning rate of 15.2/1,000 births at the Hôpital National du Point-G in Mali's capital, Bamako, whose patients are primarily Bamana (Dolo et al. 1990: 25–31). This 15.2/1,000 rate is not significantly different than the 17.9/1,000 rate reported in 1968.

While monozygotic twinning rates are constant at 3.5/1,000 births across most population groups, those for dizygotic twins vary greatly. Because dizygotic twins contribute two-thirds of all twin births, they account for these population rate differences. While routine DNA testing can often differentiate monozygotic from dizygotic twins in developed countries, it is not currently possible in much of Africa. Thus, one can only compare overall twinning rates between African populations and those in the United States and Europe.

The prevalence of spontaneous (i.e., without assisted reproduction) twin births in the United States and Great Britain is about 10.5/1,000 births, of which two-thirds are dizygotic (Kiely and Kiely 2001: 131–133). Historically, twin birth rates in the United States and Europe have risen along with advancing maternal ages up until the age of 39 years. Since the 1990s, older age at childbearing and the use of assisted reproduction have greatly contributed to the overall dramatic rise in multiple gestations. By 1997, twin birth rates in the United States had risen for white women to 28.8/1,000, for Hispanic women to 19.5/1,000, and for African American women to 30.0/1,000. The overall rate was 26.1/1,000 compared to the historical rate of 10.5/1,000. Historically, African American women in the United States had a twinning rate of 14.0/1,000, well above the national average of 10.5. This historical rate reflected in part the higher spontaneous rates of twinning long observed among the various African populations, especially the Yoruba of Nigeria (Martin and Park 1999: 70–85). However, with assisted reproduction and later age at childbearing, that rate has more than doubled.

A number of medical researchers have documented high rates of twinning among the Yoruba, Ibo, Hausa, and Fulani of Nigeria. Foremost among them is Percy Nylander, who was a lecturer in the Department of Obstetrics and Gynecology at the University of Ibadan. He found rates as high as 45.9/1,000 among the Yoruba. He determined that the high rate of twinning in western Nigeria was due to an increased proportion of dizygotic twins. While the causes of monozygotic twinning have not yet been fully elucidated, it has now been shown that spontaneous dizygotic twinning is associated with an increased serum concentration of follicle-stimulating hormone (FSH) in the mother. These levels are much higher in Yoruba women than in women in Great Britain matched for age, and they vary with geography, season, ethnic origin, and increasing parity (number of children). They are also higher in tall, heavy, and older women (Nylander 1970: 457–464). It has also been documented that spontaneous dizygotic twinning runs in families and that in such instances the higher levels of FSH are inherited either as an autosomal dominant or autosomal recessive trait.[2] It has also been demonstrated that 7–15 percent of the population carries a gene that is dominantly inherited and which predisposes to dizygotic twinning (Lewis et al. 1996: 237–246).

A Broad Concept of Twinning

The Bamana and Maninka are well aware that twins are often born prematurely and that when born at term are often smaller than singleton infants.

This recognition of higher rates of prematurity and low birth weights and their association with higher infant mortality no doubt contributed to the elaboration of beliefs and practices favoring twin survival. Among the Bamana and Maninka, babies born in pairs are accorded a privileged status that provides them and their parents greater than usual access to a variety of resources. Such access is not extended to those with disorders of sex development (hermaphrodites and pseudo-hermaphrodites) or albinos, who are also considered twin beings. For unlike what we would call twins, who are regarded as a gift from the supreme deity (known variously as *Pemba*, *Bemba*, or *N'gala*) and as extraordinary beings with unusual powers, the individuals affected by these three pathologies are thought to be the result of aberrant social conduct. Unlike twins, they are sometimes feared because of their powers and viewed with ambivalence because they are seen as the result of behavioral departures from societal norms.

The basis for considering four distinct groups of individuals as twins is *Bamanaya*, a corpus of essential spiritual and cosmological beliefs and a mode of living that define someone as Bamana or Maninka. To embrace *Bamanaya* is to believe in the centrality in one's life of *nyama* (vital life-force, energy, or power) and *boliw* (ritual objects which are regularly given blood sacrifices). *Boliw* (singular *boli*) are great reservoirs of *nyama* whose powers are increased and renewed through regular sacrifices. However, it is in the legend of creation and in its principal deity, *Faro*, that the duality of human nature (good and bad, male and female, strong and weak) and the concept of twinning are both elaborated and codified for the spiritual belief system that is at the heart of *Bamanaya*.

Twins, Hermaphrodites, and Albinos and the Legend of Creation

There are two major variants of the Bamana legend of creation, and subtle regional differences within them. The legend in the southern region is depersonalized compared to its analogue in the north (Paques 1954: 80–83). While the southern legend revolves around nonhuman forces, in the north the story is centered on supernatural personalities embodying known human virtues and vices (De Ganay 1949: 181–201; Dieterlen 1950: 1–55; Zahan 1963a: 116–120; Zahan 1974: 1–6). It is within the context of this northern Bamana creation narrative that societal values, attitudes, and practices concerning twins, those with disorders of sex development, and albinos are given metaphysical importance and historical legitimacy.

Zahan (1974: 1–6) summarized this northern creation legend beginning with belief in a supreme being known as *Bemba*, *Pemba*, or *N'gala*, which we will here call God. There are several supernatural beings associated with God and his act of creation; most prominent among them are *Mouso Koroni Koundyé* or *Nyalé, Faro,* and *Ndomadyiri.* From a certain perspective, these beings are also manifestations of God. During the first phase of creation, known as *dali folo* (first putting in order, first creation), the earth was naked, and God manifested himself as a grain (*kise*) known as *Pemba.* A *balanza* tree (*Acacia albida*) grew from this seed. But when it became fully grown, it withered and fell to the ground. Eventually, all that remained was a long beam of wood, known as *Pembélé.* This wooden beam secreted mildew that accumulated beneath it. Pemba mixed this mildew with his own saliva to create a new being, a female, known as *Mouso Koroni Koundyé* ("little old woman with a white head").

Mouso Koroni then engaged in the creative process, engendering vegetables, animals, and human beings. The latter were at first immortal. Her creativity was characterized by disorder, confusion, and haste. This is excused by some Bamana on the grounds that she wanted to populate the earth with beings as rapidly as possible. Finally, Mouso Koroni planted the *Pembélé* in the ground, and he became a tree once again. Men worshipped Pemba, now a *balanza* tree, the tree that eventually introduced them to death. In time, men transferred their worship to *Faro,* another supernatural being and manifestation of God, who is the master of water.

Some Bamana believe that Mouso Koroni disappeared at this point, after spending a wretched life on earth authoring disorder. Others, however, believe that she continues to live, the personification of air, wind, and fire. She is also the "mother of magic," the first sorcerer, and as such is called by another name, Nyalé.

Mouso Koroni was originally created with a soul that had two parts, a *ni* and a *dya,* like those of all human beings. But at the time of her creation, while God gave her the *ni,* he entrusted its double, the *dya,* to Faro. Thus, Mouso Koroni was incomplete from the moment of her creation. Nonetheless, she authored the first phase of creation, characterized by prodigious growth and fertility. As Zahan (1974: 5) notes, as Nyalé, she gives strength to newborns and hastens the ripening of grain. She is the source of all human ideas which have been or will be given to man, and represents energy, activity, and desire. But she is also the source of all malice, misunderstanding, treachery, deviancy, and sorcery. She is an extravagant being, unruly, uncontrolled, and excessive. She causes all creation to proliferate, but in an uncontrolled manner. The hasty nature of Mouso Koroni's creative efforts resulted in defective beings. She is the author of numerous anomalies, both physical and psychological.

In entrusting Mouso Koroni's *dya* to Faro, God in effect set limits on the amount of disorder in the world. He also deprived the primordial female being of coherence and made her defective. It could be cogently argued that the ancient Bamana conceived of this component of the myth to rationalize woman's imposed inferior position in their society and the necessity for male dominance.

The second phase of creation, called *dali flana* (second putting in order, second creation), was dominated by Faro and Ndomadyiri. The former represents equilibrium, and the latter stability. Faro is believed to be androgynous and to live in water. In some drawings and sculptures, he is represented in female form with long black hair, breasts, a white face and head, a fish tail, and flippers covering each ear opening. In other sculptures, he has a white human head and trunk, female breasts, and either a piscatorial or reptilian body. His fin-shaped tail and breasts are made of copper (Dieterlen 1950: 41–42).

Faro is the original albino, having stolen his white face from *Téliko*, a lesser deity associated with whirlwinds and dust devils. As detailed by Dieterlen (1950: 41–42), Faro was originally composed of sound, a voice in the waters of the sea. Téliko, a lesser deity, who was a winged albino and who is associated with whirlwinds, dust devils, and the air, attempted to fly across the world in order to dominate it. Warned about this by the dogfish (*oulou-dyégué*), Faro decided to take Téliko's body as his own and at the same time vanquish his challenger. Téliko gnawed at his own flesh in order to nourish himself to a point where only his bone marrow remained. Eventually, his body was transformed into red copper, and he fell into the sea. The dogfish, who was lying in wait for him, sang in order to draw him closer. Téliko, sensing a trap, flew back up into the sky until he reached its limits. Losing strength, his *dya* (double) fell into the sea where his body was seized by Faro, except for the external male genitalia, which Faro gave to the dogfish. Thus it was that Faro acquired an albino head and trunk and a copper tail. Faro's right hand is male, and the left female. He has no apparent external genitalia, but impregnated himself and gave birth to female twins when water first flowed on the earth. (Dieterlen 1950: 42, 88). Thus, he is the author of twinning and also the original hermaphrodite.

Although Faro's role is to perfect the world, organize it, put it in equilibrium, and give it eternal life, he is closely associated with twinning, albinism, and hermaphroditism. He was born from God's vaporous breath, from a bubble of saliva while God was pronouncing the words of creation (Zahan 1963a: 118). Faro is God's visible countenance and his word. However, during this second phase of creation, this word was unintelligible to humans, consisting of a language in which all the words were connected. It was Ndomadyiri, the divine blacksmith, the third supernatural person after Mouso Koroni and Faro, who made this primordial word into useful language. He is, as Zahan (1974: 5–6) says, what is left, the earth, after the evaporation of water (Faro) due to the action of the wind (Nyalé). This provokes the notion of fixity, of remaining in place after the withdrawal of his previous associations.

The third phase of creation is that of the present. As Zahan (1974: 5–6) observes, it is the stage when human beings and things confront one another. The formation of human societies results in confusion and disorder due to men asserting themselves and expressing their wills and emotions. However, Ndomadyiri, as a blacksmith, is omnipresent, stabilizing society through his supervision of its religious rites.

Mouso Koroni, who had retreated during the second phase of creation, appeared again during the third as Nyalé. While the second phase was characterized by order, balance, and harmony, the third has great potential for a resurgence of the disorder and confusion characteristic of the first phase because of her presence. Again, we can see how this male-dominated society that relegates women to an inferior political and social position has produced powerful religious and metaphysical reasons for so doing.

Knowledge of these myths of creation was on the wane during the 1960s when one of us (Pascal James Imperato) began conducting field research in Mali. The triple forces of the rural exodus of young people to cash economy employment in the cities and plantations of the Ivory Coast, conversion to Islam, and the influence of modernization have played a major role in the demise of knowledge of these myths among the Bamana and Maninka. Similarly, these forces have also led to the decline of *Bamanaya*, a way of life and understanding of the world encompassing religious and philosophical beliefs and elaborate cults in which blood sacrifices are often of great significance.

Jean-Paul Colleyn is a prominent French anthropologist who began his field studies among the Minianka people in Mali in the 1980s. He has since conducted important studies of Bamana art linked with contemporary field research. Colleyn's work must be viewed in light of his preference for framing his anthropological interpretations and discourses within a framework of Derridian deconstruction. Such an approach encompasses a reliance on relativism, a deconstruction of received knowledge, varying interpretations of historical evidence, and a tendency to create revisionist narratives. It also embraces an affinity for formulating discussions within a hermeneutics of suspicion and anti-foundationalism. Some of Colleyn's writings reflect an effort to deconstruct ethnicity as an objective reality in central Mali, in part by overemphasizing cross-culturally borrowed commonalities among diverse peoples and by deconstructing the distinct and different social, religious, political, and artistic characteristics that separate them.

Colleyn's tendency toward deconstruction has understandably resulted in analyses and conclusions at variance with those reflected in the studies of eminent pioneer French structuralists such as Marcel Griaule, Germaine Dieterlen, and Dominique Zahan. Their extensive field research in Mali antedated Colleyn's by several decades. Recently, the latter posited that most Bamana today are ignorant of the creation myth, Faro, and Mousso Koroni. He claims that "*Mousso Koroni* is neither a unique figure nor an individualized divinity, but a stereotype" and that "*Faro* appears as a divinity only in Segou" (Colleyn 2009: 50). This statement is of interest because it departs radically from the conclusions of Colleyn's structuralist predecessors. However, it also evidences the challenges inherent in corroborating past realities that gradually vanished from the collective cultural Bamana memory over the ensuing decades since they were first documented.

As Eamon Duffy (1992: 593) has observed in his *The Stripping of the Altars: Traditional Religion in England c. 1400–c. 1580*, the Protestant reformation in England resulted in the "death of the past" and "a relentless carrying away of the landmarks of a thousand years." In a few short decades, "whatever the instincts and nostalgia of their seniors, a generation was growing up which had known nothing else, which believed the Pope to be Antichrist, the Mass a mummery, which did not look back to the Catholic past as their own. . . ." So it is now with the Bamana myths of creation, which are no longer known to most contemporary Islamized and secularized generations, but whose past reality cannot be denied by current absence.

An Overview of Disorders of Sex Development and Albinism

The language used to describe human physical conditions can be a delicate matter. In 2009, the Intersex Consensus Conference on Intersex issued a "Consensus Statement on Management of Intersex Disorders" (Lee et al. 2009: e488–e500). This consensus conference advocated a reexamination of long-used nomenclature to describe disorders of sex development (DSD). This recommendation was based on the important advances that have been made in the identification of the molecular genetic causes of abnormal sex, as well as recognition of ethical issues and patient advocacy concerns (Lee et al. 2009: e488). The conference observed that terms such as intersex, hermaphroditism, pseudo-hermaphroditism, sex reversal, and gender-based labels are increasingly controversial and are potentially pejorative to patients and confusing to medical practitioners (Lee et al.

2009: e488). That said, the proposed revisions in nomenclature primarily substituted chromosomal identifiers for these conditions (Lee et al. 2009: e489). While these are certainly preferable within the context of medical science, they are more challenging for lay people to comprehend. Hence, here we use the older nomenclature familiar to most lay readers.

Disorders of sex development arise because of abnormalities in the karyotype of cells. The karyotype is the organization of a cell's chromosomes in relation to number, shape, size, type, and arrangement, such as 46,XX (female) and 46,XY (male). While these karyotypes are those in normal individuals, they are also present, but in abnormal forms, in hermaphrodites and pseudo-hermaphrodites (Kristic et al. 2000: 580–583; Wiersma 2001: 397–399; Krob et al. 1994: 2–10; MacLaughlin and Donahoe 2004: 367–378).

"Genotype" means the genetic makeup of an individual, while "phenotype" refers to their physical and physiological traits. Determination of a person's true sex cannot be made on the basis of the phenotypical characteristics alone; genotypical characteristics must also be determined because not all of these are expressed in the phenotype.

In the preindustrial world of rural Bamana and Maninka, people are not able to distinguish between true hermaphrodites and pseudo-hermaphrodites. In true hermaphrodites, both ovarian and testicular tissues are present in a variety of patterns. The karyotype may be female (46,XX) or a mosaic (46,XX/46,XY). However, about 80 percent of true hermaphrodites are 46,XX (female). True hermaphrodites often have an ovotestis and ambiguous external genitalia. In industrialized societies, the sex of rearing—the sex that the child is identified with—is often dictated by the phenotype, which is usually female (Kristic et al. 2000: 580–583; Wiersma 2001: 397–399; Krob et al. 1994: 2–10; MacLaughlin and Donahoe 2004: 367–378).

True hermaphroditism is a relatively rare disorder in most parts of the world except sub-Saharan Africa, where it is not uncommon (MacLaughlin and Donahoe 2004: 367–368). In a study of 96 cases described in Africa, 96.9 percent showed a female (46,XX) karyotype. The 46,XY karyotype (male) is extremely rare but not unknown (Krob et al. 1994: 2–10). Although the sex of rearing is dictated by the phenotype, in practice this means that most are raised as females (MacLaughlin and Donahoe 2004: 367–378). The causes of true hermaphroditism are not fully understood.

Pseudo-hermaphroditism is by comparison a more common disorder. In male pseudo-hermaphrodites, the karyotype is 46,XY (male), the gonads are testes, but the external genitalia are incompletely virilized, ambiguous, or female. There are several gene mutations responsible for the various types of male pseudo-hermaphroditism. These affect a number of protein and enzyme systems which result in intersex anomalies (MacLaughlin and Donahoe 2004: 367–368).

In female pseudo-hermaphroditism, the karyotype is 46,XX (female), the gonads are ovaries, but the external genitalia are virilized. Most cases of female pseudo-hermaphroditism result not from genetic mutations, as is the case with the male counterpart disorder, but from exposure of the female fetus to the virilizing effects of androgens *in utero*. The most common causes of this endocrine dysfunction are congenital adrenal hyperplasia, placental aromatase deficiency, masculinizing maternal tumors, and the administration of androgenic drugs to women during pregnancy (Minh et al. 1993: 1735–1740).

There are several other genetic mutations that result in intersex anomalies. However, the Bamana and Maninka would classify individuals with any of them as hermaphrodites. For the purposes of this discussion, they are all grouped under the rubric of hermaphroditism.

The genetic basis of albinism is complex. Currently, twelve different genes have been identified that result in different types of albinism when mutated. The best understood of these diseases and the most common is oculocutaneous albinism type 1 (OCA1) due to a total lack of the enzyme tyrosinase. This enzyme is essential for melanocytes in the skin to form melanin, the pigment that gives human skin its color. In individuals with this disease, the skin and hair are white, and the irises of the eyes a blue-gray or pink, depending on light source. They also have defective vision, significant light sensitivity, sunburn easily, and are prone to skin cancers. In those with tyrosinase-positive albinism, the enzyme is not totally lacking. Their hair may turn yellow over time, and their irises turn a light brown, although their skin is never darker than a cream or pink color. However, in a third form of the disease, tyrosinase-variable albinism, the infant has white hair, pink skin, and gray eyes at birth but later develops light tanning of the skin and yellow or light brown hair over time (Oetting et al. 2003: 307–311).

The Bamana and Maninka refer to those with OCA1 and tyrosinase-positive albinism as *yéféguéw*. These are albinos whose skin never tans but may burn on exposure to the sun (Dieterlen 1950: 88). However, they use the term *gomblé*, derived from *gon* (monkey) and *blé* (red), to signify "a red man" for those with tyrosinase-variable albinism. Sometimes the term *gomblé* is used to describe those with OCA1 albinism because they can develop severe sunburns and turn red in color. However, strictly speaking, the term is reserved by most for those with the milder form of the disease. Most people are not aware of the genetic and biochemical causes of these different forms of albinism. However, they are very familiar with their phenotypic or outward expressions.

Complicating the mosaic of albinism are several syndromes associated with systemic pathology. These forms of albinism are not associated with defects in melanin production, as is the case with oculocutaneous albinism, but with genetic defects in the packaging of melanin and other cellular proteins (Scheinfeld 2003: 5–15). Known as syndromic albinism, these genetic diseases also affect other organ systems, sometimes severely. However, those with these rare autosomal recessive disorders would be considered as *yéfégué* by the Bamana and Maninka because of their skin color.

Faro: *The Paradigm for Twins, Hermaphrodites, and Albinos*

In general, twins are referred to as *flaniw* (singular *flani*), which means "two little ones." A male twin is often referred to as *flanityema* and a female one as *flanimousoma*. Twins are considered a gift from Faro, who gave birth to the first twin pair, who were female. As a result, they do not inherit their spiritual elements, the *ni* (soul) and the *dya* (double), like everyone else does according to Bamana reincarnation beliefs. Those beliefs hold that at death, one's true *ni* goes to rest on the family altar while the *dya* enters water, where it is protected by Faro (Dieterlen 1950: 58). The first newborn following the death of a family member inherits their *dya* as a *ni* and their *ni* as a *dya*. These twin elements, which all humans possess, are either male or female. In the case of boys, the *ni* is male and the *dya* female; the opposite is true for girls. Thus, a human's spiritual elements reflect both twinning and androgyny.

In the case of twins, hermaphrodites, and albinos, these spiritual elements are not inherited from the most recently deceased family member, but rather directly from Faro, who is the source of an infinite reserve of them (Dieterlen 1950: 58, 88). In addition, the *dya* of these individuals does not enter their bodies, but rather remains under Faro's protection in water (Dieterlen 1950: 85). As a result, the *dya* is constantly protected from evil *nyama* and other malevolent forces.

Ni *and* Dya *and the Concept of the Double*

At another level of understanding, the *dya*, one's double, is a powerful reminder of both eventual death and reincarnation. For, upon death, the *dya* of the deceased is reincarnated into the first family newborn as their *ni*, or spiritual essence. This duality of spiritual essence is reflected in rituals of the *N'Tomo* initiation society, which is comprised of male children who have not yet been circumcised. The members of the *N'Tomo* society represent the primal human from first creation, uncircumcised, androgynous, innocent, and possessing both male and female character-istics. When a child leaves the *N'Tomo,* he is circumcised and no longer androgynous because his foreskin, the seat of his femininity, has been removed (Zahan 1974: 16).

Contemporary age-group associations (*ton*) put on secular entertain-ment performances with ritual *N'Tomo* masks that often reflect these beliefs. Sometimes, those accompanying the masked dancer carry a mir-ror so that he can look into it. The purpose of the gaze is both to permit the masked dancer to affirm his innocence and to be reminded of his dou-ble, his *dya,* that represents both death and reincarnation (Imperato 1980: 82). On some occasions, instead of using a mask, two dancers perform simultaneously with almost identical masks, each affirming the innocence of the other, and reminding one another of their *dya* and its presaging death and reincarnation.

Frequently, contemporary dances employing two *N'Tomo* masks are described as representing twins. However, this would seem to be a more recent interpretation distanced by the adoption of Islam from the older symbolism rooted in *Bamanaya* (Imperato 1980: 52).

FIGURE 2.1. Bamana masqueraders wearing twin masks representing techni-cal assistance personnel of the People's Republic of China. The Chinese were depicted in this fashion because they often dressed similarly, and appeared in public in pairs and never alone, 1971. *Photo: Pascal James Imperato.*

Beliefs and Practices Concerning Twins

There are a number of beliefs and practices surrounding twin births and twins. These have been described in detail by us and other authors (Imperato and Imperato 2008: 40–49; Imperato 1975: 52–60, 83; Imperato 1971: 154–159; Zahan 1974: 7–9; Dieterlen 1950: 86–87; Travélé 1931: 99–102; Henry 1910: 96–97). What is presented here is a synopsis of these beliefs and practices, some of which have been either modified or else abandoned. At the same time, newer practices have emerged.

Within the first hour after delivery, twins were ritually washed by the first wife of the oldest living village blacksmith. She used a mixture of tepid water and a solution made from the leaves of the *nama ba* (*Pileostigma thonningii*). (This ritual has also for the most part been abandoned; in only two out of seventy-four villages surveyed in the 1960s and '70s was there a history of the washing having been performed in the past decade.) Once the prayers and washing were completed, the father of the twins or one of his brothers went to the village blacksmith to order the twin altar, known as *sinzin* (literally, "support"). During our field studies, considerable regional variation was found in the physical form of the altar. (Imperato 1971:154–159; Imperato 1975: 52–60, 83)

It was believed that twins could walk on the surface of water because their spiritual double abided there. They were considered invulnerable to many other dangers, and it was common practice for Bamana and Maninka chiefs to have them march at the head of their troops in time of war. Twins served as intermediaries in settling disputes, and were thought capable of telling the future and of changing themselves into scorpions, a creature that symbolized twinness with its eight legs representing the eight limbs of a pair of twins. Many of these beliefs and practices have either been considerably altered or else have completely vanished. In Islamized areas, it is common for twins to solicit gifts on Friday, the Moslem day of religious observance. Robert M. Pringle, a former U.S. Ambassador to Mali, observed when he was there around 1990 that a woman with twins was given preference in approaching passengers on a riverboat for gifts when it docked (personal communication, New York City, April 11, 2008).

Twins are always considered a special blessing from the creator God under the protection of Faro. As such, their parents are referred to as *kunandi* (privileged ones). Following their birth, their mother places a white cotton band (*dyala*) around her forehead to demonstrate that their *dyaw* are guarded by Faro (Dieterlen 1950: 85–86). It is important to emphasize that twins represent man's original androgynous nature for the

Bamana and Maninka, and hence their close association with Faro, the androgynous deity (Zahan 1963b: 351–353).

Beliefs and Practices Concerning Hermaphrodites, Pseudo-Hermaphrodites, and Albinos

Hermaphrodites and pseudo-hermaphrodites are both known as *tyé-témousotéw*, which literally means "not male and not female." This term can also be used for both male and female homosexuals. However, the use of other additional terms for male homosexuals distances them from being in the same category. The term *mouso flana*, meaning "the second female," is sometimes used, and censorious Moslem Bamana often use the Wolof word *gorjigen*, meaning "male female." In using the latter term, Bamana are attempting to demonstrate that male homosexuality is alien to the Bamana world, and that it was imported from the Wolof people in Senegal (Koné 2002: 22).

Hermaphrodites and pseudo-hermaphrodites are considered both male and female, and as their own twin, with unique *ni* and *dia* just like each half of a twin pair. They are considered a duality in one being, and androgynous like Faro and the first humans ever created (Dieterlen 1950: 87). Unlike twins, who are respected as unusual beings, hermaphrodites and pseudo-hermaphrodites are viewed as the Other, and very much on the periphery of Bamana society. This marginalized social position relates not only to their physical characteristics, which preclude their being fully integrated into adult Bamana society through either circumcision or excision, but also to their spiritual essence. In this regard, they are analogous to uncircumcised children and hyenas (*surukuw*), who are also considered to be androgynous (Zahan 1963a: 115). Androgyny in these cases is not merely physical as reflected in the unusual appearance of the external genitalia of hyenas and hermaphrodites, or in the uncircumcised foreskin of a boy or the clitoris of a girl. All these beings are also closely associated with a dominant *wazo*, a spiritual element that is a powerful negative force encompassing ignorance and separation from higher intellectual planes (Zahan 1960: 49–50).

In addition to a *ni* and a *dya*, the Bamana believe that each living being possesses a *tere*, which is a positive force comprised of conscience and character, and which reflects Pemba the creator God. At death, the *tere* is released as *nyama*, a powerful force. Each being also possesses a *wazo* (also called *wanzo*), a negative force which originated with Mouso Koroni. The *tere* and *wazo* are joined in most humans, where the former places controls on the latter. In albinos, hermaphrodites, and pseudo-hermaph-rodites, the two are not joined together. Thus, the *wazo*, which is mani-fested by ignorance and a range of undesirable character traits, exerts greater influence in these individuals. It is through circumcision that the *wazo* is released, because it resides in both the clitoris and prepuce, where it impedes fertility (Dieterlen 1950: 64). Once released in the blood of cir-cumcision, the *wazo* enters the multi-horned masks of the *N'Tomo*.

Thus, it is through circumcision that children lose both their *wazo* and androgyny, and are put on the road to becoming responsible adults in Bamana society. Hermaphrodites and pseudo-hermaphrodites retain both their androgyny and *wazo* because they are not generally circum-cised or excised. As a consequence, their inability to marry and procreate is caused not merely by their physical androgyny, but because they retain their *wazo*, which prevents fertility.

Hermaphrodites and pseudo-hermaphrodites derive no social advan-tage from being considered twins and androgynous like Faro. More impor-tantly, their gonadal dysgenesis (abnormal development) closely associates them with Mouso Koroni's chaotic, disordered, and defective creative pro-cesses. The Bamana see them as reflections of her and the world of cre-ation as it was before *dali flana*, the second phase of creation dominated by the equilibrium of Faro and the stability of Ndomadyiri. Their frequently permanent uncircumcised/unexcised state condemns them to retain their *wazo*, which confers on them a permanent state of infancy—ignorance and sterility. As a result, they can never be given access to the ever-increasing levels of spiritual knowledge required for responsible adulthood. Thus, they are placed in a permanent pariah position in Bamana society. Most live out their lives within the extended families into which they are born.

The Bamana and Maninka believe that albinos are the result of sexual intercourse occurring in midday when the sun is at its zenith and the sky almost bright white in color. This midday sky is called the sky of Faro's anger (Dieterlen 1950: 88). Sexual intercourse at this time of day is prohib-ited among those who adhere to *Bamanaya*, and results in the conception of an albino. This single individual, with white skin that reflects Faro's own and the color of the sky under which it were conceived, is considered a twin being. At the time of such a sexual infraction, Faro unifies twins in the woman's uterus and removes the color of the skin. As an avatar of twins, albinos receive their spiritual elements directly from Faro rather than from a recently deceased relative, as is the case with twins and hermaphrodites. Because albinos are born from an act of transgression, their *ni* and *dya* are not linked together, and like hermaphrodites they have a powerful and

When a surviving twin marries, another statue is often sculpted in the opposite sex from the deceased twin and placed alongside of it. This spousal statue is called *flanitokélétyema* if male and *flanitokélémousoma* if female, respectively meaning "husband of the *flanitokélé*" and "wife of the *flanitokélé*."

Differentiating *flanitokélé* from spousal figures is difficult to impossible unless one is familiar with the history of the sculptures. Confounding matters is the fact that while *flanitokéléw* are often sculpted in the sex of the deceased twin, they are equally as often sculpted with prominent female breasts even if the individual was male to reflect the intimate association of twins with androgyny. In some villages, a simple wooden rod several inches long is made to represent the spouse of the *flanitokélé* instead of an anthropomorphic statue. In the southwestern Bamana country, such wooden rods are sculpted in place of actual figures to represent both deceased twins and their spouses.

There are regional variations in the size and styles of *flanitokéléw* (for a detailed description see, Imperato 1975: 54–56; Imperato and Imperato 2008: 47–48).

FIGURE 2.3. Bamana *flanitokélé* statue, Arrondisement of Farako, Cercle of Segou, 38.1 cm. (15"), Imperato Collection. *Photo: Robert E. Mates.*

In height they range from two to eighteen inches on average. The larger ones are often dressed and decorated with jewelry and are sometimes presented with gifts equivalent to those given to the surviving twin. Henry (1910: 98) recorded that five cowrie shells were usually given to the statue whenever a gift was presented to the surviving twin. At that time, cowrie shells were used as currency in the colonial French Sudan (contemporary Mali).

For the Bamana and Maninka of Mali, albinos, hermaphrodites, and twins are all considered double beings. This chapter has explored the religious and cosmological beliefs that frame beliefs, social attitudes, and practices with regard to these three distinct groups of individuals. From the perspective of modern medical science, twinning is considered a normal departure from singleton births, while the various forms of hermaphroditism and albinism are known to result from genetic abnormalities. The Bamana and Maninka, however, perceive all three as double beings, intimately linked to Faro, the androgynous albino deity who conceived and gave birth to the first pair of twins. This conception and birth were not parthenogenetic (i.e. asexual) in character because Faro is believed to be simultaneously both male and female as well as an albino. It was through Faro that the Bamana and Maninka found an explanation for these three manifestations of the human condition and elaborated a complex web of beliefs, attitudes, and practices concerning them that have endured over time.

Despite the inexorable adoption of Islam by the Bamana and Maninka, practices related to twins and rooted in *Bamanaya* still persist in many rural villages. Similarly, attitudes toward albinos and hermaphrodites remain unchanged in many areas. However, modernization and Islamization have for some time now formed the basis for continuous transition and change in Bamana and Maninka society. This has resulted in the gradual disappearance or decline of the *sinzin* rituals in a number of areas, and theological syncretism in which Faro has become a benevolent Islamic water genie who resides at the bottom of the Niger River and in ponds, lakes, and wells. For many Moslem Bamana and Maninka, blessings once sought from Faro through *sinzin* sacrifices are now provided through the rituals of Islam.

NOTES

Special thanks are extended to the late Djigui Diakité, the late Makan Fané, the late Bafing Kané, and the late Moussa Kanté for their assistance with field investigations conducted in the 1960s and '70s. Much appreciation is also extended to Modibo N'Faly Keita, Kolékélé Mariko, and Amadou Sanogo for their valuable help in those years, and with more recent field investigations conducted from the 1980s through 2006. We also wish to acknowledge the assistance of Boubacar Doumbia in interpreting several *Bamanan-kan* expressions, and that of Austin C. Imperato with various aspects of our research.

    1. The term epigenetic control refers to heritable variations in gene expression not caused by changes in DNA sequences.

    2. An autosomal dominant trait is one that can be expressed if just inherited from one parent. On the other hand, an autosomal recessive trait requires inheritance from both parents.

WORKS CITED

Boklage, Charles E. 1990. "Survival Probability of Human Conceptions from Fertilizations to Term." *International Journal of Fertility* 35: 75–94.

Colleyn, Jean-Paul. 2009. *Bamana.* Paris: 5 Continents Editions.

De Ganay, Solange. 1949. "Aspects de mythologie et de symbolique Bambara." *Journal Psychologie Normale et Pathologique* 2: 181–201.

Dieterlen, Germaine. 1951. *La Religion Bambara.* Paris: Presses Universitaires de France.

Dolo, A., N. G. Diall, and F. S. Diabate. 1990. "Apropos of 507 Pregnancies and Twin Deliveries in the District of Bamako." *Dakar Medicine:* 35 (1): 25–31.

Duffy, Eamon. 1992. *The Stripping of the Altars: Traditional Religion in England 1400-1580.* New Haven: Yale University Press.

Hall, Judith. 2003. "Twinning." *Lancet* 362: 735–743.

———. 1996. "Twins and Twinning." *American Journal of Medicinal Genetics* 61: 202–204.

Hay, Sylvia, and Donald A. Wehrung. "1970. Congenital Malformations in Twins." *American Journal of Human Genetics* 22: 662–678.

Henry, Joseph. 1910. *L'Ame d'un peuple africain: Les Bambara, leur vie psychique, ethique, sociale, religieuse.* Munster, Germany: Aschendorff-schen Buchhandlung.

Imperato, Pascal James. 1971. "Twins among the Bambara and Malinke of Mali." *Journal of Tropical Medicine and Hygiene* 74 (4): 154–9.

———. 1975. "Bamana and Maninka Twin Figures." *African Arts* 8 (4): 52–60, 83.

———. 1980. "Bambara and Malinke Ton Masquerades." *African Arts* 13 (4): 47–55, 82–85, 87.

———. 2001. *Legends, Sorcerers, and Enchanted Lizards: Door Locks of the Bamana of Mali.* New York: Africana Publishing Co.

Imperato, Pascal James, and Gavin H. Imperato. 2008. "Twins, Hermaphrodites, and an Androgynous Albino Deity: Twins and Sculpted Twin Figures among the Bamana and Maninka of Mali." *African Arts* 41 (1): 40–49.

Keita, Daouda. *Service de Santé.* 1968. Bamako, Mali: Ministère de la Sante Publique et des Affaires Sociales.

Kiely, John L., and Brian Kiely. 2001. "Epidemiological Trends in Multiple Births in the United States, 1971–1978." *Twin Research* 4: 131–133.

Koné, Kassim. 2002. "When Male Becomes Female and Female Becomes Male in Mande." *Mande Studies* 4: 21–29.

Kristic, Zoran D., Z. Smoljanic, D. Vukanic, and G. Janjic. 2000. "True Hermaphrodism: 10 Years' Experience." *Pediatric Surgery International* 16: 580–583.

Krob, G., A. Brown, and U. Kuhnle. 1994. "True Hermaphroditism: Geographical Distribution, Clinical Findings, Chromosomes and Gonadal Histology." *European Journal of Pediatrics* 153: 2–10.

Lee, Peter A., Christopher P. Houk, Syed F. Ahmed, and Ieuan A. Hughes. 2006. In collaboration with the participants in the International Consensus Conference on Intersex organized by the Lawson Wilkins Pediatric Endocrine Society and the European Society for Paediatric Endocrinology. "Consensus Statement on Management of Intersex Disorders." *Pediatrics* 2006; 188: e488–e500.

Lewis, Cathryn M., Sue C. Healy, and Nicholas G. Martin. 1996. "Genetic Contribution to Dizygotic Twinning." *American Journal of Genetics* 61: 237–246.

MacLaughlin, Diane T., and Patricia K. Donahoe. 2004. "Sex Determination and Differentiation." *New England Journal of Medicine* 350: 367–378.

Martin, Joyce A., and Melissa M. Park. 1999. "Trends in Twin and Triplet Births: 1980–1997." *National Vital Statistics Reports* 47 (24): 70–85.

Minh, Hoang Nhok, Joellean Belaisch, and Andrée Smadja. 1993. "Female Pseudo-hermaphroditism." *Presse Medicale* 22: 1735–1740.

Myrianthopoulos, Ntinos. C. 1975. "Congenital Malformations in Twins: Epidemiologic Survey." *Birth Defects Original Articles Series* 11: 1–39.

Nylander, Percy P. S. 1970. "Twinning in Nigeria." *Acta Geneticae Medicae Gemellologia* (Roma) 19: 457–464.

Oetting, William S., James P. Fryer, S. Shriram, and Richard A. King. 2003. "Oculocutaneous Albinism Type 1: The Last 100 Years. *Pigment Cell and Melanoma Research* 16: 307–311.

Paques, Vivianna. *Les Bambara*. 1954. Paris: Presses Universitaires de France.

Scheinfeld, Noah S. 2003. "Syndromic Albinism: A Review of Genetics and Phenotypes." *Dermatology Online Journal* 9 (5): 5–15.

Travélé, Moussa. 1931. "Usages Relatifs au Jumeaux en Pays Bambara." *Outre mer* 3: 99–102.

Wiersma, Rinus. 2001. "Management of the African Child with True Hermaphroditism." *Journal of Pediatric Surgery* 36: 397–399.

———. 2004. "True Hermaphroditism in Southern Africa: The Clinical Picture." *Pediatric Surgery International* 20: 363–368.

Zahan, Dominique. 1960. *Sociétés d'Initiation Bambara: Le N'Domo, Le Korè*. Paris: Mouton & Co.

———. 1963a. *La Dialectique du Verbe Chez les Bambara*. Paris: Mouton & Co.

———. 1963b. "Note sur lá gémelléité et les jumeaux en Afrique noire." *Bulletin de la Faculté Lettres Strasbourg*: 351–353.

———. 1974. *The Bambara*. London: J. Brill.

CHAPTER THREE

Twins and Intertwinement

Reflections on Ambiguity and Ambivalence in Northwestern Namibia

STEVEN VAN WOLPUTTE

I tell you, no rains this year.
  We had three twins last season.
            —KAKORO HEPUTE, UNRECORDED INTERVIEW, OCTOBER 1996

Tsjanakambendje and Tjiwende—his (adoptive) father—had gone to the riverbank, where a group of travelling laborers had set up camp, including an improvised brewery for *tombo* corn beer. On the afternoon of this cold and cloudy day I caught up with him there; like the others, Tsjanakambendje was on rather wobbly legs. He sang me a song or two, and we were talking and drinking when I heard thunder rolling in the distance. To tease him, I put my hand on his shoulder and nodded at the dark horizon. "Shouldn't you be on your feet?" He got up immediately. "Father!" he shouted. "The rains are coming." The two drunken men appeared to be sobered up in an instant; they went to the fire, looked for a suitable piece of charcoal (it had to be *mopane* wood), and started to mark the heads and temples of everybody in the drinking party.

This encounter, set in November 2006, reminded me of one of the first times I met Tsjanakambendje, some ten years before. We were sitting near our tent when suddenly he jumped toward our cooking pot, threw some porridge into the fire, carried the pot away and emptied its contents outside the compound, exclaiming: "Come! Eat! Bring us rain!" (*Inyo! Rya! Et' ombura!*). Tsjanakambendje was the youngest of twins (hence his name), and twinship regularly popped up in our nightly conversations. He and my then field assistant, Kataeko (himself a first-born twin) explained that twins have to "throw porridge" and mark the heads of those present with charcoal as soon as they see or hear the rain is coming.[1] Other dos and

FIGURE 3.1. Portrait of Tsjanakambendje as I came to know him in 1996. In Northern Namibia, ideas on twinship are expressed not in statues but on the body. *Photo: Steven Van Wolputte and Grite de Bondt, © RMCA Tervuren, Belgium (accession no 96.06.03.28.)*

don'ts of twins included that they cannot grind charcoal when it rains; that they wear a particular but simple necklace (called *omutombe* or *ozombe*); and that only twins and their relatives can drink the milk from the "firestick cow of the labor pains" (*ondumehupa yozongama*, discussed further below). Yet, my interviewees denied that twins have special powers. It is a matter of respect, they explained, for the ancestors. If they are not respected, they will withhold the rains.

These anecdotes demonstrate that twins occupy a special position in Himba life. It is also an ambiguous position: Tsjanakambendje's twin sister died at birth from spina bifida, and Tsjanakambendje suffered repeated bouts of illness until adolescence; his mother did not conceive again after she had her twins, and his older sister's first-born died soon after birth. Also, she became seriously ill during her second pregnancy, at a time when people in Omirora realized that the much-needed rains would not come that year. Like Tsjanakambendje's relatives, I could not but link these different events: the blessing of twin birth also cast a dark shadow on the members of Tsjanakambendje's "house" (*ondjuo*, the matrilineage, but also a woman's dwelling).[2]

This ambivalence (doubly blessed also means doubly cursed) makes up the point of departure of this essay, the principal ambition of which is to document twinship among the Himba, a group of mostly seminomadic cattle pastoralists. Together with other Herero-speaking groups (such as the Ngambwe, Zemba, Kuvale, and Herero proper) they inhabit the arid and mountainous landscape of northwest Namibia and southwest Angola. Yet, in line with the worldview predominant in the rather rural setting I worked in, I regard the birth of twosomes as an unambiguously joyous occasion that testifies to the fertility and reproductive powers of the "house." In this context, the ambivalence of twosomes seems not to reside in some innate quality ascribed to twins, but rather in the general idea that there is a limit to good fortune, or that for each better there also is a worse. In popular lore, menstruation is a condition necessary to attaining new life; desiccation is needed in order for it to rain. These contradictions and paradoxes are not anomalous, but integral to everyday life. To paraphrase Max Gluckmann (1955: 291vv), this *need* for ambiguity is not particular to Himba society: it is crucial to any society's functioning; it is not a consequence of upheaval, but of everyday, ordinary life.

Part of the argument is that the patriarchal bias of the traditional ethnographies on the Herero (among which the Himba reckon themselves) or on the region caused them to regard the patriclan or patrilineage as the sole player in the domain of spirituality and religion (see Broch-Due 1999; Hodgson 2000). Faced with the "problem" of double descent, these first (missionary) ethnographers associated the matriclan and matrilineage with the this-worldly life, with the domain of moveable property (animals) and inheritance. No doubt inspired by their own religious calling, these ethnographers linked the patriclan (*oruzo*) to religion and the sacred (as in sacred fire, sacred animals), and the matriclan (*eanda*) to he profane (see Van Warmelo 1962; Malan 1973, 1974). Yet, as we will see, the so-called profane matrilineage is crucial in linking the world of the living with the sacred world of spirits and the deceased. It is this intertwinement that is brought to the fore whenever a child is born, and especially in the case of multiple births.

I found a similar kind of interarticulation expressed in the work by Bracha Lichtenberg-Ettinger (1995: 15). She coined the notion of matrix to indicate a relationship that is characterized by "difference in coemergence," by otherness *and* sameness. Thus she addressed the need to go beyond a dominant paradigm that emphasizes difference, distinction, and absence as a necessity to enter the social realm, and that is evident in concepts such as "the name of the father" (psychoanalysis) or *habitus* (sociology) (also see Motzafi-Haller 1998). Like the notion of belonging (that implies both a recognition of difference—one belongs *to* something—and an affirmation of oneness) the matrix concept acknowledges boundaries and differences, and the ability or desire to transgress them. Transposed to this volume's case studies on twinship, it evokes the image of twins as both doubles and couples, as being "two" but also "one" without, however, this ambivalence being perceived as problematic. On the contrary, as in the case presented here, it is an ambivalence that permeates the life-world, and that is perceived as being at its source. As I have argued elsewhere, matrix and belonging operate on the level of the imaginary, of metaphor, rather than on the level of symbolic discourse (Van Wolputte 2004: 258–259). This matrixial principle refers to subjectivation, to experience and embodiment rather than to symbolic exegesis, to the life-world rather than to cosmology (see Csordas 1994; Jackson 1996; Kirmayer 1993).

This ambivalence (of being both "one" and "two") is symbolized for instance by the *mopane* tree (*Colophospermum mopane*), ubiquitous in northwestern Namibia's mountain savannah. In Himba daily life and ritual, it evokes both feminine and masculine reproductive powers. The green (or "wet,"—*tarazu*) leaves appeal to notions of female reproduction and bodiliness, but feature prominently in ceremonies (notably circumcision, burial, and commemoration) that involve the patrilineal forebears. The wood, in contrast, is associated with masculine capacities (such as dryness, hardness, and strength) and is therefore the only wood that can be used in the fire at the ancestral shrine (also see this chapter's opening scene). Yet, it also is the wood women construct their houses with, and that they use to kindle the fire inside. This ambivalence is visualized in the double *mopane* leaf, which like all things fertile comes in twos.

The notion of matrix offers a useful metaphor to discuss the paradoxes and other "problems of meaning" (Flax 1990: 222) encountered in ritual symbolism and material culture in a rural setting in northern Namibia. After a quick glance at the importance of doubles in Himba daily life and a brief introduction to Himba double descent, I will present an ethnography of giving birth, both to singletons and to twins, among the Himba.

The Premium of Opposition

The Herero feature prominently in Isaac Shapera's oft-cited article on twins in Southern Africa. For the Herero, Shapera writes, the birth of twosomes is a joyous occasion; he eloquently describes the rituals of seclusion and reintegration of twins and their parents, and emphasizes the priestly and other privileges twins and fathers of twins enjoy (Schapera 1927: 119–122).[3]

Missionary ethnographer Heinrich Vedder (1966: 176), on the other hand, maintains that for the Herero of central Namibia the birth of twins is a joyful event only at a superficial level. In line with his overall depiction of precolonial history as a period of barbarism, feud, and fear (see Lau 1981), Vedder argued that people celebrate and donate cows out of fear, not respect, for the powers twins and their genitor must possess. Carlos Estermann takes a similar position (1981: 22–24; 59–60). He describes how for the Otjiherero- and Oshiwambo-speaking groups of southern Angola, the birth of twins is categorized as an ominous event, together with breech births and, especially, births that occur with no menstruation intervening between the pregnancy and the mother's previous birthing. Across the different groups he refers to, these three occasions require similar purification rites and the intervention of a *kimbanda* or ritual specialist. His account also claims that anomalous births in the past led to infanticide (see below).[4] What these three early ethnographies on northern Namibia and southern Angola have in common is that they depict the birth of twins (or, in case of Estermann, also other ominous births) as an unusual event that triggers strong reactions, whether of joy or fear, implying that the others they describe are less equipped to deal with the unexpected and the unforeseeable (also see Danner 1988). One could also point out, however, that these early ethnographers were less equipped to deal with the ambiguous and the hazy.

This is precisely the endeavor Victor Turner (1969) embarks on in his *Ritual Process*. In linking twinship and twin rituals to contradictions and tensions in Ndembu social structure, he set the terms of the anthropological debate on twinship, even if contemporary scholars are of the opinion that his emphasis on a tensed unity or *Gestalt* between pairs of opposites is ahistorical (as it obliterates ongoing social and political tensions) and homeostatic (as this play of forces keeps opposite tendencies in balance) (Turner 1969: 83–84; Renne and Bastian 2001: 3).[5]

Scholars have since continued to emphasize twosomes as the embodiment of the dissonances experienced in social life now and over time. As Diduk (2001) remarks, the attention for multiple births exemplifies a postmodern moment in that it exposes the many possible, multilayered meanings of twinship (as the latter includes, but is not limited to, multiple births). The recent approaches, with the exception of Turner's, emphasize how these meanings have been and are changing under the expansion of various influences: Christendom or Islam, globalization, inequality, or violence (see, for instance, Diduk 1993, 2001; Kamanzi 2007; Masquelier 2001; Houlberg and Renne, chapters 13 and 15 in this

FIGURE 3.2. Portrait of Ingewe Tjiningire, herself a twin, married to a twin, and a mother of twins. *Photo: Steven Van Wolputte & Grite de Bondt, © RMCA Tervuren (accession no 96.05.26.27A).*

volume). This—unfortunately—is not the place for an extensive review of the anthropological or art historical literature on twinship (see, instead, Imperato and Imperato 2008; Peek 2008, and his introduction to this volume; Renne and Bastian 2001). Here it suffices to point out that recent scholarship has probed into the historical and contextual dimensions of ideas and practices associated with twins. They focus, inter alia, on competing ideologies and political regimes, economic disruption, or on gender and generational tensions (see in this regard the special issue of *Ethnology* on *Twinship in Africa,* Renne and Bastian 2001).

Another strain of recent scholarship has been revisiting the art historical evidence on material representations of twinship, articulating new insights into African perceptions and theories of personhood (Peek 2008). "Double" statues and Janus (double-faced) masks represent the intertwinement of the visible and invisible worlds. Like divination, couples and doubles in African art reveal a knowledge of "the other side," of invisible forces that govern the visible world. In West Africa, twin imagery in material culture also evokes the multiplicity of the self, the this-worldly self complemented by a shadow double in the that-worldly realm (Peek 2008; for Southern Africa, see for instance Jacobson-Widding 1991). The sections below will continue to elaborate on this intertwinement of the visible and invisible. Following Peek's (2008) advice not to shun structural analysis if it aids our understanding of African cultures, these sections confront not the demon of analogy (Bourdieu 1977), but the demon of ambivalence that permeates the Himba life-world.

The Ultimate Paradox: The Oneness of Twins, or the Banality of Ambivalence

This analysis tries to turn the tables by looking not at the dissonance invoked by multiple births, but at the consonance. It does not claim that the rural Himba life-world is characterized by homeostasis and harmony; on the contrary, precisely because ambivalence and paradox belong to the domain of everyday life, twin births are not exceptionally threatening. Formulated in a blunt and unsophisticated way, the general point of departure here is that much of Himba cosmology is preoccupied with doubles. To name but a few examples: a homestead consists of two concentric fences, but with their main entrances in opposed directions; only animals with two horns are edible; one is a simultaneous member of both a matri- and a patriclan; a married woman belongs to both her father's and her husband's patrilineage; people have life-force (*ounomasa*), but also life-breath (*omuinyo*); spirits protect but can also turn against you; and prosperity and good fortune (*erau*) are the result of witchcraft, but they will also inevitably provoke envy (*eruru*) and incite witchcraft against you.

In general, the dominant Himba cosmology sees life itself as the result of a double movement. On the one hand, there is a horizontal movement, mainly associated with the matrilineage and femininity; on the other, there is a vertical movement, associated mainly with the patrilineage (including its ancestors), masculinity, and elderhood. The first is a movement back and forth (-*tuka*, hence *orutuku*, womb, or *okutuka*: to churn, to tan) between homestead and cattle post, dry and rainy season, husband's and father's patrilineage. It is a uterine movement, like birth, also exemplified in the daily trek of the cows, marriage, or in the women's daily chore of churning buttermilk. The second is a movement upward; it refers to the transmission of life through the male line, and it materializes, for instance, in the smoke from the fire at the ancestral shrine, the central, supporting pole of the house, or the central tree in the homestead. The first, uterine, movement is reflected in the making of butter and buttermilk. This milk is not associated with ancestral interdictions and taboos, and anybody can drink it. The second, agnatic, movement is reflected in curdled milk; this milk is not churned, but left to stand and ferment. This is the "firestick" milk (*ondumehupa*) mentioned above. It comes in many varieties, but each one is associated with particular interdictions; one example is the "firestick milk of the labor pains" (*ondumehupa yozongama*), that can only be drunk by twins and their ascendants (see Van Wolputte 2000, 2003).[6]

This general perspective also transpires in almost subconscious, matrixial motives and themes that permeate Himba material culture. "Wetness" (*outarazu*) or fertility, especially the reproductive powers of the minor matrilineage or "house" (*ondjuo*), are evoked or reflected in the use of pairs or even numbers; for example, a woman's belt is bordered by a double row of metal beads (but a man's is not). After their menarche, women wear a headdress (*erembe*) that consists of four pairs of ear-like "horns" (*ozonya*) cut from of the delicate skin of a newborn (some say unborn) lamb, preferably a twin.[7] At that occasion, she also receives a pair of metal bead anklets, tied together with a single leather strap. After her second child, when she is considered adult and mature, the single strap will be replaced by a double one. Married women keep a double supply of butterfat (one red, one black portion) which they keep in a double container connected by four strings of metal beads. This "doubleness" is also reflected in, for instance, the pendants (*ohumba*) young and adult women wear (they come with a front- and a backside), or in the double leaf of the *mopane* tree (*omutati*).

In contrast, garments referring to marriage (as people say, an agreement between lineages) or, even more in general, to agnatic or patriarchal authority, usually display uneven numbers. For instance, the marital headdress (*ekori*) has three "ears," the marital apron is decorated with three circles or fan-shaped motifs, and so on. A like motif also is found in ritual: uneven children (the first-born, third, . . .) are given a ceremony of, in Pidgin English, "the special child" during which their father asks for special protection from the lineage ancestors (in this regard, see Diduk 2001: 31). As a final example: each house has a double set of milking goods, one for the cows of the churning gourd, one for the firestick animals. However, there is only one funnel (*ombako*) through which the various kinds of milk are poured into their corresponding calabash. This funnel is carved by the head of the homestead.

Twins, then, are both "one" and "two"; they are both even and uneven, and as such twosomes are a token of extra-ordinary fertility and good fortune.[8] The ambivalence of twinship lies not with the fact that twins are both good and evil; it is in the dominant perception that each form of good fortune, whether in cattle, children, or simply "being lucky" (*erau*), is either the result of ancestral protection (a blessing that can always be withdrawn) or of witchcraft (in which case the selfish witch has to continue to "kill" in order to feed his former victims).[9] In both cases, moreover, such a good fortune may attract (other) witches or malevolent spirits. This is why women have to be silent when going through labor, or throughout the seclusion period after they birthed twins.

Also, this idea underlies the ideal of a Himba "big man" (*omuhona*): he draws his authority in the public sphere partly from convincing his followers that he does not derive his power from witchcraft but from the ancestors. Therefore, he should be magnanimous and generous, and be careful to respect the interdictions and taboos the spirits impose so as not to offend them (for more on Herero big men, see Durham 2002: 143–145). Any form of selfishness or greed can (and will) be interpreted as a form of witchcraft. Taking into account that in Himba society witchcraft belongs to the ordinary facts of life (everybody is or can be a witch), it then functions as a moral critique of power, a leveling mechanism aiming (that is, ideally) at the biggest discrepancies between haves and have-nots.

Many of my interviewees expressed the idea that blessings are counted, and that any given "balancing imbalance" (*outanaura*) may tip over in any direction at any time. In Himba thought, this is expressed in the verb *okutanaura*, "to turn around," referring to the idea (or fear) that anything may turn into its opposite at any time.[10] Though twosomes are welcomed, the ambivalence of twinship is concealed in the common conviction that the display of blessings will attract witches and bring misfortune, or that ostentation could lead to accusations of witchcraft.

Omen and Anomaly?

Shapera (1927: 134–135) already pointed out that twin customs cannot be explained solely by referring to the abnormal character of multiple births, and that twin rituals can only be understood in reference to the birth of singletons. Even if Himba see a multiple birth as uncommon, they first of all perceive it as a birth, a mythopoeic act that takes one back to one's origin, to—as it were—a presymbolic, preancestral world. It is important to note that the birth of a child makes part of an ongoing exchange (between patrilineages, between ancestors and their descendants. . .). Noteworthy, too, is that even the birth of a single child is ambiguous—both a token of prosperity and a risk—and that it thus rehearses the matrixial motif of double and two. These ambivalences are amplified in the case of multiple births.

During her final weeks of pregnancy, an ancestor (*otjiruru*, as a pregnant woman is referred to during this time) returns to her mother's house, most often located in her father's homestead. Gradually, over the course of the weeks she spends there, she will put down most of her garments and jewels. When the labors announce themselves, all men leave the homestead; they will avoid the vicinity of the house of birth for the duration of the seclusion. With its mother seated near the back of her mother's house, the child is born a first time in the homestead's most "upstream" or eastern location. Giving birth takes place in silence, so as not to attract the attention of witches and malevolent spirits. For the same reason, the mother secretly buries the umbilical cord in a nearby riverbed. The food for mother and midwife is cooked separately; they will only leave the house at dawn and at dusk. This seclusion lasts until "the two bodies have closed again," marked by the umbilical cord falling off the infant. Then the child's father presents his son or daughter to the ancestors at the shrine. He gives him or her a name—until then the child was referred to as a "small wild animal" (okapuka)—and donates a heifer from his herd.

This is when the child is born a second time.[11] In case of a first child (oku-veripa, to give birth a first time), the young mother (omwari) is endowed with the paraphernalia referring to her newly acquired status (from etere, a childless young woman, to omberipa, "mother-of-one"). When (or if) she bears a second child, she is considered as an adult, mature woman (omukazendu), a position also reflected in the garments she wears.

Giving birth is part of an ongoing exchange between patrilineages, as the husband reciprocates the gift of childbirth by giving a cow (orutombe, "the cow of pregnancy") to his wife's father. Thus it reflects a movement to and fro between lineages, and across different realms. If the customs around single births already articulate the hidden theme of twoness and intertwinement, these themes are made even more explicit in the case of multiple births. The following condensed plot (see Turner 1969: 50) of the Himba twin birth ritual was constructed with the help of three women (two of them being themselves mothers of twins, one—their mother—having acted as a midwife) after one of the neighboring villages experienced a twin birth in the course of October, 1996.

A long time ago, my informants confided, babies born in pairs were killed at birth. If it was a boy, the body was not buried but dried, ground up, and kept in a bag inside the woman's house. These women, however, relegated infanticide to a mythical past, when, as they say, there were neither animals nor ancestors, when we lived without culture (also see Estermann 1981: 22–24, 59–60). Nowadays people celebrate the birth of twins (and, they added, for omarongo or triplets the feast is even bigger), even if they remain adamant that a few extra precautions need to be observed. The mother enters seclusion not in the village but outside it, in the bush (*mokuti*); she is accompanied by her children and midwife. The two women are not allowed to talk to anyone else but themselves, and food for them is left behind in the bush, where the midwife picks it up. Also when a cow gives birth to twin calves, the animals are secluded: the person who finds them takes the animals to the bush until the village decides it is time to return. He or she cannot talk to others, and eats food left for pickup by relatives.

In seclusion, the mother undresses and puts down all of her garments. Dressed only in three pieces of red cloth (around her head, waist, and stomach), she also unties her braids and abstains from the use of ochre. The children's father, in the meantime, also unties his hairstyle (*ondumbo*) and wears a piece of red cloth instead. Thus the women await the end of the seclusion period, before they return to the village in procession. By then, all the stock from the neighborhood has been gathered there.

As the community awaits the arrival, water is poured into a big woven basket (*oruako*), and with twigs and branches from two different kinds of trees it is used to bless animals and herds; these twigs then are placed in the milking utensils and tied to the drinking trough at the water place. Then two women carry two *otuako* (one of which is filled with water) to the seclusion shelter, place the twins in the empty one, and return to the village carrying the vessels on their heads. They are joined by the new mother and midwife. In procession they enter the village, chanting (as one of them demonstrated):

Otjiwa koyetu	Good things to us
Otjivi kovakwetu	Bad things to our equals
Epaha	Twin
O ri yetu oweni	Do not eat [kill] us
O ri otaate	Do not eat our father
O ri o maama	Do not eat our mother
Ekurukuru	Old, very old
Ekurupaha	Old old twin

As the procession reaches the homestead's entrance, people start shouting and running; they start a ritual stone-throwing fight (*okupera omakamba*), but after a while everybody sits down. The parturient now marks her forehead, chest, arms, and legs with ashes. She tastes milk from all the different firestick gourds (an act called *okumakera*, usually the prerogative of the lineage elder); the two children are brought to the ancestral shrine where also they "taste" all the firestick milk in the homestead and beyond. The head of the homestead gives them their twin names; also, he will make one of his cows "the animal of the labor pains." Twins and their ascendants (their parents, grandparents, and everybody regarded as such) also each receive a twin necklace, a simple string of (white) ostrich eggshell beads and (black) wooden pearls. The necklace not only refers to multiple births: it is also worn after a breech birth (*ombiru*), or in case of a child born with no chance for the mother to menstruate before the pregnancy (*ohengwa,* also the first milk given by a mother), instances that are equally seen as signs of exceptional fertility and fortune. In case of twin calves a sheep is slaughtered, and a twin necklace tied to the cow's calabash. On the day twins are born, everybody drinks firestick milk. A big ox is slaughtered, and only after the head is eaten (i.e., when there is no meat left) the new mother takes on her usual garments, jewelry, and hairstyle. Soon after, though, the twins are separated (as a "mother can only carry one child on her back"), one of them being adopted by a member of the mother's matrilineage.

Twins and Intertwinement

One could analyze these condensed ritual plots, following Evans-Pritchard's or Turner's lead, by pointing out the structural tensions that underlie contemporary Himba society (between, for instance, juniors and seniors, or between matrilineal inheritance and patrilocal residence). One could analyze them in terms of the homologous dichotomies they evoke: masculinity is dry and cool; femininity is hot and wet; pregnancy, for instance, is to "light a fire" (*okuyakisa*). Or one could look not at the dyads, but the triads they bring to mind (see Jacobson-Widding 1991). One such a triad would consist of the colors red, black, and white—for fire, coal, and ashes; or women, men, and ancestors.

However, postmodern approaches have pointed out that such approaches assume a closed symbolic system, obliterating the metaphoric undercurrent of the performative dimension of ritual; they stress that such metaphors do not necessarily lead to understanding and criticize (post) structuralism for its logical fallacy in equating logical, discursive, categories with lived reality (see Csordas 1994; De Boeck 1994; Jackson 1996).

The modest point this ethnography of twin ritual among the Himba tries to make is that most approaches to ethnographies of twinship overemphasize the disturbing character of multiple births, perhaps because they focus too much on overt, public discourse, and too much on difference and opposition. This essay refrained from characterizing multiple births as disturbing anomalies; instead, it looked at multiple births primarily as "births." This does not imply that Himba life is homeostatic or characterized by the absence of structural or conjectural tensions—quite the contrary.

Most Himba feel that life is, at best, caught in a precarious balance that may tip over in either direction any time. From this perspective, then, rituals (especially those relating to life and death) offer an opportunity to momentarily integrate different aspects of a fragmentary life-world and self (for instance, in relation to one's double belonging to both a patri- and matriclan). From the perspective taken by this essay, such a partial integration is achieved through matrixial motifs (such as "even" and "uneven") and metaphors (such as "moving back and forth," "red" or "black") that constitute ritual and that percolate into daily life. These metaphors are not outspoken; they are not part of the exegesis provided by ritual specialists. Rather, they belong to an unconscious cultural repertoire.

One of these matrixial, subjectivating motifs is, for instance, the idea that the ritual role of the patrilineage is most outspoken when it concerns the making of distinctions (e.g., name-giving, circumcision, and other stages of the life-cycle). These distinctions are inscribed on the body by particular (temporary) hairstyles or finery. The role of the matrilineage, however, is most prominent when the ritual occasion revolves around inclusion and embracing. Matriclans do not have particular motives traceable in garments or hairstyle. Whereas patriclans are associated with interdictions (e.g., on who is allowed to drink the firestick milk, or even with regard to diet or to cattle colors), matriclans are not. These interdictions, or particular hairstyles or motives in material culture, evoke the memory of a known patrilateral forebear, and often, a history of fission. Myths of origin relating to the matriclan, however, place their members in a genealogy that traces people back to a common (nameless) genetrix who gave birth to two daughters. Patriclans refer to a "small tradition"; matriclans evoke a "big," encompassing, tradition. The funerary and commemoration ceremonies, for instance, are headed by a member of the matrilineage of the mother of the deceased. These occasions mirror the idea that children are born twice: people also die twice. And just as the second birth takes place after the two bodies have closed again, mourners mark the end of the mourning period by reclosing (*okupata*) their hairstyle, collars, and other garments that were opened or untied at the moment of death.

Twins stand out not because they hold special privileges or possess special powers—except perhaps when dark clouds gather at the horizon—but because they embody the simultaneous articulation of "one" and "two," of interdiction and belonging. They bring to the fore a matrixial maelstrom of submerged images and associations evoking life-transmission and fertility. Also, they embody an ambivalence that dominates Himba cosmology and everyday experience. This ambivalence is at the source of culture and sociality; it is articulated in the matrixial motives of Himba material culture; it is evoked in pregnancy—the woman about to give birth *is* the ancestor—and childbirth, especially in case of multiple births. Twosomes in particular articulate or evoke this intertwinement of the human and spirit world, of the visible and invisible, of life-giving and life-taking forces.

This balancing imbalance could be interpreted as a moral economy of good and evil, or a spiritual economy of blessing and curse in which good fortune (*erau*) is a limited good (Foster 1965) that can be secured through ancestors and spirits. An important caveat to such approaches would be that they tend to locate "choice" and "behavior" within the individual. For the Himba, however, agency is dividual (see Strathern 1988; Van Dijk 2002; Van Wolputte 2004), and at least partly located "outside" the acting subject: animals, ancestors, kin, and spirits, too, are regarded as sources of self. Maybe the importance of twins is that they personify this experience of a self shaped not only from within, but also from without.

NOTES

The material for this chapter stems from anthropological field research conducted from 1995 up to present among the Himba in an area (Omirora) located in the western, rural parts of the northern Kunene Region, Namibia, and in the semi-urban setting of a small town, Opuwo. While the chapter was completed when enjoying a Fellowship at the *Internationales Kolleg Morphomata* at the University of Cologne, Germany, the field research was made possible by successive postdoctoral fellowship and research grants by the Research Foundation Flanders (FWO). I would like to thank Kaviruka Mahurukua and Mungandjo Katjanga for their friendship, comments and assistance. I am also grateful to Philip Peek, Katrien Pype, and Filip De Boeck for their suggestions and comments. However, all mistakes and shortcomings are entirely mine.

1. In northern Namibia, twins bear distinctive names. In Otjihimba and Otjiherero, the first-born is named Kataeko, the second-born Tsjanakambendje. In Otjizemba they are referred to as Kataeko and Okaviyu, respectively. These names are gender indifferent, and are used together with other names women and men acquire at birth or throughout their lifetime.

2. Himba and Herero society are characterized by double descent. This means that every woman or man simultaneously belongs to a matrilineage (*ondjuo*, "house") and a patrilineage (*osano*, expressed in the name). A matrilineage (patrilineage) is a kinship group that traces descent to a common ancestress (ancestor),

with membership being passed on through the mother (father). Different matri-lineages (patrilineages) are grouped together to form matriclans (patriclans) that, too, go back to a common ancestor.

3. Noteworthy perhaps is that, in the same year as, and in contrast to, Shapera's article, Steenkamp (a medical practitioner and Member of Parliament in South Africa) published a booklet that expressed the anxiety and popular myth in South (and West) African policy circles that Herero women were committing "tribal genocide" by refusing to bear children or by undergoing abortion (Steen-kamp 1927; see also Almagor 1982).

4. For more recent analyses of myth, cosmology, and twinship in southern Africa, see Hammond-Tooke (1977, 1988, 1992); Kuper (1987).

5. In Turner's defense, one could point out that he aimed at understanding the Ndembu worldview in Ndembu terms, not at providing a distant analysis of the tensions he describes. Still, his ethnography fails to account for the ideological dimension of the plot of Ndembu twin rituals and worldview.

6. The Himba cattle herd knows two major subdivisions. On the one hand, "firestick animals" (*ozondumehupa*) embody and present the ancestors and the patrilineage, expressed in the prohibitions associated with these animals and their produce (milk, meat, skins, etc.). On the other hand, the "cows of the butter gourd" (*ozondyupa*) embody the "house" or matrilineage, and are not associated with taboos. Their milk (*omatuka*, buttermilk) is offered to travelers and strang-ers, does not need to be tasted, and so on.

7. Like tanning, churning (both *okutuka*, "moving back and forth"), knotting, braiding or weaving (basically, all movements that imply a to and fro) are consid-ered feminine activities.

8. These same qualities (at once "one" and "two," a sign of good fortune and riches) are also attributed to the metal or plastic bead fan-shaped motive (*eha*) found as decoration on garments, necklaces, and milking pails; made from ("white") metal beads, these *omaha* are often colored with black and red butterfat.

9. It needs to be noted that witches in rural Himba society are not persecuted, except when they "kill" (*okuzepa; okuroya;* also *okurya,* "eat") outside their matri-lineage, and that older informants maintain that witchcraft has "democratized": unlike in the past, nowadays everybody is or can become a witch.

10. Two of my informants, for instance, bore the name "Kautanaurwa." This name was explained as "May heaven and earth not turn around / May the sky stay up, and the earth stay down."

11. "To give birth" is translated as *okukwata* (for men and animals) or as *oku-panduka* (for women).

WORKS CITED

Almagor, Uri. 1982. "A Note on the Fertility of the Mbanderu Women." *Botswana Notes and Records* 14 (23–25).

Bourdieu, Pierre. 1977. *Esquisse d'une théorie de la pratique: Précédé de trois études d'ethnologie Kabyle.* Genève: GenèveDros.

Broch-Due, Vigdis. 1999. "Creation and the Multiple Female Body: Turkana Perspectives on Gender and Cosmos." In *Those Who Play with Fire: Gender, Fertility, and Transformation in East and Southern Africa*, ed. Henrietta L. Moore, Todd Sanders, and Bwire Kaare, 153–184. London School of Economics Monographs on Social Anthropology 69. London: Athlone Press.

Csordas, Thomas J. 1994. "Introduction: The Body as Representation and Being-in-the-World." In *Embodiment and Experience: The Existential Ground of Culture and Self*, ed. Thomas J. Csordas, 1–26. Cambridge: Cambridge University Press.

Dannert, E. 1880. "Customs and Ceremonies of the OvaHerero at the Birth of Twins." (South Africa) *Folklore Journal* 2 (104): 114.

De Boeck, F. 1994. "Of Trees and Kings: Politics and Metaphor among the Aluund of Southwestern Zaire." *American Ethnologist* 21 (3): 451–473.

Diduk, Susan. 2001. "Twinship and Juvenile Power: The Ordinariness of the Extraordinary." *Ethnology* 40 (1): 29–34.

———. 1993. "Twins, Ancestors and Socio-Economic Change in Kedjom Society." *Man* 28 (3): 551–571.

Durham, Deborah. 2002. "Uncertain Citizens: Herero and the New Intercalary Subject in Postcolonial Botswana." In *Postcolonial Subjectivities in Africa*, ed. Richard Werbner, 139–170. London: Zed Books.

Estermann, Carlos. 1981. *The Ethnography of Southwestern Angola III: The Herero People.* New York: Africana Publishing Co.

Flax, Jane. 1990. *Thinking Fragments: Psychoanalysis, Feminism, and Postmodernism in the Contemporary West.* Berkeley: University of California Press.

Foster, George M. 1965. "Peasant Society and the Image of Limited Good." *American Anthropologist* 67 (2): 293–315.

Gluckman, Max. 1955. *The Judicial Process among the Barotse of Northern Rhodesia.* Manchester, U.K.: Rhodes-Livingstone Institute of Northern Rhodesia / Manchester University Press.

Hammond-Tooke, W. D. 1977. "Lévi-Strauss in a Garden of Millet: The Structural Analysis of a Zulu Folktale." *Man* 12 (1): 76–86.

———. 1988. "The 'Mythic' Content of Zulu Folktales." *African Studies* 47 (2): 89–100.

———. 1992. "Twins, Incest, and Mediators: the Structure of Four Zulu Folk Tales." *Africa* 62 (2): 203–220.

Hodgson, Dorothy L. 2000. "Introduction: Gender, Culture, and the Myth of the Patriarchal Pastoralist." In *Rethinking Pastoralism in Africa: Gender, Culture, and the Myth of the Patriarchal Pastoralist*, ed. Dorothy L. Hodgson, 1–28. Oxford: James Currey.

Imperato, Pascal J., and Gavin H. Imperato. 2008. "Twins, Hermaphrodites, and an Androgynous Albino Deity." *African Arts* 41 (1): 40–49.

Jacobson-Widding, Anita. 1991. "The Encounter in the Water Mirror." In *Body and Space: Symbolic Models of Unity and Division in African Cosmology and Experience*, ed. Anita Jacobson-Widding, 177–216. Stockholm: Almqvist och Wichsell International.

Jackson, Michael. 1996. "Introduction: Phenomenology, Radical Empiricism, and Anthropological Critique." In *Things as They Are: New Directions in Phenomenological Anthropology*, ed. Michael Jackson, 1–50. Bloomington: Indiana University Press.

Kamanzi, Speratus. 2007. "Twin Phobia among the Haya of Northwestern Tanzania: Interpreting it Within the Mimetic Theory." *Journal of Religion* 37 (1): 53–63.

Kirmayer, Lawrence J. 1993. "Healing and the Invention of Metaphor: The Effectiveness of Symbols Revisited." *Culture, Medicine, and Psychiatry* 17 (2): 161–195.

Kuper, Adam. 1987. *South Africa and the Anthropologist.* London: Routledge and Kegan Paul.

Lau, Birgitte. 1981. "Thank God the Germans Came: Vedder and Namibian Historiography." Collected papers of the African Seminar, Centre for African Studies, University of Cape Town, South Africa.

Lichtenberg-Ettinger, Bracha. 1995. *The Matrixial Gaze.* Leeds, U.K.: University of Leeds, Department of Fine Arts, Feminist Arts and Histories Network.

Malan, Johannes S. 1973. "Double Descent among the Himba of South West Africa." *Cimbebasia (B)* 2 (3): 81–112.

———. 1974. "The Herero-speaking Peoples of Kaokoland." *Cimbebasia (B)* 2 (4): 113–129.

Masquelier, Adeline. 2001. "Powers, Problems, and Paradoxes of Twinship in Niger." *Ethnology* 40 (1): 45–62.

Motzafi-Haller, Pnina. 1998. "Beyond Textual Analysis: Practice, Interacting Discourses, and the Experience of Distinction in Botswana." *Cultural Anthropology* 13 (4): 522–547.

Peek, Philip M. 2008. "Couples or Doubles." *African Arts* 41 (1): 14–23.

Renne, Elisha P., and Misty L. Bastian. 2001. "Reviewing Twinship in Africa." *Ethnology* 40 (1): 1–11.

Schapera, Isaac. 1927. "Customs Relating to Twins in South Africa." *Journal of the Royal African Society* 26 (102): 117–137.

Steenkamp, W. P. 1927. *Is the South-West African Herero Committing Race Suicide?* Cape Town, South Africa: Unie volkspers.

Strathern, Marylin. 1988. *The Gender of the Gift: Problems with Women and Problems with Society in Melanesia.* Berkeley: University of California Press.

Turner, Victor. 1969. *The Ritual Process: Structure and Anti-structure.* London: Routledge and Kegan Paul.

Van Dijk, Rijk. 2002. "Modernity's Limits: Pentecostalism and the Moral Rejection of Alcohol in Malawi." In *Alcohol in Africa: Mixing Business, Pleasure, and Politics,* ed. Deborah F. Bryceson, 249–264. Portsmouth, N.H.: Heinemann.

Van Warmelo, N. S. 1962 [1951]. "Notes on the Kaokoveld, South West Africa, and its Peoples." Ethnological publications no. 26. Pretoria, South Africa: Government Printer.

Van Wolputte, Steven. 2004. "Hang on to Your Self: Of Bodies, Embodiment, and Selves." *Annual Review of Anthropology* 33: 251–269.

———. 2003. *Material Culture in Himbaland, Northern Namibia.* Tervuren, Belgium: RMCA.

———. 2000. "In Between House and Cattle Pen: Moving Spaces in Himbaland." In *People, Cattle and Land: Transformations of a Pastoral Society in Southwestern Africa,* ed. Michael Bollig and Jan-Bart Gewald, 369–400. Köln, Germany: Rüdiger Köppe Verlag.

Vedder, H. 1966. "The Herero." In *The Native Tribes of South West Africa,* ed. C. H. L. Hahn, H. Vedder, and L. Fourie, 153–211. London: Frank Cass and Co.

Part Two

Doubles and Dualities

CHAPTER FOUR

Sustaining the Oneness in Their Twoness

Poetics of Twin Figures (Ère Ìbejì) among the Yoruba

BABATUNDE LAWAL

The notion that reality has two aspects (i.e., spirit/matter, visible/invisible, male/female, good/evil, essence/existence and so on) is a universal phenomenon dating back to the dawn of human history. However, its implications vary from one culture to another. In some, the two aspects are thought to be interdependent—as in the duality of twins or the primordial couple whose union gave birth to humankind. In others, the two may be viewed as complementary—as in Hinduism; mutually independent and sometimes antagonistic—as in the eschatological dualism of the Zoroastrian, Manichaean, and Christian Gnostic doctrines of good and evil in which the one is expected to overcome the other in the end; or eternally coexistent—as in the Cartesian epistemological distinction between mind and body.[1]

This chapter examines the notion of duality among the Yoruba of Nigeria and the Republic of Benin in West Africa, focusing on how it resonates in their attitudes toward twins, causing them to use carved figures/memorials (ère ibeji, hereafter referred to as twin memorials) to maintain the spiritual bond between living and deceased twins. My interpretation is based on field observations and interviews, iconographic analysis, and Yoruba oral traditions about twins—most especially songs (orin ibeji) composed by parents to honor them. I have also made use of popular sayings (òrò awon àgbà) handed down from the past and known to reflect the worldview or folk belief of the Yoruba, and divination verses (esè Ifá) often cited by diviners (babaláwo) to explain the origins and significance of natural, supernatural, and cultural phenomena to their clients.[2] The significance of these verses in the study of twin images and rituals cannot be overemphasized since (in the past) parents of twins were expected to stay in touch with diviners because of the unusual nature of their children.

The Power of Twoness

The popular Yoruba saying *T'ako, t'abo, èjìwàpò*, "The male and female in togetherness" (Lawal 1995: 45) is loaded with meanings. In addition to hinting at the life-producing potential of the couple—the source of the family—it recalls the Yoruba conceptualization of the cosmos as a "big gourd with two halves" (*Igbá nlá méjì s'ojú dé'ra won*).[3] The top half signifies maleness (*ako*) as well as the sky/heaven (*isálórun*)—the realm of invisible spirits. The bottom half represents femaleness (*abo*) and the primeval waters out of which the physical world (*ayé*) was later created. A mysterious power called *àse* is thought to hold the gourd in space, enabling the sun and moon to shine, wind to blow, fire to burn, rain to fall, rivers to flow and both living and nonliving things to exist. This power emanates from a Supreme Deity known (among others) as Aláse (Owner of *àse*), Olórun (Lord of the Sky) and Olódùmarè (the Eternal One and Source of All that Exists). The bipartite nature of *àse* is evident not only in the top and bottom halves of the cosmic gourd (*igbá iwà*), but also in the benevolent and malevolent forces of nature and in the oppositional complementarity of day and night, hot and cool, wet and dry, right and left, north and south, east and west, and life and death, among others. Many of the deities (*òrìsà*) who personify different aspects of Olódùmarè's *àse* are deemed to have two sides—at times male and female or sometimes positive and negative.[4] Even humanity (*èniyàn*) has similar manifestations. Besides, every living person is thought to have a spirit double (*enìkejì*) in heaven, in addition to being an interface of spirit and matter—that is, a physical body (*ara*) and a soul (*èmí*) that enlivens it. The bilateral symmetry of the body is sometimes said to reflect the contributions of one's parents to the self, the right (*òtún*) being identified with the father, and the left (*òsì*), with the mother.[5] Some parts of the body manifest this twoness as well. For example, bone (*egun*) is identified as male, and flesh (*eran*) as female; semen (*àtò*), male, and breast milk (*omún*), female. The head (*orí*) has two aspects as well— namely, an outer layer (*orí òde*), consisting of the hair, forehead, eyes, nose, cheek, mouth, chin, and ears; that is, those features that physically identify a person. A naturalistic portrait focuses on these visible details of the self, which may also include the whole body. The inner head (*orí inú*), on the other hand, refers to an inner, spiritual core (*ipònrí*), which, to the Yoruba, enshrines the *àse* or the life-force on which depends one's success or failure in life. The symbol of this inner core is called *iborí* (altar to the head). Its abstract form hints at the mystical nature of the spiritual self, though a stylized sculpture with an emphasis on the head may also allude to the preeminence of the *orí inú*.[6] The belief that the latter controls the outer head is evident in the popular prayer: *Kí orí inú mi má ba t'ode jé* ("may my spiritual head not spoil the physical one") (Drewal, Pemberton, and Abiodun 1989: 26; Olajubu 2003: 33).[7] The eye (*ojú*) is thought to have two layers, namely the *ojú òde* (outer eye), which has to do with normal quotidian vision and *ojú inú* (inner eye) or *ojú okàn* (mind's eye), associated with insight, intuition, meditation, critical analysis, and the like (see Lawal 2001: 516–517).

The Yoruba idea of beauty (*ewà*) also has two components, *ewà ode* (physical beauty) and *ewà inú* (inner beauty). *Ewà ode* refers to visual appeal, and *ewà inú*, to character or moral worthiness (*ìwà*). The high premium placed on the latter can be discerned from the popular saying: *Ìwà l'ewà* ("character determines beauty"). The reason for this is obvious: physical beauty (*ewà òde*) is a natural endowment, and thus to make it (*ewà òde*) the sole criterion for judging the beautiful is tantamount to penalizing the physically unattractive for a biological fact they could not have personally prevented. The stress on character, on the other hand, affords everyone an equal chance of living up to a moral ideal in order to be fully admired. Self-discipline thus becomes the key to social mobility, enabling an individual to make up for a physical deficiency or maximize the potentials of a natural endowment.[8] The key point here is that, to the Yoruba, success in life depends largely on the act of balancing or harmonizing the two aspects of the self, in addition to employing spiritual means to reinforce one's life. It partly explains why they consider the number two sacred, believing that (in a ritual context) *twoness* has the potential to influence the supernatural and bring about a desired result. As a divination verse puts it:

Èjì kòkò Ìwòrì, Olúwo Ìsálòrun! . . .	Ìwòrì-The-Formidable-Two, Master Diviner of Heaven! . . .
Ki o kó reree tèmi wá á fun mi	Bring me my blessings.
Èjì kòkò Ìwòrì	Ìwòrì-The-Formidable-Two,
Kí o gbé òrun gbà a wá síle Ayé	Bring them [my blessings] from heaven to earth.
Bálé bá lé, a fojú fóorun	When the night falls, Sleep takes over our eyes.
Èjì kòkò Ìwòrì	Ìwòrì-The-Formidable-Two!
Súré tete wá koo wá fire tèmi fún mi	Move swiftly and bring me my blessings
Èjì-kòò-kòò-kòò, Ìwòrì!	Ìwòrì-The-Formidable-Formidable-Formidable-Two!

(Adeniji 1982: 96, my translation)

Another text described "The-Sacred-Two" as "The one who left home as a wretched person, but later returned with good fortune" (Olatunji 1984: 44). So it is that the Yoruba are world-famous for their adoration of twins (*ibeji*), regarding them as spirit children with special powers that can protect as well as attract good fortune to their parents:

Èjìré Òkín Ará Ìsokùn	Twins, beautiful egrets, native of Isokùn town,
Ilé Alákìsà l'óti kí won	You entered the house of the poor.
Èjìré so alákìsà di aláso	Twins turned the poor into the rich.
O so alágbe di olóúnje	You turned the beggar into somebody with food to eat.
Ó so òtòsì di olórò . . .	You turned the wretched into the wealthy . . .

(Daramola and Jeje 1975: 282, my translation)

The Spirit Double Incarnated

To fully understand the significance of twins among the Yoruba one must be aware of their ancient belief that every living person has an unborn spirit double in heaven. The following testimony recorded by Raymond Prince during his field research in Yorubaland in the 1960s sums up the concept:

God created a man in two parts, the being here on earth and a spiritual double (Eleda or Ikeji) in heaven. Before entering the world, a man makes a contract with his double, agreeing to stay away from heaven for a certain period, to do a certain kind of work, to have a certain number of wives and children—in fact all the details of his future life in the world are agreed upon with his spirit double . . .

Once in the world, the man cannot, of course, remember his contract, but should he fail to fulfill it he will not prosper or may even fall ill. If, on the other hand, the man abides by his agreement, the double, like a guardian spirit, ensures his good fortune and protects him from trouble and illness . . . (Prince 1964: 93).[9]

As Marilyn Houlberg (1973: 23) has observed:

In the case of twins, the spirit double has been born on earth. Since there is no way of telling which is the heavenly being and which is the mortal, both are treated as sacred from birth. As one 45-year-old-man from

Ibadan commented: "We do not think of each twin as having its own counterpart in heaven; they are the counterparts of each other." Thus, everything that is done for one must be done for the other.[10]

In other words, the prenatal bond between an individual and his/her spirit double was such that one could not leave the other behind. As a result, both were born together; hence their name *ibeji* (double-birth) or *èjìré* (the intimate, inseparable two). The first to be born, Táyéwò or Táíwò (The-One-Who-Tastes-the-World), is regarded as the junior and a scout for the second, Kéhìndé (The-Last-to-Come), the senior. The cry of Táyéwò is often interpreted as a signal to Kéhìndé that it is safe to come out; otherwise, Kéhìndé would not follow. The silence of Táyéwò signifies problems and could result in stillbirth or the death of both twins soon after delivery. On the other hand, the loud cry of the two at birth is a cause for celebration, implying that they are delighted, as it were, to disembark. This unusual circumstance of their birth partly explains the Yoruba perception of twins as "spirits in human flesh" (*abàmì èdá*) or deities (*òrìsà*) who must be pampered (Daramola and Jeje 1975: 280). They also believe (as stated in the above song) that twins have the capacity to transform a "beggar into somebody with food to eat"—which is understandable in view of the many gifts that some Yoruba mother of twins (*iyá ibeji*) receive from well-wishers in the course of dancing round the town with their children.[11] Yoruba diviners (*babaláwo*) often prescribe this ritual dance because, according to popular belief, it makes twins happy and prevents them from dying prematurely. At the same time, the gifts they receive from well-wishers have a votive significance, as the latter expect twins to reciprocate and bless them with their metaphysical powers (Abimbola 1982: 73–75). Given the strong spiritual bond between twins, their parents are expected to dress them up in identical clothing, in addition to paying them equal attention. To love one more than the other is to incur the displeasure of their patron deity (*Òrìsà ibeji*).[12] Hence, having twins constitutes a kind of "double trouble" for the parents in view of the duplications and expenses involved in their upbringing—feeding two mouths; buying dresses, toys, and other things two at a time. On the other hand, giving birth to them could be a double blessing as well because having twins not only saves time, but also enables parents, according to popular belief, to benefit from their spiritual powers.

Twin Figures (*Ère Ìbejì*)

If one of the pair should die, tradition requires that a memorial (*ère ibeji*) be procured to localize the soul of the deceased so as to maintain

FIGURE 4.1. Pair of Twin Memorials (Ère Ìbejì). Yoruba (Nigeria, Republic of Benin), nineteenth–twentieth century. Wood, glass beads, string, paint. Each: 10½" x 2¾" W x 3" D (26.6cm x 7cm x 7.6cm). Virginia Museum of Fine Arts, Richmond, Va.; Adolph D. and Wilkins C. Williams Fund. *Photo: Katherine Wetzel © Virginia Museum of Fine Arts (Obj. 81.24.1-2).*

the spiritual bond between the living and the dead. The memorial, which should reflect the sex of the deceased, is usually commissioned from a carver (*gbénàgbénà*) on the recommendation of a diviner. On completing it, the carver would soak the figure in an herbal mixture and then rub it with a special ointment before handing it over to the bereaved mother.[13] Tradition requires her to treat the memorial like a living child and, among others, feed it symbolically at the same time the surviving twin is having his/her meals. If she buys a new dress for the surviving twin, a miniature of it would be made to dress the memorial. The carving may sometimes be given to the surviving twin to play with—evidently to minimize the natural instincts in twins to want to see one another after a long separation. If the surviving twin should ask about the deceased, it is forbidden to say that he/she had passed; one excuse or the other would be fabricated. More often the surviving twin is told that the deceased had traveled out of town and had left the memorial behind as a surrogate to indicate that he/she would soon be back. Although the symbolic feeding and dressing of the memorial may continue indefinitely, it could be stopped when the surviving twin comes of age or no longer asks about the whereabouts of the deceased. The memorial may then be placed in a shrine under the tutelage of the family deity (òrìsà). In the event of both twins dying, a second memorial would be commissioned (figure 4.1) and their mother would continue to treat them like living children in the hope that they will soon return to her either singly or as a pair (if she is still within childbearing age), and that they will continue to bless and protect her with their spiritual powers.

It should be pointed out at this juncture that not all the twin figures on a given altar commemorate the dead. Some perform other functions. For instance, the image of a living twin may be commissioned and placed beside that of his/her deceased partner to keep the latter company, most especially in the still of the night or when the living twin is out of town or is traveling and needs the spiritual protection of his/her deceased partner.[14] The image becomes a memorial on the death of the living twin. Secondly, not every woman who keeps what appear to be twin memorials can be regarded as bereaved, because a childless housewife may sometimes be advised by a diviner to procure a pair of twin images in order to harness their spiritual powers to restore her fertility (Picton 2003: 56). Thirdly, the deceased souls of twins are believed to be very close to, and run errands for, major deities such as Èsù-Elégba (divine messenger and keeper of the crossroads) and Sàngó (lord of the thunderstorm, also associated with social justice). As a result, images of twins may be commissioned by priests and herbalists and sorcerers and placed on the altars of such deities to perform specific functions such as mediating between the terrestrial and celestial worlds or tracking down and punishing wrongdoers.[15] To reinforce these functions, such images often bear motifs identifiable with Èsù-Elégba and Sàngó.[16]

Mythico-Historical Background

That the Yoruba once abhorred the birth of twins is reflected in an ancient Yoruba divination phrase Esin bí méjì, o sìse; èniyàn bí méjì, ó hàn òrò" ("The horse that bears two at a time is abnormal; any human being who bears twins is in trouble") (personal communication from Babalawo Babalola Fatoogun, Ilé-Ifè, Nigeria, 1982). Legend has it that the Yoruba killed newly born twins in the past partly because they associated a multiple birth with animals and partly because of the fear that one of the pair was a spirit partner and therefore a bad omen for a given community.[17] According to the Yoruba historian Samuel Johnson, the practice "received its death blow" when the wife of Aláàfin Àjàká, the king of Old Òyó, gave birth to twins. Instead of having them killed, Àjàká ordered that the woman and her children be sent into exile accompanied by a large number of servants, friends, and relatives. To cut the story short, the twins survived in the wilderness and eventually became the kings of towns now known as Èpé and Òndó (Johnson 1921: 25). Unfortunately, the time of Aláàfin Àjàká's reign is uncertain; various academic speculations place it somewhere between the fourteenth and fifteenth centuries AD. However, another version of the same legend claims that it was Odùduwà, the first divine king of the Yoruba city of Ilé-Ifè—not Aláàfin Àjàká of Old Òyó—who fathered the exiled twins that eventually became the kings of Èpé and Òndó.[18] Again, the date of Odùduwà's reign in Ilé-Ifè is yet to be determined, though some scholars speculate that it may be much earlier than that of Aláàfin Àjàká. It suffices to say that no one can say precisely when the killing of twins stopped (Johnson 1921: 25). In fact, the practice continued well into the nineteenth century in some parts of Yorubaland (Smith 1988: 52; Olupona 1991: 23–24; Abimbola 1982).

A second and more popular legend traces the beginning of twin adoration among the Yoruba to some Yoruba traders who founded a settlement near the Ègùn town of Àjàsé (now Porto-Novo, the capital of the Republic of Benin) (Sowande and Ajanaku 1969: 50; Daramola and Jeje 1975: 281; Chappell 1974: 250–265; Thompson 1971b: ch 13/2; and Pemberton 2003: 31–49). The traders named the settlement Ìsokùn, after a popular district of Old Òyó. One of their women later gave birth to twins and decided to keep them as such children were not forbidden in that area at the time. Nevertheless, the parents consulted a local diviner, who advised them to perform certain rituals, including dancing around the town with the twins. While doing so, they received a lot of gifts and eventually became well-to-do. The news soon spread to different parts of Yorubaland that the preserved twins had attracted good fortune to their parents, thereby inspiring others to follow in their footsteps. According to Tim Chappel, the Ìsokùn incident would seem to have occurred about the mid-eighteenth century, apparently before the town of Àjàsé and its environs came under the direct political control of Old Òyó, where twin infanticide had hitherto been practiced (Chappell 1974: 254–255; see also Pemberton 2003: 35–36). This is not unlikely, especially since an elderly woman he interviewed in the Ìsokùn quarter of modern Òyó in the 1960s also traced the origin of twin veneration among the Yoruba to a town near Àjàsé. Unfortunately, all attempts to locate this town have so far been unsuccessful.

A third account claims that the adoration of twins actually began at the Ìsokùn quarter of Old Òyó before spreading to the Yoruba settlement near Àjàsé. As Robert F. Thompson has observed, "Song after song salutes . . . twins as hailing from a quarter of the city of Oyo called Ishokun. The ruler of the Ishokun quarter is said to have fathered twins nine times in nine places!" (Thompson 1971b: ch. 13/3). Another legend avers that a queen from the quarter gave birth to six sets of twins in a row and the king of Òyó honored all of them with royal titles,[19] thus encouraging his subjects and other Yoruba to revere twins. However, no one remembers when this event happened or the names of the principal characters. But many of the elders I interviewed in modern Òyó in the 1970s insisted that the popular nickname for twins *Edunjobí* (i.e., "relatives of the Colobus monkey," called in Yoruba *Edun*) originated in the Ìsokùn quarter of Old Òyó. The animal is associated with twins for two main reasons. First, it often gives birth to two at a time and carries one on the back and the other on her breast—just like Yoruba mothers of twins. Second, there is a widespread belief that twins may reincarnate as monkeys.[20] Besides, the Ìsokùn district of Old Òyó reportedly had such a large population of *Edun* (Babalola 1966: 107 n1) that (in the view of some informants) it inspired the following praise song for twins:

Èjìré ará Ìsokùn	Èjìré, natives of Ìsokùn
Edun jo bí	Relatives of the Colobus Monkey,
Edun a gbó orí igi référéfé	Colobus Monkey of the treetop,
Àtètèjí tí onílègbálè	Who rises early in the morning to meet the sweeper.
O sónú kò b'éjìré	The hard-hearted one cannot give birth to twins.
Onínúre ní mbí Edun	Only the good-hearted one will give birth to the Colobus monkey,
Ó f'esé méjèjì bé sí ilé alákísà	Who jump with both feet into the house of a ragged person
Ó so alákísà di aláso.	And thereby turn that ragged person into somebody with a rich wardrobe.

(Sowande and Ajanaku 1969: 50, my translation)

According to a divination verse collected by Wande Abimbola (1982: 10, 59), "It was . . . Edun [the first twins and half-human relatives of the Colobus Monkey] who founded all the towns known as 'Ìsokùn'" (towns bearing the name "Ìsokùn" can be found near Abéòkúta, Osogbo, Sakí, Iséyìn and Ilé-Ifè). Little wonder that some informants speculate that the now extinct Ìsokùn of the Àjàsé area may be no more than one of early sites where migrant Yoruba traders decided to keep their twins. One report says that the elaborate rituals and public celebrations for twins in this former Yoruba enclave were such that they attracted pilgrims from different parts of Yorubaland (Daramola and Jeje 1975: 281). The question then arises: did these festivities enable the enclave to overshadow the original Ìsokùn at Old Òyó or elsewhere?

Simply put, it is difficult at the moment to answer this question and to say exactly when the Yoruba stopped killing twins and started adoring them. Chances are that the transition occurred at different times in different parts of Yorubaland. That the adoration might have begun much earlier than the eighteenth century is suggested by the fact that two British explorers, John and Richard Lander, visiting the Yoruba town of Ìbèsè in 1830, observed many women carrying twin memorials and making it evident that the adoration of twins was already well established by this time (Lander and Lander 1832: 107).[21] Moreover, its documentation among Yoruba captives in the Americas during the mid-nineteenth century (Ortiz 1906: 745; quoted in Thompson 1971a: 11) may very well indicate that the practice had been transplanted to the New World by the late seventeenth century when the Yoruba began to be exported there in large numbers.

By and large, the change in Yorubaland from an era of killing twins to one of adoring them resounds in the following declaration from the divination verse (Èjì Ogbè):

Èjèèjì ni mo gbè   From now on, I will favor the collaborative two
Ng ò gbènìkan soso mó.   I will no longer favor the solitary.
(Abimbola 1982, my translation)

Could there have been other factors, apart from the legends cited above, that caused this paradigm change? For example, recent scientific studies by geneticists reveal that, though genetic and environmental variables cannot the ignored, the high incidence of twins among the Yoruba (in the past and today) may equally be due to their consumption of yam (*Dioscorea* sp.), which produces the hormone phytoestrogen that stimulates multiple ovulation in women. As a result, the Yoruba are reputed to have the highest birthrate of twins in the world (Nylander 1969; Akinboro, Azeez and Bakare 2008: 41–47; see also chapter 1).

Is it possible then, that the killing of twins occurred when the *Dioscorea* species of yam was scarce in Yorubaland? If so, did its abundance cause the birth rates of twins to increase, thereby contributing to their acceptance as normal children in spite of their association with the spirit double (*enìkejì*)? Let us hope that future research will shed some light on these questions.

Metaphysics of the Twin Figure

Undoubtedly, the use of art to localize the soul of a deceased twin has been influenced by the Yoruba cosmogony that identifies the human body (*ara*) as a piece of sculpture (*ère*) created by the artist deity Obàtálá and animated by the soul—a vital force (èmí) breathed into the image by the Supreme Being Olódùmarè.[22] Thus, an individual is alive as long as the soul dwells in his or her body. Although the withdrawal or forcible expulsion of the soul from the body will result in death, the soul is believed to live on in a dematerialized state and can reincarnate as a child in a new body to start a new life on earth. Alternatively, a consecrated human-made sculpture can be used to metaphorically re-embody the soul and then function as a remembrance of the deceased. This explains why twin memorials (ère ìbejì) are considered vital to the maintenance of the spiritual bond between a surviving twin and his/her deceased partner.

Material Metaphor

The wood of the West African rubber tree (Funtumia elastica), known locally as iré, is considered the most ideal material for carving a twin memorial (ère ìbejì). This is apparently because of its sticky latex (ojè), which, according to popular belief, has the power to sustain the oneness in the twoness of twins. Yoruba carvers divide the wood of the tree into three categories—namely the savannah type (iré òdàn or iré líle), which is very hard; the saturated type (iré bàsàbàsà), which is rather soft; and the medium type (iré onà), which is not too soft nor too hard (personal communication with the famous Yoruba carver Lamidi Fakeye, Ilé-Ifè, Nigeria, 1982; Fakeye, Haight and Curl 1996: 70–71). Most Yoruba carvers prefer the third type (iré onà) because it is easier to carve and decorate with patterns. The Yoruba association of the West African rubber tree with twin memorials is reflected in the popular saying:

Òjé l'àpébo Òòsà	Lead is the most sacred symbol of Òòsà [the artist deity Obàtálá]
Irin l' àpébo Ògún	Iron is the most sacred symbol of Ògún [deity of tools and weapons]
Ide l' àpébo Òsun	Brass is the most sacred symbol of Òsun [goddess of the Òsun river]
Iré l' àpébo Ìbejì.	The wood of the West African rubber tree is the sacred symbol of twins.

(Personal communication with the Yoruba diviner Babalawo Babalola Fatoogun, Ilé-Ifè, Nigeria, 1982, my translation)

The etymology of "iré," the Yoruba name for the West African rubber tree, reveals deeper meanings; for it derives from the root verb "ré," meaning "to unite, befriend or reconcile." It is not surprising therefore that the same verb occurs in *èjìré* (the inseparable two), a nickname for twins, and it is also taboo for twins and their mothers to eat any food cooked with the wood of *iré*. The general notion that the tree has the spiritual power to bring two people together in friendship explains why its leaves, branches, bark, roots, and latex are used in making charms aimed at bonding two people, reconciling former enemies or simply promoting cordial relationships in a community. This phenomenon is reflected in the popular incantation: *"Iré oko, lóní kí o wá bá mi ré"* ("*Iré* of the forest commands you to befriend me") (personal communication with Babalawo Babalola Fatoogun, Ilé-Ifè, Nigeria, 1982; see also Babatunde Lawal 1989: 12). Note the prominence of the root verb *"ré"* in words such as *òré* (friend) and *irépò* (social harmony), which further stresses the spiritual intensity of the oneness in *èjìré*, the nickname for twins. Needless to say, assorted charms may be attached to a twin memorial to make it more potent in its ritual functions. Beaded vests may be worn for some to convey parental love or reflect the high status of a given family in the community.

Form, Meaning, and Style

Usually rendered in the nude and standing erect, barefoot or occasionally wearing a pair of sandals, and with the arms at the side, a typical twin memorial is either male or female and measures between six and eleven inches in height. The head, with its elaborate hairdo, almost always dominates the figure, alluding to its importance as the seat of the soul (*èmí*) and the site of identity, communication, and perception.[23] The otherworldly station of the deceased is reflected in the bulging, almond-shaped eyes, big flat nose, protruding lips, and highly simplified body. The smallness of a typical memorial is both symbolic and functional; on the one hand, it reflects the fact that, in the past, most twins died in infancy; on the other, the small size facilitates portability, especially when the image is given to the surviving twin to play with or when the mother dances with it in honor of the deceased twin.

In general, most memorials are made to look like individuals in the prime of life, with physically mature features—despite the fact that most Yoruba twins died young. Note their frontal, dignified, and iconic poses.[24] They are a study in composure and spiritual beauty, reflecting the Yoruba tendency to canonize the dead. As a popular adage puts it: *Ojó a k'u là á dère, ènìyàn kò sunwòn láàyè* ("It is death that turns an individual into a beautiful sculpture; a living person has blemishes") (Sobande 1970: 26).[25] In other words, tradition requires the Yoruba artist to idealize and ignore accidental physical features or blemishes associated with the living when creating a memorial. Even if deceased twins were not identical, the artist is expected to give their memorials similar facial features in order to reflect, sustain, and celebrate the *oneness* in their *twoness*. Unfortunately, some old memorials have lost much of their original facial features due to the ritual handling, feeding, washing, and anointing associated with their daily use.

Admittedly, twin memorials from different parts of Yorubaland share common characteristics in their small sizes and stylized features with an emphasis on the head. Yet certain details, such as facial marks, pierced pupils and ear lobes, flattened or protruding lips, as well as the treatment of the chin, may be used to identify individual styles and regional substyles.[26]

Recent Developments

Despite the enormous impact of European colonization, Western education, modern technology, and urbanization on their culture, many Yoruba have not totally abandoned their traditional beliefs. Mass conversion to Islam and Christianity, both of which associate twin memorials with paganism, has led many women to use imported or locally manufactured plastic dolls as substitutes and so avoid being viewed by friends and neighbors as "superstitious" or "backward." One of the most striking innovations is in the field of photography. For instance, if a twin should die without having a photograph taken of it, the surviving twin may be photographed in the dress of the deceased, becoming the latter's proxy in

FIGURE 4.2. Symbolic photograph of living and deceased twins. Girl (right) wears male dress (left) to represent her deceased twin brother. Yoruba, Ila Orangun, Nigeria, 1975. Mounted black and white print by SIMPLE PHOTO, Ila Orangun, Nigeria. *Photo courtesy of Marilyn Houlberg.*

the photograph whether or not the two are identical. This photographic image thereafter serves as a means of maintaining the twins' togetherness in life and death. If the twins are of the same sex, the photographer sometimes exposes the image of the surviving twin twice on the same paper, so that the living and the dead (represented by the living) appear to be sitting side by side in the print.

But if the twins are of the opposite sex, the surviving twin is photographed in a male dress and then in a female's. The two images are eventually combined in the final print as if the twins had posed together. Such photographs are thought to have spiritual powers and are sometimes placed in shrines, receiving offerings of food like the carved statuettes (Sprague 1978: 57).[27] As Marilyn Houlberg observed in the field: "The life of the survivor is said to depend on the existence and veneration of the photograph, just as it would be in the case of a wood image" (Houlberg 1976: 18). Through this photomontage technique, contemporary Yoruba photographers perpetuate old values in new forms, especially the tradition of giving twin memorials identical facial features so as to sustain the *oneness* in their *twoness*. (For more on these practices, see chapter 7.)

To lose two children at the same time, or one after the other, can be more than a traumatic experience for a woman in a culture, such as that of the Yoruba, that places a high premium on having many children because they guarantee immortality. However, their belief that the souls of departed twins live on in carved images or, nowadays, in photographic and other modern substitutes, offers some solace to a bereaved mother. In the Yoruba view, to have once had a child is a shade better than not being able to have any at all. And for a woman who has passed the age of childbearing, the memorials *double* as her "living children."[28]

NOTES

This chapter is an expanded version of a section of an article first published by the author as "Èjìwàpò: The Dialectics of Twoness in Yoruba Art and Culture," *African Arts* 41 (1), Spring 2008, 24–39. Special thanks to the editor Philip Peek for reading the first draft and making useful comments.

1. For a review, see Eliade (1969), Bianchi (1978), and Lovejoy (1996).

2. On the significance of Ifá divination verses, see Bascom (1969) and Abimbola (1976).

3. Another saying describes the cosmos as *Igba nla meji, ade isi: aiye ati sanma* ("Two mighty calabashes, one on top of the other, representing earth and sky"). See Ojo (1967: 196).

4. For other ramifications of twoness in Yoruba art and culture, see Lawal (2007: 24–39).

5. See also Idowu (1994: 183) and Epega (1971: 16).

6. For more on the significance of the head in Yoruba art, see Lawal 2000 (93–109).

7. Thus, a person who fails to succeed in spite of hard work is said to be troubled by his inner head. See Idowu (1994: 181–182).

8. For more details, see Lawal (2005: 161–174).

9. See also Idowu (1994:182–183); Houlberg (1973: 23); and Abimbola (1987).

10. See also Thompson (1971a); Lawal (1989); and Chemeche (2003).

11. For a collection of songs dedicated to twins, see Olayemi (1969).

12. The idea of Òrìsà Ìbejì (patron deity of twins) varies from one part of Yorubaland to another. In some areas, it refers to the collective souls of deceased twins in the Afterlife; in other, twins are venerated as deities (òrìsà) in human flesh. See also Simpson (1980: 44–45); Adeoye (1989: 345–351); and Pemberton (2003: 39–41)

13. See also Fakeye (2003: 27–29). Although the carver usually hands over the finished memorial to the bereaved mother, in some cases the latter may take the memorial to a diviner or herbalist for a second ritual treatment. This explains why some memorials have special charms attached to them.

14. For an image representing a living twin, see Picton (2003: 55, fig. 9).

15. See also Simpson (1980: 45).

16. For an image of twins bearing Èsù-Elégba motifs, see Lawal (2007: 38, 66).

17. See also Abimbola (1982); Daramola and Jeje (1975: 280); Talbot (1926: 722); Chappel (1974: 251, 256); Peel (2000: 97–98); and ch. 15 below. The fate of a mother of twins is said to have varied from one town to another. In some, she was killed along with her children; in others, she was sent into exile. There are stories that some parents kept the birth of twins a secret, killing one of them before neighbors found out.

18. See also Talbot (1926: 722); Chappel (1974: 251, 256); and Peel (2000: 97–98).

19. See also Abimbola (1981: 88).

20. On monkeys and twins, see also Sowande and Ajanaku (1969: 50); see also Ojo (1967: 167) and ch. 5 below.

21. According to Chappel (cited in Pemberton 2003: 48n3), it is possible that the women described by the Landers might not be Yoruba but immigrants from neighboring Ègùn towns.

22. For more on Yoruba cosmogony, see Idowu (1994); Drewal, Pemberton, and Abiodun (1989); and Lawal (2007).

23. For more details, see Lawal (2000: 93–109).

24. For more details on the idealization of form in Yoruba art, see Thompson (1973).

25. See also Lawal (2001: 513; and 2007: 66).

26. See Thompson (1971: chap. 13); Fagg and Pemberton (1982); Chappel (1972, 1981, 1997); Stoll and Stoll (1980); and Chemeche (2003).

27. See also Houlberg (1973: 26–27; and 1976: 18–19) and Vogel (1991: 44–47).

28. See also Lawal (1977).

WORKS CITED

Abimbola, Wande. 1976. *Ifá: An Exposition of Ifá Literary Corpus*. Ibadan, Nigeria: Oxford University Press.

———. 1977. *Awon Ojú Odù Mérèerindínlógún*. Ibadan, Nigeria: Oxford University Press.

———. 1982. "From Monster to King and Divinity: Stories of Ìbejì in the Ifá Literary Corpus." Paper presented at the Symposium on Yoruba Carving Styles: Ère Ìbeìi, Department of Art History and Archaeology, University of Maryland, College Park, Maryland.

———. 1997. *Ifá Will Mend Our Broken World: Thoughts on Yoruba Religion and Culture in Africa and the Diaspora,* interviews with an introduction by Ivor Miller. Roxbury, Mass.: Aim Books.

Adeniji, David A. A. 1982. *Ofò Rere (Àgbà Oògùn)*. Ibadan, Nigeria: Ibadan University Press.

Adeoye, C. Laogun. 1989. *Igbàgbó àti Èsin Yoruba*. Lagos, Nigeria: Evans Brothers.

Akinboro, A, M. A. Azeez, and A. A. Bakare. 2008. "Frequency of Twinning in Southwestern Nigeria." *Indian Journal of Human Genetics* 14 (2): 41–47.

Akinjogbin, Isaac (ed). 1992. *The Cradle of a Race: Ifè from the Beginning to 1980*. Portharcourt, Nigeria: Sunray.

Babalola, S. Adeboye. *The Content and Form of Yoruba Ijala*. London: Clarendon Press.

Bascom, William. 1969. *Ifa Divination: Communication between Gods and Men in West Africa*. Bloomington: Indiana University Press.

Bianchi, Ugo. 1978. *Selected Essays on Gnosticism, Dualism and Mysteriology*. Leiden, the Netherlands: E. J. Brill.

Chappel, T. J. H. 1974. "Yoruba Cult of Twins in Historical Perspective." *Africa* 44 (3): 250–265.

———1972. "Critical Carvers: A Case Study." *Man* 7: 296–307.

———1987. "A Woodcarving from Abeokuta." *African Arts* 15 (1): 38–43, 86–87.

———1997. "Akinjobi of Oke-Odan: An Egbado Yoruba Carver." *African Arts* 30 (1): 32–39, 94.

Chemeche, George, 2003. *Ibeji: The Cult of Yoruba Twins*. Milan: 5 Continents Editions.

Courlander, H. 1973. *Tales of Yoruba Gods and Heroes*. Greenwich, Conn.: Fawcett Publications.

Daramola, Olu, and Adebayo Jeje. 1975. *Àwon Àsà àti Òrìsà Ilè Yoruba*. Ibadan, Nigeria: Onibonoje Press.

Drewal, Henry J., John Pemberton, and Rowland O. Abiodun. 1989. *Yoruba: Nine Centuries of African Art and Thought*. New York: Center for African Art.

Eliade, Mircea. 1969. *The Quest: History and Meaning in Religion*. Chicago: The University of Chicago Press.

Epega, D. Olarimiwa. 1971 [1932]. *The Basis of Yoruba Relgion*, rev. ed. Lagos, Nigeria: Ijamido Printers Work.

Fagg, William, and John Pemberton. 1982. *Yoruba: Sculpture from West Africa.* New York: Alfred A. Knopf.

————. 2003. "How Ere Ibeji are Traditionally Commissioned in Yorubaland." In *Ibeji: The Cult of Yoruba Twins,* ed. George Chemeche, 27–29. Milan: 5 Continents Editions.

Fakeye, Lamidi O., Bruce M. Haight, and David H. Curl. 1996. *Lamidi Olonade Fakeye: A Retrospective Exhibition and Biography.* Holland, Mich.: Depree Art Center, Hope College.

Houlberg, Marilyn H. 1973. "Ìbejì Images of the Yoruba." *African Arts* 7 (1): 20–27, 91.

————. 1976. "Collecting the Anthropology of African Art." *African Arts* 9 (3): 18–19.

Idowu, E. Bolaji. 1994. *Olódùmarè: God in Yoruba Belief,* rev. and expanded ed. New York: Original Publications.

Johnson, Samuel. 1921. *The History of the Yorubas.* Lagos, Nigeria: CMS Bookshops.

Lander, Richard, and John Richard. 1832. *Journal of an Expedition to Explore the Source and Termination of the Niger.* London, 1832.

Lawal, Babatunde. 1977. "The Living Dead: Art and Immortality among the Yoruba of Nigeria." *Africa* 47 (1): 50–61.

————. 1989. "A Pair of Èrè Ìbejì (Twin Statuettes) in the Kresge Art Museum." *Kresge Art Museum Bulletin* 6 (12): 10–15.

———— 1995. "A Ya Gbo, A Ya To: New Perspectives on Edan Ogboni." *African Arts* 28 (1): 37–49, 98–100.

————. 1996. *The Gèlèdé Spectacle: Art, Gender, and Social Harmony in an African Culture.* Seattle: University of Washington Press.

————. 2000. "Oríloníse: The Hermeneutics of the Head and Hairstyles among the Yoruba." In *Hair in African Art and Culture,* ed. Roy Sieber and Frank Herremann, 93–109. New York: The Museum for African Art / Munich: Prestel.

————. 2001. "Àwòrán: Representing the Self and Its Metaphysical Other in Yoruba Art." *The Art Bulletin* 83 (3): 516–517.

————. 2005. "Divinity, Creativity, and Humanity in Yoruba Aesthetics." In *Before Pangea: New Essays in Transcultural Aesthetics,* ed. Eugenio Benitez, 161–174. Sydney, Australia: Sydney Society of Literature and Aesthetics.

————. 2007. *Embodying the Sacred in Yoruba Art: Featuring the Bernard and Patricia Wagner Collection.* Atlanta, Ga.: High Museum / Newark, N.J.: Newark Museum of Art.

Lovejoy, Arthur O. 1996. *The Revolt Against Dualism: An Inquiry Concerning the Existence of Ideas.* New Brunswick: Transaction Publishers.

Molade, Timothy. 1971. "Ibeji Customs in Yorubaland." *African Arts* 4 (3): 14–15

Morakinyo, Olufemi, and Akinsola Akiwowo. 1981. "The Yoruba Ontology of Personality and Motivation: A Multidisciplinary Approach." *Journal of Social and Biological Structures* 4 (1): 19–79.

Nylander, P. P. S. 1969. "The Frequency of Twinning in a Rural Community in Western Nigeria." *Annals of Human Genetics* 33: 41–44.

Ojo, G. Afolabi. 1967. *Yoruba Culture: A Geographical Analysis.* London: University of London Press.

Olajubu, Oyeronke. 2003. *Women in the Yoruba Religious Sphere.* Albany, N.Y.: State University of New York Press.

Olatunji, Olatunde O. 1984. *Features of Yoruba Poetry.* Ibadan, Nigeria: University Press Limited.

Olayemi, Val. 1969. *Orin Ibeji: Songs in Praise of Twins.* Ibadan, Nigeria: Institute of African Studies, University of Ibadan.

Olupona, Jacob K. 1991. *Kingship, Religion, and Rituals in a Nigerian Community.* Stockholm: Almqvist and Wiksell International.

Ortiz, Fernando. 1906. *Los Negros Brujos (Apuntes para un Estodio de Etnología Criminal).* Madrid, Spain: Editorial America.

Peel, John D. Y. 2000. *Religious Encounter and the Making of the Yoruba.* Bloomington: Indiana University Press.

Pemberton, John. 2003. "Ere Ibeji: An Affirmation of Life in the Face of Death." In *Ibeji: The Cult of Yoruba Twins,* ed. George Chemeche, 31–49. Milan: 5 Continents Editions.

Picton, John. 2003. "Seeing Double." In *Ibeji: The Cult of Yoruba Twins,* ed. George Chemeche, 50–59. Milan: 5 Continents Editions.

Prince, Raymond. 1964. "Indigenous Yoruba Psychiatry." In *Magic, Faith, and Healing,* ed. Ari. Kiev, 84–120. New York: Free Press.

Simpson, George E. 1980. *Yoruba Religion and Medicine in Ibadan.* Ibadan, Nigeria: Ibadan University Press.

Smith, Robert S. 1988. *The Kingdoms of the Yoruba.* Madison: University of Wisconsin Press.

Sobande, Adegboyega. 1970. "Ìsìnkú ni Ilè Yoruba." *Olókun* 9: 26.

Sowande, Fela, and Fagbemi Ajanaku. 1969. *Orúko Amútorunwá.* Ibadan, Nigeria: Oxford University Press.

Sprague, Stephen, F. 1978. "Yoruba Photography: How the Yoruba See Themselves." *African Arts* 12 (1): 52–59.

Stoll, M., and G. Stoll. 1980. *Ibeji Zwillingsfigures der Yoruba/Twin Figures of the Yoruba.* Dusseldorf, Germany: Hoch.

Talbot, P. Amaury. 1926. *The Peoples of Southern Nigeria,* vol. 3. London: Oxford University Press.

Thompson, Robert F. 1971a. "Sons of Thunder: Twin Images among the Oyó and Other Yoruba Groups." *African Arts* 4 (3): 8–13.

———. 1971b. *Black Gods and Kings: Yoruba Art at UCLA.* Los Angeles: University of California Press.

———. 1973. "Yoruba Artistic Criticism." In *The Traditional Artist in African Society,* ed. Warren L. d'Azevedo. Bloomington: Indiana University Press.

Vogel, Susan (ed). 1991. *Africa Explores: 20th Century African Art.* New York: Center for African Art / Munich: Prestel.

CHAPTER FIVE

"Son Dos los Jimagüas" ("The Twins Are Two")

Worship of the Sacred Twins in Lucumí Religious Culture

YSAMUR FLORES-PENA

Ever since I can remember I always wanted to have a twin brother. In my mind all my difficulties in relating to people could be solved by having a twin brother who could fill the void I always felt. My mother, a healer and priestess of the goddess *Ochún* in our Lucumí religion, always listened and said nothing. It was not until I myself was consecrated as a priest that the strange history of my longing for a twin emerged. The spirit of a brother I did not know existed came to light during part of my *Itá* or initiation ceremony.[1] More surprising still, this brother was my age! When I asked my mother, she confirmed that when she was pregnant with me she miscarried one child, my twin brother. After many treatments, I was carried to term. Why my mother never told me is beyond me, and she never explained. But on that day a weight was lifted from me. I had a twin, and my longing for that twin had a basis in reality.

Of course, that did not fill the hole I felt in my soul, but it began my life-long fascination with twins. As a rule, every time I encounter twins anywhere I always give the parents some sort of monetary gift. This is my way of acknowledging my other half who is staring at me from the other side of the mirror. Twins are one of those mysteries of life; they evoke a wonder so deep that even though science explains how they occur, it cannot explain away the fascination twins produce in others and themselves. I am still wondering about the connection I developed with the wish to have a twin brother, and in a way this curiosity has driven my investigation into the role of twins in my culture. This essay will explore the meaning and importance of twins, *ibeji*, in Lucumí religious culture.

I will explore the issue of how Lucumí religious culture codifies the concept of twinness through ritual art, narrative, and religious performance. At the same time I will explore how the corpus of stories, rituals, and performative behaviors, especially spirit possession, reflect the idea of a dual universe that can only be understood as a twin revelation. Finally, how can a member of the Lucumí religious community find personal or general meaning through the concept of dual equality? By dual equality I mean a concept in which both parts are of the same importance regardless of how similar or dissimilar they may be, either by opposition or complementation. This idea of complementation is part of a larger paradigm of balance, also known in Lucumí as coolness, in which one reality is always followed by its opposite, and just because one cannot perceive it does not mean it does not exist. The complementing opposite is never truly absent; when not physically present, it must be assumed to exist in another level.

Lucumí religion and culture are the result of the Yoruba experience in Cuba during and after the slave trade. Colonial documents very early used the designation *Lucumí* to refer to slaves brought from the Yoruba cultural area in West Africa, and the term has since been adopted by practitioners. Other designations are also used, both among academics and members of the culture, including *Santería, Regla de Ocha,* and *La Ocha,* but *Lucumí* is the emic designation of choice.

Everything in Lucumí religious culture begins and ends with a *Pataki,* a ritual narrative. The religious narrative explains, justifies, and makes sense of the universe for devotees. In the case of twins—*ibeji, beji, melli, jimagüas*—there are specific narratives that characterize and place them in the religious universe.

There was a devil (or monster) at the gates of the kingdom of the Santos.[2] All the Santos gathered to discuss how to face this crisis since no one could enter or exit the kingdom. The Ibejis, the smallest and youngest of the Santos, had an idea but no one paid attention to them. One by one each of the Santos attempted to defeat the devil at the gates and failed. "We have an idea" cried the twins, but their words were not listened to. Finally, tired of being ignored, while the elders deliberated, the twins decided to confront the demon. Once they were outside, the demon confronted one of the twins (the other was hiding) to devour it. "One moment," said the child, "let's have a dancing contest. The first one to get tired will become the servant of the other." Now, the demon looked at the child and thought to himself that there was no harm in humoring the child since it would tire soon and then he could devour him. The contest began and both were dancing and drinking to the rhythm of the drum. Unknown to the demon the other twin was hiding close by and every time one got tired they exchanged places. For days the drumming and dancing went on and the Ibejis changed places every time one got tired. Meanwhile the demon became increasingly exhausted. Finally, about to collapse, he said "Wait, I cannot dance any longer, you win, name your terms." "Leave the town in peace, and any place we enter you cannot stay." "Granted," said the demon. Triumphant, the Ibejis entered the meeting of the Santos to announce the end of the siege. Surprised, the Santos realized the folly of ignoring the Ibeji because of their age and granted them the right to be the standard bearers of the Santos. (Lucumí Odu Corpus,[3] my translation)

Another version (also found in Cuba) of this *Pataki* was recorded by Natalia Bolivar Aróstegui:

The Twins enjoy themselves greatly. It is not by accident that they are the children of Changó and Ochún [both *oricha*]. For some time they played two small magical drums given to them by Yemayá [another *oricha*], their adoptive mother. Around the same time the devil placed traps in all the roads and began to devour all the humans caught in them. Men, women, and children—none escaped his voracity. The Ibejis planned a strategy and Taewo [Taiwo] took to the road while Kainde followed him through the bush. Taewo went on playing the drum with such pleasure that the devil was spellbound, and warned him to be careful not to fall on the trap and began to dance. However, when Taewo got tired, Kainde came out of the bush and took his place. The problem was that even though the devil was tired, he could not stop dancing as long as the drums kept playing. When he was exhausted, the Ibejis made him swear to remove the traps. That is how the Ibejis saved humanity and gained fame for being powerful, since no other Oricha has ever been able to win a fight against the devil. (Bólivar-Arostegui 1990: 123, my translation)

It is important to note that in this version both twins follow the meaning of their names: Taiwo, "the one who comes to taste the world," and Kainde, "he who follows." This is exactly the same naming tradition the Yoruba of Nigeria practice. Even though Taiwo is born into this world first, Kainde is considered the elder. In this story the twins demonstrate their abilities as tricksters. Tricksters, often twins, have figured in the mythology of many nations since time immemorial. Pelton describes the motif: "Loutish, lustful, puffed up with boasts and lies, ravenous for foolery and food, yet managing to always to draw order from ordure, the trickster appears in the myths and folktales of nearly every traditional society, sometimes as a god, more often as an animal" (1980: 1).

The phenomenon of twins has intrigued and fascinated societies to such an extent that they have been both worshiped by some and declared by others to be an aberration that must be eliminated to preserve society. In the case of the Yoruba, the literary record indicates that both events occurred. Folk tales tend to identify twins as children of monkeys (*omo edun*): "Twins were believed to be fearless and unpredictable, deriving their spirit from monkeys" (Thompson 1971 ch. 13/2; see also ch. 4). It is essential to remember the role of monkeys in Yoruba folktales as tricksters. Many tales portray monkeys as challenging the status quo and exposing the deep contradictions of societal life. Roger Abrahams relates one such narrative. In "Monkey Steals a Drum," the Colobus monkey desecrates the royal animal, the leopard, by making dew rain on his head (in Yoruba tradition kings, diviners, and titled elders must not allow dew to fall on their heads, setting them apart from the commoners who get wet by dew on their way to the fields). "Father climbed through the branches, gẹtẹ gẹté gẹté, using both his legs and his arms to grip the tree. He declared he would shake the dew off onto the head of an elder. Leopard stared at him in surprise. All the dew on the tree rained down on Leopard's head. Leopard said, 'I've really been defeated.'" (Abrahams 1983: 55). This story is told on both sides of the Atlantic. Furthermore, a Lucumí *oriki* [praise song] states: *Mejila omo edun, Belli loro omo edun, Beji, Beji la o be kun yare* ("The twins are the children of monkeys, the twins console a grieving mother").

This idea of the double nature of twins (human and animal) becomes central to their identity as both familiar and foreign, natural and unnatural, divine and human. All these traits are summarized with the phrase *omo edun* (children of monkeys). Once their nature is decoded as the ultimate statement of duality it is very easy to understand why twins sometimes are treated as an aberration and as such ritually and physically excised from society—with understandably mixed results. According to Thompson:

> This takes us back, according to Yoruba traditions shared with the writer by the Araba of Lagos, to the foundation of the twin cult, centuries and centuries ago, when only the poor and the wretched were believed to be the progenitors of twins, and when twins were put to death at birth. Then came the day when the children of the Oyo people in the region of Ajashe—the modern Porto Novo—began to die mysterious deaths and alarmed parent[s] consulted the oracle. The . . . word of the oracle was

clear: cease killing the twins at once and honor them to persuade them from killing other children. And it was done. (1971: ch. 13/2)

In Lucumí religious culture the same event is recorded but the Santos serve as proxy for the human population:

> When Ochún had the Ibeji everyone told her that they (the Ibeji) were a bad omen and that she must destroy them. Unable to carry out such grim act, Ochún gave the babies to Yemayá, for her to raise them. After that, Ochún fell into despair and sadness. Olofin [the supreme deity] saw her sadness and sent her Ideu—the third twin—to console her. From then on all Ibeji dolls are dressed in red gingham and blue gingham. Ideu, being Ochun's beloved, always remains at her side dressed in yellow gingham.
> (Lucumí Odu Corpus, my translation)

This story brings us to the idea of Ideú, the third twin. Ochún having lost the twins to societal impositions, Ideú became the sole recipient of her maternal love and devotion, and in Cuba is identified with the child Jesus whom Our Lady of Charity carries in her arms. He is the bearer of wealth. In one *Patikí,* when Ochún loses Ideú she loses everything, all her possessions and her zest for life. Because of the unusual nature of multiple births, triplets create an even greater wonder than twins, and a "third twin" or triplet is always considered a child of Ochún [*Omo Ochún*]. A child born after twins is considered one with its brothers or sisters whether or not he or she is born with them (as literal triplets) or comes from a separate pregnancy altogether. All three children are always spoken of as a unit, *ibeji,* twins. Kainde, the oldest twin, wears blue in honor of Yemayá, while Taiwo wears red in honor of Changó.[4] The order of twins is then: Taiwo, Kainde, and Ideú.

As the story above shows, the correctness of killing twins is denied by Ochún's refusal to kill the twins and her choice to instead give them to Yemayá, the mother goddess, to raise as her own. In Cuba, the Lucumí tradition has transformed the ritual killing of the twins to a fate more in accordance to the horror of slavery: abandonment. The transatlantic trade with its fragmentation of families and lineages created an epistemological vacuum that is reflected in the abandonment motif. Although the Lucumí never officially resorted to infanticide, there are historical reports of mothers aborting their babies to prevent them from a life of slavery in a strange land. According to Rina Cáceres Gómez, "Many researchers agree that these women controlled their fertility through abstinence and contraception. On occasions [they also] practiced infanticide and abortion to prevent or avert the subjugation of their children through slavery" (2001: 232).

In Lucumí culture *ibeji*, also called *bejis*, are feasted and celebrated everywhere they go. They are spoiled and their antics are tolerated more than those of other children. *Bejis* are sacred and they are the physical embodiment of a natural order that is conceived as dual. They are messengers of wealth, triumph, and good fortune in Lucumí religious culture. As protectors of children, the Ibeji are always represented as babies, and some devotees in Venezuela, for example, place their Ibeji dolls and pots into toy play-pens. Although represented as children, they are also considered to be warriors and, therefore, in the ritual progression of praise songs (*oriki*) they are honored with the other warriors of the pantheon (see chapters 13 and 14 for representations of the "divine children" elsewhere in the African Diaspora).

Becoming initiated into the cult of twins is no longer reserved only for twins or their parents. The Ibeji are considered *Santos de Adimú*, meaning that anyone can be initiated even before the *kari-ocha* (initiation into the priesthood). Contradictory accounts about the Ibeji further the belief in their power.

Ritual Aesthetics

Anyone familiar with Lucumí religious culture knows about the emphasis on the construction of sacred spaces (altars, thrones) to celebrate, mask, and reveal the divine. These altar areas (or "thrones") are mediated places that provide a snapshot of heaven to the community and allow the *Pataki* to be presented through visual and aesthetic devices. The Ibeji altar follows the aesthetics of the warriors (Elegüá, Ogún, and Ochosi); that is, the wilderness (*el monte*) comes to the ritual place. The classic dichotomy between the bush and the village is visualized in these assemblages by including on the one hand foliage and food suitable for travel, and on the other, food that needs an urban setting to be consumed. The Ibeji inhabit, along with the warriors, a liminal area in which the town meets the awesome powers of the forest and its supernatural inhabitants. The foundational *Pataki* story of the *Odu Otura-Di*, recounted above, is evoked through the use of foliage and the presence of rum and other hard liquors as part of the decoration, and its childish aspect is revealed in the use of toys and candies. The personality of these archetypical Ibeji is captured by the offering they most appreciate: a *jícara* (gourd) filled with a mixture of rum and honey. Overall then, the altar for the Ibeji is a summary of their exploits.

Paramount in the altar is the use of identical dolls, either both females, both males, or one female and one male. The presence of identical-looking dolls to represent the Ibeji was first noted by Fernando Ortiz[5] as early as 1905: "The Jimaguas or twins are also idols [sic] of great power for the sorcerers . . . they are nothing else but two dolls crudely carved in wood, sometimes painted black (the color of their race) and dressed in a red fabric. Some sorcerers tie both Jimaguas with a cord, undoubtedly to further express their twin character" (Ortiz 1905: 71, my translation).[6] These ritually live dolls are an important part of Ibeji aesthetics. They are considered alive and therefore are accorded (as among the Yoruba) all the respect and consideration due to *fundamentos*—a term that refers to the ritual paraphernalia and sacred stones of the deities.[7] These *ere Ibeji* dolls are the visual manifestation of the mystery of twins.

There are many personal experience narratives told by devotees of these "dolls" moving of their own accord and performing other mischievous deeds. The concept that the Ibeji are in some way connected spiritually is a constant motif in Lucumí art and literature. The close proximity in which their *fundamentos* are kept serves as a reminder of this spiritual contact. One must remember how in the Lucumí story recounted above, one Ibeji danced while the other remained hidden. The exchange between them without uttering a word further emphasizes their spiritual connection: no words are necessary when spirits are united. Other scholars have recognized this concept. Ortiz, for example, uses it to identify a certain pair of figures as the Ibeji, not only because they were made to resemble each other like a mirror image but also because they are connected by a rope, like a mystical umbilical cord, emphasizing the connection that is fundamental in the theology of the Ibeji—an analysis that I agree with. According to Lucumí tradition, the Ibeji are associated with the major *orichas* Changó, Yemayá, and Obatalá. The Ibeji are always physically close to these *Santos,* since they are considered to be the children of Changó and Ochún. The abandonment of the Ibeji by their mother is reenacted by representing them close to their father and their surrogate mother, Yemayá.

Physical Presence of the Ibeji

Cuban folklorist Lydia Cabrera mentions what are perhaps the most famous *Olorichas* (priests) in the culture, *Los Jimagüas del Palenque.* According to Cabrera:

> In the 1880s on a farm in the Marianao jurisdiction called El Palenque, that [eventually] became an African neighborhood beyond Lisa, and in front of a house known as "the priest's house," lived many Lucumí and creoles all of whom were children of the famous Ibeyes [Ibejis]. Two were very important Santeros Jimagüas [twin saints] with innumerable godchildren in Havana. They were called "los Papás Jimagüas" [the twin fathers], Perfecto and Gümersindo. (1983: 25, my translation)

The importance of these famous *Olorichas* goes beyond just a successful ritual practice. That would suffice as a reason to include their individual names in the *Mojuba*, the ceremonial recitation of priests', priestesses', and ancestors' names. However, the title that precedes their names, *Jimagüas,* also identifies them as twins and as possessors of the mystical powers that not only Lucumí but almost every Cuban ritual society ascribes to the twins.

As a rule, *ibeji* in Lucumí religious culture are celebrated as living marvels. Their presence is noted and they are considered the living manifestation of the spirits worshiped in the *Santo Room* where the religious ceremonies take place. Whether or not they are consecrated as priests, the *Batá* drums salute them upon their arrival. When twins are initiated and receive the sacred symbols of the Ibeji, there is no carved figure because they themselves are considered to be the living images (*ere*) of the Ibeji. If one is dead or dies, then the doll or image is added. Also consistent with Yoruba tradition, the first-born is the junior, Taiwo, and the second born is the senior, Kainde. The way elders explained this to me is a great lesson in folk medicine. According to them, the first fetus to form will move further up into the uterus to leave space for the second fetus. This was exemplified by using the metaphor of a box. The first things to go into a box are the last ones to come out of it. Therefore, the first *ibeji* to be born is the youngest because he or she formed last and lower in the uterus.

It is fascinating that a similar theology exists in Vodou (see chapter 13) in regards to twins and their spiritual unity. Alfred Métraux (1972: 146), after explaining that twins have supernatural powers in Vodou, goes on to say of third children born after twins: "(the dosu if a boy and dosa if it is a girl) unites in its person the power of both twins and therefore can dispose of greater power than they." As explained above, in Lucumí religious culture this child, Ideú, is always dedicated to the goddess Ochún, and is also conceptualized as a third twin. This unity of both or all three Ibeji is a fundamental aspect of this shared theological universe, a key element when creating places to house their *fundamentos,* where food and offerings are presented using the same vessel. This sacred unity between sister religious practices allows for a greater understanding of belief diffusion in the Yoruba/Fon cultural continuums.

Links to Other Religious Systems
Catholicism

Since Herskovits advanced the concept of syncretism (the blending of similar traditions from different cultures) in *The Myth of the Negro Past* (1958), many hypotheses have been advanced regarding the survival of the Yoruba *oricha* through syncretic practices. When it comes to the Ibeji, there is some overlap with the Catholic Saints Cosmas and Damian, but on the other hand there is a general absence of syncretic values in visual representations from these two cults. It is true that many scholars, following the lead from Brazil and Haiti, tend to identify the Ibeji with Saints Cosmas and Damian.[8] There is a logical reason for finding this linkage, since, like the Ibeji, Cosmas and Damian are twins and healers in their own right, and, if we are to believe the legend, tricksters as well. According to Lanzetta et al.:

> In the third century AD, St. Cosmas, a physician, and St. Damian, a surgeon, removed the malignant and gangrenous limb of an aged sacristan of the church. While the sacristan slept, these two doctors successfully transplanted the leg of a recently deceased Ethiopian Moor to the leg stump of the dreaming patient. Whilst one brother removed the diseased leg with a saw, the other went to the pagan gladiator graveyard on Vatican Hill at the Circus of Nero where St. Peter's Cathedral now stands, exhumed the body of a recently buried Ethiopian man, procured one of his legs and returned to the church. The saints joined the Ethiopian's leg to the dying man's stump. The sacristan, on waking, discovered he had a new, healthy, although black leg. (Lanzetta et al. 2007: 3)

This miracle, along with the fact that the twin doctors were able to defeat death, I am certain found resonance in Lucumí hagiography.

However, even though the Catholic Twin Saints are found in Haiti and Brazil, I have never seen the chromolithographs that characteristically represent them in any Lucumí house I have visited in Cuba, Puerto Rico, Venezuela, Mexico, or the United States. If other researchers found this visual reference, it must have been an idiosyncratic acquisition by their informants.

In terms of ritual practice, the syncretism is much more pronounced. The cult of The Twins in Brazil is a key component of both the popular

FIGURE 5.1. Two images of the Catholic Saints Cosmas and Damian (one chromolith on metal, the other in plaster) from Bahia, Brazil, 2010. *Photo: Philip M. Peek.*

and religious culture. During my visit to Brazil, the first official Candomblé celebration I attended both as a priest and as a twin was a celebration for *ibejis,* a feast to Saints Cosme and Damiao. The celebration, as in Lucumí practice, included foods sacred to twins as well as toys and kids' favors. Eventually everyone turned from the religious aspect to a more secular celebration. I was presented with a chromolithograph and a medal as a memento of this event. What is interesting is the fact that the twins are celebrated throughout the Diaspora but the emphasis varies (for more, see chapters 13 and 14).

The importance of the Twins transcends their identity as deities. In some houses, when a person is initiated into the Ibeji cult they are given also Christian names, but again custom emphasizes their identical nature by naming them the same thing—and if the dolls are male and female, they receive masculine and feminine versions of the same name. For example, if the male is named Francisco, the female will be Francisca.

Yoruba Divination

The Ibeji are directly referred to the *Ifá* oracular system and the *Dilogún* divination system of Lucumí. *Ifá* as a system is based on a set of sixteen paired *Odus,* figures with specific symbolic meanings, which result from casting shells or palm nuts or manipulating a chain. The various possible permutations of these figures derive 256 combinations. William Bascom said apropos of *Ifá*: "Ifa is the most respected, in many ways the most interesting, system of divination of five to ten million Yoruba in Nigeria and millions more of their African neighbors and their descendants in the New World" (1969: ix).[9] The "senior" *Odus* are called *Meji,* which points to the repetition of the same *Odu* twice, i.e., as a twin. When the same divinatory figure repeats itself, it is a sign of great strength as it represents itself twice as an identical message and force. Considered by *Ifá* worshipers as the foundation of all wisdom, these divination figures derive their seniority from the fact that they repeat themselves and are considered very potent in their manifestation. *Dilogún,* short for *Erin Merindilogun,* is similar; the name refers to the objects used, sixteen cowrie shells.

The way the *Odus* are written and organized in terms of progression and seniority differs somewhat between *Ifá* and the Lucumí *Dilogún,* but they are clearly related systems. I consider the difference mainly a matter of graffics—*Ifá* kept its older style, while the *Dilogún* transformed and creolized, perhaps adopting the Arabic numeration system even though the naming of the figures remained Yoruba.

Twinness in the Cosmos

Although twins occur throughout the world, the Lucumí concept extends its sense of wonder deep into the epistemology of the culture. The conceptualizations of pantheon, society, divination systems, and life itself all point to a basic duality. The concept of hot/cool is a good example of this duality. Even though coolness (*ntutu*) is the paramount virtue in the Lucumí cosmos, its coexistence with hot is assured in the idea of a dual complementarity. There are cool *orichas* and hot *orichas,* distinguished by their colors. Drewal and Mason point to these values in what they call Yoruba chromatics: "Yorùbàs distinguish three chromatic groupings: funfun, pupa, and dúdú. Inadequately translated as white, red, and black, respectively, each group includes a range of colors and hues (as we understand them in Western culture) as well as various values (shades or tints) and intensities of each color" (1998: 18).

The Ibeji, by the color of their garments (red and white/blue and white), epitomize the hot/cold paradigm. This paradigm is further mediated by the inclusion of Ideú, the child born after the twins, who is dressed in yellow, the color sacred to their mother Ochún, representing the closeness of mother and child. Because of the dual nature of Yoruba/ Lucumí cosmogony, the presence of the Ibeji points to cognitive code. They are the masters of balance, hence coolness. Because there is no possibility of eliminating the contradictions of our dual universe, the Twins represent the sense

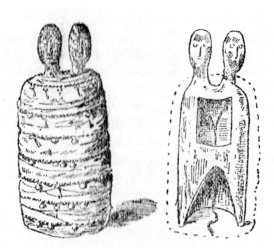

FIGURE 5.2. "Jimagüa idols. Drawing from original." (First published in Ortíz 1905: 72.) Twinness here demonstrated by a carving of conjoined figures, although pairs of figures were also created reflecting the continuity with the Yoruba use of *ere* (sculptures) to represent twins.

of *ntutu,* coolness that recognizes the perfect harmony between opposites. It is through this balance that humans can negotiate the contradictions of their own existence and thrive. One must agree with Peek when he claims, "I am proposing that images of the twins especially in relation to divination, are metaphors as well as vehicles for enhanced awareness, perfect knowledge and completed self identities" (2008: 21).

This "enhanced awareness" is the realization that everything in the universe is dual, and in order to understand it one must consider the positive and the negative, the image and its mirrored reflection. This duality, as a *Babalawo* (diviner) once explained to me, is exemplified by the Ibeji. "The Ibeji" he said, "are the masters of the world. They rule all aspects of nature and our world that are duplicate. Hence, the body, in order to function, both Osi and Otun [left and right] must be acknowledged."

A striking visual representation of the concept of the unity and differentiation of the Ibeji in Cuba was documented by Fernando Ortiz while researching his ethnography of so-called "magic," *Los Negros Brujos* (1905). He discovered an icon with an unusual form in which the Ibeji share one body with two heads (see figure 5.2).

"The idols in this case are united forming one body. The carving was destined to be wrapped and leaving only the two heads visible. The only real union of the two Jimagüas in one piece; perhaps due more to the construction of the idol than to a symbolic meaning" (Ortiz 1905: 72, my translation). If we accept this icon as a representation for the Ibeji, the image speaks volumes. The idea of one body with two heads references the cosmic concept of the Ibeji's soul as a unit split in two as they come into the world. The icon moreover appeared together with other ritual objects in a cavity; thus grouped, the *fundamentos* appear as a unit, reinforcing the idea of unity within duality that the Ibeji represent.

The fundamental unity of the Twins discussed by Ortiz becomes visualized by using one body and two heads. The twins move in a universe that is physically unified by dualities beyond our comprehension. The double-headed figure is then a way of illustrating the idea of humans inhabiting a cosmos that is visible and invisible, dark and light, cool and hot, good and bad, male and female, and so on. If the trickster Echu, both in Yoruba and Lucumí cultures, is at the crossroads of the universe, then Ibeji are the center of the center.

Marilyn Houlberg observes:

> In the case of Twins, the spirit double has been born on earth. Since there is no way of telling which is the heavenly being and which is the mortal, both are treated as sacred from birth. As one 45-year-old-man from Ibadan commented: "We do not think of each twin as having its own counterpart in heaven; they are the counterpart of each other. . . ." (1973: 23)

Ibeji are then spiritual beings made visible, a mystical concept made accessible by the reality of their split nature revealing itself twice at the same time.

If the Ibeji in Cuba are to be understood, it is paramount to place them in the Lucumí epistemology. The fact that twins are an almost universal archetype attests to the importance of such a phenomenon worldwide. Moreover, the idea of the Ibeji in Lucumí culture also points at a social concept of equality in diversity. As shrine icons the Ibeji can be paired male/male, female/female, and male/female. Gender creates no seniority but order of birth does. The cosmos is an immense reflection of this principle and the Ibeji are the localized and objective example of the same notion: the universe is double and exists in unity; if one aspect is not apparent, it must be assumed it is manifested somewhere else. If one Ibeji is present the question becomes, is the other one in this world or in the other? The principle of duality is active from cradle to grave and informs issues of gender and religious politics in the culture. Perhaps no other phenomenon epitomizes this better than trance possession. According to Lydia Cabrera, "The ego of an individual who is [possessed] by the santo is taken out, thrown away by it out of his body or his head 'Orí' which is the one who commands the body is annulled and is substituted by the Orisha [*oricha*], the Npungu, or the Fumbi" (1983: 28).[10]

This trance experience, in which the divine manifests itself using the human body as a vehicle, creates its own sense of twoness. Consistent with the idea of being divine and human, here and in heaven at the same time, the person who experiences possession creates a double image that is identical in all senses. As a mirror image the individual reflects a divine reality that is transcendent and immediate. The body is doubled by reflecting a divine reality which all present can see, touch, and experience, negating the boundaries of what the onlooker considers real and factual. In that sense a divine twin, the spirit double, becomes visible through the human twin. Temporality defines what it is atemporal and sublime. We must agree with the claim: "Dual nature is a condition of completeness" (Mercier, in Micheli 2008: 75).

In Lucumí culture the notion of doubles is the foundation of life. Nothing can be explained in any other way. How else can the culture explain the double manifestation of the *Odu* as a *Meji* and then through their permutations obtain, still as doubles, the 256 combinations that form the corpus' revelations? Yet, these permutations are but mirror images that allow the diviner to read the *Odu* as distinct realities backward and forwards, right and left, and obtain information that is distinct by changing the positions. Following that logic in the *Dilogún* divinatory system the *Odu Ofún-che* (10-5) is a different reality than the *Odu Oché-Fún* (5-10).

Ibeji, Meji, Jimagüas—whatever they are called, they are a great mystery in their familiarity. Warriors, protectors of children, and protectors of the temple house, *Ilé*, they embody the notion of duality so essential to Lucumí cosmology. Even though they can be paired in different ways, they are always considered to be identical, including the third Ibeji, Ideú. Powerful as they are, the source of their power resides in their ability to mediate opposites and keep the same visage.

In a quasi-alchemical permutation all humans embody them in every double organ that exists in the body. Lucumí folk medicine is keenly aware of this and they are invoked in maladies that affect any organ that is double in the body. *Son brujos los Jimagüas* ("the twins are sorcerers") claim some healers. This sorcery is accessed by translating their duality and warrior-like nature to fight the diseases that befall worshipers. Their theology, based on the idea of dual reality, considers the possibility that what we see in them is not what is there. Eternally childlike and eternally daring, their cosmic childhood moves in and out of a universe that is dual with the possibility of a third point, a point where tricksters and facilitators concoct human realities.

In my particular case the discovery of an identical but physically absent half guided me to further my studies and journey into the healing aspects of plants. I was initiated into the cult of Osain, the *oricha* of herbalism, magic, nature, the environment.[11] My journey has taken me from the realization of a missing part of myself to an exploration of what it means to be here and not here at the same time. The writing of this chapter has been very auspicious because in the near future I will be presiding over the initiation of a twin who by his order of birth is like me, *Kainde.* As I help him prepare for his journey into the Lucumí ritual universe our conversations always end at the same place; the "strange" place in which being a twin places the individual. Society has always been fascinated by the idea of twins; however, to talk about the experience is both familiar and foreign to me. I remember having an invisible friend whom to this day I consider very real and who would come and play with me. In my mind it was my twin and we were very much alike! Strange that the source of my longings has helped me to seek what lies on the other side of the mirror, so close and yet so far. The question as I preside over this initiation is, am I making the journey along with him and at the same time discovering what is behind the experience? No one knows, but one thing is certain: today the twins are not consoling a grieving mother but a grieving being whose half is somewhere behind the mirror, so far and yet so close!

Lucumí tradition allows for the comprehension of the twin's phenomenon to be accessible through cognitive constructs that allow people to experience the split that occurs when all opposites collide and become mediated by the realization of a universe that is fundamentally created out of identical opposites that complement each other. Moral values, life experiences, and ultimately becoming an ancestor is the price we pay for our bifurcated life. In Lucumí epistemology what is real is measured by how much we comprehend its opposite. The strength of Lucumí culture lies in its ability to always recognize itself is an Ibeji creation: African and Creole, Caribbean and continental, black and white, with the possibility of an in-between; glorious. Perhaps that is the lesson to be derived from the *Patakí* that opened our chapter; the mistake the monster at the town's gate made was his inability to recognize that everything is dual and hence the song *Son dos los Jimagüas . . .* The twins are two . . .

NOTES

To Taiwo, a brother I missed before I knew he existed

1. *Itá* is a divination session held on the third day of a consecration using the *Dilogún* (sixteen cowry shells) divination system. People who are consecrated as priests or priestesses are called *Olochas, Iyalochas* (females), *Babalochas* (males), or *Olochas*—"those with Ocha."

2. An alternative name for the *orichas,* deities of the Lucumí pantheon, *santo* is also the Spanish word for saint, as in saint of the Catholic religion. I will use the word *Santo* instead of saint to reference the deities of the *Lucumí* pantheon, following common parlance. The term may be further clarified by distinguishing between an African *Santo* and a Saint of the Church: *Santo Africano, Santo de la Iglecia.* Furthermore, I will use Creole orthography when referring to Lucumí terms.

3. *Odu Corpus,* a collection of sacred stories that serve as the basis for Lucumí epistemology and revelation. These stories, the majority memorized by diviners, are the basis for ritual and orthodoxy in the religious culture.

4. Yemayá is the mother goddess and owner of the ocean and motherhood; Changó, the god of thunder and fire, and a great warrior.

5. This particular text, *Los Negros Brujos,* was later disowned by the author for the racist remarks and inaccurate claims it contains. However, the ethnographic information he collected makes it a good record of the early attempts by Cuban society to document and "study" Afro-Cuban traditions.

6. The carving Ortiz describes, even though he identifies it as being a representation of the Ibeji, is in my opinion closer to the iconography of *Ògbóni edan.* The *edan* are symbols of the Ogboni secret society. This society is associated with the cult of the earth, and the *edan,* a kind of anthropomorphic staff (always male and female), had social control uses as well as being a symbol of their office and authority. Even though there is no official documentation of the Ogboni cult in Cuba, it is more plausible to speculate that the illustration is a retention of the Ogboni motif than that it represents the Ibeji.

7. *Fundamento* literally means "foundation materials"—they embody the mystical power of the spirit and serve as a visual pun on their presence. See Robert Farris Thompson's *Flash of the Spirit: African and Afro-American Art and Philosophy* (Edison, N.Y.: Vintage Books, 1984).

8. Lacahtañeré refers to the deities: "*Obeyes* [*Ibejis*] Catholic Saints: St. Cosmas and St. Damian" (1992, 139), while Natalia Bólivar-Arostegui states: "Catolización [Catholic reference] St. Cosmas and St Damian (Taewo and Kainde)" (1990, 123).

9. Bascom, 1969: 3. For a more detailed discussion see Bascom's characterization of *Ifá* and its sources in *"Ifa" Divination: Communication between Gods and Men In West Africa* (Bloomington: Indiana University Press, 1969).

10. *Npungu* and *Fumbi*: names given to the spirits of the *Palo Monte* tradition in Cuba.

11. *Ile,* the earth, is considered female and the natural world it sustains is *Osain.* The trees, plants, insects, animals, and all the wild elements of the natural world are under his patronage and he is viewed as male, another example of this continuous duality. The Yoruba *oricha* of medicine, Osanyin, would seem to be the origin of this deity.

WORKS CITED

Abrahams, Roger D. 1983. *African Folktales: Traditional Folktales of the Black World.* New York: Pantheon Books.

Bascom, William R. 1969. *Ifa Divination: Communication Between Gods and Men in West Africa.* Bloomington: Indiana University Press.

Bólivar-Arostegui, Natalia. 1990. *Los Orishas en Cuba.* La Habana: Ediciones Unión.

Cabrera, Lydia. 1983. *El Monte: Igbo. Finda Ewe Orisha. Vititi Nfinda Notas Sobre las Religiones, la Mágia, las Supersticiones y el Folklore de los Negros Criollos y el Pueble de Cuba.* Miami, Fla.: Ediciones Universal.

Caceres Gomez, Rina. 2001. *Rutas de la Esclavitud en Africa y América Latina.* San José, Costa Rica: Asociación Pro-Historia Centroamericana.

Drewal, Henry John, and John Mason. 1998. *Beads, Body, and Soul: Art and Light in the Yoruba Universe.* Los Angeles, Calif.: Fowler Museum of Cultural History.

Herskovits, Melville J. 1958. *The Myth of the Negro Past.* Boston: Beacon Press.

Houlberg, Marilyn. 1973. "Ibeji Images of the Yoruba." *African Arts* 7: 1, 20–27, 91–92.

Lachatañeré, Rómulo. 1992. *El Sistema Religioso de los Afrocubanos.* La Habana: Collección Echbí.

Lanzetta, M., et al. 2007. "Second Report (1998-2006) of the International Registry of Hand and Composite Tissue Transplantation." *Transplant Immunology* 18: 1–6.

Lawal, Babatunde. 2008. "Èjìwàpò: The Dialectics of Twoness in Yoruba Art and Culture." *African Arts* 41: 1, 24–39.

Métraux, Alfred. 1972. *Voodoo in Haiti.* New York: Shocken Books.

Micheli, Angelo C. 2008. "Doubles and Twins: A New Approach to Contemporary Studio Photography in West Africa. *African Arts* 41: 1, 66–85.

Peek, Philip M. 2008. "Couples or Doubles? Representation of Twins in the Arts of Africa." *African Arts* 41: 1, 14–23.

Pelton, Robert D. 1980. *The Trickster in West Africa: A Study in Mythic Irony and Sacred Delight.* Berkeley: University of California Press.

Ortiz, Frenando. 1905. *Los Negros Brujos: Apuntes Para un Estudio de Etnologia Criminal.* Madrid: Sociedad Española de Librería.

Thompson, Robert Farris. 1971. *Black Gods and Kings: Yoruba Gods.* Los Angeles: Regents of the University of California.

CHAPTER SIX

Twins, Couples, and Doubles and the Negotiation of Spirit-Human Identities among the Win

SUSAN COOKSEY

The Win people, who are also known as the Southern Toussian, frequently employ two conjoined elements, objects, or images to enhance the efficacy of spiritual intervention in order to achieve harmony, unity, and balance between spirits and humans. Characterizations of these dual forms as twins, couples, or, more abstractly, as doubled potential are often conflated in Win interpretations. Closer examination of Win thought about these doubled entities reveals that they represent discrete agents whose powers and effects on humans vary considerably. Human twins are particularly powerful beings that are also highly volatile; they may be beneficent or malignant toward their families. When two figures are construed as a couple composed of male and female, however, they are emblematic of the cosmic order that is essential to psychic and physical wellbeing. Looking closely at interpretations of twins, couples, doubles and the practices for harnessing their powers for human wellbeing reveals that negotiations between humans and spirits link health, personhood, and self-identity for the Win.

The Win inhabit southwestern Burkina Faso. They are strategically located on the margins of the Mossi plateau, which is traversed by numerous rivers and streams. The topography allows for lush forested areas, stable agriculture, and abundant livestock, and most of the population is engaged in agricultural production or animal husbandry. The Win also live close to the dramatic cliffs of the Falaise de Banfora, which have served as a refuge from numerous invaders over the centuries, including the Jula and the French, and as a site for religious rites. The population is concentrated in the villages of Toussianba, Yerokofesso, and Nianhaba and surrounding farming hamlets. The Win are closely linked to the Pentobe, and both are culturally and linguistically linked to the Senufo, who have intermarried with these groups, so that both Toussian groups are identified in Western literature as the Northern Senufo, despite distinct differences. The Tagwa Senufo are neighbors to the northwest and the south. Win kinship is patrilineal and Win families are largely patrilocal. While the Win are not endogamous, marriages were traditionally arranged between first-born daughters and paternal uncles up until a generation ago. Christianization in the early twentieth century, led by Catholics, challenged this marital system and created many converts in the process. Win clans have both Win names and corresponding Jula names, with each traditionally associated with quasi-hierarchical community roles (J. R. Hébert 1959, 1972). Governance on the local level was traditionally shared among the village chief, the customary chief, and the earth priest. Although these titles are maintained and respected, chiefly authority has greatly diminished since French colonization in the early twentieth century. Autochthonous religion, Islam, and Christianity have nearly equal numbers of adherents, although the Catholic mission and school established by the Pères Blancs in Toussianba in the 1930s continues to have a profound impact on religious, social, and economic life. Toussianba is the largest Win community, and has a large population of non-Win members, including expatriates from Africa and Europe.

Win cosmology includes a supreme god, Liyele, ancestral spirits, minor deities, and earth spirits called *setan* (singular: *setōn*). Do is the predominant local earth deity, but Boro, Koruba, and other spirits who are associated with the agricultural cycle are vital forces in the community. Spiritual leaders who are still in place work in alliance with a powerful hieratic group comprised of the great diviners, or *sanpu gbe,* and the lower-ranked *sanpu* (Hébert and Guilhem 1964, 1965; Cooksey 2004). Diviners, as a general rule, assist individuals in mediating between the human and spirit realms. The Win hierarchical diviners are instrumental in determining spiritual identity for individuals. Each individual is allied with a *setōn* before birth, and lives with it until being born into the human world. *Setan* are both male and female, and humans may have a *setōn* of either gender. The choice of a human counterpart was explained as a matter of spirit preference, and not a mutual decision, although a human may be attracted to spirit attributes and habitats.[1] Spirits may come from one of three domains: water (usually described as the river), forest, and mountains.[2] When a child is born, no one knows the origin of her *setōn*. It is up to the parents or the individual later in life to consult a diviner to determine the identity of his *setōn*. Most people are said to have water *setan,* or to "come from the river," but a minority of others, including some healers and some diviners, are said to "come from the forest" (Cooksey 2004; J. Hébert 1997).

Win beliefs as to how the spiritual origin of twins differ from those of ordinary individuals vary. Some people believe they are sent by the supreme being, Liyele. Others, such as Dobé Barro, a Kwen diviner (also known as a blacksmith diviner), of Toussianba, said twins are empowered by the same spirit realm from whence all humans and their spirit others emerged, that is, from the water, the forest, or the mountains.[3] When twins are born the parents are both delighted and anxious, as they know that the spirits are singling them out for special attention. By giving the family twins, the spirits are offering the chance of good fortune, but it is contingent on how the twins are treated. If neglected or ill-treated the twins may become angered, and the spirits will punish the family. Parents and anyone related to twins, including siblings, should honor them with equal offerings. A family that faithfully honors twins will reap the rewards of abundant health and wealth, but any inequity or lack of attention can provoke their wrath, bringing any number of misfortunes, including failure of crops, lack of fertility, a fall in social or economic status, disease, and even death upon family members. Normally, when twins are born, the family consults a diviner. In rare cases, if there are no problems like recurrent illnesses to concern them, a family may not consult a diviner while the twins are young, but they will inevitably consult a diviner sometime during the twins' lifetimes. The diviner identifies the twins' *setan* as associated with the rivers, forests, or mountains, and the appropriate locations and types of offerings for them that can be used routinely, or in the case of illness, the sacrifices needed for a particular cure.

All twins are thought to be powerful beings, but the Win distinguish between the potential negativity of same-sex twins versus opposite-sex twins. (They do not differentiate between fraternal or identical twins, however.) Although both types of twins may evoke fear and anxiety, same-sex twins are considered to be more threatening. Twins have what could be described as an Oedipal complex, desiring to bond with the parent of the opposite sex and kill the one of the same sex.[4] Opposite-sex twins counteract each other's patricidal and matricidal tendencies, but same-sex twins may conspire to kill the parent of the opposite sex, and, unchecked by the twin who seeks the love of that parent, one of them may successfully murder a parent. To avoid the risk of having their twins eliminate one of them, parents of same-sex twins must make sacrifices designed to cleanse the twins' minds of such evil actions. One sacrifice is called *pe yah wu,* or "wash the face."[5] Washing the face is also a protective measure for any child who may be vulnerable to the spirits. For example, a child who has visions or dreams of the spirits is thought to be lured to the spirit world—that is, to die and live with the spirits in their world—and must have her face washed to eliminate this potentially dangerous situation. A healer prescribes an herbal solution and regimen for washing. To strengthen its effect, the diviner will prescribe a twin ring—two metal bands fused together—that is placed in the solution. When twins grow up, they are less likely to cause problems, and the need to perform face-washing or offer sacrifices to twins diminishes. However, when a twin dies, regardless of her age, there is extra reason to be alarmed. The deceased twin who migrates to the spirit world will try to lure the other twin to join him/her there. The family is obliged to consult the diviner for instructions on how to ensure the safety and longevity of the living twin. Often the living twin will be instructed to make the proper sacrifices.

The prevailing feeling about twins in Win society is a persistent uneasiness. Family members are simultaneously compelled to please the twins' spirits and to protect against their machinations. The face-washing ritual, which is meant to cleanse a child's mind of the spirits, as well as make him or her more aware of their guiles, is also described as a way of obliterating memory so that they will not remember the instructions of the spirits. As such it identifies twins as unwitting agents of the spirits. Driven incessantly by the spirits, and filled with the memory of the spirit world, they are perceived as only partially in the human world but still closely tied to that world whence they came. Awareness of their dual identity is the deciding factor in determining which side will prevail. The malicious machinations of the spirits and their effect on the twins' behavior and thought must be revealed through divinatory and parental intervention, and their negativity must be neutralized by sacrifices, particularly amulets, that are reminders of the twins' spirit and human identities.

Among the most striking objects prescribed by diviners to propitiate twins are brass anthropomorphic amulets. Such amulets may feature two figures for twins, called *kepi niin,* three for triplets, and four for quadruplets or double twins, called *kepi yɛ.*[6] Double figural amulets are most commonly cast as bracelets, rings, and pendants. The four-figure twin amulets only appear as large, flat pendants. Twin amulets may be worn on the body or kept in the home, perhaps suspended from the rafters or in another discreet location, hidden from anyone who may wish the family harm.[7] Recent examples of quadruplet amulets are enhanced with repeated

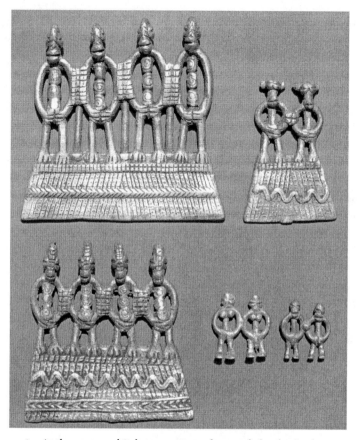

FIGURE 6.1. Anthropomorphic brass twin amulets made by the Soulama work-shop of Bounouna, Burkina Faso. Clockwise from upper right: a) Twins with serpent motif. b) Miniature male twins and miniature female twins. c) Double twins with serpent motif, spirals, and herringbone pattern. d) Double twins with spirals and grid patterns. *Photo: Susan Cooksey.*

grid patterns, spirals, or herringbone patterns that may be ornamental or that may signify both gender and spirit origin (i.e., in the water, forest, or mountain). Singly, a spiral represents the water turtle, and double spirals are symbolic of female twins. Double spirals appear as pendants and on rings either alone or with other motifs. For example, one type of cast brass ring combines the double spiral with a single female figure, a python, and a triangular initiation sign. Three spirals, however, may allude to males, in keeping with local numerological symbolism. A quadruplet or double twins amulet with three spirals mounted on each of the figures' abdomens suggests a unification of male and female elements, but whether they do in fact correspond to the notion of gender complementarity or of opposite-sex twins is open to further inquiry.

Analysis of salient visual features of twin amulets seems to indicate that they function as mnemonic devices that illustrate the powers and attributes of twins. Above all, twin figural amulets emphasize the twins' physical similarity and connectedness to illustrate their strong spiritual bond. They stand at equal heights, closely together, arms linked at the elbows and rounded so that they form a circle around the body. They stand firmly, and are usually mounted on a sturdy trapezoidal base. On some examples, a serpent—a powerful symbol of the forest spirits—undulating below the figures could be seen as slithering on the earth or swimming in water. Because both the forest and the water are the homes of the spirits, the *setan*, the combined iconography could allude to the coalition of these spiritual domains, as it situates the twins, portrayed as human figures, in both human and spirit worlds. Images of quadrupled figures further emphasize the attributes and linkage between humans and spirits. Their imposing stature and extra ornamentation on the arms; the elaborate hairdos or headdresses; and the spirals indicating water turtles, water spirits, and female twins all signify their status as beings both human and divine.[8]

The charged images of twins that appear as brass amulets are not merely a means of averting the anger of their *setan* and ensuring the safety of their families but serve other purposes as well. Small versions of twin amulets may be worn or kept in the house, where they avert recurrent illnesses and bad dreams. Four-figure amulets are prescribed for couples who have quadruplets or two set of twins, and they are installed inside the homes of couples who want many children. Thus, twin amulets are not only apotropaic (evil-averting), but they are also used proactively for enhancing mental and physical health and fertility.

Twin amulets seem to express Win beliefs about twins as a convergence of concepts of morality, gender complementarity, and cosmic balance.[9] The frightful power of same-sex twins emanates from their gender imbalance, which defies social norms and has cosmological implications as well. One wonders why the spirits would be so antagonistic toward humans that they would burden them with an ever-present and living reminder of this principle. Inexplicable and indefensible as it may seem, this imbalance is a catalyst for enhanced energy in many directions, generating additional spiritual engagement, more self-awareness, more action, and greater aesthetic expression. The act of doubling, as manifested in twinning, is not simply a provocation for humans to counteract a cosmic prank, but also offers opportunities for enhanced dialogue and production. In effect, the presence

of twins intensifies human social interactions, and enhances or reinvigo-
rates human alliances with the spirit world. Victor Turner noted a similar
effect of twinship rituals, which he saw as a play of seemingly antithetical
elements manifested in twinning, ultimately exposing a transcendent social
order by "activation of an ordered succession of symbols, which have the
twin functions of communication and efficacy" (Turner 1969: 93).

The anthropomorphic brass amulets are but one of the representations
of twins that aim to avert their antagonism and promote their benevolence. Other twin-related images include the male and female interlocutor
figures called *tasie* that are used by *sanpu* diviners, who are also referred to
as *gbintalesawo* (singular: *gbintalesanpu*) or handholding diviners.[10] A primary purpose of *sanpu* divination is to resolve people's problems, specifically problems resulting from an unintentional infraction against a spirit,
usually a personal spirit (*setōn*), who is also referred to as a spirit double.
The diviner's task is to contact the *setōn* and get instructions on the nature
of the infraction and how to make amends for the disjuncture between the
client and the *setōn*.

Tasie are essential to the divination process, and although they appear
as human male and female figures, they embody the diviner's personal
spirit or *setōn*. When a diviner contacts the spirit world, it is her *setōn* who
calls on the client's *setōn* to reveal the cause of the client's problem. The
setōn may communicate that he/she is dissatisfied with the client's lack
of attention or that a malignant spirit unleashed by a witch or sorcerer is
to blame. The *tasie* are representative of the diviner's *setōn* and his or her
spouse or lover. Both male and female must be represented, for if only
the diviner's *setōn* were presiding over the spiritual affairs in the divination chamber, the spouse or lover would be jealous. On rare occasions the
figures may also represent twins, but if they do, it is because the diviner's
setōn has demanded them to be so. Twin *tasie* figures must be made from
the same tree, unlike the "married" *tasie*, which are made from different trees, according to gender. The Win carver Bernard M'Pie Barro told
me that the *setan* preferred that the *tasie* were made of either mahogany
(*afzelia Africana*) or a lighter-colored wood that he called *wlameri* without specifying a type of tree (available light woods include kapok, *Bom-
bax pentandrum*, baobab, *Adansonia digitata*, and acacia—*Mimosoideae
parkia biglobosa*, locally called *nere*).

Barro's assertion that *tasie* might be depicted as anything, because spirits who determine their appearance can appear as anything they choose,
throws yet another light on the *setan* and their relationship with the
human world. The carver and other Win informants explained that spirits

are ubiquitous, transient, and unpredictable in their choice of locations and appearances. They may appear in dreams or visions as children or other beings, or may even assume the guise of a particular human being in real life. A spirit may decide to wreak havoc on someone by causing recurrent illness or other misfortune. On the other hand, it might choose to impersonate someone in order to reap the benefits of that person's life. Appearing as real human beings, the imposters are perceived as identical to a known individual, and are so convincing that they easily fool his family and friends, much to everyone's consternation. Only diviners can determine the cause of the affliction as a spirit double, because they perceive the true appearance of the spirit as one who "walks on his eyes," that is, upside-down. Conversely, the double can benefit the person and bring them fortune and good health. Spirit doubles can remain as long as they are undetected and undeterred by the diviner's medicines.

Spirits can imitate anything they like, but their impersonation of humans is the most blatant reminder that human and spiritual identities are inseparable and at times even indistinguishable. Yet, at the same time, random spirit double visitations challenge an individual's sense of what these identities are and stimulate further investigation of the parameters of self and spirit in relation to each other—and also in relation to other humans, who have to determine the true identity of the person they thought they recognized. Like spirit imposters, twins represent an encroachment of spirits into human territory. However, it can be argued that twins, and particularly same-sex twins, pose a more palpable threat to individuals and families than spirit doubles. At the sighting of a spirit double, it may be desirable to seek spiritual counsel to address the problem of shifting spirit-human identities, but at the birth of same-sex twins it is more crucial that families find a way to reaffirm those boundaries and identities to prevent the death of the parents or other losses—though some may be inevitable. Divination is the most accessible and effective means of determining such parameters by first informing the client about the identity of personal spirits and their characteristics, and then as the next step suggesting appropriate means for the client to reveal his or her own identity to the spirits.

In their role as interlocutors, *tasie* represent the status quo of spirit-human relations, and, if not completely controllable by humans, are at least not constantly confrontational. The notion that the *tasie*, who can be either couples or twins, are always equally paired would suggest that each has perfectly complementary attributes, as one sees in other cosmologies. For example, the Fon of Benin attribute to their twin male and female creator gods, jointly referred to as Mawu-Lisa, the female traits of fertility, coolness, wisdom, and light, and the opposing male traits of aggressiveness, strength, and darkness (Mercier 1999: 219). The Fon deities' status as twins, who are considered to be the ideal progeny, ensures that they hold conflicting powers in equilibrium. In contrast, while the Win think of the male/female couple as the reflection of the natural order, and their pantheon includes both powerful male and female deities and spirit beings, they do not consider male and female humans to be equally matched. Men are thought to have strength and all privileges of power in Win communities, while women are obliged to be subservient to men, have no political or economic power, and are thought to be less intelligent and physically weaker. Women who undermine this model by not suppressing their natural abilities out of respect for men are characterized as domineering and disrespectful. Those who do not openly vie with men, however, may express their powers covertly. Of these, some are thought to become sorcerers who can be more malicious than male sorcerers. Thus, the model of social order or harmony is realized not by the pairing of equally powerful beings, but by a dominant male accompanied by a submissive female. The imbalance of power in a couple does not hold true for twins; rather, opposite-sex twins are considered to hold each other in check. Twins represent the lack of social discord rather than true social harmony; the couple represents the attainment of social harmony only through the juxtaposition of dichotomous attributes of powerful and weak, of vocal and silent, rather than through a truly complementary relationship.

Despite gender power imbalance in Win society, the dominant interpretation of *tasie* as a married couple underscores their key role in the divination as mediators between disparate beings—spirits and humans—and their worlds. The two figures represent cooperation in the human world that is as essential to the divination process as the collaboration between humans and spirits. In this sense, one could say the *tasie* are metaphors for the gender collaboration which is essential to natural and cosmological balance and order. Their presence reflects the state of psychological wellbeing that the diviner seeks to restore to the client's life.

The use of doubled imagery that pervades Win spiritual practices illustrates a dualistic and mutual relationship needed to forge a bond between the individual and the personal spirit. Arguably, the same representations also serve to remind the spirits of their human counterparts. This reciprocity compounds the importance of the role of doubled imagery in bringing spirits and humans together, and underscores spirit-human relationships as the basis for ideas about self-identity and personhood for the Win.

Doubled images confront the client from the moment he enters the diviner's chamber. On the wall of the chamber and on the floor are images of male and female couples. The subtle wall reliefs, usually sculpted out of clayey soil from a termite mound, are depicted as two schematized figures studded with either cowries or peanut shells, positioned side by side. Except for the suggestion of male genitalia on one, the figures appear to be the same in terms of proportion, size, and gender. Below the wall figures, *tasie* are positioned on the diviner's altar on stone plinths or against the wall where they are barely visible. They are wrapped with locally made cloth—usually with a pattern called *win pwo*, "guinea fowl" (or more commonly in Jula, *kami fani*), which is preferred by the spirits—and adorned with bead necklaces. Over time, the figures may become encrusted with sacrificial offerings of blood, feathers, millet beer (*dolo*), and dirt, to the point of being completely covered. When placed in the dark recesses of the altar, they are nearly invisible. Any identifying features at that point are obscured completely, and one can barely make out the presence of two discrete but seemingly androgynous forms.

One could conjecture that the foregrounding or obfuscation of the figures has to do with the diviner's sense of their potency and the need to either protect them or bring them forward as needed to invoke the spirits. As in many sacred spaces, manipulation of powerful objects, by concealing and revealing at strategic times, occurs throughout the divinatory performance. The most powerful substances for the diviner are her sacred roots, which are kept concealed within two pots, one upturned on the other, and the diviner's power object, or *k'degue*, made with an animal tail and other medicines, which are kept completely hidden at certain times and brought out at others.

Location of the figures is relevant to their status and gender. An elder diviner, Yabile Traoré, said of the *tasie* that they were a married couple and belonged together as husband and wife. According to Traoré, carved figures may sometimes be placed close together, at other times far apart in the chamber, which mimics the way that married couples do not always share quarters. Indeed, in Toussiana, wives and husbands live in the same compound but have separate houses for sleeping. Traoré noted also that the male figure should always be placed by the larger of the medicine pots (*sepine*) to indicate his superior status, which she compared to the dominant role of men in Win households. It is also possible for the *tasie* to have offspring, which are represented by small figures. These children of the *tasie* are not only signs of the spirit's desire to reproduce but are evidence of the diviner's desire to expand her practice. *Tasie* and other

types of objects needed for practicing divination are acquired gradually
and reflect a diviner's desire to augment her powers. The addition of these
objects is comparable to the acquisition of higher degrees of education as
a means of attaining a higher level of employment.[11] It is up to the *setōn*
of the diviner to tell her what to acquire to attain a certain level of power;
figures are but one of the objects that a *setōn* may demand. The diviner
may commission *tasie* from a local carver, or may inherit them from a
deceased diviner. When a diviner dies, the elder diviners agree to let a
junior diviner have them after she makes the proper sacrifices and con-
secrates them with offerings of fowl, water, and millet beer. The diviner
Serge Ouattara received his *tasie* pair from a deceased diviner, and also
inherited a pair from his mother, who was a highly respected and powerful *sanpu*. His altar with four *tasie,* each with its own *kdegue* beside it and
ceramic medicine pots, or *sepine,* was an impressive display for his clients.
Doubling in this case was apparently a means of augmenting the diviner's
power twofold. Invoking his mother's presence and power as one of the
late great diviners, by juxtaposing her *tasie* with his, was a strategy for
enhancing his status immeasurably.

As in divinatory consultation, the theme of complementarity, the metaphoric association of male and female elements, and the linkage to twins all
appear in sacrificial offerings to the spirits. In some sacrificial objects and
performance these are central and essential concepts. One example is the
use of textiles fashioned into garments as prescribed by the diviner. Usually the client is directed to have a garment made by traditional methods,
meaning that it is a cotton, hand-woven, narrow strip cloth produced by
local weavers. The diviner recommends the number of strips in the cloth,
and the type of pattern, as well as the specific method and time for wearing the cloth. For example, a woman may be asked to wear a guinea fowl–
patterned cloth (*kami fani*) wrapper made up of seven strips. By wearing
such a cloth, a client can reveal her allegiance to the *setan* and her desire
to maintain the order and beneficence of the spirit world in two ways.
First, *kami fani* is the cloth preferred by the spirits, both male and female,
as evidenced by the fact that it adorns both the diviner's interlocutor figures. The cloth is favored by the spirits because it resembles the speckled
guinea fowl, which is a highly desirable sacrifice.[12] Twins are particularly
fond of guinea fowl and demand them as sacrifices; thus, the cloth bearing
this name is also a favorite of twins. Wrappers of *kami fani* are composed
of seven strips, showing the combination of the numbers four and three,
which are symbolic of the female and male principles respectively.[13] Men
may be told to wear a tunic made of seven white hand-woven cloth strips,

with a *kami fani* strip in the center. Other combinations, using multiples of three and four combined—eleven or thirteen strips for example—are variant types. Such garments are worn to solve a problem with a member of the opposite sex, or with twins; but they are understood and interpreted within the wider framework of gender complementarity as a sign of striving toward cosmological unity and balance.

Gender complementarity and twinning are subtly reiterated in a widely used amulet referred to as man and wife, or *ce ni muso*. The *ce ni muso* amulets are made as either bangles or rings made of twisted silver-colored metal (usually aluminum) and copper strands. Diviners prescribe them for clients who have problems with a spouse or lover. The two strands of different colored metals are intertwined to symbolize the constant and necessary alliance of members of the opposite sex. The *ce ni muso* is a means of bringing the two together in a simple, elegant form. Diviners have also mentioned that they symbolize the relationship one must have with one's *setōn*, who may be of the opposite sex. Worn as a bangle or ring, tightly clinching the wrist or the finger, it is a constant reminder to the wearer of his commitment to the cause of harmonious gender relations and his obligations to his *setōn*. Compared to other amulets that are often concealed under clothing, the *ce ni muso* is a conspicuous expression of an individual's effort to improve his relationship with other humans, particularly with twins, and with the spirit world.

The benefits bestowed by twins and couples may be enhanced through the act of doubling, as in doubled *tasie* on a diviner's altar or double twin-figure amulets. However, doubling other kinds of images, not overtly associated with twins or couples, is another means of augmenting spiritual blessings. In some cases, non-differentiated doubled images are clearly considered to be twin-related, as in the small conjoined wooden or ceramic cups or baskets that are used to propitiate twins—either male or female, living or deceased—on personal altars. One woman whose twin sister was deceased buried a twin cup beneath a personal altar, explaining that she had paid homage to her twin for years by pouring libations on the altar over the area where the cup was buried. The twin containers display no visual differentiation of gender but are for both same- and opposite-sex twins. The role of these objects is clear—but other, less obvious, images are also known to be signs of twins, for example, doubled images of animals that also lack any gender reference.

Belief in the efficacy of doubles is also manifested in the proliferation and variety of double-imaged amulets made of brass (or cuprous alloys), iron, copper, aluminum, or other metals depicting zoomorphic and other

FIGURE 6.2. Double turtle/chameleon composite brass amulets. The triangular forms with two spirals represent double chameleons. *Photo: Susan Cooksey.*

non-anthropomorphic forms. Single and double versions of the same type of amulet are generally said to bring about healing or good fortune, are prescribed both as cures for specific ailments that are diagnosed as physiological and for more complex problems that involve a range of physical, psychological, or social problems. One explanation for the doubled forms is that they are required for the relatives of twins.

A collection of amulets that I acquired from the brass-caster Yerisige Soulama of Bounouna and other market vendors in and around Toussiana from 1998–2005 included a wealth of zoomorphic and geometric shapes, and natural found objects cast as doubled objects: turtles, tortoises, chameleons, locusts, bells, spirals, and composites of these and other forms. Although the iconography of these amulets has been explored in the literature on the Senufo (Glaze 1981; Förster 1987), scholarly studies on Win usage and interpretation are limited (Trost 1993; Hasselberger 1969).

The most common double-imaged amulets I saw in use in the Win area included those with turtle and chameleon motifs.

The types of turtle amulet are differentiated according to species, as befits their associations with the different spirit domains. The tortoise, with its shell covered by a pattern of semi-spirals, is differentiated from the turtle, which has a shell designed as a large single spiral, sometimes overlaid by two crossed lines and a central boss. The tortoise lives in the forest and is thus associated with the forest *setan*. A diviner's client who has a problem with a forest *setōn* may have to wear a tortoise pendant.

According to an elder Win diviner, Maman Coulibaly, the spiral shell signifies a large turtle that ripples the water when it swims. She said that an
individual who doesn't realize that he has a water *setōn* and catches a turtle, an animal sacred to the water spirits, incurs the anger of the *setōn*. The
setōn's punishment is so severe that the offender has to seek the help of the
diviner, who reveals the identity of the spirit and why it is displeased. The
diviner may tell the client to go to the bank of the river sacred to his particular *setōn*, place the brass amulet on the altar made up of three stones
symbolizing the power of the river, and make a sacrifice of a chicken while
praying to the *setōn* of the river. Afterward, the client may then take the
amulet (*kinkwegue*) to wear. If the sacrifice is insufficient, the river may
ask for more extravagant offerings, such as a goat or a cow. These turtle
pendants are produced by brass-casters and used by diviners throughout
the area from northern Côte d'Ivoire to southwestern Burkina Faso. Other
styles of turtle pendants also exist in this region, such as those with variously adorned square shells.[14] The larger turtle amulets may be worn on
the waist or neck, and smaller ones are worn on the neck or as rings.[15]

Not only diviners, but many local residents know about the functions
and meanings of various forms of double turtle amulets, both large and
miniaturized. A Win elder, Adama Ouattara, whose father was a diviner
and a chief priest, said that the single turtle amulet and the double turtle
amulet—which he called a "twin turtle"—are meant to bring good fortune.
According to Ouattara, the double amulet indicated that one has sacrificed
two turtles on the shore of the river and consumed the meat. This act of
goodwill toward the river brings wealth and bountiful harvests. According
to Ouattara, parents are obliged to wear the double turtle pendant on their
necks so that it is visible during ceremonies celebrating a son's circumcision
or daughter's excision. Musicians playing xylophone-like instruments are
hired to perform at the ceremony, and they are allowed to demand extra
payment if they see a parent wearing the double turtle pendant.[16]

One of the most spectacular brass amulets is one that depicts two turtles joined at the side of the shell and linked to three consecutive isosceles
triangles. The triangles have spirals on each acute angle and are covered
with small bosses. Yerisige Soulama interpreted the image and symbolism
of these amulets (Cooksey 2004: 181; Blandin 1988: 69), noting that the
triangles represent two chameleons.[17] As Soulama explained, the triangle
with small bumps represents their merged bodies, and the spirals their
curled tails. Soulama also reported that this double turtle and chameleon
amulet is used by Gouin diviners, who place it next to them in consultations to expedite communication with the spirit world.

Both the turtle and chameleon are considered sacred to the spirits, and both are primordial beings, sacred to many peoples, including the Win. According to Win creation mythology, turtles glided through the newly formed waterways, as chameleons stepped lightly and cautiously on the earth to test its firmness. Because of this, the chameleon is thought to possess the patience and wisdom of the elders, and is held up to youngsters to counteract rash behavior. Cool-headed, the animal is also thought to be cool-skinned, which is a sign of good health.[18] This idea parallels the multivalent image of the chameleon in Senufo iconography as the symbol of transformation, primordial knowledge, communication with the spirit world, and healing powers represented as "cooling" (Glaze 1986: 76). The chameleon's extraordinary capacity to change its skin color and its rotating eyes are further evidence of the spiritual powers that allow it to vanish instantly and to be omniscient.[19]

As a testimony of its powers, and the desire to harness them, both single and double chameleon images are depicted on numerous types of brass amulets, including rings, bracelets, pendants, and freestanding figures. Stylistic variations range from realistic freestanding sculptures to highly abstracted triangle-spirals, which are found in single, double, and triple forms. A semi-abstracted curvilinear style, with a knob-like head and unarticulated body with similar bumps on the surface, which Leo Frobenius collected in 1908 and identified as a "waist ornament," seems to be a transitional style between the highly abstracted triangular style and more representational versions.[20] Hasselberger interpreted these abstract forms in describing a 1908 drawing in the Frobenius Institute as a "belt ornament consisting of two spiraling, intertwining horns, perhaps an abstract image of a pair of chameleons in coition" (Hasselberger 1969: 217). In Toussiana, diviners did not display chameleon sculptures but said they recommended chameleon amulets for clients. I documented people of both sexes, both children and adults, wearing the amulets from 1997–1999, and during that time it appeared to be one of the most widely used amulets. Although the chameleon, as a reptile, is a land-dweller, in Toussiana, chameleons function as emblems of water *setan,* as evidenced by an elder *sanpu* diviner recommendation of a double chameleon ring for an elder male client so that "the river would protect him"—meaning that he was allied with a water spirit.[21]

The turtle and chameleon images may serve as symbols of varying approaches to enhancing awareness in divinatory processes. Each animal embodies distinctly different but complementary abilities that may be likened to different cognitive modes employed to achieve alternate levels of awareness, as described by Peek (Peek 1992: 205; Peek and Winkelman 2004: 11). The movements the animals make, chameleons deliberate and slow, swimming turtles swift, may be metaphoric of complementary aesthetic qualities, and of different kinds of sensory processing through complementary cognitive modes. In the course of a divination consultation, diviners continually introduce sensory information to their clients in the form of images and objects with heightened aesthetic properties. On some level they must be aware of the role of this influx of sensations in the client's experience, and how important it is to process them by using a spectrum of visual and other senses with differing capacities. What could be more visually astute than an animal with revolving, multidirectional eyes? What could suggest a more fluid, linear movement than a turtle gliding through the water, or the perfectly concentric geometry of the ripples it creates? A consultation works because the diviner presents sensory information, and prescribes a partly rational, partly irrational course of action for his client that is derived from communication with the spirit world. It is up to the client to further analyze this message to comprehend its meaning for his own life.

Although I never heard Win diviners or other Win informants explicitly compare the extraordinary powers of turtles and chameleons to those of twins, I surmise that they may be regarded as equally effective envoys. For the notion of these animals, whose constant and close communication with one another is enabled by their mutual connection to the spirits, is analogous to that of twins, whose close spiritual alliance accounts for their shared knowledge of one another and the rapid, even simultaneous transmission of knowledge between them. The idea of twins as messengers is reiterated by Eileen Suthers in her study of a Djimini divination system that closely parallels that of the Win *sanpu* (Suthers 1987). Suthers asserts that the Djimini believe that because the twins have perfect knowledge of one another they can function as highly efficacious mediators. Casting twins as super-mediators who have joined their forces with the extraordinary powers of the chameleon and the turtle produces a complex, multivalent device for negotiating human-spirit relationships.

While the essential purpose of divination is to ameliorate an individual's relationship with the spirit world, even the most efficacious practices can offer only temporary respite from the demands of the spirits and the potential negative force of the spirits embodied by the twins. As the *sanpu* tirelessly attempt to cajole unruly spirits with imagery and performances that affirm cosmic order, they must constantly engage these spirits who

have the prerogative of breaching cosmic boundaries to create chaos and
suffering in human life. Twin images, male and female couple imagery,
and doubled images play a critical role in an intensive dialogue between
humans and spirits that heightens self-awareness as it alternately challenges and validates ideas of human and spirit interdependence.

NOTES

1. For example, I was told by a diviner that I had a male *setōn* from the
river.

2. An elder whose ancestors were diviners and priests, Adama Ouattara,
stated that the spirits were originally all from the water, although they may be
divided into the three categories of forest, water, and mountains (personal communication, 1998). Many people said that the *setan* live in the water with their
human counterparts before they are born, but there was no clear answer about
those that come from the forest or mountains and if the *setan* and human counterparts lived there together before birth.

3. Madeleine Traoré of Toussiana interviewed Dobe Barro in February 2008.
The interview was translated by Celestin Coulibaly for me in a personal communication, February 2008.

4. The Oedipal complex as theorized by Freud (1935: 184) includes the incestuous urge of male children to have sex with their mothers, as well as to then
commit patricide. The female version as theorized by Freud and named the
Electra complex by Jung in 1913, which holds that daughters seek to bond with
the father and are matricidal, is also applicable to the Win parent-twin relationship. I refer to this aspect of the psychoanalytic theory only as it is relevant to the
basic Win concept of the hostile, incestuous twin and corresponding child-parent
relationship.

5. The face-washing ritual involves the parent bathing the child's head with
the infusion. The explanation and Win translation (along with a Jula translation
of it as *ka o gnya ko*) were supplied by Madeliene Traoré and Celestin Coulibaly in
personal communications March 18 and May 30, 2008.

6. An alternate spelling is *képiníni*, meaning "the twins" from Barro, Ketandi.
Coulibaly and Weismann (2004: 55).

7. According to Trost, some examples of amulets he found in Toussiana caves
had loops. He also mentions that the larger twin anthropomorphic amulets are
worn on a band on the hip but not worn by the Toussian as pendants as they
are, according to A. Maesan and Til Förster, by the Senufo (Trost 1993: 84). An
example of a quadruplet figure from the Wheelock collection (Roy and Wheelock 2007: 441) has finer features, but has loops in the back, indicating its use as a
pendant.

8. A grid pattern, often configured as three rows of eight squares, is seen on
the twin figures and also on turtle figures. However, older examples have different

configurations and patterns; see for example the four figure amulet, catalogue no. 385, in Roy and Wheelock (2007: 441). They suggest that certain patterns may be related to a Bobo symbol of the lunar calendar and a reference to menses as described by LeMoal (1986) in his discussion of the *sabi na fre,* or "things of the soul" amulet.

9. The case for opposite-sex twins as representing an ideal couple who symbolize social and cosmic order is strongly supported by a story told to me by a Win woman, Madeleine Traoré. She said that her sister had two sets of opposite-sex twins, but in the first set the male died *in utero* and in the second set the female died at six months. The family surmised that the second male twin was in fact the "husband" of the first female twin and had come back later to join her.

10. The *sanpu* and *sanpu gbe,* or great diviners, together form a double-tiered, hieratic system of divination in Win communities. Hébert and Guilhem first wrote about this hieratic system in 1964. My study of Toussiana divination systems (Cooksey 2004) revealed that this system, as along with other types of divination practices, was still vital in the community. Clearly the Win *sanpu* are related to the Gouin diviners, who are called *Sando,* and the Senufo diviners described by Glaze (1981) and others, but they differ notably in their use of wood and brass display objects and their status as defined in comparison to the senior *sanpu gbe.*

11. Celestin Coulibaly, who interviewed diviners, used this analogy to clarify the addition of objects to the diviner's repertoire (personal communication, March 18, 2008).

12. The guinea fowl is preferred as a sacrifice because of its resilience. When its throat is slit it continues to struggle long after a chicken would. The way the bird lands when it expires demonstrates the spirit's acceptance of the sacrifice. No explanation was offered to me about why the duration of the death throes are appreciated except that they heighten the drama. Dieterlen also remarks on the use of an indigo and white cloth as representing the complementary properties of *le vide et l'obscurité; les blancs, la plentitude, et la lumiere* ("emptiness and darkness; white, fullness, and light"). Furthermore, she says a cloth known as *konwo, buguni,* or *kami* (guinea fowl) is used in divination and healing, and that it "expresses hope—the impure or weak man hopes to become pure, strong, full" (Dieterlen 1986: 134).

13. See for example Griaule and Dieterlen (1986: 53) and Deiterlen (1986: 43) on the cosmologies and gendered numerological symbols of the Dogon and Bamana, respectively.

14. According to Yerisige Soulama, square turtle pendants are used by Turka diviners but not given to clients. It is possible that other groups may use these as well; however my research did not encounter Win or other diviners with knowledge of these pendants. I also never saw the square turtles as rings or miniaturized. When Soulama refers to Toussian, he is probably including both

the Northern Toussian and Southern Toussian, that is, both the Pentobe and Win.

15. According to Maman Coulibaly (personal communication, December 16, 1998), the turtle pendants with axial lines on the shell are for sacrificial offerings, whereas the ones without lines are worn as adornment and have no religious significance. Most of the newer turtle amulets I saw from 1997–1999 did not have lines. However, they were more coarsely made than the earlier turtle amulets, which had very finely coiled spirals and smaller feet and heads. It may be that the later versions have dropped the iconographic cross motif simply due to a more minimal, less technically challenging approach to brass-casting.

16. Adama Ouattara, from Tebenaso, reported this in 1998. He recognized the double turtle with the pendant triangles but did not know the meaning of the triangles. I interpreted his statement to mean that the turtle pendant signified the wealth of the owner, and thus the musicians felt they could reasonably ask for higher payments than they normally received.

17. Blandin's source for much of the metalwork in southwestern Burkina Faso was the Soulama family, primarily Fangoman Soulama, the elder whom I met in 1997 and whose son, Yerisige Soulama, was the primary informant for my research on brass amulets in 1997–1999.

18. Coolness is a significant sign of health, which makes sense in a hot, dry Sahelian climate where long dry seasons bring respiratory infections and these as well as other diseases prevalent year-round result in fevers. Handholding diviners (*sanpu*) are sensitive to a client's body temperature and will comment on it during a consultation. It seems that a clear advantage of the handholding technique is in its diagnostic as well as its therapeutic role.

19. Not all diviners claim to be clairvoyant, as it is thought to be a special gift from the spirits.

20. This type of chameleon amulet and other brass amulets collected by Frobenius are now in the Museum für Völkerkunde, Munich. Hasselberger (1969) also mentioned a collection in the Frobenius Institute.

21. A local informant suggested that chameleon pendants were worn around the waist or neck of a child for curing a recurrent illness.

WORKS CITED

Barro, Ketandi, Soungalo Coulibaly, and Hannes Wiesmann. 2004. *Wīn wɛl ɔ dúkúri, Dictionnaire toussian-français*. Banfora, Burkina Faso: SIL.

Blandin, Andre. 1988. *Bronzes et autres alliages: Afrique de l'Ouest*. Marignane, France: A. Blandin.

Cooksey, Susan. 2004. *Iron Staffs in the Crossroads: Art and Divination in Toussiana, a Southwestern Burkina Faso Community*. Ph.D. dissertation, University of Iowa.

Coulibaly, Soungalo, and Yannes Weismann. 2004. *Dictionnaire Toussian—Française*. Banfora, Burkina Faso: SIL.

Dieterlen, Germaine. 1986. *Essai sur la religion Bambara*. Bruxelles: Editions de l'Université Bruxelles.

Förster, Till. 1987. *Glanzend wie Geld*. Berlin: Museum fur Völkerkunde, Staatliche Museen PreuBischer Kulturbesitz.

Freud, Sigmund. 1935. *A General Introduction to Psychoanalysis*. New York: Liveright Publishing.

Glaze, Anita. 1981. *Art and Death in a Senufo Village*. Bloomington: Indiana University Press.

———. 1986. "Dialectics of Gender in Senufo Masquerades." *African Arts* 19: 3, 30–39, 82.

Griaule, Marcel, and Germaine Dieterlen. 1986. *The Pale Fox*. Chino Valley, Ariz.: Continuum Foundation. Originally published as *Le Renard pale*. Paris: l'Institute d'Ethnologie, 1965.

Hasselberger, Herta. 1969. "Bemerkungen zum Kuntshandwerk in der Republik Haute Volta: Gourounsi und Altvölker des äußersten Südwestens." *Zeitschrift für Ethnologie*, 94 (2): 171–230. Translation by Andrew Witter, unpublished, 1997.

Hébert, Jean. 1972. "Organization de la societé en pays Toussain." *Notes et documents Voltaique* 5 (July–Sept.): 14–48.

———. 1997. "Representations de l'âme et de l'au-dela chêz les Toussian (Burkina Faso)." *Anthropos* 92 (1/3): 183–190.

Hébert, Jean R. 1959. "Les Noms en Pays Toussian." *Notes Africaines* 84: 110–113.

Hébert, Jean R., and Marcel Guilhem. 1964. "Une 'Nobelsse' Hereditaire en Pays Toussian: les Devins." *Notes Africaines* 104 (Oct.): 97–106.

———. 1965. "Note Additive sur Les Devins en Pays Toussian." *Notes Africaines* (July): 92–95

LeMoal, Guy. 1986. "Naissance et rites d'identification: Les objects." (Vienna) *Archiv für Völkerkunde* 40: 75–92.

Mercier, Paul. 1999. "The Fon of Dahomey." In *African Worlds: Studies in the Cosmological Ideas and Social Values of African Peoples*, ed. Daryll Forde, 210–234. Oxford: James Currey.

Peek, Philip 1992. "African Divination Systems: Non-normal Modes of Cognition." In *African Divination Systems: Ways of Knowing*, ed. Philip Peek, 193–208. Bloomington: Indiana University Press.

Peek, Philip, and Michael Winkelman, eds. 2004. *Divination and Healing: Potent Vision*. Tucson: University of Arizona Press.

Roy, Christopher, and Thomas Wheelock. 2007. *Land of the Flying Masks: Art and Culture in Burkina Faso, The Thomas G. B. Wheelock Collection*. Munich: Prestel.

Suthers, Eileen Moore. 1987. *Perception, Knowledge, and Divination in Djimini Society, Ivory Coast*. Ph.D. Dissertation, Universtiy of Virginia.

Trost, Franz. 1993. *Ethonarchäologie in Südwest Burkina-Faso.* Graz, Austria: Akademische Druck- und Verlagsanstalt.

Trost, Franz. 1986. "Bemerkungen zur religiosen organization der Tussian (Burkina Faso)." (Vienna) *Archiv für Völkerkunde* 40: 99–114.

Trost, Franz. 2001. "Sê pil-eine Holzplastifk der sudlichen Tussian (Burkina Faso) from Tunis, A (Hg.)." In *Faszination der Kulturen,* 5–322. Berlin: Reimer.

Turner, Victor. 1969. *The Ritual Process: Structure and Anti-Structure.* Ithaca, N.Y.: Cornell University Press.

CHAPTER SEVEN

Double Portraits

Images of Twinness in West African Studio Photography

C. ANGELO MICHELI

All studies in art history, anthropology, or any human science conducted in West Africa inevitably encounter the artistic and cultural issues associated with twins. My interest in double portraits as twin images obviously originates in careful and repeated observation of the numerous photographs produced by Western African studios. After Marilyn Houlberg's founding works on *ibeji*, it was two studies, one by American researcher Stephen Sprague and one by French anthropologist Jean-François Werner, that prompted me to investigate the question of twinness in photography on a sub-Saharan scale. Sprague claims that "Yoruba photography certainly shares similar categories of subject matter and formalistic conventions with other West African societies" (1978: 54). Werner believes that "the reason for the fascination for twinness" as it is expressed through the several examples of double portraits should be explained "by the specific contribution of Yoruba photographers who supposedly initiated this practice within rituals related to twins, rather than a cultural common trait to all West African societies" (1996: 103). Though I am far from wanting to elide or ignore the undeniable diversity of African cultures, I had to acknowledge that these double portraits not only showed similarities to me but were also produced and perceived in similar ways by the people who made them in different West African countries, and therefore they constitute a specific feature in the aesthetics of portraiture. They may appear to be family photography stereotypes, studio "tricks," or transcultural images that could belong to photography from any continent, but double portraits soon reveal a semantic depth when considered in their local context. This semantic depth has no equivalent in production outside Africa and is characteristic of the authors' thought and creation. These studio portraits are not exclusive to renowned photographers such as Malians Seydou

Keita or Malick Sidibe. Many lesser-known photographers compose pictures that respond to their customers' desires and arouse their imaginations in similar ways. In studio windows, photographs of two similar or identical figures are often displayed as double portraits. Widespread for several decades, double portraits are more than mere entertainment or a passing fad. They raise specific issues about representation in photography and, as portraits, question the notion of self-definition while suggesting links with other artistic productions and cultural meaning. They are therefore an artistic phenomenon worthy of an art historical analysis.[1]

At the Edge of Art and Anthropology

Though they are acknowledged to some extent by anthropologists and historians (Houlberg 1973; Sprague 1978; Vogel 1991; Oguibe 1996; Werner 1996; Behrend and Wendl 1997; Buckley 2000–2001; and Nimis 2005), double portraits in photography have not yet been approached as a specific aesthetic production in research on West African studio photography. Most publications only allude to the subject, usually focusing on one population (the Yoruba) or one country, and on one formal aspect, namely the duplication of one person's image into two identical figures (corresponding to the *ibeji* portrait the Yoruba have long created in different media for cultural purposes). Both Werner's and Behrend and Wendl's studies have identified another type of double portrait, "duo portraits" (two persons appearing as look-alikes or clones), and have extended their research to a larger number of countries. Vogel and Oguibe also discuss the aesthetic aspects of double portraits. Still, all studies seem to center on the Yoruba invention, which, for reasons yet unknown, gained many followers in West Africa. In most cases, these portraits are only seen as bearing witness to history, society, and family, while the medium is seen as the signature of modernity. Yet, photography is more than the simple recording of visual data about a culture and can be studied as a cultural phenomenon of its own. Photographs can be studied as cultural artifacts, art productions, and for their significance within a specific cultural context. In this chapter, I will place the photographic works on which I based my study within a more comprehensive context, placing them within the history of double portraits in Europe and in both African sculpture and photography, and within a body of collective imagery inspired by myths and practices related to twinness. In other words, these portraits will be analyzed in regard to their contexts of both production and reception.

This study is based on a collection of 300 photographs dating from the end of the 1960s up to the present day. I chose to begin with the 1960s because they coincide with the emergence of numerous portraits made by and for Africans. Moreover, among the photographs of one person and his or her doubled image that I collected and studied—or that were mentioned to me during my research—the first date back to this period. Thoroughly examining the phenomenon of double portraiture from this starting point until today allows me to capture its full dimension, and to appreciate its endurance and the great popularity it continues to have. The collection was gathered in four sub-Saharan francophone countries (Togo, Benin, Burkina Faso, and Mali)[2] as I journeyed from the coast to the interior, following the route taken by photography itself as it spread throughout the continent. The photographs were collected from studio clients but mainly from eighty photographers who have been overlooked by researchers up to now. No distinctions were made regarding sex (though most happen to be male), age, talent, or position of the photographers, nor regarding the size of studios or towns where the photographs were collected. It would have played into the hands of Western art market institutions to focus only on artists who are singled out for their style or undeniable talent. Moreover, this would have left out anonymous artists who have remained on the margins of the evolution of the history of double portraiture. Minor or imperfect photographic works that are nevertheless relevant to African photography would also have been omitted. As well as photographers, I interviewed studio clients, local inhabitants, and people involved in the cultural life of the places I visited, though not without some difficulties, as studio clients rarely came back to the studios where I collected the photographs. Some clients might just have wanted to sit for the photographer regardless of the result. Some had simply forgotten about the photographs or had not claimed their portraits either because they could not pay or did not like them. Others had moved away or were deceased.

The Art of Double Portraits

The generic term "double portraits" covers two categories of portrait, one in which the figures are similar, one in which they are identical. In the first category, the case of similar figures, an attempt is made to create a twin-like resemblance between two different people by using identical clothing, attitudes, and poses. I will call this category "paired-figure portraits" (see figure 7.1). In the second category, identical figures appear so because the portrait of one person has been reproduced twice on the same print, either symmetrically or in juxtaposition, by double-exposing the same photo paper in the darkroom; these I call "duplicate portraits" (see figure 4.2 in chapter 4). Today they can easily be done with a computer (figure 7.2), although computer-assisted duplicated portraits are quite rare. In the same category, the figures are also identical when one person is photographed in two different poses (the film is exposed twice during shooting), creating "double-exposure portraits" (figure 7.3), or reflected, in the case of "mirror portraits" (figure 7.4) (see also Micheli 2008).

The different kinds of double portraits are popular among the West African photographers I have met, and most of them are familiar with the conventions of studio portraiture as well as with the multiple exposure technique. They often own the same kind of studios, and sometimes even similar settings and props. On the one hand, "paired-figure portraits" (figure 7.1) have been common since the beginning of studio photography in Africa, as they require no specific technical skill and because people just love being photographed with someone else. According to photographers Ibrahim Sanlé Sory (born in 1948, he settled in Bobo Dioulasso, Burkina Faso, in 1968) and Michel Hounkanrin (born in 1954, he opened his first studio in Cotonou, Benin, in 1977 and started digital photography in 1998), full-length paired-figure portraits are very popular because they allow more creative freedom in terms of poses, location, and settings. Sory and Hounkanrin are well known for their spectacular settings, which are created by artists. Sory uses painted backcloths while Hounkanrin uses montages made with Photoshop. Full-length paired-figured portraits are more impressive in size and give more information about the sitters in terms of their physical appearance, whereas bust portraits, though regarded as more modern by clients who prefer closer shots, only give a fragmented image. On the other hand, for duplicate, double-exposure, and mirror portraits (figures 7.2, 7.3, 7.4) both kinds of framing are equally popular. Full-length portraits with effects date back to the 1970s. But shooting and obtaining the desired visual effects is simply easier with bust portraits: the settings are simpler and the joint between the two pictures is less important, which facilitates continuity between the two shots. This second category, as observed in the studio windows and in the personal archives of photographers and clients, represent only 10–20 percent of all photograph production. The percentage is due to several factors. Photographers are aware of double exposure and duplicated portraits but some of them do not know how to do them. Some West African towns and villages are far from the trade routes along which artistic ideas, like these portraits, travel. These types of portraits can go out of fashion—without

FIGURE 7.1. El Hadj Tidiani Shitou. Two Peul (Fulani) sisters, 1987. Mopti, Mali. "Paired-figure portrait." Black-and-white negative film scanned (2⅓" x 2⅓"). *Collection of the artist.*

FIGURE 7.2. Michel Hounkanrin. Communicants, 2004. Contonou, Republic of Benin. "Duplicated portrait." Numeric print. *Collection of the artist.*

FIGURE 7.3. Koda C Labara Foto. Venavi. 2002. Lomé, Togo. "Double-exposure print." Color print (4⅛" × 5¼"). *Private collection.*

FIGURE 7.4. Koda C Labara. Untitled, 2002. Lomé, Togo. "Mirror portrait." Color print. (5¼" × 4⅛"). *Private collection.*

disappearing altogether—in countries where photography and its commercial artifices has been present for a long time, particularly in Benin and in Togo, while they are frequently seen in the more isolated countries like Burkina and Mali. The percentage can reflect local customers' feelings about modernity. For some of them modernity is epitomized by photographs emphasizing the uniqueness of a single portrait (double exposure is seen as too old-fashioned), for others, by complex images in which one appears duplicated, reflecting the multiplicity of the individual. Nevertheless we must avoid thinking in dichotomies like modern/archaic, towns/villages, south/north. Things are not so simple, and I heard diversified and mixed thoughts everywhere. For instance, if double-exposure portraits were always considered old-fashioned or outdated, photographers Hounkanrin and C. Labara Koda (born in 1977, he opened his studio in Lomé, Togo, in 2001), whose studios are situated in two southern countries, would not produce so many of them. Hounkanrin fashions very creative posters as well as funeral portraits in large formats in light-boxes, like neon street signs, and equipped with wheels so that they can be moved from one room to another. The younger Labara thinks that double exposures are not only a very attractive means to develop his business, but also potentially more artistic than classical portraits. Sory used to like double exposures when he practiced black and white in his studio and was able "to manipulate trick-photos and create like a magician"[3] in his darkroom. Now, obliged to resort to Korean color labs, he can no longer control the results and has therefore abandoned double exposures. Yet, double portraits are still appreciated and considered to be modern and pleasant images, especially when they are in color.

Images of Twins or Twin Images?

Closer examination of paired-figure portraits (figure 7.1) brings to light a whole range of stereotyped pictures in which poses, clothing, accessories, and symmetric composition display a formal and symbolic doubling. Clients—the protagonists of this doubling—never go to a studio in twos by chance. They may be brought together by special occasions, public (mainly religious, such as Tabaski and Christmas) or private ones (baptism; rites de passage such as Christian communions, Islamic circumcisions and endogenous religious rites; weddings, funerals, reunions), for which they wear clothes made from the same fabric, a common tradition in the four countries studied which signifies that close people are also cut from the same cloth. Different types of relations exist between the two sitters, sometimes familial but also possibly affective, intimate, or social relationships. Whatever the nature of the relationship portrayed, it has been created for and occasioned by the picture, and therefore transcends the existing ones. Thus, for instance, co-wives who do not necessarily live in harmony may nevertheless appear united in the picture. There are many different types of relationships between people that reflect some aspect of twinness. This can be observed in daily life and many examples have been identified in anthropological studies. These are too numerous to be exhaustively cited in the present essay, but I may nevertheless mention some special types of relationship. *Senankuya* is a word in the Mali languages that signifies a bond between two populations like Bozo and Dogon, or between two families, like the Koulibali and the Keita. The *senânku* is a kind of twin to any individual belonging to the other group; he has in him a portion of his partner, and vice versa (Dieterlen 1988: 97). More specifically we must notice the special case of *mãgu, "parent à plaisanterie,"* someone allied or related to you by cathartic practices of joking and humor (Dieterlen 1973: 212). In Mali as well as Burkina Faso, two boys circumcised at the same time, even if they are not the same age, are considered *flâ* and will be friends or *flani:* twins all their lives (Dieterlen 1988: 204). The same relationship can be observed in other countries between two communicants who want to look like twins (as in Benin, figure 7.2). In a commercial relationship the man who sells and the man who buys are considered twins among Dogon people (Griaule 1966: 201). Among the Bobo in Burkina Faso, the two children of two co-wives born at the same time or with very little time interval are considered twins (Le Moal 1973: 200), and the same holds true in Mali. The Drewals note, after R. F. Thompson, the virtue of comradeship in the pairing of Yoruba's Gelede masqueraders (Drewal and Drewal 1983: 134–136). They write: "When two partners make a pact and adopt a common secret name, they often choose to dress alike and may be mistaken for twins" (ibid.: 136). It should also be noted that throughout this area, *badenya* or brotherly love describes a twin-like intimacy between two individuals as if they were born to the same mother: *ba* (mother) + *ny* (child). Although the term comes from countries that share Manding traditions (Mali and Burkina), it is understood and used today by people in French-speaking countries (Benin and Togo). Finally, M. Cartry (1973: 29) observes that the idea of twinship largely transcends the field of twins themselves in West Africa.[4] For Cartry, even a person born single participates in a twin-type structure. The structure of social institutions (trade, some relationships, initiations) and the world structure are themselves based on this model.

In the paired-figure portraits (figure 7.1) studio clients want to be seen with their alter ego, their "second self," in a twin-like relationship. They don't need to be real-born twins but to be seen and considered as twins, according to their cultural models that regard twins as God's blessing. In terms of image, what is important is the closeness of same-sexed persons and the tangible likeness—or the likeness that the photograph creates—between two persons pictured together. Thus, it is usually people of the same sex who are paired in the studio. The reasons for this are symbolic (linking and belonging, specific friendship between two men or women), social (decency—male and female sitters rarely show themselves dressed in the same way unless they are married, and moreover, in order to avoid gender confusion, they do not appear on the same photograph dressed alike), and above all formal, because a stronger likeness and thereby a perfection of the doubling is thus created. The construction of these doubles involves all the conventions and techniques of studio photography: *boubous* (male and female robes) and traditional dress bought from a nearby tailor or lent by the studio when customers do not possess identical clothes, similar props and accessories placed to emphasize an axis and bilateral symmetry, and, more effectively, conventional and geometrical composition which produce flat images that lack spatial depth but are not without semantic depth. This flatness is increased by resorting to specific poses in which the gravity of the figures standing side by side, their body postures reduced to graphic signs along with lighting that smoothly harmonizes the whole scene, generates a sense of formal balance, restrained energy, and rhythm within stability. All these elements contribute to compose icon-like images. They may have indexical value, but for sitters who are sensitive to the play on resemblance and illusion, symbolic dimension and reference to twin images, they are mainly wish fulfillment.

Duplicated portraits and double-exposure portraits (figures 7.2 and 7.3) are sometimes requested by the customers in order to mark a life event, like a birthday, an anniversary, an achievement in school, or a professional or commercial success. But what usually brings clients to the studio is simply the desire for a beautiful and distinctive portrait. As I was studying these double-exposure and duplicated portraits, it came as no surprise to hear them often called "twin portraits" (*flani foto* in Mali and Burkina Faso, *kinkirsi foto* and *foto wooin* in Burkina Faso, *foto venavi* in Togo, *foto hohovi* in Benin, and *foto ibeji* among Yoruba-speaking people in Mali and Benin). Ostensibly, they show two images of the same person in a formal and visual sense. But in reality, they reveal a twin of the same sex absent from this world, a twin who has remained invisible in the tangible world.

For many clients, completion of the self implies the presence of one's twin: a living twin like a friend or a family member felt as a twin, or a missing twin they feel inside themselves and who is part of the definition of the "person." This belief is attested by numerous studies on notions of "the individual" carried out in West Africa: "dual nature is the condition of completeness" (Mercier 1999: 232). Even a unique child has a twin in the other world (Bonnet 1982: 426); placenta (Dieterlen 1981: 222) can be the missing twin.[5] According to the photographers, it is possible to create a photographic twin of the opposite sex by using appropriate clothing, but this can also be viewed with suspicion—as one informant saw it, it "would disrupt the effect of an illusion obtained by perfect similarity."[6] Living in a parallel spirit world, whether missing or imaginary, the twin is "a double inside" who needs to be figured by the photo-portrait, which can restore the intimate dimension and vision of self without being suspected of invention. This is because photography and its specific artifices, as a modern means of showing oneself—as an index and an icon (Krauss 1990: 142–143)—can create illusions and play with likelihood and presumed reality. Techniques of double-exposure during shooting or duplication during developing enable the photographer to compose a formal and symmetric picture. He may also sometimes introduce an element of dissimilarity in the composition, a subtle difference—this technique is recommended by Labara and Sory. Twin illusion can emerge out of this discrepancy, to such an extent that it is eventually impossible to determine which figure is the original or which is the duplicated one.

The formal double thus achieved is sometimes so ambiguous that it may be difficult to differentiate a portrait of actual identical twins from a portrait of two friends, or a portrait of two friends in a reflecting pose from a mirror portrait or a duplicated portrait, or even a paired-figure portrait from a duplicated portrait, specifically when the artist combines two techniques, for example by duplicating identically the body of one of the two friends, yet keeping the two faces distinct (figure 7.2)—Sory, for instance, is very fond of these fusions-and-confusions. The photographer's intention and the sitters' desires come together to produce the illusion, reached in every kind of portrait by using identical poses and symmetric attitudes. "You must keep symmetry in mind," Tidiani Shitou (1933–2000, born in Nigeria, he settled in Mopti, Mali, in 1971) used to tell his son, whom I met. "Use props along the axis, arrange the sitters, think of triangular or rectangular compositions."[7] A specific feature of West African photo-portraits lies in the staging of two people side by side in the same attitude like identical twins, and indicates a use of formal and aesthetic patterns in reference to doubles pertaining to twin symbolism. The twin images, and not images of twins, produced by double portraits and considered to be lucky charms, are regarded as beautiful because they feature an idealized and harmonious relationship with one's Other or one's Self. Devised in the studio's intimate space, where dreams and illusions are composed, these lifelike pictures take shape not through mimesis but because of their fidelity to a mental image. Thus the essence of verisimilitude of the double portrait is not transparency but efficaciousness, the fulfillment of an intent beyond the materiality of the image. The reality of the photographic world becomes a substitute for the real world, setting up the limits of an aesthetic universe within the picture frame. Moreover, dynamic dimension induced by doubles, coupled to a rhythm generated by the replication of (even motionless) figures, is bound to provide visual pleasure. It should also be noted that whereas creating photographic doubles remains a game for some photographers, for others it represents an artistic strategy and a means to initiate thinking on representation and demiurgic power. The motif of the double is thus a genuinely aesthetic construction, though at the same time indivisible from its social uses.

We must bear in mind that most double portraits are for family albums or for friends. They are initially intended for private use. Yet, they become public when they are exhibited on the studios' outside walls, displays or windows, and are therefore exposed to the view and comment of any passer-by. People commission double portraits on social occasions or simply when needed, but they are not only the products of circumstances. Even when less complex images might be found adequate, double portraits have a meaning that extends beyond single or functional portraits and have developed their own artistic form. In choosing stereotypical patterns conveying conceptual models prevalent in many West African countries,[8] the sitters assume that when their portraits are viewed or used people sharing the same cultural code will understand their meaning. As for the skill exhibited by photographers, it stimulates business and demonstrates their talent. Some of them pretend to have invented the processes and techniques used themselves, bust most admit they owe their knowledge to Yoruba and Ghanaians or acquired it from European manuals. Overall, photographers mainly want to prove that they know the conventions of double portraiture and are capable of following and developing them. Replication and repetition of these patterns, sometimes with subtle changes, does not show a lack of inventiveness, but demonstrates an artistic strategy that should be viewed as analogous to the use of replication in sculpture.

The Aesthetic Patterns
Western Art Travels to Africa

Stemming from portrait painting—such as *The Cholmondeley Ladies* (c. 1600–1610), in London's Tate Gallery, portraying identical Tudor women side by side in bed holding their identical babies—the paired-figure portrait motif makes an early appearance in the history of studio photography. It responds to a desire to show family resemblance and possible twinness, whether real or fantasized, in which resemblance comes from closeness or juxtaposition. The duplicated and mirror portrait motifs have been a part of studio activity and artistic research since the invention of photography. Studio photographic fancies were very popular both in Europe and in the United States throughout the nineteenth and up to the beginning of the twentieth century. The historian Clément Chéroux notes the profusion of such photographic games, in which, "through extensive use of double exposure over black backdrops, twins and look-alikes multiplied" (1999: 36). We should keep in mind that these pictures belonged to a cultural movement that held the belief that everyone had a double. "Every Man His Own Twin!" boasted one advertisement (American Museum of Photography 2003). Notions of the doppelganger, essentially drawn from literature, or of an existing clone, were materialized through photography. Perceived as humorous or disturbing make-believes, these doubles made their appearance in photographic studios as the artifacts of photography's powers. Mirror portraits also gave artists and studio photographers the opportunity to probe the notion of an alter ego and to show an invisible world. They were produced to such an extent that they and duplicated portraits became commercialized standards in France up until the 1970s. They still recur periodically in advertising today. One of Labara's mirror portraits (figure 7.4), like Cecil Beaton's mirror portrait *Gertrud Lawrence* (1930) at the London National Portrait Gallery, shows a special pose in which the arms makes a geometrical form that brings the two spaces of the model and her reflection together, in order to form a whole where the twin figures converge. Many twentieth century artists, from avant-gardes to surrealists, up to the practitioners of "plastician photography," developed a deep interest in these portraits.

Western photographers probably introduced such innovative and surprising techniques to Africa, and some motifs were diffused by missionary and colonial postcards, which were a very popular and widespread medium from the end of the nineteenth century up to the 1950s (Geary 1998: 147–162). They certainly reached the coasts of Liberia and Sierra

Leone (see Vididtz-Ward [1999: 36], who points to the introduction of "modern technology and late photographic styles"), and also reached the coasts of Benin and Nigeria when Afro-Brazilian Yoruba returned home. We could also think of stereo photographs that offered double images in nineteenth century Western photography. But I found no oral or bibliographical proof that this trend could have exercised an influence on African double portraits. The first generation of French-speaking African photographers received photographic training in French professional studios implanted in Africa or in France itself, as soldiers, or through apprenticeship. During the post-independence years, the next generation, opened to modernity and its flow of images, adopted Western fashions. These photographers developed an interest in photo magazines and in camera instruction manuals as well as in other media such as cinema and advertising, both of which flourished in the 1970s and more and more frequently featured doubles. The well-known *Photo trucages* (1982) by Pierre Monier and the *Cokin* manual (*Cokin* 1978), which explained techniques of double exposure, were used by some photographers I met in each country, ranging from older practitioners such as Sory (who has kept his own *Cokin* manual copy since 1979), to younger ones like Labara. Sory was also trained by Yoruba and Ghanaian photographers passing through Bobo Dioulasso. Yoruba photographer Shitou often traveled across West Africa seeking contact with Westerners and African colleagues. Hounkanrin has traveled in Europe, received training in Nigeria and learned much from the media. Since the pictures were circulated between Africa and the other continents, this suggests that the portrait conventions used in them originated both outside and inside Africa, where they were adapted and reappropriated to fit in with local tastes and intentions of meaning. Yoruba photography is a good example of this process.

Yoruba Photography

The Yoruba (who live mainly in Nigeria) provide an interesting case study for several reasons. They started practicing photography at an early stage and combined the formal qualities of Victorian-style pictures with their own sculptural aesthetics, as exemplified by the hieratic poses and symmetrical composition of their photographs (Sprague 1978: 107).[9] In the 1970s, and perhaps earlier, they used photography in the *Ibeji* cult of deceased twins, assuming that duplicated portraits could fulfill the same function as ritual figures, as noted by Marilyn Houlberg: "A recent development in Ila-orangun, Igbomina, is the use of photographs to represent deceased twins. The use of the photograph as an active link with the spirit world is unprecedented in the history of photography as far as I know, and certainly warrants further study" (Houlberg 1973: 27).

Yoruba photographers were traders and tireless travelers and many of them emigrated to other countries. They opened professional studios and trained other photographers. They popularized duplicated portraits or *foto ibeji,* and in so doing changed a cult practice into a secular one. Erika Nimis indicates that in the 1970s "these photographic curios were emulated in all the countries hosting Yoruba photographers" (2005: 168). The powerful expression of Yoruba artistic, cultural, and commercial talents and the notable authority bestowed upon them by researchers in West Africa and the U.S.A. certainly explain why they have been the focus of all studies on photographic doubles.

The Influence of Sculpture

Many other photographers besides the Yoruba borrowed aesthetic forms from sculpture. A survey of West African arts might well demonstrate that some formal poses are inherited from sculpture traditions. In double portraits produced by the West African studios, the frontal, symmetric, and hieratic figures standing or sitting with hands on knees, composed and well-balanced, clearly establish a link between photographic portraits and artistic works which preceded them. The former are linked to the latter through a formal and aesthetical legacy, which underlines symbolical and conceptual content, while both have their roots in twin imagery. These links can be observed in many sculptures: in the sculpture commissioned by King Behanzin of Dahomey (1844–1906) representing his ancestors as a pair of twins; in some Dogon figures whose gestural symbolization of twinship is echoed in many portraits; in a Lobi Bateba sculpture evoking the formal and symbolic fusion of twins through a two-headed figure, a frequent composition in photography; in Yoruba, Nago, and Akan sculptures of twins' mothers, whose maternal attitudes find a radical and modern counterpart in similar images representing proud fathers with twins; and finally, in Bambara, Ewe, Fon, and Yoruba twin figurines. In perpetuating (whether consciously or not) certain forms of statuary, photographers have devised representational schemes that are acknowledged and understood by all users. When they were shown pictures of the above-mentioned sculptures, photographers did not deny the connections, and some, like Sory, even openly acknowledged them. We must take into account that the designation and function of these sculptures will vary according to culture and context, and, with Alisa LaGamma, admit that not all couples are necessarily twins. Yet, we must agree with Philip Peek that in "those images variously termed couples, pairs, doubles, dyads, and so on, [. . .] more often than previously recognized twinness is the intended representation" (Peek 2008: 15).

Thus, in perpetuating similar forms, photographers reactualize the acknowledged symbols and images of sculpture, but also secularize their religious dimension using photography's models, means, and techniques. Many examples can be found in the golden age of black-and-white studio photography as well as in today's color and computer-assisted era. The aesthetic and formal origins of twin portraits, along with the circulation of ideas and cultures, point to various sources of inspiration and therefore suggest syncretism. This question of the origins would be irrelevant if we did not analyze the underlying reasons and necessities that have encouraged West African acceptance and use of double portraits—a genre coming partly from Western countries where their cultural context and meanings were different—as twin images for several decades.

A Collective Imagery

Feared and honored in the several cultures of the four countries I am studying, twins are associated with a multitude of rituals that are still practiced today. Twin births have different meanings for each population, but as expressions of power and danger they often echo the origin and order of the world. And in the countries concerned here, this order is perceived as an unstable and unbalanced binary system of sames and opposites in which twinness plays a fundamental role, either because the creator gods are twins, or because twins are protected by the gods (Peek 2008). Twinship once awakened mistrust, awe, and respect, and still does. The occurrence of a twin birth in a family or a social group often led to the group's rejection (de Heusch 1973: 240; Pemberton 2003: 32).[10] Whatever twinship signifies to the people of the four countries studied (identical twin birth, expression of a twin-like relationship between two persons, or definition of oneself as one of a set of real or imaginary twins), it belongs to and permeates artistic, cultural, social, and family life, down to the most ordinary routine. Obviously, twinship, owing to its paradoxical aspect, generates a collective imagery (in the sense of a set of visible and invisible images) shared by cultures reaching beyond the actual borders of West African countries. Though there is variation specific to each culture, I found similar beliefs about twins in several countries and discovered common

cultural ground. Twin imagery relates to mythical, religious, and historical narratives in which twins, seen as gods or human beings, people from
the tangible world or imaginary doubles, are the protagonists. These narratives generate shared images of twins. Hence the pervasiveness of a paradigm that underlies many rituals and practices which create their own
cultural items (now considered by many as artwork) and which produces
objects such as double photo-portraits.

West African twin imagery has abandoned the negative aspects twins
once conveyed, while retaining the paradoxical aspects. This is partly due
to the influence of missionaries who valued all births and regarded them
as positive gifts, but has mainly been the result of the modernization of
West African societies, which have transcended negative superstitions by
distancing themselves from ancient beliefs and rejecting obscurantism as
society became secularized. Through this process, twin imagery has left
visual traces imbued with beauty and protection that are the source of the
images many photography customers now look for. Several studios in Mali,
Burkina, and Togo are named "Jumeaux Color" or "Venavi Photo," thus
placing them under the protection of twins. What is imagery, if not a body
of images selected by people because they are evocative, free their creative
imagination, and reflect who they are (knowingly or unknowingly) at some
point of their history? Traditional and mythical African meanings of twins
do not compete with religions (Christianity and Islam) or cultures adopted
from Western countries. Since they are open to adopting and syncretizing
a variety of cultures, the people I observed and spoke with often give two
names to their twins: a Catholic one drawn from the Bible or a Muslim one
from the Koran, and a local one from ancient African culture. They can
also believe in two different religions (an ancient African one and a recent
African one) without seeing any conflict between them, indeed finding
connections, especially concerning twins: twins are very important, they
appear in every religious history, are protected by God(s), are signs from
the divine, and have special powers. And particularly, they accept two different ways of representing twins with images: by traditional statuettes
derived from very old, local traditions, and through photography coming
from Western cultures. Some examples prove that people are aware of this
mixing of practices, which creates their modern way of living.

Pierre Verger, for instance, noticed and photographed ceremonies dedicated to the Catholic Saints Cosma and Damian, which were syncretized
with the *Ibeji* cult by Afro-Brazilian Yoruba and Fon who had returned to
Benin (Verger 1995: 388).[11] In Porto Novo, I met a Christian family who
had a Vodou shrine dedicated to twins in the yard of their compound,

and named their twin sons Cosma and Damian. In Timbuktu, the Djinga-reiber mosque (built 1325–1330, with architectural elements evoking twin-ness) is highly frequented, for it houses the tombs of twin saints named Allassan and Alousseini (two of the 333 Muslims saints of this old, holy university city). They are honored and respected by all the Tuareg peo-ple, and by many Muslim travelers and Koran scholars coming from Mali as well as the neighboring countries. Allassan and Alousseini are sup-posed to resolve problems and bring happiness because they are twins, and because this twinship recalls Hassan and Hussein, the Prophet Ali's sons, who are considered as twins by Muslim people all over West Africa. Some very popular male twin names not only name, they also describe the person with a condensed and symbolic sentence. For Christian people living in southern countries (Benin and Togo), Cosma and Damian—as well as Jacob and Esau—are obvious references to great twin saints. So are Adama and Awa for female Muslims twins, a reference to Adam and Eve, seen as the twin couple at the origins of the world. In Bobo Dioulasso, Honoré Badjo, who is Catholic, showed me the *Bihionna* protector statue commissioned by his father and his father's twin, who happened to live apart, and which represented the two brothers united. Such a represen-tation, like those of the joined bodies featured in double portraits, as we have already noticed, echoes Victor W. Turner's assertion: "Twinship pres-ents the paradoxes that what is physically double is structurally single and what is mystically one is empirically two" (Turner 1990: 50).

Twin imagery has positive connotations in contemporary societies, especially when it is rendered by symbolic and visually explicit twin images of same-sexed persons. Twin images, as dreams and objects of fantasy, are considered so beautiful, powerful, and beneficial, that people often look for, adopt, and recreate them. From Burkina Faso to Mali, it is not rare to see Muslim children who, even though they are not actual twins—but same-sexed siblings or companions—beg and live as twins usually do at cross-roads, bus stations, and in front of the mosques. They present this twin-like image because they are very attracted by the vision of themselves as twins; as twins they will be able to give and receive blessings. In Bobo Dioulasso, I met two non-twin sisters who are expected by their family to reenact a beautiful and ideal twinship; they are supposed to replace the "missing twinship" resulting from the death of their brother, and thus disruption of both family and social order will be avoided. In Ouagadugu, photog-rapher Joseph Ouedraogo has twin sons named Gilles and Constant, but he also calls them Gueswen and Wenpuire, for the full name/phrase *Gues-wenpuire*, meaning "Look, this is God's share"[12]—in other words, they are

God's sign of a unique soul divided in two male bodies. Joseph Ouedraogo also asserts that he has "twin daughters," showing me their photo taken during their First Communion. The two girls in the picture are in fact his daughter Karine and her younger friend Pascaline, who were brought up together as twins—and regularly photographed as such, which contributed to building their twin-like relationship. Similarly, Ida Mehomey (a photographer in Porto Novo) says that her best friend is her twin sister: "we often buy the same dresses, the same shoes, jewelry, and mobiles; and we ask for our portrait, which fixes the twin image and makes us sure to be seen so."[13] In 2006, the African Cup of Nations opening match (Egypt v. Lybia) was refereed by the famous Burkinabe twin referees Lassana and Housseini Pare (variations on the names Hassan and Hussein), who were invited in order to bring good luck to the football (U.S. soccer) competition. In Mali, an advertisement for Lobo tea uses the duplicated portrait of a man having tea. This strong image of two identical men aims at conveying the friendliness of two same-sexed friends having tea together—and they are perceived as twins. In a Burkinabe schoolbook, a drawing of two identical girls growing up, very similar to a duplicated portrait, is used as a perfect image of twins to illustrate lessons on time scales.

The imagery of twinness described here, which derives from myths, religious beliefs, and mundane aspects of life, is a cultural source that generates many flattering images, which are then demanded as examples and models whenever the self-exhibition of one or two persons in photographs is at stake. In both cases, the portraits commissioned reconstruct twinness by summoning up an actual twin (perceived in another person of the same sex) or an absent, invisible one (but present within oneself and conjured up in the picture with photographic effects). Twinness, as a reflection of the logic of the world and existence, embodies an in-between of merged identities (the Self and the Other), which is essential to achieve oneness. As stereotypes, they are a reflection of the cosmogony myths, a reflection of the world order made of tensions and conflicts, and echo the sacred within the secular. The pictures produced are considered beautiful by their viewers, for they correspond to usage and fulfill aesthetic expectations. As Hounkanrin says: "When I make a duplicated portrait, people think they are looking at a twin portrait. They are not really surprised, because they know a lot of twins, and find them attractive-looking."[14] In these images of twinness people need to look like identical twins and to be seen as twins. Since they resort to shared codes and memories across numerous countries, twin-like photo-portraits are known, recognized, and understood by all. However, they are not simply depictions of twins, in iconographic terms, but function as positive visual representations of role models (even while conveying relationships of precarious stability) that derive from concepts of twinness.

Double portraits may be found in other cultures outside Africa. Christopher Pinney (1997: 124–129, 183–196) refers to a similar tradition of studio portraits in Nagda portraiture (India). According to him, double portraits in Nagda do not intend to represent the twin relation between two persons, but rather suggest "a different conceptualization of the subjects," whose double or triple images are "more likely to represent bodies and faces as infinitely multiple" (1997: 196). Marilyn Houlberg (1988: 3–8; 1992:) finds them in Haiti and links them to Yoruba culture. Although she identifies similarities in the specific uses of photography in both cultures, they are soon put into perspective when she considers them as universal in the context of photographic production, relating, for instance, Haitian double images to surrealist and Dadaist collages, fragmented and juxtaposed images (1992: 65). Yet, she presents an interesting portrait of a woman holding a picture of what seem to be her twin sons. The photograph's caption, "Woman, multiple printed, holding a double image of her son as if he were one of a set of twins. Casimir Photo, Port-au-Prince, 1986" (1988: 8), makes clear that we are seeing the doubled image of a single child. We may think of the Haitian divinities *Marasa* (the Twins), whose powers and mysteries are very close to those of twins in Benin Vodou and in Yoruba culture. *Marasa,* which are sometimes represented by Saints Cosma and Damian, are very familiar in Haitian arts, as exemplified by Pierre-Louis Prospere's paintings (Lerebourg 2000: 68) (for more, see chapter 13). Finally, contemporary artists living in Africa or abroad assert and perpetuate the powerfulness of twin imagery in their works: Rotimi Fani-Kayode's (1955–1989) *Half Opened Eyes Twins* (1989, in Mercer 1996: 34) and Fatima Tuggar's *Lyali (Family)* (1998, in *Rites sacrés rites profanes* 2003: 78) in photography, or Gérard Quenum's *Les jumeaux fantômes* (2000, on www.abawe.com) in sculpture. Fani-Kayode, who was born in Nigeria to a family of Yoruba ancestry and worked for some time in England, owes much to his exploration of Yoruba history, civilization, and cosmology, which inspired some of his most sensitive works. He says that through his investigations "[he] re-discovered and re-assessed some aspects of [his] experience and [his] understanding of the world" (in Mercer 1996: 34). Tuggar (a Yoruba from Nigeria now working in New York) questions the exoticism of an "African" *ibeji* photograph and reverses it in a "trick" photograph, in which she features a framed photographic duplicated portrait of a white American family on the wall behind a black family sitting in an African interior.

Quenum (who lives and works in Porto Novo) uses discarded dolls collected from Western children to represent the Yoruba twins (*ibeji*) or Gun
and Fon twins called *ohovi*, in order to depict a world of horror, suffering,
and violence.

As ordinary studio portraits or souvenir photos, double portraits are not
windows opening onto the outside world but frames within which an
imaginary world may be devised, frames within which "the obvious intent
is not to concede transparency to the photographic image but to recognize
and underline, instead, its nature as chimera" (Oguibe 1996: 246). Double
portraits result from the merging of reappropriated techniques and local
customs. They achieve synthesis by offering a modern conception of the
individual that makes playful use of photography's trickery through twin
figuration, while remaining faithful to the notion of the individual, and
incorporating twin patterns into contemporary forms. Thanks to these
modern forms people invent and control their own image. It is image made
with—and not simply taken by—the image maker, for whom photography
is regarded and employed in the same manner as sculpture or as painting.
Photography as a new artistic means, less clinical than manipulable, is not
associated with objectivity but with the possibility and necessity of illusion. Therefore, the double portraits are at the core of both twinness and
photography and consequently must take their rightful place within the
history of African artistic productions.

NOTES

1. I previously developed such an analysis in an *African Arts* issue (Micheli
2008: 66–85).

2. Surveys were carried out in cities of various sizes: Bamako, Segou, San,
Djenne, Mopti, Tumbuctu in Mali; Bobo Dioulasso, Boromo, Ouagadugu in
Burkina Faso; Cotonou, Porto Novo, Pobe, Abomey, Ouidah, Come, Grand Popo
in Benin; Lome, Aneho, Atakpame in Togo.

3. Interview with Sanlé Sory at Studio Volta Photo, Bobo Dioulasso, February 2004.

4. In the north and south of the geographical area I study, among the Hausa
people from Nigeria, the word *aboki*'s first meaning is "my friend," but when it
refers to a twin, it means "second twin" (interview with Chaibou Baraze, Nigerian
tradesman in the Great Market, Cotonou, January 2006). Robert Brain refers to
a possible link between close friends and twins among the Bangwa people from
Cameroon (1971: 215).

5. It is outside the scope of this chapter to fully develop the concept of the
"person's double." Briefly, however, it is the person's image, shadow, or reflection,

sometimes his twin, which is captured by photography. Through photography, individuals construct their identities, both single and multiple, and do not only aim at expressing twinship. This ever-changing identity is composed of different strata, like a palimpsest, combining tradition and modernity, collective and private history. Different traditional aspects of the "person" are given in *La Notion de personne en Afrique noire* (1973), and Marie (1997).

6. Interview with Koda C. Labara, at Studio Image Plus, Lome, Togo, January 2005.

7. Interview with Ibrahim Shitou, at Studio Photo Kodak, Mopti, January 2003.

8. These models have been noticed as stereotypes in Gambia (Buckley 2000–2001: 84), Côte d'Ivoire (Werner 1996: 103), Ghana (Wendl 1999: 152), of course in Nigeria (Sprague 1978: 59; Nimis 2005: 168), but also in the Democratic Republic of the Congo (Fall 1996: 33).

9. Sprague published one of the first *ibeji* photo-portraits in this article: an anonymous late twentieth century photograph now in the collection of the University of Arizona (1978: 56)

10. One must note that in eastern Nigeria and among people from southern Nigeria, twins were sometimes killed because their existence threatened social and family order or because they were considered as adulterous offspring.

11. See also http://www.pierreverger.org/fr/photos/photos_themetree.php.

12. Interview with J. Ouedraogo, at Photo Video Neb-Nooma, Ouagadougou, January 2006.

13. Interviews with I. Mehomey, at Studio Photo Vedette, Porto Novo, January 2006 and 2010.

14. Interview with M. Hounkanrin, at Zoom Photo service, Cotonou, January 2005.

WORKS CITED

Abawé. Gérard Quenum Webpage. www.abawe.com/fr/butinage/creation_579 _2.htm

American Museum of Photography. 2003. "Seeing Double: Creating Clones with a Camera." http://www.photographymuseum.com/seeingdouble.html.

Behrend, Heike. 2001. "Fragmented Visions: Photo Collages by Two Ugandan Photographers," in "Photographies and Modernities in Africa." *Visual Anthropology* 14 (3): 301–320.

Behrend, Heike, and Tobias Wendl. 1997. "Photography: Social and Cultural Aspects." In *The Encyclopedia of Africa, South of the Sahara,* vol. 3, ed. J. Middletown, 409–415. New York: Simon & Schuster.

Bonnet, Doris. 1981–1982. "La Procréation, la femme et le genie (Les Mossi de Haute Volta)." *Cahiers de l'O.R.S.T.O.M., Sér. Sciences Humaines* 18 (4): 425–430.

Brain, Robert. 1971 [1969]. "Friends and Twins in Bangwa." In *Man in Africa,* ed. Mary Douglas and Phyllis M. Kaberry, 214–228. London: Tavistock.

Buckley, Liam. 2000–2001. "Gambian Studio Photography." *Visual Anthropology* 16 (2, Fall/Winter): 71–91.

Cartry, Michel. 1973. "Introduction." In *La Notion de personne en Afrique noire,* ed. Germaine Dieterlen, 15–31. Paris: C.N.R.S./L'Harmattan.

Chéroux, Clément. 1999. "Avant l'Avant-garde: Une archéologie de la modernité photographique." In *Vive les modernités,* Catalogue of the XXXeme Rencontres Internationales de la photographie d'Arles, 35–43. Arles, France: Actes Sud.

Cokin, Creative Filter System. 1978. Photography manual in several languages. Paris: Cokin. (A recent version can be consulted on the Cokin website: www.cokin.fr/.)

De Heusch, Luc. 1973. "Le Sorcier, le père Tempels et les jumeaux mal-venus." In *La notion de personne en Afrique noire,* ed. Germaine Dieterlen, 231–242. Paris: C.N.R.S./L'Harmattan.

Dieterlen, Germaine. 1973. "L'image du corps et les composantes de la personne chez les Dogon." In *La notion de personne en Afrique noire,* ed. Germaine Dieterlen, 205–229. Paris: C.N.R.S./L'Harmattan.

———. 1981. "Jumeaux: l'un des thèmes dominants des mythologies d'Afrique occidentale." In *Dictionnaire des Mythologies,* vol. 1, ed. Yves Bonnefoy, 614–617. Paris: Flammarion, 1981.

———. 1988 [1951]. *Essai sur la religion bambara.* Bruxelles: Editions de l'Université de Bruxelles, 1988.

Drewal, Henry John, and Margaret Drewal Thompson. 1983. *Gelede: Art and Female Power among the Yoruba.* Bloomington: Indiana University Press.

Fall, N'Goné. 1996. "Le Maître du Studio: un Passeur de Rêves." In *Photographies Kinshasa,* ed. N'Goné Fall. Paris: Revue noire.

Geary, Christraud M. 1998. "Different Visions? Postcards from Africa by European and African Photographers and Sponsors." In *Delivering Views: Distant Cultures in Early Postcards,* ed. Christraud M. Geary and Virginia-Lee Webb, 147–177. Washington, D.C.: Smithsonian Institution Press.

Griaule, Marcel. 1966. *Dieu d'Eau: Entretiens avec Ogotemmêli.* Paris: Fayard.

Houlberg, Marilyn. 1973. "Ibeji Images of the Yoruba." *African Arts* 7 (1): 27.

———. 1988. "Feed Your Eyes: Nigerian and Haitian Studio Photography." *Photographic Insight* 1 (2/3): 3–8.

———. 1992. "Haitian Studio Photography: A Hidden World of Images," in "Haiti Feeding the Spirit." *Aperture* 126: 58–65.

Krauss, Rosalind. 1990. *Le Photographique, pour une théorie des écarts.* Paris: Macula.

LaGamma, Alisa. 2004. *Echoing Images: Couples in African Sculpture.* New York: Metropolitan Museum of Art / New Haven, Conn.: Yale University Press.

Le Moal, Guy. 1973. "Quelques aperçus sur la notion de personne chez les bobo." In *La Notion de personne en Afrique noire,* ed. Germaine Dieterlen, 193–203. Paris: C.N.R.S./L'Harmattan.

Lerebourg, Michel-Philippe. 2000. "L'Esprit des Loas." In *Haïti: Anges et Démons,* ed. Martine Lusardy, 7-17. Paris: Hoëbecke/La Halle Saint-Pierre.

Marie, Alain, ed. 1997. *L'Afrique des individus.* Paris: Karthala.

Mercer, Kobena, Ferek Bishton, Simon Njami, Jean-Loup Pivin. 1996. *Rotimi Fani-Kayode et Alex Hirst.* Paris: Revue noire / London: Autograph.

Mercier, P. 1999. (1954). "The Fon of Dahomey." In *African Worlds*, ed. Daryll Forde, 210-234. Oxford: Currey Publishers / Hamburg: LIF Verlag.

Micheli, C. Angelo. 2008. "Doubles and Twins: A New Approach to Contemporary Studio Photography in West Africa." *African Arts* 41 (1): 66–85.

Monier, Pierre. 1982 [1972]. *Photo trucages.* Paris: Montel.

Nimis, Érika. 2005. *Photographies d'Afrique de l'Ouest: L'expérience yoruba.* Paris: Karthala / Ibadan, Nigeria: IFRA.

La Notion de personne en Afrique noire. 1973. Actes du colloque du C.N.R.S., October 11–17, 1971. Paris: C.N.R.S./L'Harmattan.

Oguibe, Olu. 1996. "Photography and the Substance of the Image." In *In-sight: African Photographers, 1940 to the present*, ed. Clare Bell, Okwui Enwezor, and David Tilkin, 231–250. New York: Solomon R. Guggenheim Foundation.

Peek, Philip M. 2008. "Couples or Doubles? Representations of Twins in the Arts of Africa." *African Arts* 41 (1): 14–23.

Pemberton, John, III. 2003. "Ere Ibeji: une affirmation de la vie face à la mort." In *Ibeji, le culte des jumeaux Yoruba*, ed. George Chemeche, John Pemberton III, John Picton, 30–48. Milan: 5 Continents.

Pinney, Christopher. 1997. *Camera Indica: The Social Life of Indian Photographs.* Chicago: University of Chicago Press / London: Reaktion Books Ltd.

Pison, Gilles. 1988. "Les jumeaux: fréquence, statut social, et mortalité," in "Mortalité et Société au sud du Sahara." *Population* 43 (6, November–December): 1127–1134.

Rites sacrés rites profanes. 2003. Catalogue of the 5ème Rencontres de la photographie africaine de Bamako, October 20–26, 2003. Paris: Éric Koehler.

Sprague, Steven F. 1978. "Yoruba Photography: How the Yoruba See Themselves." *African Arts* (12, November): 52–59, 107.

Turner, Victor W. 1990. *Le Phénomène rituel: Structure et contre-structure.* Paris: P.U.F. (First published as *The Ritual Process: Structure and Antistructure.* Chicago: Aldine Publishing Co., 1969).

Verger, Pierre Fatumbi. 1995 [1954]. *Dieux d'Afrique.* Paris: Revue Noire.

Vididtz-Ward, Vera. 1999. "Les Créoles de Freetown." In *Anthologie de la photographie africaine et de l'Océan indien*, ed. Pascal Martin Saint Léon and N'Goné Fall, 34-41. Paris: Revue noire.

Vogel, Susan. 1991. "Digesting the West." In *Africa Explores: Twentieth-Century African Art*, ed. Susan Vogel, 14–31. New York: Center for African Art / Munich: Prestel.

Wendl, Tobias. 1999. "Portrait et décors." In *Anthologie de la photographie africaine et de l'Océan indien*, ed. Pascal Martin Saint Léon and N'Goné Fall, 152. Paris: Revue noire.

Werner, Jean-François. 1996. "Produire des images en Afrique: l'exemple des photographes de studio." *Cahiers d'études africaines* 36, 1–2 (141–142): 103.

Part Three

The Centrality of Liminality

CHAPTER EIGHT

Forever Liminal

Twins among the Kapsiki/Higi of North Cameroon and Northeastern Nigeria

WALTER E. A. VAN BEEK

Twins and the Color Red

Twins, the Kapsiki[1] say, crave the color red and react so strongly to it that nobody should wear red in their vicinity. During the dance for another twin, a young woman, Kwandè, herself a twin, suddenly faints on seeing a small boy with a slightly reddish shirt. People flock around her, rip the shirt off the boy, put it on her head and start dancing around her: "*Kwalerha* that came to dance, *kwalerha* to dance." The mother of the twin for whom the festival was organized searches out some *sesele* and *tere* grasses,[2] calls her loudly: "Stand up, twin, stand up," and beats her with the twigs. After some time she starts trembling all over her body. People then help her stand on her feet, and she slowly opens her eyes. Finally she walks away, unsure on leaden legs.

Kwandè described the event to me:

> When I see something like that, everything becomes dark around me,
> and I hear the voices of everybody from very far away. Everything I really
> like—meat, red necklaces, red clothes, but also white clothes when they
> are beautiful—I should not look at them. It only happens when I fix my
> eyes upon it, when I keep on looking, but sometimes I cannot help it. To
> bring me around, another twin, or the father of a twin, has to beat me with
> *tere* grass. Once I did the same to another twin woman who had fainted,
> I beat her with the grass, but when she regained consciousness, I fainted
> myself. If something is really beautiful, two twins might faint at the same
> time.

FIGURE 8.1. Kwandè is brought out of trance, Kila 1973. *Photo: Walter Van Beek*

The Fascination of Twins

Though twins do occur more often in Africa than anywhere else, this demographic fact alone does not adequately explain the deep cultural involvement of Africa with double births. After all, scarcity can as easily account for cultural fascination as can relative abundance. Twins are Africa's fascination, and it shows: both in African literature and African ethnography twins feature far beyond their demographical importance. African literature both oral and written is replete with twins. In his recent novel *Measuring Time* (2007) Helon Habila tells the story of a pair of twins, two brothers with very different characteristics, one suffering from sickle cell anemia, the other a rambunctious youth. Together they make up more or less one whole character, and the captivating story uses the "double personality" to weave together the many strands of Nigerian society. As for oral literature, folk tales abound with twins in a huge variety of roles (Merolla 2007; Savary and Gros 1995).

The main aspect that strikes the eye in ethnography is ambivalence. For Central and Southern Africa Schoffeleers has compared the mythic roles of twins versus those of unilateral figures, finding an association between symmetry and social strife, while asymmetry seems to stand for social order (Schoffeleers 1991). And twins are the epitome of symmetry. Dugast points to the Bassar of Togo for a ritual association of twins with diviners and murderers (Dugast 1996). But also more mundane than myth, ambivalence reigns around twins. In many African cultures twins have their own special names, either as a variant on birth order names, as in Dogon, or as an expression of the frequency of twin births in a family. And, more mundane still, the judicial system in many parts of Africa wrestles with twins. In Zimbabwean colonial history the murder of twins by their mother was an offence the colonial administration struggled with (Zimudzi 2004), while also the apparent conflict between twinhood and rules of primogeniture provided some intricate legal puzzles (MacClendon 1997). In Nigeria, closer to the lands of the Kapsiki, the whole gamut of ambivalence of twin treatment can be found, from special veneration to "mercy killing," which today is constructed as "euthanasia" (Onimhawo 1996).

So, what is the matter with twins in Africa? It is not so much identical twins that fascinate Africa; that particular fascination is for the scientific West with its deep involvement in genetics and its insistence on the uniqueness of the individual (Zazzo 1993). In Africa it is the fact of being born together that is relevant: children born of the same mother at the same time whether identical or nonidentical twins are equally significant (Gros 1995: 30). Whereas the West wonders about two people without individualized biological differences, Africa is obsessed with the notion of two people sharing the same social space and time, two people with identical relations. In these kin-based societies identity stems from relations with preexistent groups, so the existence of two people who occupy the same space at the same time is essentially problematic. How does a society deal with the definition of personhood for these kinsmen? How does this "overflow of fertility" affect the relations between their kinsmen, and how do the rituals and symbols address the problems of identity construction?

In this contribution I want to focus on the way the Kapsiki of North Cameroon and northeastern Nigeria solve this problem of identity construction. Ambivalence and liminality will be shown to be dominant aspects, offering a window into Kapsiki conceptions of personhood and dynamics of identity construction. This we shall explore through an analysis of the symbols and rituals surrounding the twin birth, for these constitute expressions of and signals for the space to be allotted to these "double persons."

Interpretation of ritual is notoriously difficult. My approach sets off from the notions of positional and exegetical meanings of symbols (Turner 1975), in which the meaning of symbols is not treated as a cryptography, but as an emergent reality, specific in time and setting (Sperber 1975). But the theoretical position on ritual has shifted since Turner and Sperber. Ritual theory has developed through the work of Staal (1989), Rappaport (1999) and Bell (1997), while the general position of ritual inside religious theory has received a boost from the "modes of religiosity" theory of Harvey Whitehouse (2004, 2007). My approach is the following: in principle ritual has no evident message (Van Beek 2007) but forms a self-referential system in which a semantic vacuum is created that invites participants and analysts to attribute meaning themselves. So any analysis is for a large part a construct in which I attribute meaning to rituals and symbols, based upon informants' expressions, my observation, the internal logic of symbols both in the ritual action and versus each other (these are Turner's "positional" and "exegetical" meanings), and my proclivity toward systematization. For example, most symbols analyzed are part and parcel of the general ritual corpus of the collective *rites de passage* and my attribution of meaning derives from their position in that corpus. Some symbols are highly specific for births or for twins, and these demand separate interpretation. So I use rituals and symbols as a "monitoring instrument" (Van Beek and Blakely 1994: 11) to glean insights into cultural definitions of "double selves."

Twins and Other Special Births

The Kapsiki distinguish five kinds of special births: breech births, *ghi* (no prior menstruation), *matini* (no intervening menstruation), multiple births (i.e., twins and the much rarer triplets), and *dlave*. The latter term refers to a child born with a caul, where the birth membrane remains on its head. The Kapsiki call this *dlave,* as if it has a piece of "cloth" on its head. The *dlave* will be removed, dried, and put in a medicine container, worn either on a bracelet or a *mblaza,* a medicine container worn around the waist. These children are the ones that will be rich, and if male marry a lot of women, beget a great number of children, and gain a lot of money, making them rich in both Kapsiki senses, in people and in material goods. Also, their curse carries a lot of weight, as does the curse of all "special people".

A breech birth is considered mainly a problem during birth, as the reversed position will endanger the lives of mother and child. However, if the baby survives, it will still present some danger to both parents. To avoid problems, they will have a blacksmith make two specific bracelets which they will wear for the rest of their lives, each consisting of two parallel strips of iron, one straight, one twisted. For twins, as we shall see, the double-stranded type is indicated for the parents, either as a bracelet or as a ring.

A child conceived without prior menstruation of his mother, known as a *ghi,* is a big hazard. Such a child presents an extreme danger for the father, for he runs a serious risk of dying before the child is initiated. However, there is no risk that cannot be combated. In case of a *ghi* baby, the father makes a hole in the straw roof of his own hut, and then pushes the baby through the hole. Then he removes part of the child's left earlobe. The risk is still there but reduced. Now the father may see this boy through initiation, or this daughter through *makwa,* her first marriage.

According to the Kapsiki, for the first month after birth a woman is considered especially fertile; if the next child is conceived immediately, the first one will become a *matini,* a child without milk, as the lactation is interrupted too quickly, and its health is jeopardized. If a *matini* survives, people reckon it will stay small, puny, and not grow up well. Still, examples of *matini* growing up well are known, and avoidance is not total. The curse of such an individual is feared, which gives these weak ones some power.

By far the most important and the most complicated special babies are twins, *kwalerha.* As so often in Africa, twins are a category *sui generis.* The Kapsiki love them and fear them, are proud of them and shun them at the same time. They are not "of this world"; "twins are like *gutuli,* spirits that roam the bush, children of *shala.*" They are not easy to live with. They tax those around them to the limit. Quick to take offence, and especially quick to take a liking to some beautiful object, they get angry on the spot, and then become dangerous. They have to have their way in all things; whenever they take a liking for some object, people have to hand it over to them. If they do not have their way, the Kapsiki say they will go into a trance and faint, or in Kapsiki parlance, "die"; in doing so they heap curses upon the unhappy owner of the object. This puts tremendous pressure on the twins' parents, especially the father. Tlakema, an adult twin, described it to me: "Us twins, we are no normal people, we are from *shala.* If we 'die,' the fault is on the father; the mother has been chosen already by *shala,* but if the father does something wrong, the twin children will know it immediately. The heaviest responsibility is on the father." Not only do twins faint when people refuse them something, the thing that is refused will be spoilt as well. They have to taste the beer first, otherwise it will not ferment properly; food will rot if their presence is not honored with the first bite. All in all, having twins in the family is quite a challenge, almost a mission impossible.

Scorpions form their most spectacular power base. They "command the scorpions," which means they may send the beasts to anyone who thwarts them. Not only consciously but also unconsciously, they can harm anyone they do not really like. Scorpions cannot harm twins, as they seem to be immune to the scorpion's sting. Twins like to boast a little bit. According to Tlakema "People cannot truly keep us twins alive, as each time we want something, we get angry in our hearts. Only *shala* can keep us well, as everything spoils us." Twins, if both are alive, stay close to each other in marriage, marrying close relatives if possible, and a twin sister will not leave the village if her twin brother is still there. Marrying a twin is considered hazardous indeed: "If a man is married to a *kwalerha,* he cannot even beat her without her dying on him." Still, I have not been able to find an example of a twin marrying another twin, the obvious way out of this dilemma. Overall twins live lives like most others, though they are respected, their wishes are seldom crossed, and they always have the weapons of trance and scorpions.

So, parents of twins face a huge challenge. In order not to have the anger of the children descend too easily on their heads, the parents order four bracelets, *takase kwalerha,* from a blacksmith for themselves and the twins. As long as they wear these *takase* the twins' powers will not be harmful. The beer will be right when the twins taste it, the sorghum will flourish when they touch it, and especially the sesame will ripen when they look at it. In daily life the twins also wear a band of 'yanka grass on their wrists, and carry some cowrie shells and sesame in their pockets. Of all crops, sesame is theirs. They have to eat it often, they smell it from afar, and no one can pass them with sesame without their knowing it.

Twins are associated with rain; as an "overstatement of fertility," this is one of the obvious associations. So, during the birth of twins rain is expected to fall. All informants testified that this usually happened, and I myself witnessed three twin births; all happened in the rainy season and were accompanied by heavy rainstorms. Fundamentally, twins are not of this earth, but of heaven. More than anything else this shows in their dreams. They dream not of the "underworld" but of the "overworld"; their "shadow" does not descend into the earth when dreaming like those of normal people but ascends on high. In the words of Kwandè:

We, as twins, we dream of heaven. There we drink white water and we find people like here; they are our *shala*. One particular white-haired woman I know very well, she is my *shala,* who has created me. An old woman, her hair all white. If I die, I will know such in advance. After my death, my *shinangkwe* [shadow] will not go down into the earth, but will return to heaven. When as a twin you do not dream of heaven, you will die.

When dreaming in heaven, we see other twins. We do not fight. We do nothing in secret, everything is public. It is our *mehele* [character]; *shala* [the personal god] has made us so.

The Kapsiki recognize that twins occur more in some families than others; in Kwandè's family she can count eight pairs of twins. On the other hand, twin births seldom come as the first children of a woman. The actual births of twins should be easy and fast, quick and unexpected, and twins often seem to be born outside the house. For example, Kwatere, Belama's wife, gave birth in another ward; she was not known to carry twins, but both little girls were born healthy and sound. Later, her husband consulted the crab diviner, and following instructions sacrificed two chickens and left indigenous vinegar with some ground millet soaked in water on the spot where she had given birth. He then closed off the spot with thorns and stones, all to prevent the *shala* of the place from following her home.

Feasting a Twin

Twins have different names, eschewing the normal birth order names, and their names are usually chosen following the instructions of a crab diviner. Boys are called Pimbi, Mara, or Puhu; girls Kwandè or Kwalerha.

The actual first rites for twins follow those for a single child but are much more elaborate and use a different set of symbols. Everything is done in two: for the first announcement and naming ceremony for a twin, the father butchers two chickens, sexed according to the sexes of the twins, and has to produce two identical calabashes, two halves of the same fruit, for the babies to drink from. Word of the birth of twins rapidly spreads through the village. When the expected baby turns out to be a pair of twins, in the late evening after the actual birth the father warns his clan brothers from all over the village. They assemble in the hut of the *yitiya kwalerha* (twins' father), as he is now called, early the next morning. All come with their gift of chickens, and the younger ones bring a long band of white cloth which they string up between the huts of the father and mother of the

twins, the latter now called *miyakwalerha* (twins' mother). The two parents
are one for the rest of time, both to be addressed in their new dignity. Early
the same morning the twins' father will have asked the chief blacksmith
for some *hwèbè kwalerha,* the special strand of *Cissus quadrangularis* that
is used to ward off evil from these young children. Other measures may be
taken following the instructions of the crab diviner.

Each guest brings along, besides a chicken, a small gift for the father,
holding out to him a handful of sesame and a handful of eleusine grass (*Eleusine indica*). To the mother they present small coins and quartz pebbles,
offering them at the same time held in different hands. The sesame and
eleusine grains are cooked and eaten by the guests. After eating and some
dancing and singing they return home. That evening the father arranges
the "interrogation" of his twins. He calls for an adult twin, another Pimbi
or Kwalerha, to conduct the interview. Tlakema Pimbi, a twin of some 45
years of age, does the "interview" for the twins of Zra Dabala, a young
father of twins. Before entering the hut of mother Kuve, he asks her to lie
down facing the wall of the hut. He then enters, greeting the children with
"Good afternoon, my people." The baby closest to the door starts crying,
and both babies thrash their legs and arms and turn upon their backs. This,
says Tlakema, means that there will be dancing now. What will happen
later at the *shave,* the feast of coming out and naming, the crab diviner will
tell. Tlakema explains that the crying, thrashing, and the babies' heartbeat
give him the answers to his questions. The interview lasts two hours. Afterward Tlakema goes straight to Zra Dabala's older clan-brother to report
the interview; the twins' father, in turn, gets his instructions from his older
brother. In the case of Zra Dabala these are quite elaborate:

> You take a club and a shield, your wife Kuve takes the little mat she uses
> for the millet mush and the stick for stirring the mush, and both of you
> pretend to quarrel, really hard. Someone else should calm and separate
> you, and after that you two may never quarrel again.
>
> Once the umbilical cord falls off, you have to sleep with the twins'
> mother once, lest she becomes infertile. Then you grind some yellow and
> white sorghum in water and have the babies drink it. Do not put red clay
> on their navels, they do not like that, just a bit of oil is enough.
>
> From then on, you always have to provide two bowls of sauce, two
> pieces of mush, two calabashes with water and two bowls of meat, all of
> it for their mother. The sesame I have given you, you apply with your left
> hand on the mother's vulva and with your right hand on your own penis,
> in order to have children again.

People coming to greet you have to present eleusine grains and sorghum in their two hands. What your clan brings you keep, and your wife
keeps what her clan presents to her; if this is not done, then "simple people" [non-twins] cannot enter her hut. Pebbles have to be thrown before
her door. Everything has to happen in twos, for example two chickens
each day. Your wife has to tie a bell at her wrist to warn the babies each
time she enters their hut [i.e., her own hut]. It is not good to visit twins
without warning.

The cloth between your two huts has to have a little bit of red on it to
prevent the twins asking for red things from other people.

Now enter, Zra, I have put sesame on their mat. If they are real twins
[i.e., if they behave as twins should] then they will have the sesame in their
hands.

Zra, upon entering the hut, finds the sesame in the tiny fists of the twins,
and follows the instructions to the letter. His wife, however, is too weak for
the mock battle, and her sister replaces her. That evening the youngsters of
the ward come for the all-important dance, and sing out loud:

Our twins, people from the heavens,
Black sesame, Kwandè from heaven,
Twins for the dance, our twins,
Sesame of the heavens,
Who has come down from heaven to dance.
Why did you come, black sesame?
Thing of our ancestors; he did not start it.
There is a lizard hidden, Kwandè.
I saw the house of the rat,
But Kwandè had already seen it.

The children greet the twins the same way as the adults, with handfuls
of millet and sorghum which they put into a bowl close to the children.
Almost everybody asks: "Why did you come?" Did you come "to dance or
to cry," i.e., to live or to die? The twins' father cooks *zhazha,* a mixture of
millet grains, beans and, in this case sorghum grains, a habitual ritual dish
of which the children who greet the twins have to partake just a little bit:
two grains of millet and two seeds of eleusine.

All in all, this naming ceremony uses the format of the single birth but is
much more complicated. For single births, the father invites the next of

kin, kills a chicken, has a co-wife prepare mush with a special sauce made for the occasion. When the people from the neighborhood and his lineage brothers are gathered in his forecourt, the father expresses his gratitude in a short speech, and everybody eats. As always among the Kapsiki, the distribution of the meat—in this case the chicken—marks the occasion: the wings and toes for the new mother, the breast and feet for the baby's father and his father, and the rest for the midwife. Also, in this case, his wife will leave the compound much quicker to take up her normal tasks, and the waiting time for the next ritual is an easy one.

In the case of a twin birth, the period between this first naming and the ritual leaving of the compound is not an easy one for the father. As long as his wife remains inside the compound walls, he has to procure two chickens each day for her to eat. As she may stay inside from two to four months, this amounts to an astonishing number of fowl. If poor, he may restrict it a little, but a minimum of thirty chickens is still sizeable. But, again, his clansmen will help him. In these months Zra Dabala scours the market, from start till the night, dressed in his finest outfit, wearing a bracelet of *wetle*,[3] the same grass his wife wears as a girdle, to indicate his status as *yitiyakwalerha*, asking all kin and visitors for a gift, a contribution, a chicken. Hard work, but well worth the trouble, as he easily collects a dozen chickens at the weekly market. Later markets at the end of the seclusion period again see him "beg" but less successfully.

Whenever there is beer to drink, his will be the first calabash to be filled, before that of the chief, as bad thoughts from a father of twins count as a curse for the village. Twins are like the evil eye, and their parents share that power.

Then the time for the big festival nears, two months after birth in the wet season, four in the less busy dry season. Both father and mother of the twins separately consult the crab diviner to know the specifics for the feast, special sacrifices, special arrangements, special taboos. Zra Dabala is told he should not dance during or after the feast, nor should he brew too much beer (red beer, *tè*). His sacrifice is the following: a cockscomb; some sorghum from a man and some from a woman; the testicles of a male goat and a few hairs from a small goat have to be mixed and some of it put on the *melè*, the sacrificial jar. The rest Zra has to throw outside the wall of the compound, with the words: "You children have to be in health and remain healthy." His wife, for the twins to be well, has to grind pieces of nanny and male goat bones, and spit a little bit of the mixture on the twins and their *melè* (two stones) and throw the rest away in a similar fashion. For herself she must cook porridge from sorghum sprouts and put a jar with the porridge on the road to Ldiri, her native village. The crab diviner warns her not to visit her father's home, contrary to the typical custom before a feast. This coming-out feast, *shave,* for single children is a small thing, just for some neighbors and close kinsmen. With twins, however, it is a large event that unites both clans, and the *hwelefwe* (matri- and bilateral kin) of both parents. It is the father who sets the date, buys two goats and everything else for the feast.

At Zra Dabala's twin festival, his clansmen, the *kangacè,* flock into his compound early in the morning, with me included, for I am *ngacè* as well. The village chief is also with them to advise the young father, who has never conducted such a ceremony before and feels quite insecure. Zra has brewed twelve jars of *tè,* red beer, and—having only one wife—has asked his brother's wife to brew twelve jars of *mpedli,* white beer, as the twins are a boy and a girl. The old clansmen seat themselves in the place of honor in the forecourt and gracefully accept their two jars of *tè.* Zra, in the usual cryptic explanation the Kapsiki use on such occasions, says "This is not something common. I have made just two jars, and as you happen to be here, please taste a little bit." The village chief comforts him, "No apology is needed for the paucity of the beer. You just do what you can do and what you have to do. May *shala* help you and give you health."

When the clan elders have drunk, Zra's father's brother takes the lead in the sacrifice of the sheep, a ram, and a ewe. Two of Zra's sister's sons perform their ritual duty and cut the throat of the sheep at the same time, one at the father's hut, the other at the mother's, at the signal of the older man. They carefully collect the blood in a bowl, later to be used for the sacrifice on the jar.

They skin and butcher the animals. Their own immediate reward is the pancreas, the neck, and the colon of their beast, and they hand the third stomach to the boy that has herded the animals. The elders of both the mother's and the father's clans get the sheep heads. Zra then kills two chickens (a hen and a rooster), as is done each day for the mother of the twins. The women of Zra's lineage cook one sheep, and the women of the mother's patrilineage cook the other for their kinswoman at her hut, at the same time as the sister's sons are spending time preparing the skins to be carrying slings for the twins. Some cowrie shells are sown on the skins, two shells on each sling to symbolize a twin. The sister's sons carefully cut some strips of skin with hair from the slings. The twins will wear these, as will some of their matrilateral kinsmen. The strips with hair are called *mnta* and are a symbol of initiation, as we will see below.

The sun is already high when the preparations are complete. The sister's sons have eaten, the slings are ready and decorated, and the babies, their mother, her close kin, and the midwife wear the *mnta,* the strips of skin with hair, on their left wrists. The lineage of Kuve is gathered in her hut, the lineage of the father in his hut. The wives of both lineages are seated in the brewery, while a few guests from other clans and important elders such as the village chief are seated in the entrance hut, *dabala* (it still is the end of the rainy season), while curious visitors are scattered around the rest of the compound. Zra Dabala and his *hwelefwe* (matrilateral kinsmen) tie strips of *peha*[4] around their foreheads, the most visible sign of being connected with a twin. Then people drink and later eat. The *kangacè* in Zra's hut drink from his sacrificial jar.

After drinking and eating, the moment of *shave* has come. Yelling with delight, the clansmen take their respective twin-parents on their shoulders and carry them out of the compound. The other kinsmen, shouting and yelling, walk out of the compound and take off the twin parents' *peha* in the wall opening. Zra and his wife quietly wait for the majority of the villagers to leave, and then walk back into the house with their *peha*. With their closest kin and some neighbors assisting, the usual ritual of the *shave* of the twins themselves starts, the same way as with single children. A few women watch the mother come out of her hut with the midwife and stand in the opening of the wall, bending over. The other women rub oil and ochre over her back, and the midwife positions the young baby on the mother's back—upside-down! A loud chorus of "*awu, awu*" (no, no!) greets this "mistake," so the midwife tries again. Again "no, no," wrong position. Four times the baby is put the wrong way on its mother's back; finally the midwife gets it right; "*ee, ee*" (yes, yes!), all the women shout their acclaim. One of the sisters of the new mother then puts on the *hwetu,* the baby sling; twice wrong—"*awu, awu*"—and finally right—"*ee, ee.*" A young sister of Kuve plays the second mother for the second twin. For the first time, with the babies upright and well tied up on their backs, both women quickly walk through the wall opening, into the forecourt. Into the middle of this forecourt they throw some goat dung, and make cultivating motions with the handle of a hoe they hold in their right hand. The other women, in a similar quick trot, follow them, sprinkling water on the dung and on the mother's buttocks. As there is to be no dancing—on the instructions of the crab diviner—the guests then leave. Also, Kuve will not visit her father for some time—contrary to standard practice—as advised by the same crab diviner. In twin rituals every standard action is put into question, and divination reigns. As in the first ritual, the general format is that of the single birth, but much more elaborate and especially closely informed by divination in all relevant details. The rest of the year the twins are not shown much in the village. They remain a little bit marginal, and the mother and father will demand special attention from anyone they may encounter. This period ends with the first cutting of their hair about a year after their birth. Then the *hwelefwe* of both parents gather in the compound early in the morning, each around the hut of their kin. All kinsmen have their heads shaved while sipping the beer Zra has prepared, the "beer to shave the head." The band of cloth that linked the huts of Zra and Kuve from the very moment of twin birth now is removed. The actual feast is almost a reenactment of the *shave* ritual: two goats, male and female, are skinned, butchered, and boiled. People drink, eat, and give blessings. The young girls of the wife's clan take care of cooking the mush. Before the meal, the *yityaberhe* of Kuve, a kinsman living at close quarters and acting as a substitute father who watches over her wellbeing in her husband's compound, takes a bowl of sesame sauce, prepared by Kuve's mother's sister, and sprinkles the sauce over the two babies, who rest in the arms of two sisters: "You have to be healthy, to be healthy, to dance the *la*-festival [final part of initiation]." The mush, beer, and meat are distributed, and people drink and eat. Finally, Zra's mother's brother addresses Zra's *melè* and pours a calabash of red beer over it: "*Shala, Jigelafte,*[5] everybody must be healthy, all must marry wives and have children in order to have the *hwelefwe* continue. Let him (addressing the boy) marry a good wife who will not run away, but a good wife who stays." He pours beer on the *melè*, spits on the posts of Zra's hut, on Zra himself, and drinks. Then Zra and his other kinsmen drink.

The next morning Kuve and Zra plant two trees, *mekweda,*[6] in one of their fields. They put a hollow stone, an old grinding slab, close to the saplings, and water them regularly. Those trees will never be touched, nor will anyone ever cut their branches for firewood, as they directly represent the twins. Should anyone cut a branch, the corresponding twin will fall ill, while cutting the tree would cause the death of the twin.

Later, the twins will perform their sacrifices on those trees, using them as a kind of second *melè*. For instance, before a twin girl marries her first spouse, before performing her *makwa* rites, she will dress herself in her straw cape, her iron skirt, and wrap some cloths around her body. Then she takes two jars of *tj*, one sheep, and one goat to the trees. She cuts some branches from both trees, and then slaughters and butchers the animals on the spot, letting the blood run over the branches. She will use these branches to build the roof of the alcove of her hut.

The twins have now been introduced to their *hwelefwe*, their kinsmen, as well as to their clan and lineage. In all rituals pertaining to twins, individual rites for healing or sacrifice, as well as during their participation in collective rites, such as initiation and first marriage, the *hwelefwe* have to participate. To summarize, twin rituals are more complicated than those of "normal" people; more kinsmen have to show up; all sacrifices are made in twos; the special symbols of *peha, mnta,* and *wetle* are used; and there is an abundance of cowrie shells and invocations.

Twins and Their Symbols

Most of the symbols in twin birth are used elsewhere in Kapsiki religion, but their constellation is quite characteristic. The difference between single children and twins is especially well marked. Kapsiki symbolism centers around a few essential fields: food, plants and trees, and the division of sacrificial animals, all set inside a social-spatial symbolism of, on the one hand, the village, ward, and compound, and, on the other, of social groups such as clans, lineages, and general kin.

One main metaphor is the road, path, or *hwenkwa,* the "place toward" as it is called in Kapsiki. Within this bounded universe, from which roads branch out to similar but often inimical social spaces, the divisions of the clans, and—less relevant in this context—of wards produce the second spatially coherent social unit, the compound, *rhè.* The bordered space of the village is reproduced in the microcosm of the *rhè.* An enclosing wall surrounds the sleeping and cooking huts, their isolation mediated by a structured entrance complex, a partitioned courtyard, and an entrance hut (Van Beek 1986), and by the many drains for the disposal of household waste. The enclosing wall is a prime symbolic element, and is reflected on a smaller scale in doorways, door posts, and hut roofs. The birth rituals are intimately associated with these structures and include sprinkling sacrificial blood over door posts, lentils, and thresholds, marking the place where the birth took place outside the wall.

This focus on borders and mediations of borders reflects Kapsiki body symbolism (Van Beek 1994b), which comes out in birth ritual. The placenta, and especially the umbilical cord—the essential bridges between the body of the mother and that of the child—are the center of ritual attention. During birth the placenta and umbilical cord get almost as much attention as the baby itself; both are buried very carefully at the mother's washing place (or given to her mother to do the same at her hut), a place which is called after the midwife herself (*mewehi* and *mewete*), and they are watched closely lest someone ritually misuses them. The placenta and even more the umbilical cord signify, evidently, the bond between mother and child, but mainly the mortal, fragile side of that bond. It signifies the separation between the two that has led to the new human being. The umbilical cord is an entrance for evil after birth. The positive symbol of motherhood, usually milk in other African societies,[7] here is the baby sling, a carryall made for a single child by its father (for twins, by the father's nephews or whomever the diviner indicates). It is this *hweta* (skin) that links mother and child, close together but two separate persons.

Other metaphors center on agriculture, such as the form of the grave, which mimics one central house symbol, the plaited granary (Van Beek 1995), and the discourse on rain, relevant for twins as well, which can be read as a discourse on power (Van Beek 1997). Parallel to the distinction between twin and single births runs the distinction between the ritual, male red beer and the secular, female white beer (Van Beek 2006). The food symbols used in birth rituals are used in other rituals as well (Van Beek 1978). Their general signification is one of strength and fertility (*rhwempe* and *rhedle*) and general festivity. Eleusine grains are used in various dishes often having to do with rites of passage, but also is used in many sacrificial dishes. On the whole, the food used in single birth rituals is the same used in the sacrifices for compound, lineage, ward, and clan, a connection that underscores the entry of the child into the patrilineal system.

Animals, more than anything else, serve as markers of relationships, in birth as in other rituals. The typical Kapsiki sacrifice consists of a meal, with a sauce appropriate to the occasion, and a sacrificial animal that is distributed according to strict rules to lineages, sister's son, herding boy, wives of the clan, and daughters of the clan. This pattern dominates public meals in birth rituals as well. The distribution of the meat stresses the relationship of the baby and of its parents with the rest of its kin and with the structures of the society. The focus is on the identity of the baby as a member of a group with longstanding interests.

Rituals for twins add a quite different set of symbols. First, rituals for twins engage much larger patrilineages; in fact, the whole clan is always involved.[8] But even more significant is the central place of the *hwelefwe*, in fact of both *hwelefwe*, the new father's and the new mother's, though the one of the father dominates. The composition of this group is complex and includes one's bilateral kinsmen (*hwelefwe te za*) plus a restricted matrilineal group (*hwelefwe te male*). The group does not have a clear boundary, and is mainly important in the major rituals of passage, initiation, and burial. The twins do not belong to the patrilineal system only, but are part of the cognatic stock of both parents. This not only involves the majority of the village with the *kwalerha*, it also gives the twins a much wider

FIGURE 8.2. The twins, wearing *peha,* with their father's brother. *Photo: Walter Van Beek*

identity: they do not belong to one clan or lineage only. They are not simply a link between lineages like single children are, but constitute a force on their own; they have a separate, powerful identity in their own right, and depend ultimately mainly on their peers, other twins, to solve their problems. On the one hand their rituals demonstrate the eager acceptance of new members of the group, but on the other hand the twin rites breathe concern with the wellbeing of the whole village. Even while rejoicing in the excess of fertility there is worry about the viability of the twins. Will they die or dance? Will the parents (the father, more than the mother) live up to their responsibilities? But there is more to the presence of the *hwelefwe* than simply a larger circle of kinsmen involved.

Plant symbols give some clues to a further interpretation of these twin rituals. Sesame and *'yanka* grass are associated with the twins, *mentsehe* and *peha* with the parents. All of these plants figure in one other set of rituals only: initiation. All boy initiates, the *gwela,* dress in their traditional leather pants and adorn themselves with bronze objects, but their liminal identity as warriors is marked by donning strips of *peha* on forehead and ankles, by *'yanka* or *mentsehe* bracelets, and finishing off their attire with a long necklace of cowrie shells. Girl initiates, the *makwa* entering their first marriage, distinguish themselves from their male counterparts by wearing iron skirts instead of brass ornaments, but also wear the same grasses in their loin coverings as twins. A further, and even clearer, symbol of liminal adulthood is the *mnta*. For twins these were the strips of goat skin with long hairs; the same word is used to describe the long hairs on a ram's dewlap. These splendid shocks of hair also form the crown of the *gwela* outfit; the boy initiate "wears" them on top of his lance during the final days of his initiation. So, the positional message of the twins' symbols seems clear: the twins are not children, they are grown up. Their mature status was already clear in their interrogation; they are always addressed as adults: "our people" among twins, with their interrogator respectfully knocking on the door before entering. Twins are never small, their power and danger preclude viewing them as children. Not only are they mature, their symbols designate them as young people during initiation; they "are" *gwela* and *makwa*, initiates. It is during these rites of passage that the *hwelefwe* is the most active. During the *gwela* for boys and the first entrance of the *makwa* bride, as well as during burial rites, the *hwelefwe* takes center stage. In a way, twins are even more liminal than initiates. Not only do they wear the outfit of the initiates during their birth rituals, but they continue to wear them throughout their lives. And so, to some degree, do their parents, always wearing their special bracelets, always addressed as "parent of the twin." The sesame, as an important ritual food, points in the same direction. *Gwela* boys have to cultivate a lot of sesame during the wet season that forms part of their liminal period.[9] Twins are, from the very beginning, surrounded by sesame, and remain so. Whereas normal initiates are reintegrated into society as mature individuals without the paraphernalia of their initiation, the twins never leave their symbols of initiation behind. They are, throughout their lives, associated with the *gwela* and *makwa*. When they undergo the *gwela* and *makwa* rites, they do not change their apparel; they remain as they are.

Thus the Kapsiki solve the problem of the coexistence of two people in the same time and place in a particular manner. Just as twins are in many societies "intolerable to think" (Gros 1995) as well as a confusion for anyone approaching them (Hamard-Frichet 1995), for the Kapsiki such people with identical places in a society are not "of this world." They are the archetype of "ambiguous symbols" (Bell 1992: 182). Both for the vaunted "autonomy" of the Kapsiki (Van Beek 1991) and the many echelons of Kapsiki social identity, twins present a challenge. To assign them the status of a normal being would run counter to the cultural definitions of a person, of social relations, and of the relation between the individual and the supernatural world. So twins are never children, never adults, but forever liminals: they are born initiates, they remain so during their whole lives, forever in-between, powerful but fragile, a dangerous blessing, people from on high and not from this middle earth.

NOTES

1. The term "Kapsiki" is used throughout this chapter to indicate both the Kapsiki group in North Cameroon and the Higi in Northeastern Nigeria, who, despite their two names, form one ethnic group. Research among the Kapsiki was carried out in 1971, 1972–73, 1979, 1984, 1988, 1994, 1999, 2003, 2008, 2010 and financed by Utrecht University, grants from WOTRO (Netherlands Foundation for Tropical Research), the African Studies Center at Leiden, Tilburg University, and the Pieter Langerhuizen Lambertszoon Fund.

2. Respectively *Indigofera tinctoria L.* and *Vetiveria zizanoides L. Nash,* grasses.

3. *Saccharum spontaneum, L.*

4. A palm, probably *Phoenix reclinata.*

5. Another term for god, probably related to *jigilé,* the Mafa term for god (see Van Santen 1993).

6. *Phederbia* sp. The Kapsiki name means "my in-law."

7. The mother's milk, in the form of her breast, may be used as a powerful symbol in cursing. When a mother chews on a nipple and speaks bad words, or even thinks "bad thoughts," the results for her child will be immediate. This *bedla* of the mother is the most potent curse of all, and—quite characteristically— operates through the direct bodily contact between mother and child (Van Beek 1994a).

8. The clans are more pronounced in the identity construction in daily life anyway, than they are in the major sacrifices and rites of passage.

9. The initiation for boys usually starts in March, that of girls—first marriage—in April, and the following cultivation season is part of their initiation time. The rituals end with the reintegration into society as full adults during the *la*-festival in November–December.

WORKS CITED

Bell, Catherine. 1992. *Ritual Theory, Ritual Practice.* Oxford: Oxford University Press.
———. 1997. *Ritual: Perspectives and Dimensions.* Oxford: Oxford University Press.
Bloch, Marc. 1992. "Birth and the Beginning of Social Life among the Zafimaniry of Madagascar." In *Coming into Existence: Birth and Metaphors of Birth,* ed. Goran Aijmer, 70–90. Göteborg, Sweden: Institute for Advanced Studies in Social Anthropology.
Dugast, Stéphan. 1996. "Meurtriers, jumeaux et devins: trois variations sur le

thème du double (Bassar, Togo)." *Systèmes des pensées en Afrique noire* 14: 175–209.

Gros, Christophe. 1995. "Inclassables jumeaux, et pourtant . . . Place et signification des jumeaux en anthropologie sociale." In *Des jumeaux et des autres,* ed. Claude Savary and Christophe Gros, 25–50. Genève: Museum of Ethnography.

Habila, Helon. 2007. *Measuring Time.* London: Hamish Hamilton.

Hamard-Frichet, Colette. 1995. "Vous avez dit jumeaux? Fragments autobiographiques d'une mère de jumelles." In *Des jumeaux et des autres,* ed. Claude Savary and Christophe Gros, 270–276. Genève: Museum of Ethnography.

MacClendon, Thomas V. 1997. "'A Dangerous Doctrine': Twins, Ethnography, and the Natal Code." *Journal of Legal Pluralism and Unofficial Law* 39: 121–140.

Merolla, Danielle. 2007. *Ewe Stories and Storytellers from Ghana.* Leiden, the Netherlands: Verba Africana 1.

Pellegrini, Béatrice. 1995. "Les jumeaux dans le monde: biologie et culture." In *Des jumeaux et des autres,* ed. Claude Savary and Christophe Gros, 51–58. Genève: Museum of Ethnography.

Pison, Giles, et al. 1989. *Mortalité et société en Afrique.* Paris: Presses Universitaire Françaises.

———. 1999. "L'Afrique, continent des jumeaux." *Séminaire Anthropologie de l'enfance.* Paris: Presses Universitaire Françaises.

Onimhawo, John A. 1996. "Euthanasia: A Philosophical-theological Evaluation of Traditional Nigerian Experience." *Orita* 1–2: 106–131.

Rappaport, Roy A. 1999. *Ritual and Religion in the Making of Humanity.* Cambridge: Cambridge University Press.

Savary, Claude. 1995. "Introduction." In *Des jumeaux et des autres,* ed. Claude Savary and Christophe Gros, 11–24. Genève: Museum of Ethnography.

Savary, Claude, and Christophe Gros, eds. 1995. *Des jumeaux et des autres.* Genève: Museum of Ethnography.

Schoffeleers, Johannes-Matthijs. 1991. "Twins and Unilateral Figures in Central and Southern Africa: Symmetry and Asymmetry in the Symbolization of the Sacred." *Journal of Religion in Africa* 21 (4): 345–372.

Sperber, Dan. 1975. *Rethinking Symbolism.* Cambridge: Cambridge University Press.

Staal, Frits. 1989. *Rules without Meaning: Ritual, Mantras, and the Human Sciences.* Bern, Switzerland: Peter Lang.

Turner, Victor. 1975. *Dramas, Fields, and Metaphors: Symbolic Action in Human Society.* Ithaca, N.Y.: Cornell University Press.

Van Beek, Walter E. A. 1986. "The Ideology of Building: The Interpretation of Compound Patterns among the Kapsiki of North Cameroon." In *Op zoek naar mens en materiële cultuur,* ed. Harry Fokkens, Pieteke Banga, and Trinet Constandse, 142–162. Groningen, the Netherlands: Groningen University Press.

———. 1987. *The Kapsiki of the Mandara Mountains.* Prospect Heights, Ill.: Waveland Press.

———. 1991. "Harmony versus Autonomy: Models of Agricultural Fertility among the Dogon and the Kapsiki." In *The Creative Communion: African Folk Models of Fertility and the Regeneration of Life*, ed. Anita Jakobson-Widding and Walter E. A. Van Beek, 285–306. Uppsala, Sweden: Uppsala University Press.

———. 1994a. "The Innocent Sorcerer: Coping with Evil in Two African Societies, Kapsiki and Dogon." In *African Religion: Experience and Expression*, ed. Thomas Blakely, Walter E. A. Van Beek, and Dennis L. Thomson, 196–228. Oxford: James Currey.

———. 1994b. "A Granary in the Earth: Dynamics of Mortuary Rituals among the Kapsiki/Higi." In *Mort et Rites Funéraires dans le Bassin du Lac Tchad*, ed. Catherine Baroin, Daniel Barreteau, and Charlotte Von Graffenried, 137–152. Paris: ORSTOM.

———. 1997. "Rain as a Discourse of Power: Rainmaking in Kapsiki." In *l'Homme et l'Eau dans le Bassin du Lac Chad*, ed. Herman Jungraithmayer, Daniel Barreteau, and Uwe Seibert, 285–297. Paris: ORSTOM.

———. 2006. "Kapsiki Beer Dynamics." In *Ressources vivrières et choix alimentaires dans le bassin du lac Chad*, ed. Eric Garine, Olivier Langlois, and Christine Raimond, 477–500. Bondy, France: IRD

———. 2007. *De rite is rond: Betekenis en boodschap van het ongewone*. Tilburg, the Netherlands: Tilburg University Press.

Van Beek, Walter E. A., and Thomas D. Blakely. 1994. "Introduction." In *African Religion: Experience and Expression*, ed. Thomas D. Blakely, Walter E. A. Van Beek, and Dennis L. Thomson, 1–20. London: James Currey.

Van Santen, José C. M. 1993. *They Leave Their Jars Behind: The Conversion of Mafa Women to Islam (North Cameroon)*. Leiden, the Netherlands: VENA Press.

Whitehouse, Harvey. 2004. *Modes of Religiosity: A Cognitive Theory of Religious Transmission*. Oxford: Altamira Press.

Whitehouse, Harvey, and James Laidlaw, eds. 2007. *Religion, Anthropology, and Cognitive Science*. Oxford: Altamira Press.

Zazzo, René. 1992. *Reflets de miroir et autres doubles*. Paris: Presses Universitaires Françaises.

Zimudzi, Tapiwa B. 2004. "African Women, Violent Crime, and the Criminal Law in Colonial Zimbabwe 1900–1952." *Journal of Southern African Studies* 30 (3): 499–517.

CHAPTER NINE

Snake, Bush, and Metaphor

Twinship among Ubangians

JAN-LODEWIJK GROOTAERS

In the first part of this essay, beliefs and rituals concerning twins in the Central African Ubangi region will be mapped out. This constitutes a preliminary survey, for hardly any systematic research has been devoted to twinship among Ubangian populations. The one exception are the Ngbandi people, whose beliefs about twins have been described in detail, first by the missionary Basiel Tanghe in the 1920s. The most striking assertion of the Ngbandi is that twins are snakes—thus echoing the (non-Ubangian) Sudanese Nuer, according to whom twins are birds, as reported by Edward Evans-Pritchard. The second part of the paper reviews Evans-Pritchard's and others' interpretations of this equivalence, and considers their relevance to the case at hand. Statements such as "twins are snakes" have long been analyzed through—and taken to exemplify—lenses like "non-Western rationality" and "metaphoric language." Yet today, such analyses have lost most of their appeal. This chapter acknowledges changes in theoretical approaches over time as well as cultural shifts in twinship ideas and practices.[1]

Ubangian Twinship Beliefs and Rituals

The Ubangi River constitutes the natural border between the Democratic Republic of the Congo (D.R.C.) and the Central African Republic (C.A.R., the former Oubangui-Chari). It has given its name to a family of languages—the Ubangian languages, formerly called Adamawa-Eastern—whose speakers, a dozen peoples, live on either side (Boyd 2007). In the domain of sculpture, which includes principally figures, musical instruments, and masks, the Ubangi region can be considered as a single culture area displaying a few interrelated art styles (Grootaers, ed. 2007).

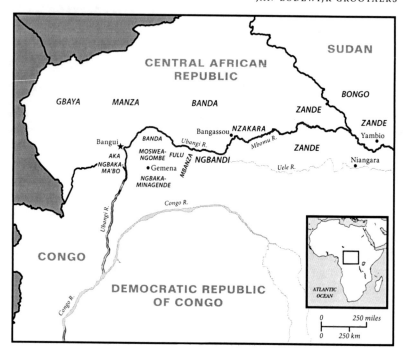

It should be noted that none of the Ubangian peoples make special carvings related to twins. Many exchanges between Ubangian populations
have taken place in the past in the domain of religious beliefs and ritual
practices. One example is the generalized adoption of puberty initiation
ceremonies, known by the same name in most parts of Ubangi (*gaza* or
ganza), another is the spread of closed associations dedicated to particular
spirits—both of which have been analyzed elsewhere (Grootaers 2007).
Here I will investigate ideas about twins, for these too seem fairly consistent throughout the Ubangi region.

   This overview is based on existing literature, published and archival,
and a couple of surveys in the field.[2] Before I outline their ideas about
twins, the various Ubangian peoples are reviewed according to their linguistic classification. Various languages are spoken in the Ubangi culture
area, a region characterized principally by wooded savanna. Most belong
to the same family, known as the Ubangian languages, which are divided
into five groups. These groups may comprise a single people or several.
Two other families of languages are also found in the region: Central
Sudanese languages and Bantu languages. Speakers of these languages are
a small minority in the area (Bouquiaux and Thomas 1980; Cordell 1983;
Eboué 1933).

Ubangian Peoples

The Banda people is made up of some fifty groups who each speak their own Banda language and live in four different countries: Sudan, Chad, the Central African Republic, and the northern Democratic Republic of the Congo (Cloarec-Heiss 1998; Daigre 1931, 1932; Santandrea 1984). This fragmentation is the result of an age-long Arabic slave trade in the past, which led to successive waves of migration from Sudan. Numerous closed associations in the Ubangi area originated among the Banda. One of the Banda groups, the Mbanza, speak a Banda language, but culturally they are more closely related to their non-Banda neighbors in the Congo, the Ngbaka (see below). These two peoples at one time used very similar masks and other ritual objects in boys' initiation ceremonies (Burssens 1958).

The Ngbaka are also known as the Ngbaka-minagende to distinguish them from an unrelated Ngbaka group, the Ngbaka-ma'bo (see below). Most northern Congolese sculptures originated with them, and there is quite a bit of information about their initiation and healing rituals (Henrix 2007; Maes 1996). Far less is known about the religious beliefs and practices of the other members of this language group, the Gbaya and the Manza, both from the Central African Republic (Tessmann 1934, 1937; Vergiat 1937).

The third group of Ubangian languages is spoken by numerous small peoples who are found throughout the area, from the border with Congo-Brazzaville to southwestern Sudan. These include the Ngbaka-ma'bo, the Monzombo, the Gbanziri, and the Sere. They were allegedly the first "Ubangians" to settle in the region, around 1600 (Maes 1984; Thomas 1970).

In the late nineteenth century, economic life in much of the Ubangi Basin was dominated by the Ngbandi, who form a separate language group. They live mainly in northern Congo (D.R.C.) and also partly across the border in the Central African Republic. Their contacts with the first European travelers and colonizers ensured that numerous objects and photographs of them reached the West early on. Catholic missionization of the Ngbandi started at the end of the first decade of the twentieth century (Tanghe 1929).

The best-known members of the last Ubangian language group are the Zande and the Nzakara. Unlike all the peoples mentioned so far, they were organized into kingdoms from 1800 onwards. They developed a court art, with decorated musical instruments and spoons, but they are also known for their small ritual figures belonging to closed associations (Lagae 1926; Evans-Pritchard 1971; de Dampierre 1967; Grootaers 2002).

Central Sudanese languages are primarily found to the north and east of the Ubangi area, but the Fulu (sometimes called Furu), a small group from Chad, settled along the Ubangi River in the nineteenth century (Maes 1984). They absorbed many cultural features from their Ubangian neighbors. To the east of the Zande, in southwestern Sudan, live the Central-Sudanese-speaking (i.e., non-Ubangi) Bongo, known for their life-size grave figures, who also carve figurines for deceased twins. They too can be reckoned in the Ubangi culture area. Their culture was one of the first to be put on record in this part of the continent, through the writings of the Russo-German explorer and botanist Georg Schweinfurth (Schweinfurth 1875; also Evans-Pritchard 1929; and Kronenberg and Kronenberg 1981).

Finally, Bantu-speakers are basically only found to the west and south of the Ubangi area. One exception is the Moswea-Ngombe, a small Bantu-speaking enclave of Ngombe in northern Congo (Wolfe 1961). Incidentally, the Aka pygmies in the Central African Republic also speak a Bantu language. They are among the earliest inhabitants of this part of the continent, and this particular group adopted a Bantu language in the course of their history (Bahuchet and Guillaume 1982). However, neither the Moswea-Ngombe nor the Aka will be discussed in relation to twinship.

Beliefs and Rituals

The Ubangians' attitude toward twins used to be complex, and this still tends to be the case today. This section, therefore, alternates between reports from the past, and present-day observations and testimonies. Twins are rarely merely accepted, but it is often difficult to tell whether they are desired or feared. Their birth is considered an exceptional event, a manifestation of the presence of higher powers among the living. It is laden with special significance and brings about a state of ritual danger. Twins are regarded as dangerous and ambiguous beings. They herald great fertility but also constitute a threat to their social environment. Among some Banda groups, for example, twins were reputed to cause harm to others, and numerous ills were attributed to their powers. One observer in the late 1920s noted that "it was not unusual to see sick people beg [young twins] to give them back their health."[3] At the same time, however, Banda twins were entrusted with the protection of major events, like the collective hunt (Eggen 1976: 49/c–49/d). In southern Bandaland, near the Ubangi River, twins were related to the rainbow (evingi or avingi). The rainbow is supposed to make its house in water, especially at sources, and in termite mounds, and it used to be implored to prevent or cure barrenness. The symbolic linking of twins with water, rainbow, and fertility is not unique to the Banda, as we will see.

Purificatory and propitiatory cults that have been described in the past continue to exist to some degree; they function both to celebrate twin births and to protect twins' parents and the community at large (see chart 1). So elaborate were the ceremonies and rites connected with their birth and life, and so great was the threat of evil in consequence of any violation of these rites, that in older days twins were often seen as a liability to the family.[4] Where twins are equated with specific animals, such as snakes, relatives and the twins themselves refrain from killing those animals or consuming their meat. The special status of twins is further indicated by their personal names, which in most Ubangian societies are fixed. The first child to be born after a twin birth is also considered to possess some of the powers ascribed to its twin siblings and usually also gets a fixed name (see chart 2). The rituals surrounding the birth of such an "after-twin" sometimes resemble end-of-mourning rituals.[5] Uniquely among the Ubangian peoples, the Ngbaka-ma'bo possess several words to designate twins: *ngbooi* is used only in the context of their birth and death, and *koda* is the usual term (Thomas 1970: 834); some Ngbaka-ma'bo groups have another word, *mee* (unpublished field notes, C.A.R., May 2004). This underscores the ideas that twins are different from other persons, that their being is not the same over time, and that they are especially dangerous at moments of major life crisis.

The special powers of twins are generally considered to decline as the children grow older, although even as adults, twins will continue to observe certain ritual precepts, while their parents remain identified as parents of twins. In order not to provoke these powers, which could cause the death of one of the twins or of other persons involved, everyone is bound to treat both twins exactly alike with respect to gifts, songs, feeding, clothing, offerings to their tutelary spirits, and so on. Most authors explain this behavior in terms of avoiding jealousy on the part of the wronged twin. Yet in one of the first sociological analyses of twins in (Southern) Africa, Isaac Schapera noted that the identical treatment of twins was one of the methods used to solve the paradox of twins' identical "social personalities," i.e., their occupying the same place in the social structure due to their simultaneous birth (Schapera 1927: 135–136). A different interpretation of this phenomenon was offered by Eric de Dampierre, a specialist on the Ubangian Nzakara people. According to him, the Nzakara abhor "identity," a sign of chaos; for them everything is—or should be—"singular." The appearance of twins thus signals, even provokes, cosmic disorder. One way to deal

People	Twins	Equated with or likened to	Rituals at birth	Rituals at death	Plants / Objects	Ref.
Banda	*amia* or *ameya* (pl.)	sometimes witches	special dance and hunt, two trees planted for offerings		*ekere-miya*, "twins plant" (*Dioscorea* sp.)	2, 4, 6, 24
Mbanza	*amea* (pl.)	snakes, sometimes mice	umbilical cords in 2 pots on 2 trees near crossroads		1 pot for each twin	6
Ngbaka-minagende	*(be) da*	snakes, sometimes witches	installation of double *ndaba* altar	buried at crossroads	2 pots for each of the twins	1, 6, 7, 8, 13
Manza	*(be) da*	related to snakes, scorpions	altar for offerings at entry of house		*kole-mia*, "twins plant" (*Dioscorea* sp.)	17, 24
Gbaya	*(be) da*	related to snakes, reptiles	elaborate coming out celebration	buried in forked tree at crossroads		9, 10, 17
Ngbaka-ma'bo	*ngbooi, koda; mee*	witches	special songs and ceremonies	buried at crossroads or in forked tree	*gila* (kapok tree)	6, 22, 23
Ngbandi	*angbo* (pl.)	snakes [same term]	special dance and songs; placentas in 2 pots at extremity of village	buried on forked poles, later at foot of twin trees	*nduru* (kapok tree), 1 pot for each twin	6, 15, 16, 20, 21
Nzakara	*abue* or *abie* (pl.)	sometimes witches	planting of shrub			3, 6, 19, 25
Zande	*abi* (pl.); *angbo* (pl.)	sometimes witches		buried by roadside		5, 6, 12, 14
Fulu	*ndani* or *dani*	snakes				6
Bongo	*runga*		fertility ceremony (*ngala runga*)		2 pots for each of the twins; 1 or 2 statues for deceased twin(s)	11, 18

References to charts

1: Crabbeck [1939]
2: Daigre (1931: 666)
3: De Dampierre (1984: 13–17)
4: Eggen (1976: 49/c–49/d, 55/e–55/f)
5: Giorgetti [Gero] (1968: 48–50)
6: Grootaers [1991–1992, 2003, 2004, 2005]
7: Henrix (2000: 41–42, *sub verbo* da; 466, *sub verbo* zi)
8: Henrix (2006, II: 41–42)

9: Hilberth (1973: 49–51)
10: Hilberth and Hilberth (1968: 56–57)
11: Kronenberg and Kronenberg (1981)
12: Lagae (1926: 173)
13: Langdon (1989)
14: Larken (1926: 26)
15: Moen (2005)
16: Molet (1971)
17: Moñino (1988: 119)

18: Nougayrol (2008) (personal communication)
19: Retel-Laurentin (1969: 62, 389–390)
20: Tanghe (1921)
21: Tanghe (1926)
22: Tessmann (1928: 320)
23: Thomas (1970: 209–235, 834)
24: Vergiat (1937: 48–50)
25: Zaal (1955)

with this anomaly is to treat the twins exactly the same, thereby restoring and underscoring their natural singularity. In the same vein, the burial of infant twins near a crossroads should enable them to choose their singular destiny.[6] Writing about the Ubangian Ngbaka-ma'bo, in the western Central African Republic, Jacqueline Thomas remarked that crossroads—where the Ngbaka-ma'bo too used to bury their twins—carry "considerable symbolic importance in relations with the supernatural" (1970: 290).

A further "issue" with twins has to do with seniority. Whereas in some Ubangian cultures the first-born twin is the youngest, having been sent out by his senior sibling to scout out the world, for most Ubangians seniority follows the order of birth. A biblical story with an interesting twist underscores the relevance of seniority among twins. In the 1940s and '50s Nzakara Protestant converts recast the biblical story of Isaac's sons, the twins Esau and Jacob. In their version, the elder of the twins is black, and at first was prevented from being born by his white brother. After an intervention of Nzapa (God), the black boy came out first and the white second: "After which the black twin, who was the elder, commanded the second one." Yet

People	Special personal names of twins	Special names of next child
Banda	Meya (1st, m. and f.); Kada, Kongbo, or Ebru (2nd, m.); Ndakela or Ngatere (2nd, f.)	Ebru or Ndakela
Mbanza	*No information available*	*No information available*
Ngbaka-minagende	Dawili (1st m.) and Kongbo (2nd m.); Dako (1st f.), and Kagu or Mbali (2nd f.)	Yangge (m. or f.), Sebutu (m.), Futu (f.)
Manza	*No information available*	*No information available*
Gbaya	Yandele (f.) and Ngonzo (m.)— and many others	Gberi (m.), Ndui (m.), Mgbutu (f.), Yapeli (f.)
Ngbaka-ma'bo	Guna-le and Sidi-le; Dinza, Meke, Mbaranga, Mboma	*Not applicable*
Ngbandi	Revealed by twins themselves through dreams	Ngere-ngbo, Nvu-ngbo, Ya-ngbo
Nzakara	Revealed by twins themselves through dreams	Fulu
Zande	Bi (1st) and Siro or Ngbo (2nd)	Furu [taken over from the Nzakara]
Fulu	*No information available*	*No information available*
Bongo	Dokay (1st m.) and Yugu (2nd m.); Makay (1st f.) and Runga (2nd f.); Yudju (m.) and Mayere (f.)	*Not applicable*

the latter fooled his father and received his blessing. Ever since this trickery, "it is the white people who are in command" (in de Dampierre 1967: 560–563). The revised Genesis story thus transposes the conflict over seniority among twins to the power relation between Africans and Europeans during colonialism. The white boy's cunning behavior is well known to the Nzakara, and to many other Ubangians as well. They all tell stories about Tule (or Ture, Tere), the local trickster, and in some instances it is claimed that the white people owe their supremacy to this Central African antihero.[7]

The gender of twins is also related to seniority. The Manza in the Central African Republic used to consider the first-born male and the second female, irrespective of their biological gender. After birth, the "male" twin received a small shield and a miniature bow, while its "female" counterpart was given a small basket with some bits of food. In the past, Manza women who were the elder of a pair of twins devoted themselves to male activities, including smithing and hunting (Vergiat 1937: 49–50; Vergiat n.d. [1997]: 214).

Twins as Snakes

The most striking characteristic of twin beliefs among Ubangians is the widespread association of twins with snakes (see chart 1). The Ngbandi people even consider twins to be snakes, and both are designated by the same term, *ngbo* (plural: *angbo*).[8] This means that the kind of statement that is found elsewhere (for instance among the Nuer, "twins are birds"—*cueek e dit*) is not possible in the Ngbandi language ("*angbo* are *angbo*" would be a tautology). Curiously, this problem has not been addressed by any authors who have written about the Ngbandi. The Catholic missionary Basiel Tanghe devoted two books to Ngbandi twin beliefs, one in Dutch in 1921 and a revised French version in 1926. Yet he mentioned that "tweelingen zijn slangen" and "les jumeaux sont des serpents"—respectively Dutch and French translations of "twins are snakes"—as if these were direct quotes from his Ngbandi informants. One explanation may be that the missionary also communicated in the Lingala language, a lingua franca widely used in the region and belonging to the Bantu language family. It would not have been a problem to express the equation in Lingala. Another solution would have been the use of paraphrases. One sometimes encounters the expressions *ayafo te angbo* to designate twins, which translates as "children of snakes" ("children of twins" is no alternative), or *ya mbi adu angbo ose*, said by the father and meaning "my wife laid two snakes" (the verb *se* being used for eggs).[9]

According to Tanghe, the Ngbandi had a cult devoted to the snake (*ngbo*), which they considered to be their most important spirit (*toro*). Offerings at the spirit hut of the snake (*toro ngbo*) were made before and after hunting and fishing, and in many songs the snake would be venerated but also insulted (Tanghe 1926: 7–8). When twins were born, they were celebrated and appeased through the snake cult. Writing fifty years later, the Protestant missionary Louis Molet, who stayed among the Ngbandi on and off between 1959 and 1970, disagreed with Tanghe's interpretation. According to him, there was no snake cult at all: "If offerings are made at the *toro ngbo*, libations poured and animals sacrificed, it is always about worshiping the power of the twins" (Molet 1971: 56). It is worthwhile to compare similar twin songs recorded by both authors. The major difference appears to be that Molet systematically translated *ngbo* as "twins" instead of "snake." Yet in this particular example grammar supports Tanghe: "twins," being plural, would have to be *angbo* instead of *ngbo*.

Mbi du ma ngbo o	I gave birth to a snake.
E we ngbo o	Let us scoff at the snake.
Ngbo ga na ne e	The snake comes with what?
Ngbo ga nzo lo o	The snake brings a good thing.[10]

Mbi du ma ngbo	I gave birth to twins.
E we ngbo	We scoff at twins.
Ngbo aga siolo	Twins bring bad luck.
Ngbo aga tapere	Twins bring trouble.
Ngbo aga nzolo	Twins bring good things.
Ngbo aga pasa	Twins bring happiness.[11]

In the past and still today, it is not the father who gives twins their personal names, as he does for other infants. The names are revealed through a dream that often comes to a relative, which can be months after their birth. Thus, contrary to most other Ubangians, whose personal names for twins are fixed, among the Ngbandi names given to twins vary (see chart 2).[12] Traditionally, a couple of days after a twin birth, a communal celebration took place in which participants adorned themselves with red powder and white patches. The red powder came from the camwood tree (*Petrocarpus cabrae*), the white color from river clay or oyster shells. One encounters these colors in many rituals throughout much of the Ubangi area, and several interpretations of their significance have been advanced.[13] Red is said to symbolize the bush, and the evil spirits dwelling there, and white stands for the river, and the more benevolent water spirits. Being used during initiation and funeral ceremonies, the red color has also been associated with moments of danger and transition, while white has been described as protecting and purifying. Even though the following pertains to the twin ritual of the Bantu Ndembu people (Zambia), it is interesting to quote Victor Turner on the intrinsically multivocal character of color symbolism: "This is yet another example of the way in which the same symbols have varying significance in different contexts. The binary opposition white/red at different episodes of [the twin ritual] represents strength/weakness, good luck/bad luck, health/disease, purity of heart/a grudge causative of witchcraft, semen/maternal blood, masculinity/femininity" (Turner 1969: 53–54). And, as Turner added, such totalizing symbols are not mere assemblages of cognitive signs, but are believed to have efficacy, to bring about change.

The various interpretations of the link that the Ngbandi make between twins and snakes will be addressed in the next section. This section ends by reviewing briefly the existence of this affinity in other Ubangian cultures as well, both nowadays, and in the past. Much of it constitutes bits and pieces of information, for which contextual ethnographic knowledge often is lacking.

The Banda cultivate a kind of yam (*Dioscorea sp.*), called "plant of the twins" (*ekere-mia*), whose double bulb is associated with twinship and which is planted near the parents' house. It has been noted that the fruit of this plant was also worn to protect one from snakebite (Vergiat 1937: 50; Daigre 1932: 166). The Mbanza people, a Banda group close to the Ngbaka-minagende, told me that "twins are snakes (*yakoro*)."[14] The Ngbaka-minagende say that "the magic force (*zi*) of twins is the snake" (Henrix 2000: 466). This *zi* should be understood as the vital force that exists in all animated beings. Other sources mention that twins are believed either to be snakes, or to be able to become snakes—hence the prohibition on killing or eating snakes for Ngbaka-minagende twins and their families (Crabbeck [1939]; Langdon 1989). Writing about Manza twins, Vergiat noted that "snakes and scorpions . . . are under their dominion" (1937: 50). The Gbaya, for their part, did not believe that two children born at the same time could have the same father: "The one born last is sired by an evil power. It comes from the marshes, from the ferns, from the abode of mystical snakes" (Hilberth 1973: 49). Moreover, Gbaya twins too were able to send snakes and scorpions to take revenge on an enemy, and it was claimed that they could cure snakebite and that they themselves had no fear of snakes (ibid.: 51). The Fulu, finally, a small Central Sudanese group surrounded by Ubangian Ngbaka-minagende, Mbanza, and Ngbandi peoples, also believe twins to be snakes.[15]

All this suggests the existence, among Ubangians, of a core of shared ideas about twinship. These do not constitute a unified and singular theory, but "a complicated network of similarities overlapping and criss-crossing: sometimes overall similarities, sometimes similarities of detail."[16] Such "family resemblance" is one of the consequences of a history of extensive migrations, intermingling, and exchanges within this Central African region (Maes 1984; Grootaers 2007).

Classification, Symbolization, and Other Twinning Issues
Social Personality of Twins

The birth of twins is, as Victor Turner put it, "a source of classificatory embarrassment" (1969: 45). Indeed, what genealogical and social position can two individuals take who occupy the same "slot"? Several (mostly South African) solutions to make twins "fit" were reviewed by Schapera (1927), the first one to deal with the question. In some societies both twins were killed, or only one was left to die, the survivor being regarded as a "normal" child; sometimes twins were removed from the kinship system and permanently assigned a particular, often sacred status; or twins got special treatment during their childhood (by being treated identically, for instance), and they participated in special rituals at their birth, marriage, and death. Most of these solutions can also be found in the literature about Ubangian twins.

We have already given examples of the special treatment of twins. The missionary Cees Zaal, who lived with the Nzakara in the 1950s, mentioned the existence among the Nzakara of "twin murder" (Zaal 1955). In his unpublished *Ethnographic Notes,* written in Dutch, he remarked that although many twins were born among the Nzakara, he had never encountered a single living pair of them.[17] The one identified as the "snake" used to be killed at once. Zaal also referred to the case of a Manza twin birth where both children were killed, concluding that Manza twins were even worse off. Yet a photograph in Vergiat (1937: facing 97) showing two infant Manza twins being breastfed contradicts this generalization. Another missionary, who later converted to ethnography, Louis Molet, wrote about the Ngbandi. He understood the fact that Ngbandi twins after birth were not presented to their ancestors as an indication of their extra-genealogical position (Molet 1971: 39, 44). This position, in turn, was interpreted by Molet as signifying Ngbandi twins' relation to the bush, a hypothesis to which we will return.

In some cultures twins are said to be other things too, further high-
lighting how twins are given a unique classification among humans. This
has always stimulated a great deal of anthropological theorizing. Evans-
Pritchard, for one, offered an exegesis of the Nuer statement that "twins
are birds" (*cueek e dit*) in a chapter of his *Nuer Religion* (1956), titled "The
Problem of Symbols." This turned out to be the problem of "something
being something else" and how these two somethings relate to a third term
(Evans-Pritchard 1956: 138, 142). The twins are not *like* birds, he was told,
nor are twins *literally* birds, with "a beak, feathers, and so on" (ibid.: 131).
We will dwell on the Nilotic Nuer case, first, because it shows great formal
resemblance to the "twins-are-snakes" of the Ubangian Ngbandi people,
and second, because it has given rise to extensive literature—unlike the
Ngbandi case.

Symbolic Correspondences

Before dealing with this type of analysis, it is worthwhile to recall a
recent critique of classical twinship studies: "Anthropologists have typically viewed twinship in Africa as a cultural text of elusive symbolic meanings" (Diduk (1993: 551). One way to counter such a tendency is to consider twinship beliefs in a more socially and historically situated manner.

The "analogical representation" of twins and birds, as Evans-Pritchard
called it, was to be explained in terms of Nuer religious thought. Even
though the Nuer do not fail to draw an empirical analogy between the
multiple hatching of eggs and the dual birth of twins (just like the Ngbandi
do with regards to snakes and twins), this is secondary to their conviction
that both twins and birds are "children of God [or Spirit]" and "persons of
the above" (Evans-Pritchard 1956). A twin is a special creation and as such
a manifestation of Spirit, associated with the air; similarly, a bird belongs
by nature to the above and is therefore also associated with Spirit. In other
words, a bird is "a suitable symbol in which to express the special relationship in which a twin stands to God" (ibid.: 132). Several personal names of
Nuer twins reflect this relationship, such as Dit ("bird"), Gwong ("guineafowl"), and Ngec ("francolin"). The fact that the latter two are walking
birds was explained by Evans-Pritchard in a footnote—"Twins belong
to the class of the above, but are below; just as guineafowl and francolin
belong to the class of birds, which as a class is in the category of the above,
but are almost earthbound" (ibid.: 129n1).

In his major monographs Evans-Pritchard was in continuous dialogue
with Lucien Lévy-Bruhl, whose theses he intended to falsify empirically.

The French philosopher had studied the psychology of non-Western collective representations and, in a series of influential books written between 1910 and 1938, set out to understand "how natives think."[18] It was especially Lévy-Bruhl's notion of "prelogical mentality," dominated by the irrational "law of participation" which is not troubled by contradictions, that Evans-Pritchard took issue with. In his first ethnography, *Witchcraft, Oracles, and Magic among the Azande* (1937), he showed Zande beliefs to be consistent and rational in their own way, even if they were mystical and therefore empirically untrue. While writing on the Zande, Evans-Pritchard critically reviewed Lévy-Bruhl's ideas and declared: "Thought which is totally unscientific and even which contradicts experience may yet be entirely coherent in that there is a reciprocal dependence between its ideas" (Evans-Pritchard 1934: 51). The coherence of apparently irrational Zande ideas and practices was further enhanced by their formal congruence with Zande social rules and relations.

Some two decades later, in his book on Nuer religion, Evans-Pritchard was less concerned with logic than with faith. The book can be seen as an attempt to show the existence of high religion and developed religious sensibility in the absence of a church. This interest has been related to the fact that some years earlier Evans-Pritchard had converted to Roman Catholicism, while his close relationship to missionaries of the American Presbyterian Mission in Nuerland—one of whom had received the book "chapter by chapter" to comment upon and add information—may also have played a role.[19] Still, the author explicitly referred to the French philosopher in his discussion of "twins are birds." It was on statements of this kind, he wrote, "that Lévy-Bruhl based his theory of the prelogical mentality of [primitive] peoples, its chief characteristic being, in his view, that it permits such evident contradictions—that a thing can be what it is and at the same time something altogether different" (Evans-Pritchard 1956: 131; also 140–141). Yet the apparent contradiction disappears to those who view the idea within the Nuer system of religious thought. In sum, twins and birds are not thought to be linked "by a mystical bond but simply by a symbolic nexus" (ibid.: 141).

One of the founding fathers of symbolic anthropology, Claude Lévi-Strauss, used the Nuer case in his interpretation of totemism. Although the "twins-are-birds" statement is not part of Nuer totemic beliefs proper, Lévi-Strauss identified the same structural principles at work. His reanalysis took up the aforementioned idea laid out by Evans-Pritchard and transposed it into a scheme of binary oppositions:

SPIRIT : HUMANS :: BIRDS FROM ABOVE : BIRDS FROM BELOW ::
PERSONS FROM ABOVE : PERSONS FROM BELOW

In this structural classification, not only do twins—as persons from above—and birds in general belong to the same celestial order, but twins and earthbound birds also occupy a similar *intermediary* position between the cosmic poles of Above and Below (Lévi-Strauss 1962: 119–120). That is why the Nuer can cogently say that "twins are birds." The choice of birds is neither irrational nor arbitrary, nor is it stimulated by naturalism. It is in this context that Lévi-Strauss launched his famous *bon mot:* "biological species are not chosen because they are 'good to eat' but because they are 'good to think with'" (1962: 132).

According to this view, the natural fact that birds hatch multiple eggs did not inspire the metaphor, nor indeed did the symbolic relation of birds to Spirit/God. The connection between twins and birds is understandable as a metaphoric correspondence of their ambiguous associations with sky and earth; specific birds are chosen on the grounds that they are able to fulfill an intellectual need thanks to their place within a mentally construed cosmos. The main critique Lévi-Strauss leveled against Evans-Pritchard was that the latter's emphasis on theological notions of *kwoth* (Spirit/God) rendered the analysis of Nuer indigenous twin theory "too closely dependent on the theology peculiar to the Nuer" (Lévi-Strauss 1962: 122). The analysis was therefore not universal enough.

Yet Lévi-Strauss himself has been criticized for his narrow, reductive interpretation of symbols. Already in 1966 Raymond Firth argued that the Nuer relation of twins to birds "is not simply an intellectual classification," since it also involved food prohibitions, shame behavior, and moral responsibility (Firth 1966: 15). Similarly, in his discussion of Ndembu rituals, Victor Turner declared: "The symbols and their relations as found in [a particular ritual] are not only a set of cognitive classifications for ordering the . . . universe. They are also, and perhaps as importantly, a set of evocative devices for rousing, channeling, and domesticating powerful emotions, such as hate, fear, affection, and grief" (Turner 1969: 42–43). Symbols are informed with purposiveness that involves the entire person, mentally and physically. Over the course of a ritual a succession of symbols are activated, which have "the twin function of communication and efficacy" (ibid.: 93).

In the same line, but pursuing the argument one step further, is Terence Turner's fundamental critique of symbolic anthropology and metaphor theory. These approaches, according to the author, analyze meaningful forms by focusing on their minimal elements (individual symbols or tropes), thereby "abstracting them from both their pragmatic contexts of social use and the more complex meaningful constructs (rituals, narratives, patterns of action) in which they are embedded" (Turner 1991: 122). The minimal elements—"twins are birds" or "twins are snakes," for instance— become reified and begin to lead a life of their own, detached from cultural discourse, social action, and historical context. In Lévi-Strauss' work such autonomous expressions become part of a mental scheme, sustaining the view of culture as essentially a "system of symbols and meanings" without relationship to concrete practice. Terence Turner's criticism echoes Arnold Van Gennep's early emphasis on "ritual sequences," as opposed to the study of isolated rites (Van Gennep 1909). Against the one-sided structuralist and symbolic approach Turner advocates a more contextually and historically situated understanding of metaphors.

Return to the Snakes

How can all this be related to the Ngbandi case, where twins are equated with snakes? The ethnographic material from the Ubangi region lacks the synchronic thickness and diachronic depth to fulfill Terence Turner's program. Still, some hermeneutic attempts have been made. Louis Molet, for one, offered an interpretation of Ngbandi beliefs inspired by Lévi-Straussian oppositions. To begin with, both twins and snakes are anomalous within their respective realms. Snakes are animals without limbs, twins are social beings without proper seniority between them. Hence *ngbo* (twins/snakes) "are freaks, a materialization of disorder" (Molet 1971: 55). Beyond this classificatory congruence between twins and snakes, the author also identified twins as partaking of the bush. The bush, a hostile world populated by wild animals and evil spirits, is opposed to the inhabited world of village and field. Yet sometimes either of them partly "invades" the other. Markets and smithies are human enclaves temporarily located in the bush, while snakes and diseases are irruptions of the bush into the village. And so is the birth of twins, according to Molet (1971: 68). After their birth, twins were excluded form the domestic space and had to live in an enclosure, their placentas were placed at the border of the village, and they were not presented to the ancestors. Their closeness to the bush, which required all these ritual observances, at the same time gave them power over the outcome of hunting and fishing.

Different readings were proposed by Tanghe and a few other authors, which relied on a wider set of symbolic linkages known to various Ubangian peoples. Partly based on questionable linguistic comparisons, Tanghe (1921, 1926) evoked a triadic relationship between twins, snakes, and chiefs.[20] The chief had a dual nature, being a private, human person, and a public figure with spiritual power. The snake too was double, being both animal and Spirit. Hence the twins' close relationship to both. Another "field of metaphors" involved water, fertility, and the rainbow (de Jonghe 1924; Leyder 1935). In a number of Ubangian languages the rainbow is considered as an animated being, and it is often likened to a pair of snakes, one on top of the other.[21] Snakes and the rainbow live in water, and water is generally associated with fertility. Twins, who are double, are a manifestation of "superfertility." According to the Nzakara, for instance, "the rainbow . . . is the metaphor of twins in the natural order" (de Dampierre 1984: 23). Nevertheless, the association of twins and rainbows among Ubangians remains tenuous at best.

The bush is home to the snakes, and contrary to the rainbow, it carries strong connotations of untamed wilderness and unregulated consumption usually associated with witchcraft. The fact that many Ubangians consider twins to be witches—sometimes snakes *and* witches—underscores the antisocial aspect of their reputation (see chart 1). In the past, the Ngbandi would not let infant twins eat the roasted intestines of a chicken sacrificed in their honor—a custom in other cases—for fear that this would trigger their "bad instinct" and make them "homicidal."[22] Normally, babies are dependent on their parents for food, survival, and socialization, yet twin babies invert this relationship: they seem to have power over their parents and other adults, and also a measure of control over game in the forest. Accordingly, it is the bush-like, unruly character of twins that partakes of both snake and witch.

Let us return, for a last time, to the non-Ubangian Nuer, where metaphoric matters turn out to be more complex than hitherto suspected. Evans-Pritchard noted that the souls of dead twins were said to go into the air—they "fly away"—and that dead infant twins were not buried but used to be covered in a reed basket that was placed in the fork of a tree. This was done, according to the author, "because birds rest in trees" (1956: 130). Yet as can be seen in chart 1, twin graves in trees or on forked poles occur in a number of Ubangian societies, none of which relates twins to either birds or creatures of the above. Even Ngbandi "snake-twins" who had died at a young age were placed in forked poles (Tanghe 1926: 69). This type of burial is thus not at all related to the avian character of twins.[23] Furthermore, Nuer twins are linked to *snakes* too. Evans-Pritchard did not elaborate on this, but he mentioned that a large number of small Nuer lineages respected snakes, including the python: "Those people I have asked about their totemic affiliation have told me that a python was born as twin to their ancestor" (Evans-Pritchard 1956: 67). The relation between twins and snakes in Nuerland appears still relevant today. A recent study evokes the Nuer treatment of snakebites by a person who is knowledgeable about specific snakebite plants: "the person who knows is someone born as a twin to a snake—some women give birth to twins, one is a person, one is a snake" (Blakeway et al. n.d. [1997]). The authors provided no further information, but the connection is clear.

In the end, one gets the impression that in Nuer studies the bird metaphor came to overshadow all other possible connections within the total structure of meaningful relations pertaining to twins. "Twins are birds" became a trope that overdetermined the argument. And while the distinction between "high" and "low" birds was pertinent in Lévi-Strauss' elegant interpretation of twins as persons "in between," we require more ethnographic information in order to make any conjectures as to why the Nuer would *also* relate twins to snakes. All of this should be kept in mind when analyzing the material from the Ubangi region—both to avoid an overemphasis on the snake metaphor, and to recognize the far greater lack of knowledge we have about Ubangian cultures.

Indeed, this knowledge is scant at best, and one of the striking features of Ubangi ethnography is that almost all the first, and sometimes only studies were written by Christian, mainly Catholic, missionaries. The same holds true for dictionaries and grammars of Ubangian languages, but the reasons for the high missionary productivity—and relative absence of non-missionary anthropologists and linguists—in this part of Africa remain unclear.[24] Anthropologists have always relied on missionary writings, yet at the same time they used to "ritually disassociate" themselves from the missionaries' alleged ideology (Rosaldo 1989: 69). Anthropologists also often kept silent about the scientific importance of missionary works, and equally silenced the missions' local impact in an attempt to conjure up visions of an unadulterated cultural order.[25] To recognize these two-way influences and interferences, however, allows for a more historically situated view of beliefs and practices.

Missionaries were (and are) agents of social change, and some of the transformations in Ubangian notions of twinship transpire through their writings. In his book about Ngbandi twin beliefs, which he linked to their snake cult, Basiel Tanghe mentioned how the people were fascinated by the Bible story in which Satan, in the shape of a snake, deceived the first humans. His listeners asked him time and again whether "God was really stronger than the snake" (Tanghe 1921: 54). The biblical link between Satan and the snake continues to be invoked today to explain the witch-like character of twins, as was made clear to me by Banda informants in the Central African Republic.[26] Gbaya Christians, on the other hand, changed their association of twins with snakes and reptiles to the belief "that twins come from God" in a way that differs from other children (Hilberth and Hilberth 1968: 57). These various cases illustrate a continued ambivalence toward twins on the part of Ubangians, yet with fundamental shifts as to how twins are being valued. When the study of certain phenomena relies heavily on research done several decades ago, it is necessary to counter the tendency to social and cultural reification. Societies and theories inevitably change over time.

NOTES

1. I would like to acknowledge the help that I received, in piecing together some of the information, from Yves Boulvert, Pascal Boyeldieu, Didier Carité, Andrea Ceriana, Guinimanguimi Paul, Marcel Henrix, Sharon Hutchinson, Pierre Nougayrol (who supplied some of the information in the tables), Péleket Jean-Bosco, and Manuel Valentin.

2. I did fourteen months of doctoral fieldwork among the Zande in the east of the Central African Republic in 1991–1992, went back for three months to various parts of that country in 2003 and 2004, and spent three months in the northern Ubangi Region of the Democratic Republic of the Congo in 2005.

3. Daigre (1931: 666). More than seventy years later I was told by Banda informants that "twins are like witches"—sorciers in French. This fits in with Daigre's observations.

4. The same holds true for other African peoples, including the Dinka (Sudan), the Nyoro (Uganda), and the Ndembu (Zambia); cf. Deng (1972: 37), Beattie (1962: 1), and Turner (1969: 44).

5. Thomas (1970: 209), speaking about the Ngbaka-ma'bo, mentions the "end of twinship," based on the model of the end of mourning. I have not encountered a similar perspective among other Ubangian peoples.

6. De Dampierre (1984: 13–17). The author developed a whole theory about the use of a particular plant (bisibili, or Trachyphrynium braunuanum) in twin rituals (1984: 14), yet it would seem that this plant played a role in the context of all births (unpublished field notes, D.R.C., November 26, 2005). Further hypotheses based on this supposed connection developed by the author therefore appear doubtful (cf. de Dampierre, ed. 1995: 186–190).

7. For an analysis of a "multiple ruse" involving the Zande Trickster and the Europeans, see Grootaers (2004).

8. The Ngbandi morpheme *(a)ngbo* is used with different tones and vowel sounds, resulting in different words with different meanings: besides "twins" / "snake," also "red," "salted," and "enclosure" or "stake." However, notably, the pronunciation of *(a)ngbo* meaning "twins" and "snake" is one and the same. Cf. Lekens (1958: 676–677, 682–683).

9. These paraphrases are scattered among various sources, including Vergiat (1937: 48), Molet (1971: 45), and Moen (2005: 51).

10. Tanghe (1926: 51, 53).

11. Molet (1971: 55).

12. The Nzakara have no fixed twin names either, as these are also revealed through dreams (de Dampierre 1984: 15).

13. E.g. Tanghe (1929: 281), Vergiat (1936: 91–92n1), Thomas (1970: 209), Molet (1971: 68–69), Henrix (2000: 190, *sub verbo* kula), Moen (2005: 139–140).

14. Unpublished field notes, D.R.C., October 26 and December 11, 2005.

15. Unpublished field notes, D.R.C., October 27 2005.

16. Cf. Wittgenstein's (1953: §66) definition of "family resemblance."

17. De Dampierre (1984: 14) confirmed the common elimination of the weaker of Nzakara twins; another Nzakara ethnographer, Anne Retel-Laurentin, denied that the Nzakara killed any of their twins (1969: 62n21).

18. E.g. Lévy-Bruhl (1910, 1938). All of Levy-Bruhl's books were translated into English; the first translation, of 1926, was entitled *How Natives Think*.

19. Evans-Pritchard (1956: ix). See also Firth (1966: 7) about the probable missionary influence on Evans-Pritchard's interpretation of Nuer thought.

20. Nothing indicates that Evans-Pritchard had read Tanghe's writings—although he certainly was acquainted with the series in which most of Tanghe's books were published—but the symmetry of the proposed "triadic relationships" involving twins in Ngbandi and Nuer cultures remains puzzling.

21. The Zande, who use the animal pronoun *(u)* for the rainbow, consider the superior rainbow male *(bawangu)* and the inferior one female *(nawangu)* (Lagae and Vanden Plas 1922: 27, *sub verbo: arc-en-ciel*).

22. Tanghe (1926: 72). The author also mentioned the Ngbandi belief in inter-twin, intrauterine anthropophagy, manifested in the birth defects of singletons, such as multiple limbs or megalocephaly (ibid: 74).

23. The Bantu Nyoro people (Uganda), who associated twins with pythons—the python was referred to as "mother of twins"—also said of a dead twin that it had "flown away *(gurraka)*, as a bird does" (Beattie 1962: 1, 11n3).

24. The list of Belgian, Dutch, French, and Italian missionary authors on Ubangi matters is long, but I limit myself to those referred to in this article: Daigre, Eggen, Giorgetti, Henrix, Hilberth, Lagae, Lekens, Maes, Moen, Molet, Santandrea, Tanghe, Van den Plas, and Zaal.

25. The past decades have seen the appearance of publications, principally by anthropologists, that deal with the knotty relationship between both groups of fieldworkers: cf. Stipe (1980), Sutlive (1985), Salamone (1986), Van der Geest

(1990). Judging from their titles, it does not seem far-fetched to view anthropologists and missionaries as some sort of twins . . .
   26. Unpublished fieldnotes, C.A.R., May 22, 2004.

WORKS CITED

Bahuchet, Serge, and Henri Guillaume. 1982. "Aka–Farmer Relations in the Northwest Congo Basin." In *Politics and History in Band Societies*, ed. E. Leacock and R. Lee, 189–211. Cambridge: Cambridge University Press / Paris: Editions de la Maison des Sciences de l'Homme.

Beattie, John. 1962. "Twin Ceremonies in Bunyoro." *Journal of the Royal Anthropological Institute* 92 (1): 1–12.

Blakeway, Stephen, et al. n.d. [1997]. *Nuer Ethno-Veterinary Knowledge: A Resource Manual, Findings of a Preliminary Study*. UNICEF.

Bouquiaux, Luc, and Jacqueline Thomas. 1980. "Le peuplement oubangien: Hypothèse de reconstruction des mouvements migratoires dans la région oubanguienne d'après les données linguistiques, ethnolinguistiques et de tradition orale." In *L'expansion bantoue*, 807–824. Paris: Centre National de la Recherche Scientifique.

Boyd, Raymond. 2007. "The Ubangian Languages." In *Ubangi: Art and Cultures from the African Heartland*, ed. J.-L. Grootaers, 104–111. Brussels: Mercatorfonds.

Burssens, Herman. 1958. *Les peuplades de l'entre Congo-Ubangi (Ngbandi, Ngbaka, Mbandja, Ngombe et Gens d'Eau)*. Tervuren, Belgium: Musée royal du Congo belge.

Cloarec-Heiss, France. 1998. "Entre Oubanguien et Soudan central: les langues banda." In *Language History and Linguistic Description in Africa*, ed. I. Maddieson and T. Hinnebusch, 1–16. Trenton, N.J. Asmara, Eritrea: Africa World Press.

Cordell, Dennis. 1983. "The Savanna Belt of North-Central Africa." In *History of Central Africa* [vol. 1], ed. D. Birmingham and P. Martin, 30–74. London: Longman.

Crabbeck, Gustave. [1939]. Ethnographic File no. 506. Ethnography Section, Royal Museum of Central Africa, Tervuren, Belgium.

Daigre, Joseph. 1931. "Les Bandas de l'Oubangui-Chari (Afrique Equatoriale Française)" [Part I]. *Anthropos* 26 (5–6): 647–695.

———. 1932. "Les Bandas de l'Oubangui-Chari (Afrique Equatoriale Française)" [Part II]. *Anthropos* 27 (1–2): 153–181.

De Dampierre, Eric. 1967. *Un ancien royaume Bandia du Haut-Oubangui*. Paris: Plon.

———. 1984. *Penser au singulier: Etude nzakara*. Paris: Société d'Ethnographie.

———, ed. 1995. *Une esthétique perdue: Harpes et harpistes du Haut-Oubangui*. Paris: Presses de l'Ecole normale supérieure.

De Jonghe, Edouard. 1924. "Associations primitives d'idées: Serpents. –Jumeaux.– Arc-en-ciel." *Congo* 5/I/4: 545–559.

Deng, Francis. 1972. *The Dinka of the Sudan*. New York: Holt, Rinehart, and Winston.

Diduk, Susan. 1993. "Twins, Ancestors, and Socio-Economic Change in Kedjom Society." *Man* 28 (3): 551–571.

Eboué, Félix. 1933. "Les peuples de l'Oubangui-Chari." *L'Ethnographie* 27: 3–79.

Eggen, Willy. 1976. *Peuple d'autrui: Une approche anthropologique de l'œuvre pastorale en milieu centafricain*. Brussels: ProMundi Vita.

Evans-Pritchard, Edward. 1929. "The Bongo." *Sudan Notes and Records* 12 (1): 1–61.

———. 1934. "Lévy-Bruhl's Theory of Primitive Mentality." *Bulletin of the Faculty of Arts* [University of Egypt] 2 (1): 1–36.

———. 1937. *Witchcraft, Oracles, and Magic among the Azande*. Oxford: Oxford University Press.

———. 1956. *Nuer Religion*. Oxford: Oxford University Press.

Firth, Raymond. 1966. "Twins, Birds, and Vegetables: Problems of Identification in Primitive Religious Thought." *Man* 1: 1–17.

Giorgetti, Filiberto [Gero]. 1968. *Death Among the Azande of the Sudan (Beliefs, Rites and Cult)*. Bologna, Italy: Nigrizia.

Grootaers, Jan-Lodewijk. [1991–1992, 2003, 2004, 2005]. Unpublished field notes from the Central African Republic and the Democratic Republic of the Congo.

———. 2002. "Politics, Music and Magic in Central Africa: Zande Culture and History." In *Forms of Wonderment: The History and Collections of the Afrika Museum*, ed. J.-L. Grootaers and I. Eisenburger, 422–445. Berg en Dal, the Netherlands: Afrika Museum.

———. 2004. "Le *Trickster* zande à la source du savoir des Européens? Une ruse plurielle d'Afrique centrale." In *Les raisons de la ruse: Une perspective anthropologique et psychanalytique*, ed. S. Latouche et al., 221–232. Paris: Editions La Découverte.

———. 2007. "Open Borders in a Central African Crucible." In *Ubangi: Art and Cultures from the African Heartland*, ed. J.-L. Grootaers, 16–103. Brussels: Mercatorfonds.

———, ed. 2007. *Ubangi: Art and Cultures from the African Heartland*. Brussels: Mercatorfonds.

Henrix, Marcel. 2000. *Dictionnaire ngbaka-français*. Ghent, Belgium: Research Centre for African Languages and Literature.

———. 2006. "Croyances ancestrales chez les Ngbaka mi-na-ge-nde" [unpublished manuscript]. Author's archives.

———. 2007. "Beliefs and Rituals of the Ngbaka People." In *Ubangi: Art and Cultures from the African Heartland*, ed. J.-L. Grootaers, 294–311. Brussels: Mercatorfonds.

Hilberth, Ellen, and John Hilberth. 1968. *Contribution à l'ethnographie des Gbaya* [Studia Ethnographica Upsaliensia 29]. Uppsala: Almqvist and Wicksell.

Hilberth, John. 1973. *The Gbaya* [Studia Ethnographica Upsaliensia 37]. Uppsala, Sweden: Almqvist and Wicksell.

Kronenberg, Waltraud, and Andreas Kronenberg. 1981. *Die Bongo: Bauern und Jäger im Südsudan.* Wiesbaden, Germany: Franz Steiner.

Lagae, Constant. 1926. *Les Azande ou Niam-Niam: L'organisation zande, croyances religieuses et magiques, coutumes familiales.* Brussels: Vromant.

Lagae, Constant, and Vincent Vanden Plas. 1922. *La langue des Azande,* vol. 2: *Dictionnaire Français–Zande.* Ghent, Belgium: Veritas.

Langdon, Margaret. 1989. "Notes on Some Ngbaka Customs" [unpublished manuscript]. Author's archives.

Larken, P. M. 1926. "An Account of the Zande." *Sudan Notes and Records* 9 (1): 1–55.

Lekens, Benjamin. 1958. *Ngbandi-Idioticon,* vol. 2: *Ngbandi en Nederlands-Frans.* Tervuren: Koninklijk Museum van Belgisch-Congo.

Lévi-Strauss, Claude. 1962. *Le totémisme aujourd'hui.* Paris: Presses Universitaires de France.

Lévy-Bruhl, Lucien. 1910. *Les fonctions mentales dans les sociétés inférieures.* Paris: Félix Alcan. Translated in 1926 as *How Natives Think.*

———. 1938. *L'expérience mystique et les symboles chez les primitifs.* Paris: Félix Alcan.

Leyder, Jean. 1935. "Association primitive d'idées: Serpent – jumeaux – arc-en-ciel au Congo belge." In *2me Congrès National des Sciences: Comptes rendus,* vol. 1, 39–44. Brussels: Fédération Belge des Sociétés Scientifiques.

Maes, Vedast. 1984. *Les peuples de l'Ubangi: Notes ethno-historiques.* Gemena, Democratic Republic of the Congo: Pères O.F.M. Capucins.

———. 1996. *Les Ngbaka du centre de l'Ubangi.* Gemena, Democratic Republic of the Congo: Pères O.F.M. Capucins.

Moen, Sveinung. 2005. *The Mongwande Snake Cult* [Studia Missionalia Svecana 98]. Uppsala: Swedish Institute of Mission Research / Falköping, Sweden: Kimpese Publishing House.

Molet, Louis. 1971. "Aspects de l'organisation du monde des Ngbandi (Afrique centrale)." *Journal de la Société des Africanistes* 41 (1): 35–69.

Moñino, Yves. 1988. "Lexique comparatif des langues oubanguiennes." In *Lexique comparatif des langues oubanguiennes,* ed. Y. Moñino, 87–146. Paris: Paul Geuthner.

Nougayrol, Pierre. 2008. Personal Communication, July 29 and 30, 2008.

Retel-Laurentin, Anne. 1969. *Oracles et ordalies chez les Nzakara.* Paris, The Hague: Mouton & Co.

Rosaldo, Renato. 1989. *Culture and Truth.* Boston: Beacon Press.

Salamone, Frank. 1986. "Missionaries and Anthropologists: An Inquiry into Their Ambivalent Relationship." *Missiology* 14 (1): 55–70.

Santandrea, Stefano. 1984. *The Banda of Bahr el Gazal (Sudan): Short Ethnological Notes.* Pro Manoscripto. Verona, Italy: Comboniani.

Schapera, Isaac. 1927. "Customs Relating to Twins in South Africa." *Journal of the African Society* 26: 117–137.

Schweinfurth, Georg. 1875. *Artes Africanae: Abbildungen und Beschreibungen von Erzeugnissen des Kunstfleisses centralafrikanischer Völker.* Leipzig, Germany: F. A. Brockhaus / London: Sampson Low, Marston, Low, and Searle.

Stipe, Claude. 1980. "Anthropologists Versus Missionaries: The Influence of Pre-suppositions." *Current Anthropology* 21: 165–178.

Sutlive, Vinson. 1985. "Anthropologists and Missionaries: Eternal Enemies or Colleagues in Disguise?" In *Missionaries, Anthropologists, and Cultural Change,* ed. D. Whiteman, 55–90. Williamsburg, Va.: College of William and Mary.

Tanghe, Basiel. 1921. *De slang bij de Ngbandi.* Brussels: Goemaere.

———. 1926. *Le culte du serpent chez les Ngbqndi.* Bruges, Belgium: Les Presses Gruuthuuse.

———. 1929. *De Ngbandi naar het leven geschetst.* Bruges, Belgium: De Gruuthuuse Persen.

Tessmann, Günter. 1928. "Die Mbaka-Limba, Mbum und Laka." *Zeitschrift für Ethnologie* 60: 305–352.

———. 1934. *Die Baja: Ein Negerstamm im mittleren Sudan,* vol. 1: *Materielle und seelische Kultur.* Stuttgart, Germany: Strecker und Schröder.

———. 1937. *Die Baja: Ein Negerstamm im mittleren Sudan,* vol. 2: *Geistige Kultur.* Stuttgart: Strecker und Schröder.

Thomas, Jacqueline. 1970. *Contes, proverbes, devinettes ou énigmes, chants et prières ngbaka-ma'bo (République Centrafricaine).* Paris: Klincksieck.

Turner, Terence. 1991. "'We Are Parrots,' 'Twins Are Birds': Play of Tropes as Operational Structure." In *Beyond Metaphor. The Theory of Tropes in Anthropology,* ed. J. Fernandez, 121–158. Stanford, Calif.: Stanford University Press.

Turner, Victor. 1969. *The Ritual Process: Structure and Anti-Structure.* Ithaca, N.Y.: Cornell University Press.

Van der Geest, Sjaak. 1990. "Anthropologists and Missionaries: Brothers Under the Skin." *Man* 25 (4): 588–601.

Vergiat, Antonin-Marius. 1936. *Les rites secrets des primitifs de l'Oubangui.* Paris: Payot.

———. 1937. *Mœurs et coutumes des Manjas.* Paris: Payot.

———. n.d. [1997]. *Noirs d'Oubangui: Traditions, mythes, et symbols; Rites sexuels et magiques* [unpublished manuscript]. Roanne, France: Musée Joseph Dechelette.

Wittgenstein, Ludwig. 1953. *Philosophische Untersuchungen / Philosophical Investigations.* New York: Macmillan.

Wolfe, Alvin. 1961. *In the Ngombe Tradition: Continuity and Change in the Congo.* Evanston, Ill.: Northwestern University Press.

Zaal, Cees. 1955. *De 'Nzakara': Etnografische aantekeningen* [unpublished manuscript]. Archives of the Congregation of the Holy Spirit, Gemert (the Netherlands).

CHAPTER TEN

Fiction and Forbidden Sexual Fantasy in the Culture of Temne Twins

FREDERICK JOHN LAMP

Things that are unspeakable and unthinkable have a way of both tanta-lizing and frightening those in their grip. None of us are free of this. The phenomenon of twins fascinates, tantalizes, and frightens. It is in this vein that I analyze art, architecture, ritual, and oral literature from the Temne of Sierra Leone that both celebrates and fears the birth of twins, especially the monozygotic (the dreaded "same sex"). Psychoanalytic literature will situate the Temne in some universal phenomena—on the fear of sexual transgression, especially incest compounded by homosexuality—in which we should all be able to breathe more freely. In the meantime, let's see how the Temne treat twins.[1]

Multiple sets of twins (*tà-bàri*, singular: *kà-bàri*), sometimes two and three sets in a family, are not uncommon among the Temne (Thomas 1970 [1916], I: 18; and confirmed in my own field research in the 1970s), and they give rise to elaborate precautions. Twin ritual among the Temne of Sierra Leone involves miniature spirit houses, miniature wooden beings, anthills as the empty shells of the dead, and elaborate ceremonies. I have found twin ritual and its effects only in the western part of Temne land, especially in Port Loko District.[2]

It is the use of the twin houses, more than the twin figures, that domi-nates Temne twin ritual. There are several types of Temne ritual houses that are miniature. This is because they are situated not in our mundane world, but in the dim, remote world of the spirits, less visible than the houses of the real world, obviously not useful to real people, not located in real dimensions or space or time (Lamp 1982: chapter 3). Among these spiritual miniature houses are the houses devoted to twins.[3] These are not where wooden twin figures are housed, but they contain symbols of twin-ship and of death, and they are the site of sacrifices, and possibly burial.

FIGURE 10.1. Pa Aluseni Kamara carving a twin figure, Making village, Port Loko District, Sierra Leone, 1979. *Photo: Frederick John Lamp.*

However, we will begin with the figures, which are situated in an elaborate body of arresting visual and performative imagery. They were still being used and carved when I did my research among the Temne from 1976 through 1980, but the practice was clearly in decline. Certainly the wars of the 1990s have disrupted much of Temne culture, so it is in question whether the carving of twin figures, or the ritual itself, has continued. Nevertheless, I have opted for the present tense here, since I though don't know for sure, I am hopeful for the endurance a group of people and a culture that I entered in all its details at the age of twenty-two, and still have great affection for.

Use of Twin Figures

Standing wooden figures, about 20–30 cm. tall, are carved as a general rule to represent the dead twin as a playmate for the live one, but also as an instrument of ritual for the mother (Anwyl 1916: 43; E. Langley 1939: 77; Thomas 1970, I: 114). In some cases figures are carved for living twins (Cole 1886: 25; Thomas 1970, I: 114), but this seems to be the exception. I have never seen a matched pair, although figures in identical style are found in separate collections (see figure 10.3).

An early reference to twin figures was recorded by an African American missionary in 1877, revealing some characteristic ritual practices involving these figures:

I was standing in front of the house. A girl passed, going toward the river, with an image ornamented with beads in her hand. . . . She said it was a woman's child, and she was going to wash it. I spoke to the king, asking him to get it for me. He sent for the woman, who said that she gave birth to twins, and one died. She had this image made, and believed that the spirit of the dead child now dwelt in it and minded the family. She could not part with it. [. . . though eventually with a little coercion she did]. (Joseph Gomer, October 2, 1877, in Flickinger 1882: 247–248)

It is the mother who maintains the figure, kept near her sleeping place (Thomas 1970, I: 114). She decorates the figure with strings of beads, usually white to represent spiritual protection, hung around the waist as small children often wear them. The figure may be placed standing before the mother when suckling the remaining child after the one twin has died. When washing or feeding the child, the figure is also washed and fed, i.e., offered plates of food. When the living twin marries, the figure is presented to him or her, and taken to the new home (Langley 1939: 77).

An expert female builder at the village of Romeni told me that when she comes to build the twin house, *ka-bangka,* she brings twin figures, puts them in a basket (*ka-blai*), places it on the family's veranda, and then proceeds to build their *ka-bangka.* Presumably the proximity of the twin figures to the construction site is significant. Hall (1928: 427) reported that the wooden figures illustrated in his article were taken from the graves of twins, suggesting that they may have been intended as companions for the dead.

Twin figures also serve other ritual purposes. A figure used by the Angbangbani association of diviners and circumcisers is said to be a twin. Healers also use twin figures, which they keep in baskets with other items, to kill witches. During boys' initiation, *Rabai,* their staffs are frequently carved with a twin figure as the finial, each chosen by the young boy himself as a symbol of sexual and social energy (Lamp 1978). It is said that anyone who plays with a twin figure may get twins (Thomas 1970, I: 114), so the figure is thought to have a great deal of creative power.

Building the House

The *ka-bangka* (also called *sòsò*) may be built for living or dead twins by the father or mother of the twins, by a female specialist in the ritual of twinship called Na-Tà-bàri (Madame Twins),[4] or by other ritual

FIGURE 10.2. Twin House, *ka-bangka*, Rogbep village, Sierra Leone, 1979. *Photo: Frederick John Lamp.*

practitioners.[5] A living twin may rebuild the house when it is needed. A house may be built for a single set of twins for one family, or a single house may be built for all the twins in the town. There may be many men who come to help build the house, and repetition characterizes the building. As soon as they finish building, they condemn the house and destroy it. This is repeated several times before the final house is left to stand, so it can take all day to finish a twins' house. Rice is then cooked with duiker skin and beans and first offered to a selection of collected anthills, and then to the builders; they condemn the rice and throw it back into the pot, then it's offered again, repeatedly.

Within and about the twins' house are a number of items important to its ritual. One anthill (*k'ɔbi*) for each living and dead twin to be commemorated or honored is placed on the ground within the house. At one village near Port Loko, there were two anthills in the twins' house for deceased *gbese* (the child born after twins), five for dead twins, and one for a remaining living twin. A white ribbon is tied around the center of each anthill to delineate the head from the body. White cloth is used to drape over and cover the anthills to keep them warm and dry, as if they were the living twins themselves.

Inside the house may be also found a number of broken white plates, glass medicine bottles, and white flour from *kà-fumàk* (a fungus).[6] The whiteness of these objects refers to the whiteness of the spiritual world. One can also find calabashes meant to receive sacrificial foods, tobacco for the spirits' enjoyment, gourd rattles, bamboo gongs (*è-buke*), snail shells, and tortoise shells (*è-kuntho*) intended to be used for providing rhythm for songs performed in twins' ritual. Buried underground within the *ka-baŋgka* are said to be containers of gun powder, fishhooks, thread, and a needle. These are all used in aggression against evildoers who would cause harm to the family. The twins are called upon to kill these evildoers if they should come, using spiritual methods invoked by the objects under the twins' house.

The twins' house is more than just a place for ritual or a commemoration of twin birth. It is a shrine, and it may be seen as a spiritual presence itself, even as a spiritual being who can be supplicated. All of these definitions seem to be suggested in song during twins ritual. The first song identifies the *sòsò* as the place where the twins live. But we know that they don't actually live in the *sòsò,* so the implication is that the *sòsò* is more than the miniature hut but is an enveloping presence, a spiritual enclosure:

de runi-e	Where are you living?
ε runi-e	Where are you living?
ε runi-e	Where are you living?
kaŋ sòsò	In the Sòsò [the twins' house].

Another song emphasizes the intense spiritual power of the twins' hut, in comparing it to the ritual house of the diviners and healers of the women's society, *aŋ-Bom.* The singer laments her exclusion from entering the *sòsò* or *ka-baŋka* (for what reason she doesn't give), but counters that she will enter the *ka-baŋklò,* the house of *aŋ-Bom,* instead:

ò wòŋ ro baŋka	He enters the twins' hut.
ò wòŋ ro baŋka	He enters the twins' hut.
ε-ε aya ye ò wòŋ ro baŋka	[exclamation] He enters the twins' hut.
kaŋ ka ò yò-yε mi sò	But he doesn't let me enter again.
i wòŋ ro baŋklò	I enter the hut of aŋ-Bom.
ò wòŋ ro baŋka	He enters the twins' hut.

A third song addresses the *sòsò* as if it were a living, responsive being, asking it to identify the mother of the twins:

kane kum ta-bari	Who bore the twins?
Ya-Mari, kònò kum ta-bari	Mother Marie, she bore the twins.
sòsò, kane kum ta-bari	Sòsò, who bore the twins?
Ya-Mari, kònò kum ta-bari	Mother Marie, she bore the twins.

In the course of one of my interviews, the practitioner of twins' ritual sang the following words, as a supplication of *sòsò*, again as if it were a spiritual being capable of granting twin birth when requested:

ò-porto kònò yema	The white man wants
kum ta-bari	to bear twins,
sòsò	Sòsò [the twins' house].

Character of Twins

Twins are said to be owned and guided by spiritual beings who share the same names. Twins have special towns located in the spiritual world, with names such as Rombangkang, Kayangka (the caves, located in the forest), Romanè, and Yengkesa (located by the water). Twins come from these towns originally, and they return eventually to their home of origin, as a song sung in twins' ritual suggests:

o-rà mà-e e	Oh, where are you?
kò ro Yengkesa	I'm going to Yengkesa.
o-rà mà-e e	Oh, where are you?
kò ro Yengkesa	I'm going to Yengkesa.
o-rà mà-e e	Oh, where are you?
ka ke-bàng ka-ti	To the sea there,
ka ke-bàng ka-ti	To the sea there,
re me kò	That's where I'm going.
kò ro Yengkesa	I'm going to Yengkesa.

James Littlejohn (1980: 228), who worked extensively on Temne concepts of spiritual space, reported a very particular spiritual origin for Temne twins which has not been mentioned elsewhere:

> . . . [T]wins are believed to be demons belonging to the family of Monitor Lizard. They are river demons who have managed to enter their mother's womb while she was bathing in the river, and have been born in the form

of mortals. The members of this family, as recounted, can live either on land or in water, and include all snakes.

Perhaps the use of the snail as the emblem of twins among the neighboring Southern Bullom (Hall 1937, F: 72; Pichl 1967: 104) suggests the same watery origin.

Twins are *thekre,* meaning they have supernatural power and vision, and are considered to be in league with spiritual forces—good or bad—that can effect change (Shaw 1982: 101, 110). They have *sòki* ("four eyes"). Even before they can talk, twins can communicate with ritual practitioners. Their powers may be used by others. In a dream, the twins' spirits may say, "We are looking for someone." This may result in a woman's pregnancy, suggesting that the twins are responsible for calling a newborn from the spiritual world. Hall (1928: 418) reported that twins' powers are specially directed to encourage human fertility. A particular story about twins (actually "three twins," *tà-bàri a-sas,* i.e., triplets) suggests that twins have enormous spiritual power to do superhuman things, such as collecting all the smoke from a burning woods inside a fishing net, extracting cool drinking water from a pot of boiling water, or connecting diverging roads to make them go the same place, and so resolving disputes (Lamp 2008: 60). Conducting the proper ritual for dead twins, or simply behaving well with living twins, can bring riches. Two songs heard in twins' ritual advise this:

Sento ngo, Sina ngo	Oh, you, Sento, Sina—
ta mai nà nga o	Let's take care of them.
man pu der de	For they've come to us.
ta mai nà nga	Let's take good care of them.
ta de bans su	Let us welcome them.
ta de bans ò-komra ò-kore	Let us welcome the pregnant woman.

Twins are known also for extremely aggressive behavior and are capable of severe malevolence. They kill people accused of being "witches." Twins can be "witches" and can cause the rice crop to fail, according to a Temne story (Lamp 2008: 57). They can cause all manner of trouble (e.g., madness) to fall upon parents if their ritual is not properly performed. Dreams about twins can be inauspicious: dreaming of a person wearing white beads passing in the night, or dreaming of planting the banana (*è-pòlòt*) presages the death of the twin (Thomas 1970, I: 88). If someone hits a twin, the twin can twist the offender's head one hundred eighty degrees (Shaw 1982: 105).

Dead twins communicate with their living partners. The spirit of a dead twin may visit a living one in dreams to give advice on financial matters or on a journey to be undertaken (Langley 1939: 77). The dead twin can torment the living twin (Cole 1886: 66).

Most commentary on the birth of twins suggests that it is dreaded, although the proscriptions are ambivalent. Certain behavior is said to elicit twin birth. If a man or woman eats a banana (è-pòlòt) from a banana tree planted for twins, the wife or the woman herself will bear twins (Thomas 1970, I: 88). It was reported in the late nineteenth century that if two women walking on the road separate to allow two men to pass between them, this would cause them to bear twins (Banbury 1888: 185). Anyone who plays with a twin figure is likely to bear twins (Anwyl 1916: 43). A story that I recorded in the village of Ropapa (Lamp 2008: 57) tells of the mother of a twin who was discovered to be a witch. All the foregoing seems to indicate that it is one's transgression that brings twins into the family. Besides, twin births promise to bring heartbreak to the family, as one song from twins ritual suggests:

ang gbàl ang-gbàthàng	They sweep the veranda
ka-ting-o	For nothing—
ka ta do-ràng a yira-o	They sit behind the house—
ang-gbàthàng an tse thò	The veranda remains empty.

Literally, the song says that sweeping the veranda is a waste of time because the men just abandon it anyway to come sit behind the house where the women are cooking. The analogy is: to bear twins can be a waste because as soon as they're born, they may just "pass behind"—i.e., die—so the mother has suffered in vain.

But a comment by one of my Temne consultants suggests that one's transgression could deny the arrival of twins to one's family: if someone in the family is not "clean," twins will go to another family to be born again. One Temne consultant said that if the mother of twins wishes to give birth to twins again, ceremonies are performed for her at the *ka-bangka,* so occasionally a family sees benefits in the birth of twins. And ceremonies for the birth of twins are expressions of pleasure.

The Ritual Care of Twins

Ritual for the twins is usually conducted by a person with the official name of Na-Gbese (Madame Gbese), a practitioner in charge of twins. Gbese is the name given to the child born after twins, who receives the same ritual as the twins.[7] It seems that a Na-Gbese is always a child born after twins herself, although this is not entirely clear.

On the day of birth, the most extensive ritual is carried out. This is the ceremony called *wòngkò*. All other twins are invited to participate. First, an anthill is put in the twin house. Then the participants fill some cups with rice flour, scatter it on the path from the *ka-bangka* to mother's house and back to *ka-bangka*. In ritual, the first-born is always handled first. The newborn twins are now carried, cushioned on a cloth in a calabash or a rice fan (*ka-theme*), from house to house. Each house gives them dual gifts. As they travel around the village they beat the musical instruments, the bamboo gongs (*è-buke*) or tortoise shells (*è-kuntho*) taken from the *ka-bangka*. The people sing a number of songs expressing great pleasure:

Song 1)
ti waŋ kò rò   I will put him there.
waŋ kò rò pepe   I will put him there in the calabash.
tse waŋ kò tete   Don't put him [undecipherable].
waŋ kò rò pepe   I will put him there in the calabash.

Song 2)
o de ba kàli-a   Oh, come and look!
o ya-e   [exclamation]
tà-bàri am pu funtha   The twins have laid down—
[chorus] *Sento, Sina*   Sento, Sina
òyò òwe   [exclamation]

Song 3)
Sento ya Bali-eng   Sento and Bali
è-è Sento ya Bali-eng   Oh, Sento and Bali
hali a than ba-yeng   Even as small as this [showing the hand]—
a bot ta mi ka am-pepe   They put [gifts] for me in the calabash.

Then they carry the twins to the *ka-bangka*. Here the diviner uses his methods to determine whether the twins have come to stay or not. It is the role of the anthills, representing particular ancestors—known only to the diviner—associated with twinship, to help to determine this. The twins are placed on the ground with their heads toward the entrance of the *ka-bangka*: it is said that if the baby lies still, its life will be short, but if it turns with feet toward the door its life will be long (Langley 1939: 76–77). Interestingly, one can barely imagine a newborn child repositioning itself, although it *is* something newborn reptiles would be capable of. When the twins are weaned, sacrifices are taken to the shrine again as at birth, and the announcement is made that they are weaned.

Annual ceremonies are held for the honoring of twins first in the middle of the rainy season well before harvest, then in the middle of the hot dry season, when harvested grain dwindles, the fruit and vegetables have not yet ripened, and food is scarce. The mother collects leaves in the woods and makes medicine with them, and cooks bland rice with no pepper in the sauce. She mixes the fungus, *ka-fumàk*, with palm oil, feeds it to the twins, places it on each twin's tongue, chest, back, and feet. She may take a piece of gold, speak to it to inquire whether anyone is wishing ill, then dig a hole inside the *ka-bangka* and bury the gold, in order to fight the potential evildoer.

At the death of the twin, an anthill is placed in the *ka-bangka*, if one has not already been placed at birth, and covered with white cloth to keep it cozy. Rice flour (*ang-gbera*), valued for its symbolic whiteness, is made and offered to the deceased, poured on the ground before the door of the twin house. A new white cloth is then hung in front of the *ka-bangka*.

Na-Tà-bàri then removes the white cloth from the anthills, leaving just a strip. The remaining strip of white cloth is used as a headband on the anthill, resembling the white headband characteristically worn by the

FIGURE 10.3. Female twin figure on a staff. Wood, 56 cm. (including partial shaft). Collection unknown. *Philip Abrams, Reston, Virginia.*

paramount chief, ò-kande. Dead twins are regarded as ò-kande. The mother of twins then goes into the woods to gather leaves and make a potion for the remaining twin. People in the village cook food to leave for the dead twin at the ka-bangka in order to restore health to its mourning mother.

The deceased twin, if an infant, is said to be buried under the wall of the family house. But earlier in the twentieth century, it was said to be buried in the miniature house, the ka-bangka (Hall 1928: 416; Langley 1939: 77). One must never say that a twin has died, only that he or she has gone to fetch salt, etc., or has gone away. When my Temne assistant, Jacob, asked an adolescent girl, Sento, where her twin was, she, not knowing that the other twin had died, replied, "My husband has gone on a trip" (I discuss the use of the spousal term below). Friends do not express sympathy but tell the mother or the remaining twin, "I hope he (or she) will have a good journey."

Speculations on Parental Fear, Fantasies, and the Sexual Aspects of Twinship

Parents are often shown to be fearful of twins, accusing them of sorcery, according to one Temne story (Lamp 2008: 57), or even trying to break them up, to the point of wishing one dead, as another story tells (Lamp 2008: 62). There are many sources of this tension. Twins can kill, twist a person's head off, make someone pregnant, cause more dreaded twin births, implicate the mother in witchcraft, and die on a whim. Their very name, tà-bàri, sets them in the noun class not of human beings (which is the ò-class) but of small animals and insects, somewhat troubling in itself. This relates to the testimony given to Littlejohn that Temne twins come from the sea or the forest and are members of the reptile family, and it recalls Evans-Pritchard's (1967: 136) data on the Nuer of Sudan that "a twin is not a person . . . he is a bird. . ." (see chapter 9).

The family with twins needs to take special precautions, or the twins can harm the family or themselves. Twins love contradictions, and parents speak to them with contradictions. This is to get them to have "separate minds" (Thomas 1970, I: 114). Twins are associated with the rubbish heap (a place usually to the west, with enormous symbolic content) because of their ambivalent power; if they cry too much, become ill, or are simply troublesome, they are placed there for a time, which would put them on the line toward the world of the dead, perhaps as a warning (Shaw 1982: 106). There are special dietary prohibitions for twins. Twins must never eat ta-titi sticks (the wood used to construct the shrine) or they will become deaf (Langley 1939: 78), nor snail (causes crawcraw, an itching skin infection), nor iguana (causes deafness) (Thomas 1970, I: 113).

These are all emblems of the etiology of twinship, so to eat them would be cannibalistic—thus evoking a fear that twins would devour each other or even themselves.

What must be equally disconcerting is the documented notion that Temne twins, while appearing to be two different people going their separate ways, tormenting each other and everyone else, are actually one and the same person. Temne inheritance law at the beginning of the twentieth century indicates this: in case of living twins, each twin gets only half a share that would normally fall to an individual heir (Thomas 1970, I: 165). They are thought to have one mind, and parents go to great lengths to force them to think separately—again, to have "separate minds." A similar conception has been found among the Fon, of the Republic of Benin, in both spiritual and mundane realms. Many gods, such as the primordial Mawu-Lisa, are often thought of as a single, bisexual being, yet alternately these gods can also be considered by some to be twins. For example, Daŋ Ayido Hwedo is/are the same. The first human beings all were cojoined twins and androgynous (Mercier 1954: 219–233). In one of the Temne stories (Lamp 2008: 60) about twins—probably monozygotic triplets to be more precise—it is stated that twins must always agree and if one says "Let's do this," the other must follow the same path:

> . . . a woman who gave birth to three twins (triplets). After she had given birth to the twins, she advised them never to disagree with one another until death, that everything that one starts, the other should support, and that if they go on a journey they should not disagree with each other. If one says "Let's do this," the other should agree. . . . After they had grown, they decided one day to go on a journey in search of wisdom. So they went on this journey, walking all day and all night. They didn't find a town. They saw nobody, just woods and animals. After they had traveled for three days, they came to a fork in the road. One said he's going to go on the left-hand road. The other said he's following the right-hand road. But the third said, "Our mother advised us never to disagree with one another. Now that we've decided to go on a journey and we've found this fork in the road, you have decided to disagree with each other. It's not right." When he was finished, the other two ignored his advice. Since they disagreed, he said he was not going anywhere. "You go on your different roads—I'm going to stay at this intersection."

The story goes on to tell of the misfortunes of the two brothers who decided to split, but the first brother at the intersection miraculously sewed together the two diverging roads and came to save his brothers.

Not only are the twins one and the same, but, in a more complex sense, they represent a sexual bond. Male and female twins are called husband and wife. As described above, the remaining twin always refers to his or her deceased twin as a spouse. When a girl twin wants to be married, her twin brother ("husband") must be paid before he gives his consent. One Temne twin figure mounted on the staff from a boy's *Rabai* initiation shows a Janus (two-faced) twin figure, suggesting that the Temne conception of inseparable male and female twins is similar to that of the Fon. In Sierra Leone oral narratives, the theme in which the twin brother prevents his twin sister's marriage is prominent. Eberl (1936: 135) tells a story from the neighboring Mende people of a twin brother who saved his twin sister from marrying a tenacious bush spirit. Although here the most explicit issue is saving a woman from an anthropophagic spirit, it is also significant that it is a twin brother refusing to allow his sister to marry. This recalls a Zulu story related by Hammond-Tooke (1992: 206) in which twins, conceived miraculously and immaculately, are born to a senior wife of the chief. The male twin will not allow his female twin to marry; for example:

> She hides the twins in her hut and instructs them always to conceal them-
> selves from the eyes of the villagers, especially the crows [who are actually
> the children of the co-wives], who scatter water and ash all over her house.
> . . . The children flourish and attain the age of puberty. . . . One day, when
> the mothers are in the fields, the twins disobey her order to remain con-
> cealed and go to the river to fetch water. . . . Suddenly a group of strangers
> appear and ask for water. This the boy gives. The strangers say that they have
> been sent to find a wife for the son of the chief and ask about the inhabitants
> of the village. The boy denies that there is a potential bride there. . . .

For the Dogon, according to the sage Ogotemmeli, the original hom-inids created by God were the eight Nummo, each one androgynous and considered a pair of twins, perfection, and the ideal unit. Twin births were the original norm, although the Nummo knew that birthing would even-tually result in errors such as single births, like that of the solitary jackal. The individual Nummo "were able to fertilize themselves, being dual and bisexual."

> The permanent calamity of single births was slightly mitigated by the
> grant of the dual soul. . . . Thus it came about that each human being from
> the first was endowed with two souls of different sex, or rather with two
> principles corresponding to two distinct persons. In the man the female

soul was located in the prepuce; in the woman the male soul was in the clitoris. (Griaule 1965: 19, 22, 24)

Inherent in Ogotemmeli's analysis is the defense of circumcision in male and female initiations—the fear of androgyny, and the need to create single-sexed individuals who could then mate with their opposites. Yet "Dogon religion and Dogon philosophy both expressed a haunting sense of the original loss of twin-ness. . . . Most of the conversations with Ogotemmeli had indeed turned largely on twins and on the need for duality and the doubling of individual lives" (Griaule 1965: 198).

Again, for the Fon, the ideal divine birth is likewise a twin birth, preferably of opposite sex, in which the two, in sexual partnership, are one "androgynous, self-fertilizing being" (Mercier 1954: 219, 231). Zulu tradition posits the existence of twin spirits, male and female, who rule the sky and the earth, respectively. A Zulu consultant said:

> . . . it is clear that one is the husband and the other the wife. . . . The sky is like a husband because the sky is above the earth. They are not only twins. Yes, they are twins, but they're also husband-and-wife. We call them twins because we do not know which one is more important. If we say twins, then we do not say that one is greater than the other. (In Berglund 1976: 34)

Another Zulu consultant, a "rain-maker," explained that "they came from the womb at the same time. . . . That is the condition of the sky and the earth. They are twins. They are both from the beginning. . . . Being twins, they are also husband-and-wife. The husband fertilizes the wife. The fertilizer is the water" (Berglund 1976: 62).

Hammond-Tooke wrote an interesting structural analysis of four Zulu stories from South Africa in which he investigated the "deep structure" that lies beneath the apparent and sometimes confusing surface structure (Hammond-Tooke 1992: 203–220). In the four stories, which are very complicated, with many "nonsense" passages, he was able to detect a pervasive pattern in each in which a male and female child, probably from the same parents, and probably twins (explicitly in one case) go on an adventure in which the male offers sour milk to the female, who rejects it. After fighting off various monsters who mediate the journey, they marry. In the first story, the girl and boy share the same name, with gendered endings, and explicitly love one another; in the second, mentioned above, a boy and girl are born miraculously together in a pot filled with the mother's blood, and the boy refuses to surrender the girl to other suitors; in the third story, twins figure in the story apparently gratuitously, but they may be transformations of the hero and heroine; and in the fourth story, a boy and girl born to separate mothers fantasize that they are twins. Drawing upon the symbolism among the exogamous Zulu surrounding the sharing of sour milk as an indicator of kinship, and the rejection of it as an indicator of non-kinship, therefore sexual availability, Hammond-Tooke interpreted these stories as attempts to reconcile the inconsistency of a strong and pervasive desire for incest, on the one hand, with the preoccupation with prohibitions against it, on the other. The fact that the stories were told to children emphasizes the obsessive need to objectivize what are seen as real existential problems (following Bruno Bettelheim) so that, early on, people can work through them and accept the ambiguities.

The concept of male/female twins as partners to one extent or another, even as husband and wife, seems pervasive throughout Africa, where they are seen as inseparable, unable to live without each other. How sexually can we interpret this? Marriage, for the Temne, clearly is a sexual bond for the purpose of bearing children, even more than an emotional bond or soulmate bond, which category is usually reserved for same-sex friends. Is (or was) Temne twin marriage a sexual unity, either conceptually or in fact? There are no data available to answer this.

Suppose the twins are monozygotic, or simply dizygotic same-sex. Does this same sexual bond (whether symbolic or physical) still hold for the Temne?

Thomas (1970, III: 75) tells a story of twin brothers who "loved each other well," and who made a pact, "that where you die, I will die" (Lamp 2008: 62). I give an excerpt:

> These twins loved each other very much. The children used to go fishing often, they learned to set traps for birds, and they used to go also to pick the fruit of a tree near the cave of the evil *ang-kàrfi* [singular: *ò-kàrfi*, a non-ancestral spiritual being]. The twins found that each time they tasted the fruit of this tree, they felt happy. . . . Their father is dead. The mother did not love the one boy, Morba. . . . [The story goes on to describe their entering initiation together by which they die and enter the spiritual world. The spirits entrust each of them with a mask and instruct them never to let the masks get wet, but their discriminatory mother allowed Morba's mask to get wet.] . . . [Condemned,] Morba took the mask, headed straight towards the woods, and entered the woods. Kereyombo said, "Wait, so that we two go and die together." Morba replied, "No, I will

go alone, go die alone, because I broke my promise." But Kereyombo said, "Oh, but I put a promise in my mind that where you die I will die."

It is impossible to know from the evidence available here exactly what is meant by the word love. Clearly much of the data indicates that a pair of twins is considered a single person, for which the implications of mutual love are complex. Among the neighboring Kuranko, same-sex twin pairs seem to be considered a single sexual entity, as twin girls must marry the same man and twin men must marry the same girl (Parsons 1964: 42).[8] In the previous Temne story of the male triplets, they were instructed to be inseparable. Mercier (1954: 231) has reported for the Fon "The ideal type of every group in the divine world is a pair of twins of opposite sex or, more rarely, of the same sex." He previously described these couplings as sexual unions, although he did not go on to elaborate upon the nature of the divine monozygotic couples. Ogotemmeli, Griaule's Dogon consultant, said that the seventh and eighth Nummo twin ancestors, both female (the first four were male and the last four were female, although all shared dual principles), gave birth to the Dogon ancestor, Lebe. "'Lebe is a new Word [act of creation] created by two females . . . It is not known which of the two, the seventh or the eighth played the part of the male'" (Griaule 1965: 60). "Ogotemmeli had often said that the ideal pair was composed of two females and consequently had the sign 8, the same as the creative Word" (Griaule 1965: 212).

Considering Temne ideas of twins as sexual couples, considering the extensive documentation on sexual prohibition in Africa, and considering the great fear and awe that many African societies have for twins, and the attention lavished on representing them aesthetically in sculpture and architecture, it seems to me that we need to factor in the sexual dimension to any discussion of the culture of twins, especially monozygotic twins, whose lives together are probably more intimate than any other coupling. Twins are associated in several ways with hypersexuality. I would like to propose that an important factor in this fear that parents have, and the elaborate ritual in which they engage, is the fear of incest and homosexuality, whether or not the fear is well founded.

Public display of affection is governed in Africa differently from the West in a number of sexual arenas. Same-sex physical affection, such as holding hands, hugging, kissing, and sleeping together is simply the African norm, displayed openly, whereas public display of affection between men and women is considered offensive. One cannot help but notice that in Angelo Micheli's analysis (chapter 7), every image of doubles and twins in contemporary studio photography is same-sex.

The conventional wisdom from European/American observers has been for long that such same-sex affection is nonsexual. I no longer accept this, based upon long experience. Yes, for some African men there would be no thought of the sexual. If we take Kinsey's continuum from heterosexual to homosexual in a ranking of one to six to apply as well to Africa (and except for the notion of absolutes, I think it can be reasonably useful to do so), then some men will have less or more inclination to take the affection further, and many would take it as far as they can with encouragement. In my experience, sensuality permeates African life, unlike in much of the West where it has been disdained, feared, and even punished. Same-sex affection for many African men is clearly titillating to some degree or another, in my experience on a quotidian level, and is, in fact, institutionalized in homoerotic ritual.

Until the past couple decades it may have been unthinkable to propose a homosexual theory of African religious practice, and to the present day, there is some extreme hostility expressed in both rhetoric and law enforcement against homosexuality in particular African countries whose leaders insist that homosexuality is alien to Africa. But recently, some of the scattered and ignored data on homosexuality in Africa has been gathered and published, with extensive, reliable documentation on the prevalence of same-sex relations among men and women alike, especially in the arena of ritual practitioners (Beckwith and Fisher 1999; Drewal and Drewal 1983; Evans-Pritchard 1970: 1428–1434; Lamp 1978: 34–49, 94; Lamp 1996; Murray and Roscoe 1998; Somé 1993). Twins are, by definition, ritual practitioners, and inhabitants of a space somewhere between the physical world of cultural norms and the spiritual world where many of our familiar codes are inverse. They are in many ways the "gatekeepers," betwixt and between dual realms. This is not to argue that ritual priesthood and ritual mediumship is by definition homosexual but simply to say that there is a significant prevalence documented in ritual contexts well above that documented in quotidian life.

Quite a few studies have shown that although homosexual behavior has been accepted in many African societies, as with many aspects of life in African thought, it is not to be discussed openly. Clear homosexual behavior has its accepted niche in ordinary Temne life, as it does in many African societies, associated with the left, as opposed to the right, the hidden and private as opposed to the open and public. This may also account for its proliferation in ritual situations, which are often closed and esoteric.

Whether the "homosexual," as a category differentiated from "homosexual behavior," is widely recognized in indigenous African thought south of the Sahara is under dispute (Murray and Roscoe 1998: 271–273). Yet homosexual preference has been documented among many ethnic groups. Isolated cases are found in traditional Africa where permanent homosexual identity and even homosexual marriage is approved, and sometimes even prescribed, for example, among the Dagara of Burkina Faso (where they are called "gatekeepers"), the Meru of Kenya, the Kongo of Angola, and the Amhara of Ethiopia (where they are called "God's mistakes"). Documentation begins as early as 1616, by Petrus Jarric, in Angola (Murray and Roscoe 1998: 22, 37, 93, 147). But same-sex marriages are, and were, certainly not common.

The arts and culture of Africa, generally, are full of homosexual and homoerotic practices. Particularly in the professions of religion, healing, dance, and mediumship, it is found in abundance, for example, among Coptic monks, Kenyan performers known as *mashoga*, the *mugawe* ritual leaders among the Meru of Kenya, *omasenge* diviners among the Ambo of Angola, diviners among the Zulu of South Africa, and in the healing ritual system known as *zaar* in Sudan. In Senegal, *goor-djigen* is a tradition among women in which close partnerships result in "twin souls," involving the fusion of bodies and identities, mutual massage, sharing undergarments, and shared erotic strategies called *tour* (Biaya 2000: 717). I have documented indigenous African same-sex phenomena more fully elsewhere, examining the role of cross-dressing, gender transformation, gender inversion, transgender roleplaying, same-sex use of artificial genitalia, homoerotic performance, wordplay, and the dialectics of same-sex thought (Lamp 2004).

Among the Baga in Guinea, where I spent two years, I have already documented the common prevalence of teenage homosexual behavior (Lamp 1996: 73–74), and it is natural to suppose that similar patterns occur elsewhere. Let's be clear, that drawing from universal experience, one can expect adolescent boys to engage in a variety of sexual behaviors that may not fit the dominant paradigm for adult sexuality. Adolescent boys everywhere are bursting with hormones and find themselves with erections at the slightest stimulus and often involuntarily. Adolescents are extremely curious, sexually and otherwise. This is a period of utter amazement by both boys and girls about the unbelievably rapid transformation of their bodies. They become eager explorers of this exotic world. Boys especially, at this point, are programmed also to distance themselves from their parents. When pubescent boys find themselves alone in small groups, especially in twos, there is frequently some sort of sexual play, and if they are alone together and nude, the likelihood that one will get an erection is high, and the likelihood that mutual exploration will take place is also high. In my three years living with the Temne, I found frequently that groups of boys left to themselves, whether at their special bathing spot at the river or piled into bed five deep, often engaged in sexual play. While in the case of both the Temne and the Baga this behavior is certainly known to, and probably expected by the adults, who, of course, all went through this phase themselves, it is not necessarily condoned. It always happens away from adult supervision. In this context, I want to make it clear that what I am describing is behavior, not necessarily sexual preference, and certainly not a permanent status as the word homosexual is commonly used in the West. I use the term "homosexual" as an adverb and not as a noun.

The study of sexuality in general is hampered by stigmas and outright opposition in Western scholarship, particularly in the United States, where the greatest funding for medical and sociological study exists. The few Western studies on homosexuality among twins and among siblings have been fraught with conflict. A study by Pillard and Weinrich (1986) showed that among male siblings, those with gay-identified brothers were four times more likely to identify as gay themselves than males without gay male siblings. Bailey and Pillard (1991) published a study that sparked considerable argument over their finding of a 52 percent concordance for homosexuality among monozygotic twins and 22 percent among dizygotic twins. That is, if one twin is gay, the other is also likely to be, to the percentage given. But their studies invited only gay-identifying subjects, not a random sampling of the general population, and they did not test for or give statistics for the rate of occurrence of homosexuality among twins as opposed to the normal rate among the general population. One might surmise that the occurrence among identical twins is one half again that of the general population if twins, taken as single entities, follow the normal rate. If not, then perhaps the rate of occurrence among twins is even higher. A recent study (Kendler et al., 2000), however, sampling twins in general and their siblings, found that male twins, both monozygotic and dizygotic, report the same percentage of non-heterosexual identity as the general male population (3.1%), but female twins report a considerably higher rate (2.5%) than the general (1.5%).

Twins have been regarded internationally as a class apart from other humans. "They are thought variously to be magical, godly, beneficent, demonic, blessed, incestuous, and/or fruits of animality or adultery" (Pector 2002: 196). The literature, both fiction and nonfiction, on sibling incest is vast, from Egyptian texts to the *Wagner Ring Cycle*. Incest between male and female twins is assumed in some cultures around the

world. For example, in Bali it is understood to take place between opposite-sex twins while they are in the womb, which prompted the researcher
J. A. Boon to say that *"twinship is the incest of birth order"* (Stewart 2000:
720, original emphasis). The theatrical piece, *I La Galigo,* directed by
Robert Wilson and drawn from traditions from South Sulawesi in South-
east Asia, is a classic tale of the dread that parents have of the incest of
their children. The male and female "Golden Twins" are separated by
their parents at birth for fear that they would consummate in life the
intimacy they had nurtured in the womb. Such twin incest would bring
disaster (Cohen 2005). In the novel *El Cuarto Mundo,* by Chilean writer
Diamela Eltit, there is the account of a twin sister and brother who vio-
late the incest taboo, and this is described as a "catastrophe." Nevertheless they repeat the act, always under the watchful eyes of their parents,
for the catastrophe is irrevocable (Hines 2001). There is some literature
traced back to Sigmund Freud on the tension between sibling desire and
guilt.

Some documentation on monozygotic twin incest exists. A sampling of
this might include Burlingham's (1949) observations of identical twin boys
in a nursery in England: "The other children of the nursery would often
watch Bill and Bert, laugh at them and with them, and sometimes would
try to join in the game; but the twins paid little attention to them; they preferred to amuse and excite each other." One researcher, René Zazzo (1984:
190) was told by two twin brothers:

> . . . to make love is a good thing but to join with a woman for life is fool-
> ishness. . . . You are not a twin, you cannot know. A man like you probably
> searches another self in love. . . . But for us twins, this "alter-ego," this dou-
> ble, we have it already and we've always had it. . . . When one has known
> the intimacy of the twin couple, any other intimacy seems incomplete,
> disappointing. . . .

Michael Meyers (1982) documented the long-standing sexual relations
between two monozygotic twins who openly declared their deep love for
each other, were erotically drawn to each other, and were intimately familiar with each other's sexual fantasies. Among female identical twins, there
have been rare cases of incest reported (Perkins 1973).

There exists quite a large body of homoerotic literature and photography in the United States involving male twins who are portrayed as sexual partners (Underhill 1999; Bianchi 2002; Keefer 2004; Weiermair et al.
1994: 33, 79; and numerous calendars and greeting cards). These are all

extraordinarily beautiful young men who demonstrate a deep, passion-
ate, unqualified affection for each other that any reader would covet for
him- or herself, but which would happen only in fantasy. In the theater
production *Dead Ringers*, directed by David Cronenberg and based on
the nonfiction book *Twins*, by Bari Wood and Jack Geasland, a pair of
identical twin men (one gay in the true account but not in the play), share
an intense sexual appetite for the same woman and their inseparability is
interpreted as mutual desire for each other ("Whatever is in his blood-
stream goes directly into mine," the one says of the other) (Oster 1999; see
Meyers 1982: 144 for another true example). In *The Bridge of San Luis Rey*,
by Thornton Wilder, the twin brothers Manuel and Esteban are plagued
with a deep shame about being identical, which overlays their forbidden
sexual relationship. When Manuel falls in love with a woman, the unity of
their being is destroyed, and it ends in the death of one and then the suicide of the other (Burlingham 1945: 209).

All these examples represent fantasies about identical twins, which
Burlingham (1945) reports to be common. Many people entertain fantasies about the relationships of twins which may or may not correspond to
reality.

> It is a conscious fantasy, built up in the latency period as the result of dis-
> appointment by the parents in the oedipus situation, in the child's search
> for a partner who will give them all the attention, love and companionship
> he desires and who will provide an escape from loneliness and solitude.
> ... This twin is meant to fulfill many of the daydreamer's longings. ...
> (Burlingham 1945: 205, 208)

Mitch Walker (1980: 23) has coined the term, "Magickal Twinning," to
describe mythological traditions on the psychological dynamic of same-
sex bonding: "The action of Magickal Twinning is a kind of duplication
where the spirit-essence of one object is infused into another, making
spirit twins, yet where the two duplicates are bound together through
their common spirit-essence into a third object, an indivisible unity."
Certainly, Temne parents of twins entertain fantasies about them, often
negative (they caused the crops to fail by witchcraft, they can make you
pregnant with twins, etc.), and they view them as a single, spiritual entity.
They are seen as two halves bound by an intense love, even as a sexual
unit.

But there is equally some opposing literature on inherited, innate sibling sexual aversion going back to Edward Westermarck at the end of the

nineteenth century, aligned with Darwinian theories of the survival of superior species, that is gaining some credence today (Richardson 2000: 558–563). All these theories had to do with heterosexual incest, and the social as well as biological implications of childbirth from such unions. Essentially, the theory goes that the elements of strangeness and the exotic play an important part in sexual attraction, and that siblings or other children raised in close contact have little interest in each other. But the question of consensual homosexual incest between siblings, which does not have all the same implications, has seldom been addressed. In some studies of male twins, however, gay-identifying twin partners overwhelmingly denied any mutuality in overt sexual relations, claiming to have developed their same-sex attraction independently and often far apart from each other (Kallmann and Baroff 1955: 308; Holden 1965: 862; Perkins 1973; Meyers 1982). Ross Brooks (2004) follows the erotic imperative that "opposites attract," citing several studies showing that gay men overwhelmingly sought men unlike themselves (passive/active, juvenile/mature, masculine/non-masculine, etc.). This would suggest that perhaps twins would only rarely turn to each other sexually. Some studies suggest that the expectation of an emotionally close relationship among same-sex twins, in which each twin's needs and feelings are automatically met and understood by the other twin, may cause anxiety and confusion for the twins who do not conform to the stereotype, and who, in fact, fight constantly and distrust their twin (Stewart 2000: 728).

Nevertheless, no two people live constantly in more intimate circumstances than twins, especially identical twins. The opportunities to be alone are numerous, and among those I have met, the mutual affection of one twin for the other is frequently expressed. To love one's twin is the ultimate narcissism, as Freud (1955: 60) suggested, "a stage in the development of the libido which it passes through on the way from auto-eroticism to object-love." Among the many aspects of twinship that may cause parents concern and even occasion great fear, the sexual prospects must be among them. Fantasy heightens these fears and may be unfounded but it can still play an important role in ritual. What people think is the case is often more important to their ritual behavior and even to quotidian behavior than what is empirically the case. For the Temne and others in Africa, elaborate rituals of precaution in regard to their twins, who are characterized as sexual mates yet expected to take on normative sexual roles in producing heirs, must be predicated in part by this tension. Raising the "river demons," the monitor lizards who have invaded the womb, who devour each other, is no easy task.

NOTES

1. Another version of this essay, with complete oral narratives, appeared as "Temne Twins (*tà-bàri*) Should Share Everything. Do You Mean Everything?" *African Arts* 41 (1, 2008).

2. My research on twin ritual was conducted initially in 1976, but more thoroughly in 1979–1980.

3. T. J. Alldridge (1901: 149–152, figure 52) described and illustrated similar twin houses among the nearby and related Southern Bullom (Sherbro) of Sierra Leone—a larger one for the first-born, and a smaller one for the second. Alldridge reported that such twin houses were found throughout the territory of the Mende and the Southern Bullom. H. U. Hall, in his field notes (University Museum, University of Pennsylvania, F-65–75) described the twin houses and ritual in some detail.

4. It is not clear whether these specialists are the mothers of twins themselves, but this was suggested at the village of Rowal.

5. As suggested at the village of Romeni.

6. *Lentinus tuber-regium* (Deighton 1957: 117).

7. The same name has been reported for the neighboring Mende (Hall 1937, F: 68) and Vai further to the south (Koelle 1854: 177), so it may be of Manding origin, although different names are reported for the Kono and Kuranko.

8. I use the nonparallel "man" and "girl" because this is commonly the nature of traditional marriage in Sierra Leone, where males generally must become financially secure before taking a wife, and females are generally offered in marriage by their families as adolescents.

WORKS CITED

Alldridge, Thomas Joshua. 1901. *The Sherbro and Its Hinterland*. London: Frank Cass.

Anwyl, T. C. 1916. "The Timne and other Tribes of Sierra Leone (or the Anthropological Report on Sierra Leone, by N. W. Thomas)." *Journal of the African Society* 16 (61, October): 36–51.

Bailey, J. M., and R. C. Pillard. 1991. "A Genetic Study of Male Sexual Orientation." *Archives of General Psychiatry* 48: 1089–1096.

Banbury, George Alexander Lethbridge. 1888. *Sierra Leone, or the White Man's Grave*. London: S. Sonnenschein, Lowrey and Co.

Beckwith, Carol, and Angela Fisher. 1999. *African Ceremonies*, vol. 1. New York: Harry N. Abrams.

Berglund, Axel-Ivar. 1976. *Zulu Thought-Patterns and Symbolism*. Uppsala: Swedish Institute of Missionary Research / Cape Town: David Philip.

Bianchi, Tom. 2002. *On the Couch*, vol. 1. Berlin: Bruno Gmünder.

Biaya, T. K. 2000. "'Crushing the Pistachio': Eroticism in Senegal and the Art of Ousmane Ndiaye Dago." *Public Culture* 12 (3): 717.

Brooks, Ross. 2004. "The Desire and Pursuit of the Whole: Testosterone, Perceived Dominance, and Sexual Preference in Men." http://www.thesympo sium.co.uk/desire.

Burlingham, Dorothy T. 1945. "The Fantasy of Having a Twin." *The Psychoanalytic Study of the Child* 1: 205–210.

———. 1949. "The Relationship of Twins to Each Other." *The Psychoanalytic Study of the Child*, 3/4: 57–72.

Cohen, Matthew Isaac. 2005. "Performance Reviews: I La Galigo." *Asian Theater Journal* 12 (1): 138-149.

Cole, John Augustus Abayomi. 1886. *A Revelation of the Secret Orders of Western Africa.* Dayton, Ohio: United Brethren Publishing House.

Deighton, Frederick C. 1957. *Vernacular Botanical Vocabulary for Sierra Leone.* London: The Crown Agents for Overseas Government and Administration.

Drewal, Henry J., and Margaret T. Drewal. 1983. *Gelede: Art and Female Power among the Yoruba.* Bloomington: Indiana University Press.

Eberl, Rudolf (Ralph Eberl-Elber, pseud.). 1936. *Westafrikas letztes Rätsel: Erlebnisbericht über die Forschungsreise 1935 durch Sierra Leone.* Salzburg: Verlag das Berglandbuch.

Evans-Pritchard, Edward E. 1967. "A Problem of Nuer Religious Thought." In *Myth and Cosmos: Readings in Mythology and Symbolism,* ed. J. Middleton, 127-148. Garden City, New York: The Natural History Press.

———. 1970. "Sexual Inversion among the Azande." *American Anthropologist* 72: 1428–1434.

Flickinger, D. K. 1882. *Ethiopia; or 26 Years of Missionary Life in Western Africa.* Dayton, Ohio: United Brethren Publishing House.

Freud, Sigmund. 1955 [1911]. "Psycho-analytical Notes on an Autobiographical Account of a Case of Paranoia." In *The Standard Edition of the Complete Psychological Works of Sigmund Freud,* vol. 12. London: Hogarth.

Griaule, Marcel. 1965. *Conversations with Ogotemmeli: An Introduction to Dogon Religious Ideas.* Oxford: International African Institute.

Hall, Henry Usher. 1928. "Twins in Upper Guinea." *Museum Journal* 19 (University Museum, Philadelphia, Pa.): 403–427.

———. 1937. Field Notes on the Sherbro Expedition. Unpublished ms., University Museum, University of Pennsylvania, Philadelphia.

Hammond-Tooke, W. D. 1992. "Twins, Incest, and Mediators: The Structure of Four Zulu Folktales." *Africa: Journal of the International African Institute* 62 (2): 203–220.

Hines, Donetta. 2001. "'Woman' and Chile: In Transition." Unpublished paper, Annual Meeting of the Latin American Studies Association, Washington, D.C.

Holden, H. M. 1965. "Psychotherapy of a Shared Syndrome in Identical Twins." *British Journal of Psychiatry* 111: 859–864.

Kallmann, Franz J., and George S. Baroff. 1955. "Abnormalities of Behavior (in the Light of Psychogenetic Studies)." *Annual Review of Psychology* 6: 297–326.

Keefer, Dean. 2004. "Twice as Nice: Twins Dayle and Doyle Are the Perfect Pair." *Playgirl*, October.

Kendler, Kenneth S., Laura M. Thornton, Stephen E. Gilman, and Ronald C. Kessler. 2000. "Sexual Orientation in a U.S. National Sample of Twin and Nontwin Sibling Pairs." *American Journal of Psychiatry* 157 (11): 1843–1846.

Kinsey, Alfred C., Wardell B. Pomeroy, and Clyde E. Martin. 1948. *Sexual Behavior in the Human Male*. Philadelphia, Pa.: Saunders.

Koelle, Sigismund W. 1854. *Outlines of a Grammar of the Vei Language Together with a Vei-English Vocabulary*. London: Church Missionary House.

Lamp, Frederick J. 1978. "Frogs into Princes: The Temne Rabai Initiation." *African Arts* 11 (2): 34–49, 94.

———. 1982. *Temne Rounds: The Arts as Spatial and Temporal Indicators in a West African Society*. Ph.D. Dissertation, Yale University, New Haven, Conn.

———. 1996. *Art of the Baga: A Drama of Cultural Reinvention*. New York: Museum for African Art / Munich: Prestel.

———. 2004. "African Art: Traditional." In *The Queer Encyclopedia of the Visual Arts*. San Francisco: Cleis Press. Also in the online *Encyclopedia of Gay, Lesbian, Bisexual, Transgender, and Queer Culture*, at www.glbtq.com (2003).

———. 2008. "Temne Twins (*tà-bàri*) Should Share Everything. Do You Mean Everything?" *African Arts* 41 (1): 50–65.

Langley, E. Ralph. 1939. "The Temne, Their Life, Land, and Ways." *Sierra Leone Studies* 22: 64–80.

Littlejohn, James. 1980. "West Africa." In *An Illustrated Encyclopedia of Mythology*, ed. Richard Cavendish, 222–229. London: Orbis.

Mercier, P. 1954. "The Fon of Dahomey." In *African Worlds: Studies in the Cosmological Ideas and Social Values of African Peoples,* ed. Daryll Forde, 210–234. Oxford: International African Institute.

Meyers, Michael F. 1982. "Homosexuality, Sexual Dysfunction, and Incest in Male Identical Twins." *Canadian Journal of Psychiatry* 27 (March): 144–147.

Murray, Stephen, and Will Roscoe, eds. 1998. *Boy-Wives and Female Husbands: Studies of African Homosexualities*. New York: St. Martin's Press.

Oster, Corinne. 1999. "Dead Ringers: A Case of Psychosis in Twins." *American Imago* 56 (2): 181–202.

Parsons, Robert T. 1964. *Religion in an African Society*. Leiden, the Netherlands: E. J. Brill.

Pector, Elizabeth A. 2002. "Twin Death and Mourning Worldwide: A Review of the Literature." *Twin Research* 5 (3): 196–205.

Perkins, Muriel Wilson. 1973. "Homosexuality in Female Monozygotic Twins." *Behavior Genetics* 3 (4): 387–388.

Pichl, Walter J. 1967. *Sherbro-English and English-Sherbro Vocabulary*. Pittsburgh, Pa.: Duquesne University Press.

Pillard, R. C., and J. D. Weinrich. 1986. "Evidence of Familial Nature of Male Homosexuality." *Archives of General Psychiatry* 43: 808–812.

Richardson, Alan. 2000. "Rethinking Romantic Incest: Human Universals, Literary Representation, and the Biology of Mind." *New Literary History* 31: 553–572.

Shaw, Rosalind. 1982. *Temne Divination: The Management of Secrecy and Revelation.* Ph.D. dissertation, School of Oriental and African Studies, University of London.

Somé, Malidoma Patrice. 1993. "Gays as Spiritual Gate Keepers." *White Crane Newsletter* 4 (9): 6–8.

Stewart, Elizabeth A. 2000. "Toward the Social Analysis of Twinship." *British Journal of Sociology* 51 (4): 719–737.

Thomas, Northcote W. 1970 [1916]. *Anthropological Report on Sierra Leone,* 3 vols. Westport, Conn.: Negro Universities Press.

Underhill, Steven. 1999. *Twins.* Berlin: Bruno Gmünder.

Walker, Mitch. 1980. *Visionary Love: A Spirit Book of Gay Mythology.* San Francisco: Treeroots.

Weiermair, Peter, ed. 1994. *Dino Pedriali.* Zürich: Edition Stemmle.

Zazzo, René. 1984. *Le Paradoxe des Jumeaux.* Paris: Stock.

CHAPTER ELEVEN

Embodied Dilemma

Tabwa Twinship in Thought and Performance

ALLEN F. ROBERTS

In a special issue of *African Arts* dedicated to sculptural and performed re/presentations of twins, Babatunde Lawal (2008) expounds upon "the dialectics of twoness in Yoruba art and culture." As he reminds us, "Yoruba are world famous for their adoration of twins" (ibid: 24), and anyone familiar with African arts will surely know of *ibeji* figures and how they articulate the living presence of twins. Indeed, if museum collections include African materials at all, they are almost certain to possess *ibeji,* so visually compelling, numerous, and long-collected are they.

The Tabwa and related peoples of southeastern Democratic Republic of the Congo, northeastern Zambia, and southwestern Tanzania also make twin figures for some of the same reasons the Yoruba do.[1] Such works are not as well known outside of their immediate contexts as *ibeji* are, however, for Tabwa and their neighbors sparsely populate the southern shores of Lake Tanganyika in a relatively isolated part of Central Africa where, for the last thirty years or so, there has been terrible civil strife. Nonetheless, with well-known Yoruba studies in mind, a discussion of a Tabwa sense of the life, physical death, and ongoing spiritual presence of twins permits fruitful understanding of their convergent logics of expression.

Commonalities first: as Victor Turner (1989: 44) noted with regard to the Ndembu people of northwestern Zambia, "there are several absurdities in the physiological fact of twinship." In particular, in societies for which kinship and lineage are essential to understanding personal identity and status, two babies born for what ordinarily would be a single position within webs and hierarchies of dependency and mutual support can reveal fundamental contradictions in the very functioning of social systems. As Turner also elucidated, culture is often built from just such schismatic dilemmas.

As we shall see, what is so striking about twins is how they and, to a lesser extent, their parents personify dilemma itself—as the dictionary has it, "a situation that requires one to choose between two equally balanced alternatives" and "a predicament that seemingly defies a satisfactory solution" (Morris 1969: 369). As such a conundrum suggests, parents may wish they could resolve the dilemma of twins by favoring one over the other to meet the expectations of kinship and other culturally determined relationships, but they simply cannot, given the everyday dynamics of a family with all the love, responsibility, exasperation, and other intangibles so implied. As dilemma personified, the doubling of twins places them inexorably *between* usual reckonings, defying but making acutely obvious how necessary choice must be in more ordinary circumstances. Of particular interest here will be the *performance* of these cultural tensions through ritual and song.

A Phenomenology of Tabwa Twinship

Reflecting the structural ambiguity and resultant ambivalence that twinship can engender, Tabwa feel that twins (called *mapacha* in KiSwahili or *bampamba* in KiTabwa) mediate between numinous supernatural forces and the absurdly limited powers and crabbed local-level politics that beset humanity. Turner (1989: 47) found that Ndembu twins

> . . . are at once more than human and less than human. Almost everywhere in tribal society they are hard to fit into the ideal model of the social structure, but one of the paradoxes of twinship is that it sometimes becomes associated with rituals that exhibit the fundamental principles of that structure; . . . indeed, one often finds in human cultures that structural contradictions, asymmetries, and anomalies are overlaid by layers of myth, ritual, and symbol which stress the axiomatic value of key structural principles with regard to the very situations where these appear to be most inoperative.

And just as Turner suggested for Ndembu, in the case of Tabwa twins the difficult circumstances of their birth and of their sustenance as nurslings prove an occasion to reflect upon the risks and harmonies of life itself.

Tabwa feel that the birth of twins may be presaged in several ways; for instance, a woman may dream of a great serpent like a python, mamba, or boomslang—all frighteningly common in their part of central Africa. Ordinarily, large snakes like these are understood to be manifestations of an *ngulu,* that is, the sort of earth spirit associated with "ecological" or "territorial" cults once (and still occasionally) practiced to assure continued access to important natural resources such as spawning runs of fish or success in hunting (A. Roberts 1984; cf. Willis 1999). Such an oneiric sign may foretell a pregnancy with twins, for it is said that they come to live with their families from the extraordinary mountain peaks, plunging caverns, lacustrine whirlpools, and other *ngulu* sites dotting the landscape as Tabwa define (that is, *construct*) and understand it (A. Roberts 1984, 1986a). In such places divinity is close at hand, and people are fearful when they find themselves in proximity to them because one can never know what strange things may occur. As soon as twins are born and have grown old enough to speak, parents ask them which *ngulu* earth spirit they have come from, and it is expected that they will name or otherwise designate an important *ngulu* recognized in the area.

It should be noted that the oft-alarming ambiguities of serpents must further inform the anomalies of twinship as Tabwa understand the institution. In shedding their skins, snakes seem "eternally reborn," and their peculiar linearity may be interpreted as "a straight line with one extremity lost in the infinity of the past, and the other in the infinity of the present" (Gougaud 1973: 125). Such a sense suggests that snakes connect divine and human realms, and as Mircea Eliade once commented, snakes are all that is "amorphous and virtual, . . . everything that has not yet acquired form" (1959: 48). Indeed, in many African systems of thought, they are intimately associated with and may even incarnate the inchoate (A. Roberts 1995: 62–65). Even as they connect they divide, however, for they also define difference, much as the sinuous centerline of a yin-yang motif instantiates the tense disjunction of dialectical principles. Such an analogy is not distant from Tabwa reckoning, as we shall see in a moment, for the human body midline—in earlier days and sometimes still set off with scarification—is sometimes thought of as a "snake" that defines the fraught asymmetries of the "right" and "left" sides of the body and all they symbolize (Roberts 1986b, 1988a). Such anomalous potential, such alarming lack of knowing what to expect matched by the tremulous hope that circumstances will prove auspicious, characterizes a Tabwa sense of twins.

Another sign that the birth of twins is imminent is when a woman dreams of dancing and the application of *mpemba* chalk to her face, as is the practice in preparation for several deeply significant rituals, but especially as an antecedent of spirit-possession in a set of performance practices called Bulumbu (see A. Roberts 1988b, 2000). Indeed, the songs of twins are often sung during Bulumbu rituals, especially in the long prelude that may occur if a supplicant is having difficulty allowing the spirit to "mount" and take possession of his or her being. One can assume that among the reasons for such use is the very ambiguity that twins represent, which may "open" the supplicant and the event more generally to other possibilities than what appears to be happening. Here, too, the association between twins and spirits (in this case both *ngulu* and the ancestors) is underscored, and when the parents of twins chalk their faces before dancing in public, an analogy is established between mediums and spirits. If a woman who has dreamed of performing such a ritual does not bear twins soon thereafter, surely someone in her family will in the near future.

It is important to understand the contributions of Tabwa color symbolism to their epistemology of twins. White (as in chalk) is one of the triad of primary colors that Tabwa recognize, and it suggests a state of grace through light and enlightenment, with poetic reference to how moonlight allows one to perceive dangers hidden—or worse yet, lurking—in the darkness. Chalk is "surrogate moonlight," and as it is applied to the face, a mask is created that provides a thin threshold between person and spirit (cf. Roberts and Roberts 1996: 187–206).

Black and red—the other two primary colors—are also significant to Tabwa twinship, for reference to any of the three always implies its mediation between the other two through an isosceles triangle generating deeply meaningful metaphors. Indeed, the color triad is a round-robin of paradox that produces meanings never settled, never assured, always at risk (to paraphrase Denis Hollier 1989: 26). Jacobson-Widding's (1979) consideration of the red-white-black symbolic triad as a "mode of thought" for Bantu-speaking peoples of Central Africa is apposite here.

"Black" refers to all that is obscure and secretive (A. Roberts 1993). As such, "black" relationships or phenomena may lead to gnawing doubt and suspicion, yet in conjunction with all that is "white," "black" can suggest the transformative potential of arcane knowledge obtained through spirit possession and other interventions of divinity. Tabwa and their neighbors also associate "black" with their culture heroes, for such figures bear both the profundity and the dangers of political power. These protagonists are members of a paradigm common to many Central African societies that is comprised of beings who are divided down the body midline. Sometimes they are half-beings, sometimes they are half human, half beeswax; but in any case, they bespeak incompletion and the need for negotiated resolution (A. Roberts 1991). In all such tales (and occasional figural sculpture), such bizarre anatomy embodies dilemma in ways complementary to twinship, and indeed, heroes and twins are variations on an essential cultural theme.

In cosmogonic myths, "black" protagonists are opposed by "red" agents of disorder, violence, and change both deleterious and necessary. "Red" tyrannies must be overthrown to establish the "black" harmonies of human culture as Tabwa and their neighbors understand them (see de Heusch 1982). "Red" antagonists may take human form in myth, and among Luba, the primordial being lives without cultured constraint, is uproariously incestuous, and possesses such a furious temper that he eventually kills his own mother. But these antiheroes are also known as (or at least intimately associated with) the greatest of all serpents, whose rainbow breath desiccates and dooms all upon whom or which it falls.

Among Tabwa this being is called Nfwimina, said to be an "endless" snake that sets the seasons by both causing and drying the rains. In many ways, Nfwimina is the structural equivalent of Nkongolo-Mwamba, the better known Luba "drunken king" (see de Heusch 1982; Mudimbe 1991). A relic of Nfwimina (or a structural substitute) is instrumental to the transformative magic of Tulunga shamans among Tabwa (A. Roberts 2000), and in earlier days, such an "activating agent" (*kizimba*) was used in powerful hunting medicines and to effect the uncanny transformation of raw ore to "cooked" bloom in the important precolonial iron-smelting industry. In turn, Nfwimina is a member of a named set of phenomena that define the discontinuities—hence the symmetries—of the physical universe, such as a great watershed that "crosses no streams" along the crests of a mountain chain while defining the difference between cardinal directions, or the Milky Way that "splits the sky in two" as it turns about the South Celestial Pole (A. Roberts 2005). In the past, the human body was perfected through scarification that rendered such indeterminacy prominent, as the body midline was enhanced through a line of scarification running from forehead to genitals, nape to buttocks. Late nineteenth century photographs of Tabwa individuals and ancestral sculptures show how important this "tegumentary inscription" could be (A. Roberts 1986b, 1988a), as do the majority of twin figures from earlier times that bear the same scarification pattern (Maurer 1986: 247–250). To complete this loop of logic, for Tabwa the "red" serpent is analogous to the human body midline that divides the "black" culture hero in two, setting "right" (masculine might, the East, and the dawning of wisdom) against "left" (feminine weakness, the West, and death)—or, in other circumstances, one faction against another through the trickster-like mediation of twins.

More Sinuosities

Before twins are born, they are said to silently confer with each other *in utero,* so as to decide when and to whom they will be born. While in the womb twins have another intimate relationship with snakes as well, for according to a Tabwa sense of anatomy, a woman's belly is home to Kisumi, a serpent that controls her fertility and conception, and that may cause injury to the mother and/or her fetus if shamanistic intervention is not sought and great care taken. Kisumi reigns within the interior landscape of a woman as Nfwimina does in the greater world, and Kisumi's production of "hot and dry" menses is structurally equivalent to Nfwimina's desiccating rainbow breath.

Twins are sometimes born prematurely and they are often dangerously small and fragile beings. They always prove physically taxing to mothers the world over who bear and nurse them. Many twins perish in birth or do not survive for long, and indeed, women sometimes die while trying to give birth to twins. Such perils must be multiplied many times over in most of the Democratic Republic of the Congo these days, given the near-total lack of biomedicine that has characterized war-torn rural areas of the sprawling republic, including the isolated lands where Tabwa live, since the mid-1970s.

The Anxiety of Loss: The First of a Suite of Tabwa Songs about Twinship

Syampundu, syampundu, wane abe mubii, ngaankumbile (repeat); *Kaletu winginina, ngulu yane kikino* (repeat). "Father of a surviving twin, father of a surviving twin, be with me, mine; that he chase away from me the bad people" (repeat). "Oh sorcerer in the forest, don't insult my *ngulu* earth spirit" (repeat). Exegesis: A mother of twins who has lost one of the two sings the praises of her husband, who has cared for her well. The death of one of the twins is frightening, since it increases worry about the other's survival. The mother warns evil persons to remain at bay and not insult the earth spirit that has sent her twins by taking the second one from her as—presumably—they have taken the first.[2]

Twins that do survive are deemed psychologically—and, indeed, psychically—different from other Tabwa individuals. I was told that twins may whisper together or communicate with each other as they plot mischief at the expense of their siblings and other close relatives. This must be very trying for parents who may feel threatened by the detached "otherworldliness" of spiritually distant offspring. These intimacies seem even more sinister, however, for the twins' odd communication can suggest something indecent, impure, perhaps even incestuous going on between them, whether or not sexual activity itself is implied. A case was brought to my attention of a woman who, shortly after giving birth to twins, was said to have been driven blitheringly mad (*bulubi*). It was said that the twins had done this to her, seemingly through their mysterious witch-like powers. Again, however, while a case like this might find its explanation retrospectively in the anomalous nature that twins are believed to possess, it was also pointed out that most twins do not do such things. Exceptions often prove rules.

Even as people may be afraid of the extraordinary powers of twins, to bear them is a triumph of one's sexuality and related physical powers, and the parents of twins are encouraged to celebrate their exceptional fecundity through raucous joking, singing, and dance. A paradox marked by ambivalence (twins as threat or as auspicious) is at play here, as is the parents' own marginality: by giving birth to twins, they have proven themselves outside the norm, and they are both permitted and expected to take certain liberties as a consequence. The hilariously crude humor invoked demonstrates the parents' release from the niceties of ordinary etiquette. Their exceptional fertility and so, it is assumed, their exuberant sexuality are brought into focus, both in the ways that people of different clans tease and joke across what may be tense differences of politics, and as a further reference to creativity itself—always an ambiguous gift.

Tabwa at Their Most Ribald

Tokolo, tokolo, tebutoko nimpemba yanio (repeat). "The little *mbegu* [seeds] in the organ of birth of a woman are not filth, they are *mpemba* [chalk]." Exegesis: People tease a woman who gives birth to twins, but she must not become angry; instead, she sings with them. They may insult her about the shape and size of her vagina, but she responds that the "seeds" inside her are not filth, for they have brought her the "whiteness" (spirit-inspired blessing) of twins.

Kapule kache, kanio kache, kabutula mpangalume (repeat). "The 'vein' of the man is small, the organ of birth of the woman is small, but they give birth to great men."

Mukipuli mwasiyapamba. Muli mukanwa ngamundibu. Mukunio mwang'inampamba. Muli mukanwa ngamundibu. "Within the 'vein' of the man, of the father of twins. Inside there, there is a mouth like that of an iron bell. Within the vagina of a woman, of the mother of twins.

Inside there, there is a mouth like that of an iron bell." Exegesis: The penis of a father of twins is huge, its opening is like the mouth of (or it "rings" like) an iron bell. The vagina of a mother of twins is huge, its opening is like the mouth of (or it "rings" like) an iron bell. You, parents of twins, your organs are so great that they allow such children to be born from them!

Kipuli kipi-kipi, leta nondo bakisambule (repeat). "Your penis is *so* short, bring us a blacksmith's hammer so we can 'forge' it!" Exegesis: This is a song to make people laugh. The women singers taunt a man and tell him that if they beat his tiny penis with a hammer, they can draw it out as a blacksmith does in pounding red-hot iron on his anvil, so that even he may bear twins.

When twins are born to Tabwa living along the shores of Lake Tanganyika, they are kept secluded in their parents' home, as are all newborns, until their umbilical cords dry out and detach themselves from the infant's belly. A twin that perishes before this can happen is not considered a whole person and is buried in a midden (*kizhyala*) at the edge of the homestead or hamlet. Women deposit ashes from domestic cooking fires as well as uneaten food and garbage in the *kizhyala*, which stands as a proleptic "nonplace" where endings and beginnings are confused and new histories can be conceived (A. Roberts 2000). Stillborn and premature infants that perish (both known as *kaonde*) are also buried without ceremony in the *kizhyala*, for like twins that die in or shortly after birth, "they are not human, but are 'just blood' (*damu tu*), 'life' itself but lacking the boundaries that would have made them persons" (Davis 2000: 62). The death of a twin is spoken of as a "return" rather than a "departure," and it is felt that because "they have never been quite of this world," they will go back to the *ngulu* earth spirits whence they came (ibid.). A deceased twin or a *kaonde* will hasten to be reborn a whole child, it is hoped and urged, and such a death is not to be mourned for it is not a death at all. In the meantime, however, the burial of twins is fraught with particular anxieties, for a *kizhyala* may be raided by both healers (*waganga*) and witches (*walozi* or *ndozi*) seeking *vizimba*, "activating agents" made from disinterred human remains that are deployed in the most potent of Tabwa magical preparations (A. Roberts 1997).

Once the umbilical cords of surviving children have fallen off, twin babies are treated in ways different from other newborns. A platform (*kaala*) of the sort usually built to dry vegetables or fish up off the ground and so away from hungry domestic animals is used to support a shallow winnowing basket (*lusele*) in which the twins are seated. Community parents who have borne twins in the past (and so, in Turner's terms [1989], who have undergone the ritual processes leading to new social identities) light a smoldering fire under the *kaala* that is made from different sorts of medicinal woods and dried plants, in a process called *kufitwila*, "to blacken," so as to "ripen" or "mature" (*kuwakomaaza*) the twins and "close their heads" to keep them from the baneful influences of *ndozi* witches (see Davis 2000; Kaoze 1942).

As the ritual continues, white *mpemba* chalk is applied to the faces and heads of the twins' mother, father, and the close kin of both parents. As with Bulumbu spirit possession, this act signifies a change of status to one inflected by supernatural powers. It also invokes the lunar symbolism of light and enlightenment. The association between twinship and spirit possession is too complex to address here (see A. Roberts 1988a, 1990), but it is significant to note that the woman (usually a wife) who assists a male Bulumbu medium is called Kapamba or "Little Twin" (or sometimes, "Mother of Twins"; see Roberts and Roberts 1996: 191; and chapter 12).

The twins' parents and their mother's kin dance together, while the twins themselves, with "cooling" ash applied to their bodies, sit in the winnowing basket placed before their home. Small gifts are offered to the children, always in pairs. Eventually the twins and their close kin dance their way to the chief's residence, where the parents dance some more, collecting gifts as they go. In the past, it is said that such dancing would continue for three days and nights. Even though they are tiny babies, it is said that the twins are aware of the recognition they receive on such occasions, for as one man had it, "they hear a lot, these are not children, they are *bakubwa*"—elders or great ones—with the implication being that twins possess arcane powers beyond those of ordinary children and most adults as well.

The Complex Choreographies of Parents Who Have Borne Twins

Sempa, tumone byang'wana tebeliwa sile. Eeyeyeye, eeyeyeye (chorus). *Kamwona wane, Kisimba umpindi munkulo* (chorus). "Dance so we can see how you do it, don't take our money for nothing. My Kamwona, Kisimba lies upside-down to my chest." Exegesis: People want to see the mother of twins dance, so that they feel their gifts are justified; but she laments that she prefers the second-born of her twins (Kamwona) because the first (Kisimba) lay in a reverse position during pregnancy that caused her pain in the chest.

At the rising of the first new moon after the twins' birth, the parents again dance and receive presents for their newborns. "The rising of a new moon" is a key metaphor of Tabwa ontology (A. Roberts 1986a). Registers of isosceles triangles decorating all manner of material culture and the body arts of scarification and hair-braiding are given this evocative name—*balamwezi* in the Tabwa language. The personified male moon is described as residing at the apex of such a triangle, forever divided by his loyalties to his wives (the eastern and western appearances of Venus) at the basal points of the triangle. The same triangle alludes to the "matrilineal puzzle" wherein a man's attachment to his wife and biological children lie at one basal point, while his dedication to his sister and his heirs (her children) lie at the other. In other words, the tensions and schisms of social life are conveyed by and contemplated through the dilemmas explored through this geometrical symbol.

Gifts given to twins at the rising of a new moon are called *milambo ya masultani,* gifts in honor of chiefs, since "twins are like chiefs." As one man said, "when a chief goes about he receives *milambo,* and so it is with twins." *Milambo* is from the verb *kulamba*—"to lick"—and refers to gifts offered as marks of deference and respect. Comparison of twins and chiefs reinforces the duality of each, for a chief is "father of his people," yet because misfortune and evil acts inevitably exist in his community, it must be that he condones and perhaps even participates in such fell deeds. Like the moon, a chief has two "faces," the one benign, the other deceitful, underscoring the dilemmas implied by both the office and the state of being.

A Song of Arrogance

Temutumwene? Tuli npazi twamingilila. "Don't you see us? We are fire ants, we are entering." Exegesis: This is sung by twins when they enter a village. "Don't run away, you must give us gifts"—or, the implication is, we will overrun and "bite" you into submission as swarming fire ants do all too often as they invade Tabwa homes.

After celebration at the rising of a first new moon, parents of twins are given the honorific titles of "mother of twins" (*ng'inapamba*) and "father of twins" (*syapamba*). Twins are always given the same personal names along the southwestern shores of Lake Tanganyika: Kisimba for the first-born, Kamwona for the second. In recognition of ambiguities, however, the second-born is deemed hierarchically "first-born," for it must have been able to oblige its less powerful other to emerge from the womb first. "Kamwona" suggests as much, for it means "the little one seen" as birth begins. These names are now understood to belong to important possessing spirits that—like twins—are felt to hail from the important *ngulu* site of Kibawa's cavern and "whose abilities are miraculous like those of twins."[3] *Kisimba* also refers to quartz crystals obtained from Kibawa's cavern or picked up while hiking in the cool of the night, when one notices moonlight reflected in their faceted surfaces as a flash of Spirit.

As the months pass, an *ng'inapamba* mother of twins dances lasciviously at the rising of each new moon as befits her status as someone of exceptional fertility. The *syapamba* father returns the twins to the *kizhyala* midden and makes them lie down and roll about, so that they become covered with ashes. The commentator telling me this continued on to explain that the twins are like *wafu* spirits of the dead; and like *mpemba* chalk, ashes are a sign of an association with Kibawa, whence the twins may have come. Ashes make both twins look identical, if for only a few moments: two is subsumed into one—yet the paradox is aggravated as the "one" clearly inhabits two bodies.[4] The twins are beaten (lightly) with a switch to make each understand that he/she is to "soften the soul" (*kuregeza roho*), in hopes that the twins will not "make trouble any more. They have been 'pierced' (*kutoboa*) by their parents so that anger will quiet in their souls" and they will henceforward avoid tormenting their parents and siblings in mysterious, witch-like ways. A trip to the midden and the twins' mild flagellation renew their association with the cooling qualities of a place of extinguished fires and substance-without-definition, thus underscoring the inchoate nature of the *kizhyala* and the twins themselves as defying definition.

The birth of twins is not a finite act, or so Tabwa parents hope, for people generally desire to continue giving birth as long and as often as possible because high infant mortality takes so many. Physical realities may intervene, however, given the trauma that twin birth can cause a woman's body. As a consequence, birth of a next child is again cause for particular celebration. Such a child is given the special term *busindi*, and receives at least some of the festive attention offered to twins, including small gifts. A *busindi*'s parents are also lauded as even more extraordinary than those only giving birth to twins. A *busindi* does not possess the dangerously ambiguous, extra-human powers of twins, however.

Celebrating the Next-Born after Twins

Kamwona ni Kisimba bapewa yabo. Elele (chorus). *Ninene pankayako napewa yane. Elele.* "Kamwona and Kisimba have been given theirs, and I, at the hour that I leave, I will be given mine." Exegesis: The twins Kamwona and Kisimba have been given gifts, and Busindi (the one born after twins) sings this cheerful song because if the ones preceding him received gifts, he/she should as well.

The Conundrum of the Crossroads

The death of a twin is not mourned, nor is its demise referred to as a "death." Rather, it is felt that the twin has "returned home" to the *ngulu* earth spirit site—the mountain, spring, or Kibawa's cavern—whence it originated.[5] Rather than in the *kizhyala* midden, older twins used to be buried at a crossroads somewhere outside human habitation, and presumably this may still be the case among Tabwa living away from Catholic and other religious missions. A *kizime* aloe would be planted over such a grave, so that even when the mound disappeared, "people would know that chiefs are buried there." *Kizime* is chosen because the hardy plant can survive seasonal bushfires, and "cannot be eliminated or made to disappear" (*haifutiki*). The fleshy green leaves are a testament to endurance, even during the "hottest" moments of violent change. And to return to the cosmological plane, such dry-season fires are associated with Nfwimina, the great ophidian antagonist, whereas the "coolness" of *kizime* resonates with the "black" culture hero and all the creative energy he implies.

A crossroads is a liminal "nonplace" of few equals. In one of his last published works, called "Crossroads of Being, Crossroads of Life" (1987), Dominique Zahan addressed life's greatest dilemma: the difference between the ways things "ought" to be and the way they are—that is, the reality that despite all reasonable expectations based upon upright behavior and hard work, surprises and disappointments are inevitable. For Zahan, the crossroads symbolized such ambiguity, for "a crossroads is, above all, a place that no one expected to be *there*" (ibid., 355). Why does my path cross this other one *here*, rather than somewhere else? How can one conceptualize the conundrum of the crossroads, where convergence immediately leads to divergence? Why such an unexpected crossing, *now*? Why such sudden discontinuity, complete disjunction, a necessity to choose, an obligation to turn, a possibility to change? Really, what *should* I do next? As one finds in many world traditions, for Tabwa a crossroads is an opening to opportunity, a place where one may encounter spiritual agents that can change one's life for the better, or the most heinous of witches who assemble there to dance upside-down and naked as they await their next prey, who just might be *you* (see A. Roberts 1996b). Some people still place a broken pot in the crux of a three-pronged fork at the crossroads outside of town, and dancing in honor of deceased twins takes place there at the rising of the new moon while offerings of food are placed in the shard as tangible evidence of exchange with spiritual powers. Burying twins at a crossroads—a nonplace that *exacts* decision—is further indication of their potential to divide and unite, destroy and create. In a way, twins personify the "crossroads of being" that Zahan evoked so eloquently, and conversely, the ready symbolism of one path meeting another helps people to think through the deeply perplexing nature of these spirit-children, with all their awesome yet frightening potential.

Fragment of a Dirge

Kine wapokwa mwana, ni minwe yalepa. Pa butanda, uliwakanosya kibuli. Biseka bitipukile, ni mwinsi undoelele. Misile mwebebe batetelwe tulimba na Leza. Nkulange kwa kufikila! Ukaye ukafikile kuli syampundu mwelelwa mu masansa. "When you have lost your child, your arms grow longer. Twisting and turning in the beds of others will only bring madness. When the maize is tender, the pestle will make you happy. I will cede my place to you, you who have received vocal chords from God. That I show you where you may stay! You will go and lodge with the father of a surviving twin, for whom the dead are thrown down at a crossroads." Exegesis: These lines are among the 132 verses of a dirge. The melancholy lyrics note how "the arms grow longer" when one's infant has perished, and warn that grief-induced sexual activity will lead to madness, however "happy" the "pestle" may be in pounding "tender maize." While the singer is ready to cede to someone known for vocal talents, a last allusion is provided: the aggrieved person is urged to go and stay with a father of a surviving twin—that is, someone who has lost the other—who buries his dead at a crossroads. The implication is that the sense of abandon and lack of purpose that characterize grief *do* have a place in Tabwa society, as embodied and practiced by the parent who has lost one twin but clings to the other in hope of its survival.

The death of a twin brings about a challenge to and a change of status for the parents, as stoic as they are expected to remain. Instead of "mother or father of twins," the parents become known as "mother and father of the surviving twin," *ng'inampundu* and *syampundu* in KiTabwa. A small wooden figure (generally around 20–25 cm. tall) is commissioned from a carver, to be carried by the mother of a deceased twin and later by its surviving mate. This practice, widespread in the area in the past (Colle 1913: 253), was continued into the 1970s along the southwestern shores of Lake Tanganyika and probably inland from there as well. At each meal, a bit of food is taken on the mother's index finger and offered to the spirit of the twin via the figure, by rubbing or touching the food to the carved mouth. Such figures are carried about in a *kipapo* cloth sling along with or instead of a living infant, until the deceased twin would have been old enough to get around by itself. Then the figure is carefully kept in the house, and perhaps eventually put in a family shrine under the eaves or in some other private corner.

The carved figures of deceased twins make tangible all the dilemmas of their being. The truncated form of the figures is their most noticeable trait, for they are attenuated below the navel and above the loins in all but one known example.[6] None have legs, and many also lack arms. By terminating the figures at the top of their hips, no reference to sexuality is made. Some twin figures possess breasts, but most are generic and may be either male or female. The navel, in contrast, is often developed as though herniated. This physical event is frequent among Tabwa children due to malnutrition, and pronounced navels last a lifetime for some people. Such an exaggeration brings attention to the navel and its link to one's mother and matrilineage. Those twin figures that do possess arms display the hands either side of the navel in a pose, also depicted by many full figures, that emphasizes matrilineal heritage.[7]

What can be made of this unusual iconography? Roy Willis provides suggestive musings in two articles, the first a classic called "The Head and the Loins: Lévi-Strauss and Beyond" (1967) in which he applies structuralist methods to his own ethnography of the Fipa people living in southwestern Tanzania, across Lake Tanganyika from the Tabwa, to whom they are closely related culturally and historically. In a second, "The Body as Metaphor" (1991), Willis reflects upon my own exposition of Tabwa sculpture (A. Roberts 1986a). For Fipa, as among Tabwa, "head" refers to intellect, authority, and rational control as most evidently demonstrated by men, while the loins represent "sexuality, reproductive power and also 'wildness,' animality and the hierarchical superiority [of "head"] over the lower, inferior 'Loins'" most readily associated with women (Willis 1991: 277). As the title of his earlier piece suggests, Willis is interested in the symbolic tensions posited by the poles of human anatomy and the ideas about which the body proves so "good to think," but as he stresses in his second paper, head and loins are mediated for Fipa by "the heart" as seat of the soul. Yet the heart is characterized by indeterminacy, since, again for Fipa, it may be as "white" as a "good" heart informed by generosity and grace, or as "black" as a witch's heart, bilious with evil (1991: 277; cf. Willis 1985). My sense is that while Tabwa twin figures do participate in such triadic discourse, their truncation places the emphasis upon what is therefore absent: the loins. Fecundity is missing, and therefore not the issue of twins themselves, as it most certainly is for the mothers who have borne them (as emphasized by the pronounced navels that most figures display). Rather, twins are caught up in the very "indeterminacy" of which Willis writes so evocatively: the positive, assertive qualities of their "heads" are mitigated by the ambivalent secrecy of their souls.

Conclusions and Beginnings

As Mary Nooter Roberts outlines in chapter 12, the Luba people living to the west of the Tabwa share a number of understandings and practices concerning twins and twinship. At least some Luba understand twins to be "children of the moon," and as the great missionary ethnographer Theodoor Theuws (1960: 132) wrote of western Luba, "it is the moon that has brought this unaccustomed fecundity that frightens people by its excessiveness." Tabwa may not be so explicit as this (or, at least, none was to me), but their conception of the nature of twins is nevertheless understood by reference to a lunar idiom. Tabwa twins themselves bear lunar names. Kisimba, the first-born who is secretly less powerful than the second, is also the name of the first wife of the great chthonic spirit Kibawa. The "real" Kisimba is there in the womb, even as its counterpart is born, yet it remains unseen within the mother's belly. In this, it is like the moon in a tenebrous, anxious period called *kamwonang'anga,* consisting of the two or three nights of utter darkness preceding the reappearance of the new moon. *Kamwonang'anga* means "the little one seen by the shaman," and refers to the fact that when unseen, the moon is present but denying people its light and enlightenment. Like Kamwona within the womb, only a shaman can see the moon in its hiding, as it restrains its light but promises its return, and only such a thaumaturge can help people escape the malicious beings that hold sway in such obscurity. Indeed, a major reason for celebrating the appearance of each new moon is that balance has been restored and grace will again protect and promote. Kamwona is born as the second (but "first") twin, for it is "the little one seen," while Kisimba brings with it the flash of spirit, signaling the powers of unseen realms.

Tabwa rituals associated with the birth of twins are rich in lunar symbolism, including the use of *mpemba* chalk and ashes that make symbolic allusion to moonlight and divine intervention. But even as twins are rolled about in ashes "so that they look alike," their duality is most apparent. As Turner remarks, rituals for twins "in some situations focus upon the duality of twins, and in others upon their unity. . . . You can examine the *process* whereby two become one. Or you can examine the converse of this, the process whereby one person becomes two, the process of bifurcation" (1989: 49, original emphasis). This is Turner's conundrum, then: two for one is one for two.

In their division, twins are different from other people, and sometimes dangerously so, for even as they focus their attentions on each other more than those about them, and so deny tenets of social interdependence, they may plot the demise of their parents and others close to them. They are "chiefs" in that they make all too apparent the dialectic of generosity and greed, and, ultimately, good and evil. They are celebrated and given gifts as befits their positive side ("moonlight"), and feared and whipped with switches in recognition of their maliciousness ("the dark side of the moon"). When the new moon rises, marking the completion of a cycle of beneficence and want, twins are covered in ash and "reunited" in appearance, but beaten so as to allay their evil thoughts and divisiveness. Twins are born when the *ngulu* earth spirits choose to send them into the world: no one knows when that will be, or what the consequences. And yet twins are fundamentally important to Tabwa logic, insofar as they personify dilemma itself.

NOTES

1. Forty-five months of doctoral research in anthropology were conducted among lakeside Tabwa people and in administrative and missionary archives of Zäire (now the Democratic Republic of the Congo or D.R.C.) in the mid-1970s, followed by archival and museum research in Belgium, England, Germany, Italy, Scotland, and the United States. Funding and scholarly support are acknowledged in A. Roberts (1986a). Conflict in the D.R.C. has precluded my return, and the "ethnographic present" of this paper refers to the mid-1970s. Tabwa ethnicity is very complex and generalities about Tabwa can be problematic; see A. Roberts (1986a, 1996a); cf. (Petit 1996, 2005).

2. The lyrics of Tabwa songs about twinship are published here for the first time. They are offered in KiTabwa, as sung for me by a woman named Konsolata

living in the town of Lubanda where I resided, followed by exegeses gained from Tabwa friends with whom I discussed the lyrics.

3. Possessing spirits do not seem to be twinned, as among Luba (see M. Roberts, chapter 12). Kibawa is an earth spirit recognized by Eastern Luba, Tabwa, and other peoples of southeastern Congo that rose to prominence—at least for Tabwa—as a nativistic response to the late-nineteenth-century trauma of the East African slave trade followed by colonial conquest. By the 1970s, lakeside Tabwa understood that the dead travel to and reside in Kibawa's cavern, where they may be consulted through an oracle. For Luba, Kibawa has become associated with the culture heroes Mbidi Kiluwe and his son Kalala Ilunga; see A. Roberts (1996a).

4. Here and elsewhere in this chapter, notions of "partitive" personhood are at play, for Tabwa and Western senses differ as to what does and does not delimit the person; such matters are among the subjects of a book in progress.

5. Pronouns in Swahili and other Bantu languages do not reflect gender. In the case of twins that die young, it seems more in keeping with Tabwa epistemology to use "it" rather than he or she, since these tragic beings are not considered fully human.

6. Object number 54.51.2 at the Royal Museum of Central Africa (Tervuren, Belgium), displays female genitalia; see Maurer (1986: 248) for this and other Tabwa twin figures, as well as Van Geluwe (1986), Afrika Museum (1995), and Cameron and Ross (1996).

7. The navels of a few twin figures are so pronounced that they might be mistaken for phalluses; see, for instance, a Tabwa figure collected by Lieutenant Glauning in 1900, now no. III E 8038 in the Museum für Völkerkunde of Berlin, or a famously "abstract" one collected by H. Tomaschek among neighboring Mambwe in 1905, no. III E 11475 at the same museum (Maurer 1986: 249 no. 200, and p. 250 no. 208, respectively). An example of a Tabwa twin figure with hands posed either side of the navel is no. 16593 at the Royal Museum of Central Africa (Tervuren, Belgium); see Maurer (1986: 248, no.186). Evan Maurer's 1986 *catalogue raisonné* of Tabwa sculpture illustrates many full figures that strike the same pose.

WORKS CITED

Afrika Museum. 1995. *Poppen spel en ritual/Dolls for Play and Ritual.* Berg-en-Dal, the Netherlands: Afrika Museum.

Cameron, Elizabeth, and Doran Ross. 1996. *Isn't S/he a Doll? Play and Ritual in African Sculpture.* Los Angeles: UCLA Fowler Museum of Cultural History.

Colle. P. 1913. *Les Baluba,* 2 vols. Brussels: Albert Dewit.

Davis, Christopher. 2000. *Death in Abeyance: Illness and Therapy among the Tabwa of Central Africa.* Edinburgh: Edinburgh University Press, for the International African Institute, London.

Eliade, Mircea. 1959. *The Sacred and the Profane.* New York: Harcourt Brace.

Gougaud, Henri. 1973. *Les animaux magiques de notre universe.* Paris: Solar.

de Heusch, Luc. 1982. *The Drunken King or the Origin of the State.* Bloomington: Indiana University Press.

Hollier, Denis. 1989. *Against Architecture: The Writings of Georges Bataille.* Cambridge, Mass.: MIT Press.

Jacobson-Widding, Anita. 1979. *Red-White-Black as a Mode of Thought.* Uppsala Studies in Cultural Anthropology 1. Stockholm: Almqvist and Wiksell.

Kaoze, Stephano. 1942. "Culte et superstitions des Batabwa." Two unpublished notebooks. Archives of the Catholic Diocese of Kalemie-Moba, Democratic Republic of the Congo.

Lawal, Babatunde. 2008. "Èjìwàpò: The Dialectics of Twoness in Yoruba Art and Culture." *African Arts* 41 (1): 24–39.

Maurer, Evan. 1986. "A Catalogue Raisonné of Tabwa Art." In *The Rising of a New Moon: A Century of Tabwa Art,* ed. Allen Roberts and Evan Maurer, 219–278. Ann Arbor: The University of Michigan Museum of Art.

Morris, William, ed. 1969. *The American Heritage Dictionary of the English Language.* Boston: Houghton Mifflin.

Mudimbe, V. Y. 1991. *Parables and Fables: Exegesis, Textuality, and Politics in Central Africa.* Madison: University of Wisconsin Press.

Petit, Pierre. 1996. "Au Coeur du royaume: Réflexions sur l'ethnicité luba." *Bulletin des Séances de l'Académie Royale des Sciences d'Outre-Mer* 42: 759–774.

———. 2005. "Art et histoire des Luba méridionaux, Partie II: Ethnicité, histoire politique, et ateliers sur les frontières sud du royaume." *Anthropos* 100: 17–33.

Roberts, Allen. 1984. "'Fishers of Men': Religion and Political Economy among Colonized Tabwa." *Africa* 54 (2): 49–70.

———. 1986a. "Social and Historical Contexts of Tabwa Art." In *The Rising of a New Moon: A Century of Tabwa Art,* ed. Allen Roberts and Evan Maurer, 1–48. Ann Arbor: The University of Michigan Museum of Art.

———. 1986b. "Les arts du corps chez les Tabwa." *Arts d'Afrique Noire* 59: 15–20.

———. 1988a. "Tabwa Tegumentary Inscription." In *Marks of Civilization: Artistic Transformation of the Human Body,* ed. Arnold Rubin, 41–56. Los Angeles: UCLA Museum of Cultural History.

———. 1988b. "Through the Bamboo Thicket: The Social Process of Tabwa Ritual Performance." *TDR, The Drama Review* 32 (2): 123–38.

———. 1990. "Tabwa Masks, 'An Old Trick of the Human Race.'" *African Arts* 23 (2): cover, 36–47, 101–103.

———. 1991. "Where the King Is Coming From." In *Body and Space: Symbolic Models of Unity and Division in African Cosmology and Experience,* ed. A. Jacobson-Widding, 249–69. *Uppsala Studies in Cultural Anthropology,* no. 16. Stockholm: Almqvist and Wiksell.

———. 1993. "Insight, or, NOT Seeing Is Believing." In *Secrecy: African Art that Conceals and Reveals,* ed. M. Nooter, 64–79. New York: Museum for African Art.

———. 1995. *Animals in African Art: From the Familiar to the Marvelous*. New York: Museum for African Art / Munich: Prestel.

———. 1996a. "Peripheral Visions." In *Memory: Luba Art and the Making of History*, ed. Mary Roberts and Allen Roberts, 210–243. New York: Museum for African Art / Munich: Prestel.

———. 1996b. "Le dernier carrefour d'un chef tabwa." In *Mort et vie: Hommages au professeur Dominique Zahan (1915–1991)*, ed. P. Erny, A. Stamm, and M.-L. Witt, 93–121. Paris: Harmattan.

———. 1997. "Anarchy, Abjection, and Absurdity: A Case of Metaphoric Medicine Among the Tabwa of Zaïre." In *The Anthropology of Medicine: From Theory to Method*, ed. L. Romanucci-Ross, D. Moerman, and L. Tancredi, 224–239. 3rd ed. New York: Bergin for Praeger Scientific.

———. 2000. "Difficult Decisions, Perilous Acts: Producing Potent Histories with the Tabwa Boiling Water Oracle." In *Insight and Artistry: A Crosscultural Study of Divination in Central and West Africa*, ed. John Pemberton III, 83–98. Washington, D.C.: Smithsonian Institution Press.

———. 2005. "Monotony and Surprise in Tabwa Cosmology." In *Songs from the Sky: Indigenous Astronomical and Cosmological Traditions of the World*, ed. V. D. Chamberlain, J. Carlson, and M. J. Young, 281–292. Bognor Regis, U.K.: Ocarina Books.

Roberts, Mary, and Allen Roberts, eds. 1996. *Memory: Luba Art and the Making of History*. New York: Museum for African Art / Munich: Prestel.

Theuws, Theodoor. 1960. "Naître et mourir dans le ritual luba." *Zaïre* 14 (2–3): 115–173.

Turner, Victor. 1989. *The Ritual Process: Structure and Anti-Structure*. Ithaca, N.Y.: Cornell University Press.

Willis, Roy. 1967. "The Head and the Loins: Lévi-Strauss and Beyond." *Man* (n.s.): 2, 4, 519–534.

———. 1985. "Do the Fipa Have a Word for It?" In *The Anthropology of Evil*, ed. David Parkin, 209–233. Oxford: Blackwell.

———. 1991. "The Body as Metaphor: Synthetic Observations on an African Artwork." In *Body and Space: Symbolic Models of Unity and Division in African Cosmology and Experience*, ed. A. Jacobson-Widding, 271–281. *Uppsala Studies in Cultural Anthropology*, no. 16.

———. 1999. *Some Spirits Heal, Others Only Dance: A Journey into Human Selfhood in an African Village*. New York: Berg.

Van Geluwe, Huguette. 1986. *Tabwa Tervuren 1986*. Tervuren, Belgium: Royal Museum of Central Africa.

Zahan, Dominique. 1987. "Carrefour de l'être, Carrefour de la vie." *Eranos* 56: 353–384.

CHAPTER TWELVE

Children of the Moon

Twins in Luba Art and Ontology

MARY NOOTER ROBERTS

The day of the rising of a new moon we do not go to the fields; we take the day off, just as you take every Sunday off to go to mass to take communion. On this occasion, we refresh the *bilembo* offering baskets, anoint them with chalk (*mpemba*), and put them on the mats in the ancestral shrines, and then we begin to drink and sing the *songs for twins.* These practices are tied to the history of our ancestors.

—KEUZI, PERSONAL COMMUNICATION, 1987

Keuzi, a Luba female diviner, recounts a ritual that unfolds every month on the night of the new moon in Luba towns and villages throughout Katanga Province of the Democratic Republic of the Congo. The ancestral shrines are cleaned and spruced, beer is brewed, and offerings are made anew. Come evening, the singing begins, with a focus on mesmerizing "songs for twins." The songs, sung in chorus and refrain, are dedicated to the *bavidye,* the tutelary spirits of Luba kingship, who are described as twins. The *bavidye* play critically important roles in maintaining social equilibrium and in sanctifying royal authority and prerogative. The "rising of the new moon" is a time of rejuvenation and hope, recognition and rebirth, and twins are conduits for the aspirations of the community as they challenge the forces of darkness that precede the tiny sliver of newly emergent light every lunar cycle.[1]

Why is so much attention directed at twins on the night of a new moon, and why do the spirits of Luba kingship take the form of twins? In Luba thought and practice, twins are perceived as ambivalent beings. In fact, they are called "children of misfortune" and/or "extraordinary" children (Theuws 1960: 131). It is considered abnormal for two beings to emerge from a single womb, and they are treated as less than human and with distinct disdain for their atypical status. In the Kinkondja region on the border of Lake Kisale, twins are always called by the names of Kyungu for the first-born and Kabange for the second.[2] "You cannot have a person by one of these two names who is not a twin (*mapasa*)." Should one twin perish, it is forbidden for people to cry for that child, for risk of causing the death of the second. So people never cry or mourn the loss of a twin unless (or until) the second one dies (Nsenga Ubandilwa, personal communication, 1988).

> In the old days, before people had their babies in hospitals, we did not cut the umbilical cord of twins, for they were children of misfortune. The cord simply detached on its own. Also, on the day when the children were brought out in public, they were completely caked in chalk and we sang insulting songs, so that they [the twins] would heal. If we did not cast insults, the twins could die. (Keuzi, personal communication, 1987)

The wife of an important deceased titleholder in the collective of Kinkondja, named Ngoi wa Nkulu, described the connection between twins and misfortune in the following way:

> If you gave birth to twins, then at the rising of the new moon you would cover them in chalk and sing the songs for twins, in other words, you would cast insults while others danced. The next morning, the mother would take two baskets and balance them on each side while circulating with them through the village. Twins are children of taboos, interdictions, and misfortune, and so people would begin to make offerings in these baskets of manioc, flour, fish, and in the old days, even beads. (Personal communication, 1987)

How can such commentaries be explained and understood within a broader Luba cosmological and ontological framework? This essay seeks to unravel the imbricated meanings linking kingship, twins, and spirituality to show that twins are vehicles for understanding contradiction and ambivalence in a complex and politically fraught world. It will also be seen that the visual arts are a vehicle for expressing multilayered interrelationships between twins, spirit mediums, and female representation, and that the regalia of kings make purposeful reference to this representational triad.

Children of the Moon

One of the names assigned to Luba twins is "children of the moon." The moon is a complex metaphor for Luba, always ambivalent because it appears and disappears, offers clarity and delivers obscurity. As Father Théodore Theuws writes, "The moon is ambiguous like life itself. . . . To be and to become, to live and to die are but two faces of the same reality." The Luba have an expression for that which is unwanted, unaccustomed, or unusual and extraordinary: *i bya malwa*.

> Anything that is outside of the ordinary, shocks the imagination, troubles the peaceful pace of life, in brief, all that reminds people of their ambiguity, all of that is *bya malwa*. The moon disappears, that is to say, the moon dies, the shadows fall upon the world for three consecutive nights: *i bya malwa*. The moon reappears—*watentama*—the forces of life return: *i bya malwa*. These lunar alternations are regular. They condition the being of humankind. They are the cause and symbol of its instability. (Theuws 1968: 11, my translation)

The notion of something regular, that one can expect every month, yet which is the cause of instability would seem to be a paradox. In this respect it is similar to the concept of *anomaly*. The dictionary definition and common usage of the word refers to something abnormal or deviant, and a departure from the norm. The word bears the Greek root *homalos,* "same" or "regular," yet this sense is negated by the prefix *a-*. In other words, system is implied even within the negation of normality. It is the negation of the rule—what is uniform, average, and regular—that causes disequilibrium. Yet the regularly irregular can also be normal. As V. Y. Mudimbe has said, normal and pathological are two sides of the same reality.[3]

The same play of difference and negation of difference can be seen in the Luba epic explaining the origins of Luba kingship. The original culture bearer of Luba kingship was an enigmatic figure named Mbidi Kiluwe, identified as a lunar hero (de Heusch 1972; A. Roberts and Maurer 1985: 29).[4] He appeared from the east and brought royal kingship practices and civilized customs to the indigenous people of the region, before disappearing, never to be seen again. During his stay at the court of the cruel and incestuous autochthonous despot, Nkongolo Mwamba, Mbidi Kiluwe had union with two of Nkongolo's sisters and left behind a son, Kalala Ilunga, who became the first legitimate Luba king. But he also left behind twins, who were born to the second sister (Burton 1961: 6). When Mbidi retreated back to his home in the east, he entrusted the children to the care of Mijibu'a Kalenga, the first Luba royal diviner, whose clairvoyance and wisdom enabled their survival. The ambivalent nature of power—which can be either benevolent or malevolent—is embodied by the moon's dualities, echoed by Mbidi Kiluwe's enigmatic appearance and subsequent disappearance, and also by his engendering of both a son and twins. Yet the son is as ambivalent as the twins, for in his genetic makeup, he embodies the two sides of Luba identity—the autochthonous side of incest, tyranny, and excess, and the refined and cultivated side of civilization imported from the east (Mudimbe 1996: 246). When Mbidi appears, order is introduced. But when he departs, the two sides battle, and the conflict is indicative of the essential paradox of Luba kingship—its dualisms, ambivalences, and anomalous origins.

Mbidi Kiluwe and his son Kalala Ilunga belong to a paradigmatic set of culture heroes throughout this vast region of southeastern Congo that are characterized as divided beings. As Allen Roberts has documented (1993: 73, 74), sometimes they are physically divided down the body midline, which is a metaphor for their dichotomous identities. But such heroes always embody dualistic principles, which cause them to have a two-sidedness that is often unpredictable and dangerous. Just like the moon, with its alternations of luminous visibility and tenebrous shadow, such culture heroes embody the paradoxes and ambivalences of power.

Songs for Twins and Spirit Possession

In addition to being sung on the night of a new moon, and at all events of momentous transformation in Luba society, including the investiture of a new ruler, funerals, and initiations, the most important function of the "songs for twins" is to induce a state of spirit possession. Practiced by diviners or members of the Mbudye historical association, possession is an altered state of consciousness when a spirit comes to mount the head and take over the identity of the possessed subject. Songs for twins, with their bawdy lyrics, are catalysts for possession. Luba spirit mediums use only song and percussive rhythms to induce a state of trance and invariably it is the rhythmic repetition of the songs for twins (*mapasa*) that enables the manifestation of the spirit.

On a certain level of ontological understanding, the moon is a metaphor for spirit possession. The verb used to describe the ascent of the moon after a cycle of interlunary darkness is *kutentama,* from the same root as the verb used to describe epiphytic plants that climb to high places, such as orchids and ferns, and mediums who become possessed by spirits, including both diviners and members of the Mbudye historical association. In all three cases, the word is the same, implying a metaphorical association between that which ascends and reaches to certain heights and states of elevated awareness and clairvoyance (Roberts and Roberts 1996: 189). As Tusulo Banze explains, "We *bambudye* have a strict interdiction to never look at the rising of the moon. We have this interdiction because the way that the moon rises is comparable to the way an *mbudye* takes possession of his spirit" (personal communication, 1988).[5]

Luba spokespersons commonly use verbs of ascent to describe the state of becoming possessed. For example, during initiation rites into the highest levels of the Mbudye association, which is a governmental body responsible for the guardianship of Luba historical knowledge, an initiate must undergo possession by one of the twinned spirits of Luba kingship. It is said that the initiate who has passed through the first two levels of knowledge and aspires to Mbudye leadership may "climb the platform" to the next stage of initiation called *lukala,* from the word for a "threshold, earthen mound, or ladder" (Van Avermaet and Mbuya 1954: 220). Ascension to this third level means that the initiate must mount an earthen throne and become possessed by one of the twinned tutelary spirits of Luba kingship. Once possessed by a twin spirit, the initiate is described to have "broken through the sky," to see beyond the place where thunder and lightning strike (Nooter 1991: 126). Following the third level of *lukala,* the initiate continues to the fourth and final level called *lukasa,* which is both the name of the beaded wooden board used for instruction into this level and the title of the highest rank or step in the process of knowledge acquisition (Roberts and Roberts 1996: 124–134).

The other major institution in which possession is a common practice is divination, which is also considered to be a branch of political authority. As noted in the epic, the children of the culture bearer were entrusted to a diviner, and the first Luba diviner was critical to the king's ascent to power. This kind of diviner, called a *kilumbu,* or by the name Bwana Vidye, undergoes spirit possession in order to perform his or her consultations. Possession is induced by songs for twins being sung throughout the session by wives (if the diviner is a man) and/or attendants (if the diviner is a woman) to sustain the presence of the spirit. Only in a state of possession by the spirit can a diviner offer clairvoyant guidance of the type that Mijibu'a Kalenga, the first Luba diviner, could offer to Kalala Ilunga as he confronted—and transcended—the intrigues of his cruel maternal uncle.

Whenever diviners enter a state of trance they must adorn themselves with white chalk, referred to as "captured moonlight" (A. Roberts and

Maurer 1985: 28), to confirm their condition of "white enlightenment."[6] Sometimes chalk is applied around the eyes, sometimes to the entire face, and usually also to the chest, shoulders, and arms. The chalk is a direct reference to the moon, for its whiteness and purity evoke the blessing of the spirits and the clairvoyance and insight afforded by its light. Chalk is applied to the body and/or face whenever a person is undergoing a transition from one state of being to another. It signals transformation and liminal passage, as well as benevolence, wellbeing, and spiritual grace.

Kapamba: The Mother of Twins

Kapamba is the name assigned to the wife of a diviner (when the diviner is a man). The name is an honorific and it is also associated with mothers of twins. The connection between the mother of twins and the diviner's wife underscores the fact that twins are considered to be spirits, both in ordinary life and in contexts of ritual and problem-solving. During divination, Kapamba is the one who calls the spirits through percussive rhythms and the songs for twins. She is also responsible for respecting the taboos, translating the possessed diviner's utterances, and generally serving as the guardian of her husband's spirits. While the diviner performs a consultation and manipulates the various object-filled gourds that are vehicles of the spirit's directives, Kapamba sings the songs for twins and strikes an iron bell in a slow rhythmic repetition to produce the circumstances necessary for the sustained presence and intervention of the spirit(s).

However, in the context of the birth of twins, the title of Kapamba refers to a particular role. The following passages are drawn from the writing of Théodore Theuws (1960), who wrote extensively about Luba twins:

> When it becomes clear that a pregnant woman will give birth to twins, a special wise woman is summoned. It must be a woman who has already borne twins, and whose twins are still living. She is called by the title of Kapamba, just like the diviner's wife. It is her role to care for the twins, to arrange for the rituals surrounding their birth, and to ensure that all prohibitions are respected. First, she runs to find some strings that she will cross over the chest of the expectant mother, the father, and herself. While awaiting the arrival of the second twin, the women call to the child in the same way that they do to the moon on the night of its rising: "Is it coming? Will it appear?" In the meantime, a healer is called upon to prepare medicinal water with which to purify the children, the mother, and

FIGURE 12.1. Kapamba shown as she summons the twin tutelary spirits of Luba royal culture and sustains their presence by singing the "songs for twins." This enables her husband, the diviner, to conduct a consultation through the enlightened wisdom of his possessing spirits. 1989. *Photo: Mary Nooter Roberts.*

the women present. As soon as the children are born, he arrives with the water and begins to cast ritual insults, specifically of a sexual variety, at the mother of the twins while sprinkling everyone with the healing water.

The twins are purified only with the earth from a termitary, whereas Kapamba utilizes chalk that she takes from a gourd honoring the tutelary spirits. Chalk is white like the moon. Twins are in effect children of the moon. Kapamba is herself called *inakwezi,* or "mother moon." It is the moon that has brought this unprecedented fecundity, which frightens people by its excess. (Theuws 1960: 131–136)

The lyrics of the songs for twins allude to the extraordinary fecundity of mothers of twins, the power of women more generally, and sometimes the cunning of sorcerers. Following are lyrics from songs that this author collected in 1989 in a village to the east of Niembo, where there is a famous father-son divining team. During the course of the performance the diviner who led the singing spontaneously erupted into a trance state, even though he was not intending to conduct a divination session, thus demonstrating the power of the songs to invoke a state of spiritual identification:

> Ngoy, with the filed teeth, from Lualaba; Ngoy with the filed teeth.
> *Chorus:* Ngoy, with the filed teeth, from Lualaba; we are calling Ngoy with
> the filed teeth.
> Oh, the head that was made for the *nkaka* [beaded headdress worn by a
> person in a state of possession],
> The nose for *mpemba* [white chalk],
> The torso for scarifications,
> The genitals red like a tender palm nut.
> Today, fall down, you look,
> Today, how you have grown,
> How God is unsympathetic!

Other songs are even more explicitly sexual in their lyrics:

> My mother, Mother of Twins
> *Chorus:* Your spoiled vagina, your vagina,
> You Mother, Mother of Twins,
> From Munza where one practices *majende* [the stealing of souls,
> a fearsome practice of sorcery],
> How I have looked and have worn myself out,
> My Mother, Mother of Twins.

> The clitoris is crying tears of sadness.
> *Chorus:* The clitoris is crying tears.
> The huge penis has gone to the army.
> The clitoris is crying tears.

The words of many other songs for twins are far more enigmatic and highly symbolic, but demonstrate the close associations between extreme fertility, anomaly, and the fear of instability that results. They also are considered to be insulting lyrics, aimed at the mother and father of twins, who are viewed as harbingers of the misfortune wrought by the birth of twins. As the missionary W. F. P. Burton writes, "in the ceremonial reviling which takes place after twins are born, the mother shrieks at her fellow-villagers, 'It is all your fault. You must have charmed me with bent millet-stalk. It will make the gardens heavy with grain, but it has made me heavy with suffering'" (1961: 104).

The ritual of insulting is central to practices associated with Luba twins, and requires a broader understanding of the social roles and purposes of insulting more generally. Edmund Leach (1979: 153–166) and Mary Douglas (1979) have both written on topics of verbal abuse and joking as used strategically and ritually in various social contexts. But insulting is a particular kind of verbal strategy aimed at reconstituting the social order. Luba themselves talk about the necessity of insults in order to ensure the health and wellbeing of twins: "We begin to sing, we insult ourselves, we sing songs to insult each other, *Kwimba masa,* until they [the twins] are healed. If you do not cast insults then one might die. You have to insult yourself and others until the twins reestablish their health and wellbeing" (Keuzi, personal communication, 1987).

A Shared Intelligence: Two Bodies, One Mind

The following account by Nsenga Ubandilwa offers insights into the nuanced ways that Luba regard twins as two beings sharing a single intelligence. This account also demonstrates the entangled perceptions of twins that have been inspired by conversion to Christianity:

They have many prohibitions, following the word of God in paradise. In the Garden of Eden there was a man and woman, and Isaac and Jacob were born together, one holding the other. They were children of misfortune because they were two beings emerging from a single womb, from which would normally emerge only a single child, and as such it is a kind of misfortune. It is also the power of God. There where people remained naked, everyone, the father, the women, and children insulted each other, and it was like it was in the Garden of Eden. The insults were cast for the children of misfortune in order that they could grow up with a complete intelligence. In the Garden, it was a white person and a black person.

They did not cut their hair. They were seated with their parents when the moon would rise and we would sing the songs for twins, according to our tradition. If we did not sing the songs for twins the children would be imbalanced because it is the intelligence of a single person that two people receive, or that is shared by two people. In order for this intelligence to be equal between the twins, one would summon a healer once the children were walking. The healer prepared medicines and performed the ceremony called *kusubula*. The children were washed and their hair was cut as well as their finger- and toe-nails. Then, the healer prepared the substances in a horn. They also prepared traditional drinks because the children stop nursing on their own. And then, we sang the songs for twins in order to balance their intelligence or the memory of two persons. . . . That is why we pray to God and to our spirits to bestow intelligence on both twins so that their memory could be complete. (Nsenga Ubandilwa, personal communication, 1988)

The account signals a philosophical conceptualization of twins sharing a single intelligence, which must be balanced in order for them to be functional and fully able to cope in the world. It offers a way of thinking about politics as well, for if Kalala Ilunga is a divided being, as are all Luba culture heroes and kings, then he is like twins who possess a single intelligence with conflicting dimensions, which must be balanced and controlled in order to survive.

A Luba diviner named Musempe made some remarks in an interview (personal communication, 1987) that demonstrate the close association between twins and kings, as revealed through the contexts of singing the songs for twins. First, he describes every test that an aspirant to the throne must undergo (initiation into the Mbudye association; ritual incest in the *koba ka malwa*, "house of unhappiness," during his investiture; the acceptance of an offering by the spirit of the lake), and how each stage is celebrated and validated by the singing of the songs for twins. Then Musempe concludes, "The songs for twins stayed here with us ever since the arrival of Mbidi Kiluwe; we sang the songs in honor of twins. We also sing the 'songs for twins' for all chiefs who are enthroned. It is like a baptism, it is like a prayer."

The Reification of Twin Spirits

A type of sculpture has been identified as a twin figure among the Tabwa, and it also exists—although rarely—among the Luba (see chapter 11; Roberts and Roberts 1996: 100; A. Roberts and Maurer, 1985: 84). A simple cylindrical shape with no limbs, the figure has the suggestion of a head and body. True to Luba artistic conventions, such figures often possess geometric patterns on their surfaces alluding to scarification marks of beauty worn by Luba women. Some even have a navel and a reference to genitalia by the placement of the scarification patterns, and one known

FIGURE 12.2. Headrest supported by paired female figures (may allude to female spirit mediums who lived together at sacred sites to serve as interme- diaries between humans and the twin tutelary spirits of Luba royal culture called *bavidye*). Luba, Democratic Republic of the Congo. Wood; height, 7 in. National Museum of African Art, Washington, D.C. Museum Purchase, Inv. No. 86.12.14. *Photo courtesy of the National Museum of African Art.*

example reveals a small hole that was most likely used for the insertion of *bijimba,* a magical charge of powerful medicinal substances. The hair is also incised with horizontal and vertical lines, and some twin figures interrupt the head and body with four supports that resemble those seen on certain Luba stools.

There are also many representations of double figures in the corpus of Luba art that seem to be related to the importance of twins in Luba ontol- ogy. It is not uncommon to see two female figures arm in arm, side by side, back to back, or entwined on the tops of staffs of office and/or supporting the platform of stools and headrests.

Luba exegesis makes it clear that such depictions, though both female, are embodiments of the *bavidye,* or twin spirits. One early archival pho- tograph by J. Van den Boogaerde of the artist and chief Twito-Kilulwe shows him holding a staff of the most ancient type, exuding palm oil from its surface and topped by two female figures, arm in arm (see Roberts and Roberts 1996: 158).[7] The chief himself wears several beaded neck- laces, including one set of beads that drapes diagonally across his chest to his hips. Ngoi wa Nkulu, the wife of a Luba titleholder in Kinkondja, explained that mothers and fathers of twins always wear strings of fiber crossed in this way over their chests. If one twin dies, then they remove one of the two strings, leaving the other to drape diagonally across the torso (personal communication, 1987). It is very common to see members of the Mbudye association and other high Luba officials donning beaded bandoliers either crossed over their chests or diagonally across the torso. Whether it is a literal reference to their being the parents of twins or a symbolic allusion to the *bavidye* twin spirits of Luba kingship depends on the individual's personal history.

Twin *bavidye* spirits are also manifest in Luba insignia in the form of Janus heads on staffs of office, cups, and headrests. Although such Janus depictions are not as clearly feminine as full figures of pairs, they nevertheless conform to female representations in Luba art in a general way.[8] Exegesis on a Luba staff by a titleholder who wished to remain anonymous indicated that the Janus heads were specifically those of Mpanga and Banze, two of the most important twin spirits in the Luba pantheon of tutelary spirits called *bavidye*. Mpanga and Banze are associated with the protection of the history and sacred prohibitions of Luba kingship, and they inhabit a sacred forest near Kabongo where the kings of the founding dynasty have been invested into office (Roberts and Roberts 1996: 166).

Why would the twin spirits be depicted as women when in oral narratives they seem to be male/female pairs? Luba explain that *bavidye* reside in sacred locales such as lakes, grottoes, forest groves, and the foothills of mountains. In order to gain access to them, female spirit mediums would intercede on behalf of humans to propitiate them. Oftentimes these mediums lived in pairs as celibate priestesses, single women who never married or bore children, but who had a special connection to the spirits. Until even the late 1980s, paired female spirit mediums were known to reside at certain sacred locations.

The practice of two women living together at a sacred site and serving as intermediaries with the *bavidye* twinned spirits is linked to the role of a particular female spirit medium, known as Mwadi in some locales and as Kifikwa in others, who is an incarnation of a deceased Luba king (see Burton 1961: 53; Roberts and Roberts 2007: 56, 57). Luba kings and very powerful chiefs are considered to be semidivine, with one foot in humanity and the other in the realm of *bavidye*. But once deceased, they join the pantheon of *bavidye*, and in the past it was documented that an ordinary woman would become possessed by his spirit and assume the title of Mwadi while she served as the king incarnate. During the course of the author's field research from 1987–1989, several Luba individuals explained that the reason spirits take residence in the bodies of women is that only the body of a woman is strong enough to hold the spirit of a king. The staff owner mentioned above stated it in this way: "the spirits responded above all to women: they were more 'favorable' to women" (Roberts and Roberts 1996: 168). The missionary W. F. P. Burton heard very similar accounts from his Luba informants.

> It is often said that a man's body would not be spiritually strong enough to support the spirit of Ilunga Mwila (a king). Only a woman's body could endure it. . . . Indeed until the advent of the white man the *kifikwa*'s influence counted largely in the appointment of a new chief, and her word was never gainsaid. The natives believe that in thus reverencing the *kifikwa*, they are still giving deference to their ancient chiefs, who live, reincarnated in the body of the medium. (1961: 54)

It is logical then that *bavidye* are mediated by women, who have a more direct relationship to spirits. This applies in other situations, as when Luba explain that most diviners in the past were women because women could embody the spirit directly without entering into a state of trance. Only in recent times has the profession become predominately male. Even now, when a Luba male diviner goes into trance, he must be assisted by his wife, Kapamba, who is responsible for calling the spirits by singing the songs for twins. It is through her intercession that he achieves altered consciousness and transformed identity. A similar distinction is made in the nonroyal form of divination called *kashekesheke,* in which a diviner and a client hold a sculpted wooden figure and the diviner analyzes its movements as responses to questions posed to the spirit. Women *kashekesheke* diviners have no need for any special preparation to serve in this role, whereas male practitioners must undergo *lusalo,* which involves the insertion of medicinal substances into the surface of the skin of the hand where the sculpted figure makes contact. This then activates the figure to respond (Roberts and Roberts 1996: 180–185).

These examples demonstrate that Luba spirit mediation is differentiated according to gender, and that Luba perceive women to have a more direct relationship to spirits. Consequently, it is women who assume the roles of spirit mediums at the sacred sites and it is they who are depicted on the regalia of kings and chiefs, titleholders and diviners, to enable such objects to serve as conduits to or vessels for spirits. Through the images of paired women, the staff, headrest, stool, or cup serves as a channel through which to receive the blessing, protection, and wellbeing of the twinned spiritual guardians of Luba kingship, who embody the contradictions and ambivalences of political power and life itself.

Luba Twins in Contemporary, Global Perspective

The relationships between twins and divination find continued expression not only in contemporary Luba communities of rural Katanga province, but also in the African Diaspora, including the American South and New York City. In May 2005, Allen Roberts and I received a package from The Twins, forty-fourth-generation divination artists of the Li-Maa Clan, which they explain to be the older name for Luba, and which they inherited from their great-great-grandfather.[9] According to The Twins, the Luba survived the transatlantic slave trade, and there are "Luba" secret societies still in existence in Texas and Louisiana. The Twins' full names are Enjai and Amnau Eele, and they currently reside in New York City. Among their most important predictions was the attack on the Twin Towers of the World Trade Center on September 11, 2001. With the codirection of Brett Berg, The Twins produced a film entitled *The Letter,* which included their divination process and a large-scale *lukasa* memory board mapped out on the inside of a door to a storage unit. By discerning the name "Atta" in Manhattan, and the decoding of letters and numbers combined with images of people, places, and events, The Twins foresaw the deadly events at the Twin Towers, and sent a package about it to a famous movie actor's studio.

The Twins work in concert to perform divination. "Eele paints events on canvas prior to them happening, and Amnau write about events prior to them happening. Once our Divinations manifest, we present our paintings and writings to society as memory boards." They explain their ancestry in the following way: "Our grandfather was known as a Luba Master Iron Artist. He was the second male only in our Clan to be born with the ability to Divine and Eele is the third male" (personal communication, 2005). Their great-great-grandfather was descended from enslaved parents, and he was said to have lived to be 116 years old.

The Twins discovered the author's book *Memory: Luba Art and the Making of History* when it appeared in 1996 to accompany the exhibition of the same title held at the Museum for African Art in New York. They state that the photographs in the book have provided information intended by the objects, which they are grateful to their great-great-grandfather for sharing with them. According to The Twins, the highest order of Luba is

twinning, and their greatest aspiration is to save lives through the predictions and visions afforded by the art of divination (personal communications, 2005 and 2006).

Luba twin practices, arts, and rituals reflect the complex ambiguities,
ambivalences, and dualities that characterize power itself. If the greatest
spirits of Luba kingship are twins, and Luba kings join this pantheon upon
their deaths, then it is clear that twinship is considered to be the highest
order of Luba existence—however anomalous it may be. What is certain is
that the anomalous must be protected by prohibitions and taboos, and just
as twin births are surrounded by such interdictions, so are Luba kingship
practices defined, even dictated, by the taboos that surround and guide
them. It is almost as if the very fabric of kingship is such that it must be
protected to remain balanced. When Kalala Ilunga was born of the blood
of Nkongolo and Mbidi Kiluwe, he inherited a conflicting dualistic heritage (Mudimbe 1996: 247). In order to balance the two sides and allow
them to share a single intellect, just like twins, he and successive kings
have had to live according to the strictest rules of behavior and proto-
col. The role of the Mbudye association was to ensure the respect of such
rules and regulations, and the *lukasa* memory board was devised to teach
and instruct all royal officials about these procedures which alone could
ensure the success and continuity of the state.

When considering how *bavidye,* or the twin spirits of the Luba universe, come to be the most exalted of beings, it is useful to consider the
words of Edmund Leach when describing how cultures construct a continuum between humans and their gods:

> The gap between the two logically distinct categories, this world/other
> world, is filled in with tabooed ambiguity. The gap is bridged by super-
> natural beings of a highly ambiguous kind. . . . These marginal, ambigu-
> ous creatures are specifically credited with the power of mediating
> between gods and men. They are the object of the most intense taboos,
> more sacred than the gods themselves. . . . So here again it is the ambigu-
> ous categories that attract the maximum interest and the most intense
> feelings of taboo. The general theory is that taboo applies to categories
> which are anomalous with respect to clear-cut category oppositions. If A
> and B are two verbal categories, such that B is defined as "what A is not"
> and vice versa, and there is a third category C which mediates this dis-
> tinction, in that C shares attributes of both A and B, then C will be taboo.
> (Leach 1979: 159)

Kalala Ilunga, the first Luba king, mediates the opposed heritages of Nkongolo Mwamba and Mbidi Kiluwe; he shares attributes of both and thus becomes taboo. Kingship is defined by taboo (*bizila*) because it occupies the ambiguous zone between human frailty and strength, corruption and refinement, excess and restraint, and other oppositions. Twins, too, are anomalous, extraordinary beings, sharing a single intelligence and signaling excessive fertility. Both twins and kings are outside of the ordinary, and thus *i bya malwa* (sources of astonishment and ambiguity). As Allen Roberts articulates with regard to the same phenomenon among the neighboring Tabwa, a Luba-related people, "Comparison of twins and chiefs reflects the duality of the latter, for a chief is 'father of the people,' yet misfortune exists in his community, and he is felt to condone if not participate in such evil. Like the moon, a chief has two 'faces,' a perplexing reality for which twins provide a convenient vehicle for reflection" (A. Roberts and Maurer 1985: 30; for more, see chapter 11). Through the female figure, which is the locus through which twin spirits take abode, spirits find residence, and through Kapamba, the mother of twins and a diviner's wife, they become manifest during the performative consultations with the diviner. Songs for twins are conduits to transformation, potentiality, and rejuvenation, just as the new moon each month affords enlightened vision and renewed hope. The children of the moon are the embodiments of this dichotomous worldview, and its complex set of cultural practices and prescriptions provide a template for political action and being in a world that is always seeking equilibrium in the face of inevitable extremes.

NOTES

1. See Allen F. Roberts (in the 1985 volume *The Rising of a New Moon,* which he coedited with Evan Maurer) for a detailed account of how the new moon serves as a metaphor for social renewal among neighboring Tabwa, who refer to the day of the rising of a new moon as "our holiday," or "our Sunday" (3).

2. These names can vary from one locale to another in the Luba region. For example, the missionary W. F. P. Burton documented in the nearby Mwanza area that twins were called Kapia and Kiungu, with Kapia always being the first to appear. However, among Luba peoples, infants are considered to be reincarnations of particular ancestors, and if a diviner determines the ancestor that is returning in the form of a new body, then only one twin bears the additional name of the ancestor (1961: 56).

3. This discussion of anomaly was inspired by a lecture offered at UCLA by Professor Mudimbe on May 1, 2008, entitled "In the House of Libya: A Meditation on Africa and the Practice of the Social Sciences," the Bi-annual Coleman Lecture

given in honor of the founder of the UCLA African Studies Center, Prof. James S. Coleman. In this lecture, Mudimbe analyzed the complex roots of the word *anomaly* and its various levels of meaning.

4. There is a great deal of analysis of Mbidi Kiluwe, and the many ways that he manifests, as a buffalo, stealthy and secretive, and black as the night (see A. Roberts 1993: 72–77).

5. In KiLuba, prefixes are used to designate plurals and singulars. The word *mbudye* refers to an individual member of the association, and *bambudye* is a reference to multiple members of the association, or the collectivity of members. Mbudye with a capital "M" is the term for the association itself.

6. Many Luba and Tabwa informants refer to *mpemba* in French as "kaolin," yet Allen Roberts suggests that the chemical composition of the substance is not kaolin in this part of central Africa, but rather is chalk.

7. The staff pictured in this early photograph by J. Van den Boogaerde taken near Mwanza between 1916 and 1918 may be the one that is now in the Seattle Art Museum or is by the same hand, which is probably that of Chief Twito-Kilulwe, who is shown holding it in the photograph. See Roberts and Roberts (1996: 172).

8. It is important to note that even when a carved head appears to be female, it could actually depict the head of a chief or king, as rulers were known to don female coiffures on the day of their investiture.

9. I would like to thank Joanna Grabski, who first informed Allen Roberts and me about The Twins after her spouse encountered their work in New York City.

WORKS CITED

Burton, W. F. P. 1961. *Luba Religion and Magic in Custom and Belief.* In *Annales* 35. Tervuren, Belgium: Africa Museum.

Douglas, Mary. 1979. "Jokes." In *Implicit Meanings: Essays in Anthropology,* 90–114. London: Routledge and Kegan Paul.

Heusch, Luc de. 1972. *Le roi ivre ou l'origine de l'état.* Paris: Gallimard.

Leach, Edmund R. 1979. "Anthropological Aspects of Language: Animal Categories and Verbal Abuse." In *Reader in Comparative Religion: An Anthropological Approach,* ed. William A. Lessa and Evon Z. Vogt, 153–166. New York: Harper and Row Publishers.

Mudimbe, V. Y. 1996. "Afterword: The Idea of 'Luba.'" In *Memory: Luba Art and the Making of History,* ed. Mary Nooter Roberts and Allen F. Roberts, 245–247. New York: Museum for African Art / Munich: Prestel.

Nooter, Mary H. 1991. *Luba Art and Statecraft: Creating Power in a Central African Kingdom.* Ph.D. dissertation, Columbia University, New York.

Reefe, Thomas Q. 1981. *Rainbow and the Kings: A History of the Luba Empire to 1891.* Berkeley: University of California Press.

Roberts, Allen F. 1993. "Insight, or *Not* Seeing Is Believing." In *Secrecy: African Art that Conceals and Reveals,* ed. Mary H. Nooter, 65–79. New York: Museum for African Art / Munich: Prestel.

Roberts, Allen F., and Evan Maurer, eds. 1985. *The Rising of a New Moon: A Century of Tabwa Art.* Seattle: University of Washington Press, for the University of Michigan Museum of Art.

Roberts, Mary Nooter, and Allen F. Roberts. 1996. *Memory: Luba Art and the Making of History.* New York: Museum for African Art / Munich: Prestel.

———. 2007. *Luba.* Visions of Africa Series. Milan: 5 Continents Editions.

Theuws, Théodore. 1960. "Naitre et mourir dans le ritual Luba." *Zaire* XIV (2–3): 115–173.

———. 1968. "Le styx ambigu." *Problèmes sociaux congolais* (81): 5–33.

Van Avermaet, E., and B. Mbuya. 1954. "Dictionnaire kiluba-francais." *Annales du Musée Royal du Congo Belge,* no. 7.

Part Four

Transformations

CHAPTER THIRTEEN

Two Equals Three

Twins and the Trickster in Haitian Vodou

MARILYN HOULBERG

Twin and trickster beliefs have traveled from various parts of Africa to the "New World." This essay examines the transformation they have undergone as they come together in the cultural gumbo in what is known in Haiti as Vodou. Among the Yoruba of Nigeria and the Republic of Benin not only are twins singled out for special veneration but so too is the child born after twins, the trickster. A similar pattern comes from their neighbors, the Fon (or Fongbe) of the Republic of Benin. The concept of the trickster child carries over into Haitian Vodou, where the twins (*marasa*) are said to be followed by *dosou* (if male) or *dosa* (female), considered to be a troublesome and very powerful child. The twins are "cool" (*rada*) and the child born after twins is "hot" (*petwo*). Paradoxically, even though smaller and younger, children born after twins are said to be "the big chiefs." This paradox is a typical trickster trait; as we shall see, the twin-trickster complex also helps to explain the paradox of how 2 = 3.

Out of this complex set of ideas comes a range of visual imagery that relates to twinness and the trickster in Vodou arts. The fact that from the sixteenth to eighteenth centuries enslaved Africans of various ethnic groups brought their twin beliefs with them to Haiti is reflected in what are termed "nations of twins." They may celebrate together but various traits remain separate. Their ritual utensils, altars, songs, foods, dances, drumming patterns, and ritual flags can reflect which nation of twins they belong to: Marasa Kongo, Ibo, Nago, Fon, etc. The concept of 2 = 3 will be analyzed in the visual arts of flags, temple murals, and contemporary paintings and sculptures in Haiti.

Haitian Vodou Background: Past and Present

Vodou, known and distorted through the popular media as "voodoo" and known in the southern part of the United States as "hoodoo," is a blend of African religions, Roman Catholicism, and various influences from Freemasonry. The term Vodou derives from the Fon word *vodun* meaning spirit, deity, or mystery. The Fon brought their religion to Haiti with them from former Dahomey, now the Republic of Benin. In Haiti, the Fon religion combined and recombined with the religions of many other African groups, among them the Yoruba and Igbo of Nigeria, the Kongo of the Democratic Republic of the Congo, the Asante of Ghana, and many others.

In *The Rainy Season,* Amy Wilenz states: "Vodou is a slave religion, much as Creole is a slave language" (1989: 164). But I would suggest rebellion has also been part of the Vodou religion, not unlike the double entendres and the cutting-edge witticisms and proverbs of the Haitian Creole language. James Clifford might have had Haiti in mind when he describes Aime Cesaire's theory of "negritude" as meaning "descending from a Caribbean history . . . that is, a history of degradations, mimicry, violence and blocked possibilities" (1988: 15). But he goes on to add that Caribbean history is also rebellious, syncretic, and creative. This, I would suggest, is particularly true of Haitian Vodou. It, too, is a political force, a religion of constant syncretizing and creative incorporation of new elements, typical of those in the Caribbean. As Clifford further describes Cesaire's Caribbean world, it is "hybrid and heteroglot" (1988: 175).

Vodou itself is hybrid and heteroglot. Its ceremonies combine elements of the Latin Mass in the *action de grace* of the Catholic liturgy which floats out over the Vodou congregation at the beginning of the service. Songs with words praising the saints blend into Yoruba, Fon, and Kongo words, and phrases and songs in Creole, a language that synthesizes French with many different African dialects and vocabularies. French Freemasonry is represented in painted symbols and rituals, and it should be noted that most urban *houngans* (priests) are also Masons.

Old themes are expressed in often startling new manners and mediums. Today, for example, you will see aerosol sprays such as "Sure" deodorant used to sanctify and purify the service. At the beginning, it is used to salute the four cardinal points, while Vodouistes are spun around and sprayed from head to toe. This modern spray takes the place of incense braziers and the rum or *clarin* which the *houngan* or *mambo* used to spray

FIGURE 13.1. Michael Jordan with Saints Cosmos and Damian painted on the back of a "tap-tap" public bus in Port-au-Prince, Haiti. 2002. *Photo: Marilyn Houlberg.*

from their mouths in a fine mist. Throw in a few commercial videographers hired by the priests so they can share the ceremonies with Haitians in Boston, Brooklyn, Miami, or Montreal, who may also have helped to pay for the service in exchange for blessings.

Twins Today

Twins are very popular in Haiti. Nightclubs, restaurants, and all sorts of shops are named after them. Their image is painted on the public buses, called "tap-taps." In figure 13.1, the song "No Money, No Love" floats above a vigorous, angry, intense Michael Jordan, NBA star. Below him the twins in their Catholic forms of the Saints Cosmos and Damian look serene holding their curative leaves. Does this tap-tap make Michael the trickster who follows the twins?

When former U.S. president Bill Clinton met with then-president of Haiti Bertrand Aristide in a televised live interview at the White House,

Aristide held up his arm and compared it with Clinton's. "We are like brothers, no [pause] like *marasa*, except on the surface you are light and I am dark but beneath the color, we are twins." Perhaps he was referring to the fact that they were both presidents or just that they were so compatible. In Port-au-Prince in the restaurant in the Plaza Hotel, all the waiters in tuxedos were gathered around one of the televisions, all eyes in the place riveted on the meeting. When Aristide said the word *marasa* everyone clapped and whistled at this Haitian touch.

The songs of the *Marasa* and other *lwa* (spirits) are frequently heard on CDs throughout Haiti. Here are a few verses from "Magique Marasa" by Papa Wawa and Azore, 1993, loosely translated from the Creole:

Bobo, father of twins, has passed away.
Bobo died and left the twins in the Vodou temple.
Some say to Bobo, "In whose hands have you left the twins?"
Don't worry, father, we are strong enough.
When you were alive, we were big chiefs.

You can even sleep at the crossroads.
Nothing can happen to either you or your children.

We are the Marasa and we never just play around with people.
We are dangerous!
So don't worry, Bobo, our father,
We control our own fate,
We control everything!

"Magique Marasa" is a song from a hit record by Haitian singer Papa Wawa, who, of Haiti's many popular groups, creates probably the most African "roots"-style music, using Vodou drums and iron gongs. Many of Papa Wawa's songs honor the Vodou *lwa*, sometimes known as *lwa Ginen*, "Guinea" being the generalized ancestral homeland of Africa, where souls are said to go when mortal death occurs. This song honors the Sacred Twins, *Marasa*, acknowledging both their magic power and their roots in Africa. The song actually commemorates the death of a famous priest, Mirabeau (or "Bobo") who was the father of twins.

In Papa Wawa's song, a number of typical Vodou twin beliefs emerge. Twins, even when young, are powerful and dangerous. They love to eat and they demand their ritual feasting; they will even trick others in order to get a more ample meal. They are associated with transitional places such as thresholds, and their magical powers are so strong that they can protect all at that most mystically dangerous place, the crossroads. The Marasa join Papa Legba as the guardians of the crossroads where the world of the above or the living meets the world of the below or the dead. The Haitian Legba derives from the West African trickster, known to the Yoruba of Nigeria as Eshu Elegbara, and to the Fon in the Republic of Benin as Legba. Both ends of the age spectrum are at the crossroads: the young, capricious but powerful twins, and the aged Papa Legba, forever on the road, with his walking stick and straw bag. Both Papa Legba and the Marasa must be invoked before any Vodou service can begin. They are the ones who have the power to open the spiritual road.

Sacred Twins in Africa

The intertwining of West and Central African concepts in the beliefs surrounding the Marasa is clear from the linguistic evidence alone. The Kongo word for twins, *mabassa*, means "those who come divided"—thus, the one who comes as two. The term *dosou* (feminine: *dosa*) meaning the child born after twins, derives from the Fongbe *docu*, meaning the child of either sex born after twins. To complicate things further, in Haiti the children that follow *dosou/dosa* are called *alaba* and *idogbe*, meaning the second and third children born after twins. The word *avlekete*, designating children with extra digits (considered a type of twin in Haiti), suggests influence from the Fon and the Ewe peoples, whose goddess of the sea is Avlekete. Sacred children and other types of spirits in many African cultures are associated with rivers or bodies of water since water is considered the essence of life.

Other African cultures have no doubt also contributed elements to the Haitian system of twins and sacred children. Fon cosmology in particular is so penetrated by dualism that Fon concepts of twins and other sacred children merit special attention. Even the head of the Dahomean pantheon, the creator divinity Mawu-Lisa, is a pair of twins. As Mercier notes, "The ideal type of every group in the divine world is a pair of twins of opposite sex, or more rarely, of the same sex. We have pointed out that among men also the ideal birth is a twin birth and that in the beginning every birth was of that kind. The twin structure of the gods is the rule . . ." (1954: 231). Herskovits establishes the importance of human twins among the Fon in this way: "By far the most prized category of births are twins, called *hohovi*" (1967: 263).

Sacred Children: Why Two Equals Three

Wherever African populations have settled in the New World, be it Cuba, Brazil, the United States, or Haiti, the importance and frequency of twin births leaves its imprint, as is amply demonstrated in this volume. In Haiti, as in Africa, the category of children called twins is broader than in Western cultures. In Haiti it includes multidigited *avlekete*. It is said that in the womb, one twin devoured the other except for the telltale extra finger on each hand or extra toe on each foot—an almost "vanished twin."

Even broader is the category of "sacred children." In Haitian Vodou, types of sacred children mirror those found in many parts of Africa. In addition to twins (including children born with multiple digits) and the children born after twins in the birth order, sacred children include breech births (i.e., feet first); children born with a full head of hair or with several teeth; albinos; those born with the umbilical cord around their neck or other parts of their body; hunchbacks; dwarfs; hydrocephalic children; and those born in the caul (amniotic sac).

In both Africa and Haiti the circumstances surrounding the birth of a child or multiple children can be read as a way of predicting the future. A child's fate and future ritual obligations may be determined at the moment of birth, based on the day of the week of the birth; the special deities invoked to conceive the child; the deities of the parents; and, of course, the mode of arriving in the world, for example, as multiple births, or feet first and all of the other variations detailed above.

The midwife or *sajfanm* ("wise woman") plays a critical role in the interpretations of the birth. She is the one who notes all of the important signs of the delivery and passes this information on to the parents. She may be a *mambo* (priestess) herself or she may be assisted by a *mambo* and any number of *ounsi* (initiates). Since few but the Haitian elite can afford to have their babies in clinics, most Haitian women use the services of the *sajfanm*. Thus, traditional African-based beliefs and rituals surrounding births, deeply imbedded in Vodou, are still very strong in Haiti today.

If twins are two children born at the same time, why is their most salient symbol a configuration of three elements, as seen in Marasa *veve*, the bowls used for twin feasts, and other items honoring or representing the sacred twins? Harold Courlander explains how twins and the children born both before and after twins are linked in a powerful continuum:

> The twin spirit has been personified in the [*lwa*] named [Marasa]. The child born after twins is believed by many Haitians to be even "stronger"

and more to be placated than twins themselves. He is known as a [*dosou*] if a boy, [*dosa*] if a girl. Their patron *lwa* are known as Marasa Dosou and Marasa Dosa. The patron of triplets is [Marasa Twa]. Triplets are regarded as a special category of twins. Some Haitians, in fact, believe that the twins are merely a partial manifestation of the group of three, which is completed on the birth of the dosou or dosa. It is also believed by some that the child born before twins is "weak" both in physical vitality and psychic powers, because his strength has been sapped by the Marasa who have followed him. (1960: 32)

Courlander concludes, "Thus twins are integrally linked to the child they bring with them in a triplet birth, or to the child born after them who may be considered a delayed triplet" (1960: 32).

Imaging the Sacred Children

Triplet births are typically quite rare in West Africa and Haiti as well as in other parts of the world, so when three children are represented on shrines or flags in Haiti they are most likely not depicting true triplets—a question I have frequently been asked.

While the substance of twin belief and ritual in Haiti comes from multiple African sources, both the imaging of twins and the calendar for twin rituals have been borrowed from European Catholicism. Mass-produced, inexpensive color lithographs of the Catholic saints are sold on the steps of churches, in nearby small shops, and at pilgrimage sites. They are hung in homes, put on the walls of Vodou sanctuaries, and used as models for large-scale murals in the *ounfo* (Vodou temple). Those who can afford it frequently have three-dimensional plaster versions of the saints as well.

Various Catholic saints are correlated with the twins in Vodou. Most prominent are the twin saints Cosmos and Damian, patron saints of physicians, surgeons, and barbers, who are linked to local twin traditions in Brazil, Cuba, and Haiti. In Haiti, the palm fronds they fold in their hands in chromolithographs (see figure 5.1) are interpreted as curative leaves used to make medicines. This connection between twins and medicine finds further support from Africa, consistent with the belief that twins—because of their lower birth weight—are vulnerable and thus need not only more spiritual and medical attention but also extra food through twin rituals.

Another saint associated with the Marasa in Vodou is Saint Nicholas, said by Vodouists to be the father of twins. Saint Nicholas is connected with

FIGURE 13.2. Beaded Vodou flag, "Les Trois Marassa Guinen," by Yves Telemaque, Port-au-Prince, Haiti. 2005. *Photo: Marilyn Houlberg.*

the sun; at ceremonies for him—especially on his saint's day, December
6—Vodouists pray to him while facing east toward the morning sun. This
linkage between saint, sun, and twins is expressed in the invocation or magical prayer to Saint Nicholas that accompanies the drawing of the *veve* for
the Marasa. It translates, roughly, "By the power of Saint Nicholas, the sun of
justice, who shines on the four corners of the earth. By the power of Marasa
Dosou Dosa, Marasa Zin Sou, Zin Sa, Marasa, Marasa" [Marasa guardian of
the bush, Marasa guardian of the house, Marasa of Africa-Guinea].

The chromolithograph of Saint Nicholas shows him standing next to
a wooden salting tub that contains two children; in one version a third
young child is kissing his foot in thanks. Saint Nicholas, a saint of the
fourth century AD, has saved them all from slaughter by a mad butcher
who had planned to sell their salted flesh as meat in the market. In Vodou,
the children in this chromolithograph are interpreted as Marasa and
Dosou/Dosa. The twins are in the tub and the child kissing his foot is said
to be the child born after twins. The association of Saint Nicholas with
Christmas and generosity toward young children by bringing them gifts
was easily brought into congruence with Vodou beliefs surrounding the
twins and other sacred children in the birth order.

Another Catholic chromolithograph associated with the twins is one
depicting three young girls in the clouds. They are known as the sisters

Faith, Hope, and Charity; the Three Graces; and the three *femme Egypt*, women of Egypt. They are martyred preadolescents said to have lived in the second century AD. Because they were beheaded, only heads and shoulders are shown floating in the sky in their chromolithograph and on Vodou flags. Sometimes the flags are inscribed with "*Marasa Trois*" (The Three Twins), or a variation, such as Yves Telemaque's "*Les Trois Marassa Guinen*" (The Three Guinean Twins) (see figure 13.2). In this spirited flag Telemaque positions a bowl in front of each one for the food they will receive as part of a ceremony symbolized by the ritual bead-covered rattle with its summoning bell, a cup for water, and a candle. Healing leaves decorate the green background.

Knowing through Doing: The Ritual Cosmos of Twins

It is through the details of ritual and ceremony that many religions are transmitted over time, particularly in Haiti, where 65–70 percent of the people are unable to read or write. Since Vodou is without creed or book, it is through ritual that Vodou is "written," over and over again, in variations, through time, space, and symbol. As Evan Zuesse (1979: 238) has observed, it is "the very concreteness of ritual [that] is its profundity. . . ." Further, he suggests that "ritual . . . is spiritually more profound than any theology; it accomplishes more for those who participate in it than any number of rarefied mystical treatises. . . ." Noting that Westerners generally fail to appreciate these very qualities, he suggests that if African religions

> . . . made less use of concrete ritual and proverbial symbolism and more use of abstract metaphysics, their cults might seem more immediately comprehensible and "profound" to us, but their efficacy and self-authenticating reality to participants would be much less. . . . *The deepest form of knowing is through doing. Being is less adequate a religious good than Becoming.* (Zuesse 1979: 242, my emphasis)

Ritual, art, and symbol interact in an elaborate dialogue surrounding the sacred children so essential to Haitian Vodou. To honor and represent twins and others, there are altars resplendent with pottery, sacrificial foods and bottles with specific drinks, special herbs, chromolithographs, sequined flags, and temple wall murals. These elements function in conjunction with others such as ground drawings, songs, and specific drum rhythms that are used to call and salute the twins and the other sacred children in the context of ceremony.

Most ceremonies centered on sacred children take place at Christmas time, the time of the celebration of the birth of the most sacred child in Christianity, Jesus Christ. December 6, the feast of Saint Nicholas, said to be the father of the Marasa in Vodou and the patron saint of children in Catholicism, marks the beginning of the twin ritual season. December 28 is another popular day for twin ceremonies, since it is the feast of the Massacre of the Holy Innocents, commemorating the young children who, by order of King Herod, were killed in an attempt to destroy the infant Jesus. On this day parents who have lost infant children may receive solace. Marasa ceremonies held on this date serve both to protect living children and to commemorate deceased ones. The season concludes on January 6 with the Epiphany—the Adoration of the Magi, the three kings who came from distant lands bearing gifts for the Christ Child.

Thus, in Haiti, the African beliefs and practices honoring sacred children are merged with the Catholic calendar and traditions surrounding infant children, including the infant Jesus. The syncreticism works because both systems share a concern for the wellbeing of infant children and for the commemoration of the spirits of dead infants.

Cap Haitien, December 28, 1985

I was invited to a ceremony by Wilfred J., an *avlekete* who showed me his six-fingered hands and recounted the common belief that one twin had devoured the other twin in the womb, except for the extra fingers. Wilfred told me that this father and his three-year-old were also born *avlekete*. Neither he nor his son would ever have their extra digits removed because they bring good luck and wealth. He was anxious to attend this ceremony in order to serve the Marasa and thus to strengthen himself.

At 8 PM, approaching the *ounfo,* we heard the drums and saw big pots of beans and rice and other food cooking over open fires. The children were fast asleep on mats at the feet of their mothers. Some sixty people had crowded into the tiny space of a 12 × 18–foot temple. The cement platform at the base of the *poto mitan* (center pole) was filled with bottles, candles, and tin kerosene lamps, and the ceiling was festooned with fringes of tissue paper, shredded colorful flowered plastic table cloths, and the ubiquitous strings of paper Haitian flags, black and red with the photographic image of Duvalier in the middle. The officiating *ougan* wore a red cowboy shirt and black cowboy hat.

Four sets of twins ranging in age from six to twelve years old were seated on the floor near some Marasa pots. A hunchbacked dwarf and a young albino man also received special ritual attention during the evening. Wilfred said that *dosou/dosa* (the children born after twins) and other types of sacred children were also present. In the course of the evening, there were about a dozen trance possessions by six *lwa,* including Gede, Ogou, Ezili, and Philomene.

The first *lwa* to appear, the longest to stay, and the most entertaining, was Gede, the trickster *lwa* of death and regeneration. Once dressed in his accoutrements—black shirt and sunglasses—Gede made his way around the peristyle, one hand on his hip, pitching forward and back on one foot. Then he would take off his sunglasses and make eye contact in a very exaggerated way, his head zooming in and out, his eyes alternatively squinting and bulging wide, making us stare death in the face. But there was also a very lighthearted aspect to his performance as he danced the *banda* with subtle, hypnotic hip movements.

Gede, as the trickster *lwa* of death and regeneration, is the special guardian of infant children and the *lwa* best able to help human beings avoid death. Gede is also able to create new life and thus an exaggerated phallus is one of his most salient symbols. His herbal curing ceremonies are considered among the most potent. Gede's services on November 1 and 2 (All Saints and All Souls Days in the Catholic calendar) commemorate the dead, both children and adults. On those days all the neighborhood children are fed in a small feast for the Twins. In fact, Gede and the Twins share the same two sacred days of the week, Monday and Friday. In many areas of Haiti, 50 percent of the children do not reach the age of five, so the linkage between the children and the spirit of death is to be expected.

Feasting and the Twins

A feast for the Twins, *manje Marasa,* may occur at times other than the Christmas season. For example, the Marasa are invoked along with Legba at the start of the week-long ceremony known as the *sevis kay* (service of the house), when all the *lwa* served in an *ounfo* are celebrated, each in a set order. The *sevis kay* is not tied to a particular time of the year. It can be done on the occasion of initiation, the making of a new *mambo* and *ougan,* and the creation of new healing bundles (*paket*).

During one such ceremony held at Mariani, near Port-au-Prince, in early December of 1985, a number of twins and other young children were gathered on a Monday morning near the entrance to the temple complex. Three deep holes were dug in the middle of the road, to be filled with various sacrificial foods (beans, peanuts, etc.) and pans of basil and water.

Terracotta Marasa pots were massed near the holes. Each hole was ringed with a circular *veve* as well as the tripartite one for the Marasa. In a way, the relationship of the three holes in the road to the symbolism of the Marasa *veve* resonated as a three-dimensional ritual diagram involving not just the four cardinal points but also the world above and the world below. These rituals are often the subject of decorative Vodou flags such as one by Antoine Oleyant depicting with ritual correctness the iconography of the *veve* interspersed between the three male figures.

After the holes were dug, a line of honey was dribbled in from the main gate at the edge of a major highway in order to lure the spirits of the Marasa to the three holes and to their sacrifices. As the drumming began, cooked beans were put on the Marasa pots in the three holes and also served in bowls and on plates to all of us who were present.

In addition to being the obligatory first ceremony of a *servis kay,* the *manje Marasa* can be occasioned by dreams, divination, and inherited ritual obligations. One *manje Marasa* I attended on March 26, 1993 was prompted by several of these factors. This long-planned ceremony took place on a Friday. Friends of the bereaved's deceased mother had reminded him that she had served the Marasa; if he was having problems, it was because he had not fulfilled the ritual obligations that had descended on him. Also, his deceased infant son, his first-born, had been appearing in his dreams, crying and complaining that he was cold, wet, and hungry in the watery world of the dead. Since the man's wife had died several years before, he planned all this with the help of his sister-in-law, Geslin Racine, who was an *ounsi* and a "twin," an *avlekete.* The ceremony took place in her home.

It should be noted that Madam Racine not only has six fingers but four of her six children have six fingers on each hand as well, including her twelve-year-old daughter described below. The day before the ceremony was spent shopping for the twins' feast foods of rice, beans, peanuts, pistachios, cashew nuts, hard candy, little cakes, sugar, molasses, honey pudding, popcorn, cassava bread, eggs, and coffee. A fine multicolored rooster called a *zenga* had been purchased several weeks before and fed well in order to provide a worthy sacrifice. Its many colors were highlighted as symbolic of the many "nations" of twins being honored and served.

This feast was attended by several parents of twins, many local children, a visiting *mambo* who did the *veve,* and, of course, the sponsor. After this, the twelve-year-old daughter of the officiating *ounsi* became momentarily possessed by the spirit of the twins. This meant that the Marasa were showing their pleasure at the feast by "passing through" her, even if only fleetingly. The rooster was then cooked and added to the pot of beans, which was placed on the *veve* for the twins next to the basket tray holding all the other offerings to the Marasa. Of the two cups of coffee only one had sugar so as to please the twins however they liked it. At about 7 PM all of the young children were invited to take from the tray and to partake of the rice, beans, and chicken being served to everyone. Later, the sponsor took some of the foods home in a large calabash to feed his own Marasa pots.

Fourteen years later, on January 6, 2007, I again attended a ceremony for the Marasa at Madam Racine's house. Everything was similar to the ceremony described above. The only difference was the prominence of twelve-fingered and twelve-toed children. One young man with twenty-four digits, Garrison, aged eleven, was featured as the most sacred child in the ceremony. He was doubly sacred because not only did he have extra digits on both his hands and feet but he was also born in the amniotic sac (the caul). Those who are born in the sac are considered to have the gift of "second vision," a type of special vision. They are said to be able to detect witches and devils wherever they go. When they enter a house, they can spot them immediately. Even at his young age, eleven-year-old Garrison's witch-finding talent is in steady demand.

The Nations of Twins

During the ceremony, Garrison had special duties such as lighting the nine candles floating in oil and also dividing the food. While there were about fifteen children present, oddly enough, there were no double-birth twins among them. The group was dominated by *avlekete*, with their shared trait passed down through the generations. The highlight of the evening was the distribution of the chicken and beans from the large pot placed next to the tray and on top of the Marasa *veve*.

The Yoruba influences on the ceremony were many. Beans are the favorite food of twins in both Haiti and Yorubaland. They are said to soothe their anger. One popular Yoruba song that mothers sing is: "I have beans, I have palm oil; I am not afraid to have twins." The twelve-digited children are called *olugbodi* in Yoruba, which indicates a sacred child. In Haiti the extra digits may or may not be removed. Madam Geslin Racine said she had them removed on her children and grandchildren, as her own had been removed at birth. The proof of the power of the devoured twin was the fact that the digit would reemerge as a "nub." At this point in the conversation she called all the *avlekete* to come and have their "nubs" photographed, which they proudly did. It may be recalled that Wilfred of Cap Haitian, an *avlekete* whose father and son were also *avlekete*, said his family tradition was *not* to remove the extra digit because it was a source of his power and strength.

The *lwa* are grouped into "families, pantheons, or . . . *nanchons*," each with its own ethos or corresponding attitudes. There may have once been as many as seventeen different *nanchons* of *lwa*, but Leslie Desmangles (1992) points out that the best known *nanchons* in Haiti today are the Rada, Petwo, and Kongo (and in some Haitian provinces, Ibo) *nanchons*. Within these categories are subsets. The Rada nation of sacred twins, generally considered to be beneficent and calm if properly served, include the Marasa Nago and the Marasa Ginen. Their plates are terracotta and are used in combination with the small calabash. The Petwo Marasa, on the other hand, is generally considered more volatile and vengeful; they are comprised of the Kongo and Ibo nations among others. The Marasa Kongo and Marasa Bwa (twins of the forest) are generally represented by three-chambered wood plates with the third chamber doweled into the intersection of the other two.

Rada/Petwo: Twins and the Birth Order

As we have seen, some nations of twins are considered Rada and others Petwo, each with their own type of ritual plates. However, the picture may be more complicated. Some Vodouists say that a given *nanchon* of Marasa, even though classified as Rada, may have a Petwo side. For example, by the addition of the term *flambo* (flaming), the Rada Marasa Ginen is transformed into the more volatile Petwo Marasa Ginen Flambo with all the attendant ritual implications. The division between Rada and Petwo is by no means clear-cut and firm although their respective characteristics are generally culturally agreed upon in Vodou.

In addition, some Vodouists suggest that the twins themselves are considered more Rada than the *dosou/dosa* (the child born after twins), who is associated with more volatile Petwo spirits. This is the same pattern found in Yorubaland where the *ibeji* (twins), considered a disruption of the normal single birthing pattern, are potentially hot and powerful until properly propitiated through ritual. The child born after twins, called *idowu* in Yoruba, however, is equated with Esu Elegbara, the very volatile trickster. A praise name for Idowu (equivalent to the Haitian Dosou/Dosa) is *Esu leyin ibeji*, the trickster behind the twins. Esu inhabits such transitional places as entrances, thresholds, and crossroads; perhaps Idowu's birth can be considered a transition back to normalcy. As one Lagos, Nigeria, father of twins explained, another single birth after Idowu is necessary to restore equilibrium: "There is always trouble with Idowu, there is always quarreling. Idowu lands fast and hard. The Alaba comes softly, softly, just floats down and then everything goes back to normal." *Alaba*, the second single birth after twins, is then followed by *idogbe*, the next single birth before all is resolved. As we have seen, *idogbe* is equated with and related to *idogwe/ dogwe* in Haitian Vodou, as the child who follows the Marasa Dosou/Dosa in the birth order and thus also brings everything back to normal.

This pattern was reiterated very clearly by a set of female triplets born in 1920, one of whom I interviewed in 1993 when they were living in St. Marc. In a discussion of possession trance, this woman distinguished between the first two born, considered twins, and the third child out, the *dosa*. Only the *dosa* triplet was expected to go into a possession state. She herself was the *dosa*. The *dosa*'s trance was described by people gathered for the discussion as a volatile performance during which she acted like a petulant child that everyone had to appease with candy and other gifts. This corresponds with what the Yoruba say about the *idowu* child, the trickster, who is always trying to upstage his or her older siblings, the twins.

Twins and Vodou Flags in the New World Context

If a Haitian *hougan* or *mambo* needs a flag or pair of flags for their temple, they will usually commission them directly from the artist and his or her workshop. Every Vodou ceremony begins with the salutations to the Marasa and Papa Legba, who open the way. The *veve* are next drawn, the two female *hounsi* carry sequined flags on flag staffs and flank the sword bearer who represents Ogun, the spirit of iron and war. They march around the center post to the drumming, and thus the ceremony begins.

The Vodou flags for export used to be sold to tourists, but with the political unrest over the last few decades, the tourist trade has virtually vanished and life has been difficult for the twenty or so major flag artists of Port-au-Prince, the center of artistic production. Now, of course, the horrendous earthquake of February, 2010, has destroyed what artistic production remained. Hopefully, this situation will improve.

The Trickster Artist: Roudy Azor

One of the best new flag artists in Haiti today is Roudy Azor, who has produced several beaded Marasa flags. In one striking flag he depicts three women emerging from a single kneeling body. Twins with white streaming hair flank the central Dosa, the "hot" child born after twins. The flaming three-legged *chaudier,* or brazier, relates to the Dosa. The three gourds at the bottom and the triple *veve* in the upper right-hand corner refer to the Marasa Trois. In another flag, "La Sirene Marasa Trois," Azor combines the Marasa, the Dosa, and the mermaid, La Sirene. In answer to why he combined the twins and the mermaid he replied that just as the twin children come in multiples so when you see mermaids in your dreams, you never see just one. "First you see one and then more keep swimming towards you."

Azor knows so much about Marasa Dosou/Dosa because he was born into a family with two sets of twins and was born right after one set and is, therefore, himself a *dosou.* As a *dosou* he has important special duties in the twin ceremonies, such as dividing food and lighting certain candles that are then presented on the floor to the twins. As he put it, "I control all the power of the Marasa. I carry their power on my shoulders and that's a heavy load."

Azor is quite a trickster not only because he is the "trickster who follows the twins," but also because he specializes in creating a large number of Gede (the trickster) flags and sometimes goes into trance when he prepares to work on them. He always keeps a camera in his workshop so that he can document or have others document him in Vodou ceremonies related to his flag-making. Azor loves to do Gede flags because, he says, "Gede is the alpha and omega" of the *lwa.* He defends Vodou as nothing to be afraid of—it is positive not negative. "It is through Vodou that all of the ancestors can come back to strengthen Haitians today." Azor is a young artist, born in 1980, who has been making flags since 1998. Inspired by the roots of Vodou and by his dreams, Azor promises to be an outstanding flag artist.

Like Gede, Azor has a sense of humor. His favorite Gede is Gede Masaka, a corporal with epaulets who goes all around the *oumfo* officiating in mocking and humorous ways. In ceremonies, of the various Gedes that possess those present, many have to do with modern technology. Azor and my friend George Rene laughed so hard when describing and imitating some of the new Gedes they have observed. "*Gede journaliste*" runs around with a fake microphone and pretends to conduct interviews. "*Gede intellectual*" usually has a briefcase and a book and with mincing steps sits down and crosses his legs and pretends to read. "*Gede medicine*" has a stethoscope around his neck and delights in sitting on women's laps "listening to hearts." "*Gede accident*" comes in with fake blood on his clothes and screams for help, "I have been in a car accident. Call a doctor!!" "*Gede internet*" calls for his "computer" and they usually bring him an old broken-down TV and Gede makes clicking sounds and tosses his head and chatters his teeth while pretending to type on an imaginary keyboard. Azor concluded this discussion about Gede with a flourishing hand gesture, "Gede—the whole world is his!!"

Dolls in Vodou Twin Arts and Shrine Contexts

Manufactured dolls represent twins and *dosou/dosa* on altars in various parts of Haiti and the U.S. In West Africa, especially among the Yoruba, twins are commemorated by small wood carvings if deceased or lidded pots if they are living. As we have seen, in Haitian Vodou, connected pots and Catholic chromolithographs are used but no wooden images. Instead, plastic baby dolls are incorporated into Marasa and Marasa Trois imagery. Artist Ronald Edmond wraps them into these sequined and beribboned configurations as shown in figure 13.3. They are destined for Vodou shrines or for the export trade. Some shrines have plastic fancy-dressed dolls straight from Toys R Us, either already packaged as twins or arranged in groups of two or three.

Haitian artist Veronique Leriche Fischetti combines dolls into various representations of the *lwa,* including the Marasa Trois. In her basement she has turned her Long Island, N.Y., home into "Little Haiti" with many spirits assembled there. As a Haitian diaspora artist she faces many challenges but has remained very connected to her roots as well as open to experimentation with new influences and resources. U.S. artist Alison

FIGURE 13.3. Wrapped and beaded Marasa and Marasa Trois dolls by Ronald Edmond, Port-au-Prince, Haiti. c.2004. *Photo: Marilyn Houlberg.*

Laird Craig, who has visited Haiti and is conversant with Vodou, has also created trilogies of the Marasa Trois.

At the core of this essay are twins and twinness. But spiraling out inevitably occurs through the entire system of sacred children, and through the other *lwa* that are associated with them, such as Gede. Paths of various artists and shrines also branch out. Oral traditions further serve to underpin the richness of belief. This has resulted in many *lwa* having their own CD's and thus traveling out into the world in their own musical diaspora.

Such an apparently simple idea as 2 = 3 has provided Haitian artists with endless stimulation. In the best Vodou mystical mathematics TWO DOES EQUAL THREE in the case of twins. Vodou flags are still commissioned for Vodou temples but are also currently on sale on the internet and on eBay. Some Haitian artists have their own web sites and were choosing to sell directly to their clients via the internet prior to the disastrous earthquake (a practice they will hopefully soon be able to restart). So, the Marasa may be set to spin out into cyberspace on a scintillating flash of sequins and beads reflecting off the spiraling planets.

The importance of twins and other sacred children in Africa and the African Diaspora continues to be a significant grounding factor in the growing importance of African-based religions in the New World. The way all the nations of twins have persisted in Haiti and by extension other parts of the Americas may prove to be an important cooperative model for how cultures can both remember and commemorate their specific, distinct heritages, and yet unite in common rituals and values. In this case, reverence for young lives is symbolized by the twins, an extra abundance of new life. As Vodou practitioners say: "The twins walk with all nations from Africa"; but then as another Vodouist in this same conversation added, "Twins walk with all nations of the world."

NOTE

Portions of this essay appear in my essay "Magique Marasa: The Ritual Cosmos of Twins and Other Sacred Children" (1995).

WORKS CITED

Clifford, James. 1988. *The Predicament of Culture: Twentieth-Century Ethnography, Literature, and Art.* Cambridge, Mass.: Harvard University Press.

Courlander, Harold. 1960. *The Drum and the Hoe: Life and Lore of the Haitian People*. Berkeley: University of California Press.

Desmangles, Leslie. 1992. *The Faces of the Gods: Vodou and Roman Catholicism in Haiti*. Chapel Hill: University of North Carolina Press.

Herskovits, Melville J. 1967. *Dahomey: An Ancient African Kingdom*. New York: J. J. Augustin.

Houlberg, Marilyn. 1995. "Magique Marasa: The Ritual Cosmos of Twins and Other Sacred Children." In *The Sacred Arts of Haitian Vodou*, ed. Donald Cosentino, 267–283. Los Angeles: UCLA Fowler Museum of Cultural History.

Mercier, P. 1954. "The Fon of Dahomey." In *African Worlds*, ed. D. Forde, 210–234. London: International African Institute, Oxford University Press.

Wilenz, Amy. 1989. *The Rainy Season: Haiti Since Duvalier*. New York: Simon and Schuster.

Zuesse, Evan M. 1979. *Ritual Cosmos: The Sanctification of Life in African Religions*. Athens, Ohio: Ohio University Press.

CHAPTER FOURTEEN

Divine Children

The Ibejis *and the* Erês *in Brazilian Candomblé*

STEFANIA CAPONE

The worship of twins in Brazil is, as are most Afro-Brazilian religious practices, the result of ancient interpenetration of elements from both African and European cultures. In Bahia, the worship of Saints Cosmas and Damian, widespread among Portuguese settlers, found its parallel in the worship of the *ibejis,* the Yoruba twins brought to the region by African slaves. This worship is known in most of the Afro-Brazilian religions, such as Bahian Candomblé, Batuque of the Rio Grande do Sul, or Carioca Umbanda.

In this chapter, I will analyze the main characteristics of this worship aimed at divine children, and its link to another "child-like" entity, the *erê* of Candomblé. We will see how this spirit, which has historically played an extremely important role in the Candomblé initiation rituals, concentrated certain aspects of the *ibejis* through a "productive misunderstanding" which entailed the association of different types of divine "children." The "childish" trances of the *ibejis, vunji, erês,* or *tobossis* seem to share some elements that stage a ritual inversion, playing a central role in the construction of what Bastide (1958) called the "structure of ecstasy."

Saints Cosmas and Damian: An Afro-Brazilian Devotion

The worship of twins has been present in Brazil since the beginning of Portuguese colonization. In the sixteenth century, the worship of the twin saints Cosmas and Damian was already quite widespread in Europe, notably in Italy and in the Iberian peninsula.[1] When the Portuguese colonizers arrived in Brazil, the first Catholic church, founded in 1535 in Igarassu, a small city of the State of Pernambouc (Brazil's northeast), was dedicated to the twin saints. From there, their worship extended to the entire Brazilian territory. Women would ask for their help during multiple childbirths and for their protection against diseases, bewitchings, and the "evil eye."

With the arrival of the African slaves, this devotion, at first European, combined with the worship of the *mabaças*[2] or *ibejis* (the African twins) "in a symbiosis so tight that it is difficult today to distinguish the actual African component from the European one in popular customs" (Bastide 1958: 181). The *ibejis*, quickly associated with Saints Cosmas and Damian, were already by the beginning of the twentieth century the African deities whose worship was the most popular in Salvador (Rodrigues 1988: 229). This worship was not limited to black families. It also concerned white families "from Bahia's upper class" who celebrated the twin saints by offering "food sacrifices" (Rodrigues 1988: 229).

In Brazil, September 27 is traditionally dedicated to Saints Cosmas and Damian. The saints are celebrated in the *terreiros* (houses of worship) of Candomblé and Umbanda, as well as in private homes, with a *caruru*—an Afro-Bahian dish made of okra which also constitutes the main offering for the *ibejis*. After having laid down the offerings in front of the saints' altar, seven young boys, specially invited for the occasion, are gathered to eat the *caruru*. They sit on the floor in a circle around a bowl filled with sacred food. The children must eat with their hands, as it is done during rituals in the *terreiros*. The seven children represent Saints Cosmas and Damian and their "brothers": Doú (also called Doum or Dois-Dois), Alabá, Crispim, Crispiniam, and Talabí. October 25 is the day consecrated to Saints Crispim and Crispiniam, who are mainly celebrated in the *terreiros* of Umbanda. The third "brother," Doú,[3] is often symbolized by a small vase or a third small character, placed between the statuettes which represent Cosmas and Damian. He is the "guardian" of the *ibejis*. In the wealthiest houses, the saints are dressed in silk and covered in jewels. They are also washed with infusions made of special leaves associated with the *ibejis*, and receive sacrifices of poultry, "like in the rituals performed for the *orixás* [Yoruba deities]" (Ramos 2001: 298).

Before the celebration, it used to be the tradition in Salvador to go out in the streets to collect money in order to raise enough funds to pay for the mass and for the preparation of the *caruru* for the twin saints. Women and children carried images of the saints in boxes or on trays decorated with ribbons and flowers. This money collection, which is less common in the present day, seems to be a sort of ritual duty since even the wealthiest people had to ask for charity, though in a symbolic way, by going to friends' houses to raise part of the necessary money. According to Arthur Ramos (2001: 298), any couple who has twin children must "exchange" (*trocar*)

FIGURE 14.1. *Ibejis* represented in Brazil as the twin Saints Cosmas and Damian, and their "brother" Doú. *Photo: Stefania Capone.*

them for the statuettes of Saints Cosmas and Damian. The twins are then represented by the statuettes, which are surrounded with jewels and coins on the altar. Likewise, their annual celebration is preceded by a visit by friends bringing gifts. This led Bastide (1958: 182) to claim that the worship of twins "led [in Africa] to a commercial exchange which, in a new country and under the pressure of the dominant religion, took the form of an exchange with God (money collection and payment for a mass)."

The "*caruru* of the saints" or "*caruru* of the seven boys" is the only public ceremony displayed on behalf of the *ibejis* in Candomblé. Every year, new worshippers can engage themselves in this ritual duty. According to tradition, the person who finds a whole okra in the ritual dish will prepare the *caruru* next year.

The *Ibejis* in the Afro-Brazilian Religions

Quite widespread, the worship of the *ibejis* has been the subject of numerous interpretations linking them to other "childlike" entities. Thus, since the 1930s, the *ibejis* have been associated with the *erês*, "childish" spirits who manifest themselves in Candomblé once the incorporation of the

the *orixás*, the African deities, has been completed.[4] Less intense than the *orixá*'s trance, the *erê* trance also plays a very important role in the Candomblé initiation rituals. This association seems to originate in the caption of a photograph in the book *O Negro brasileiro* (first published 1934 by Arthur Ramos, reprinted in 2000), which shows an *oxé* (the double-headed axe, symbol of the god Xangô) and two statuettes of the *ibejis*, called "Erê" in the text. Ramos probably used the term *erê* to denote the *ibejis* because of the similar Yoruba word used to designate the wooden votive statuettes by which they are traditionally represented: *ere*. The initiates answered the researcher's questions by saying that they were *ere*, i.e., "wooden idols," meaning that they were at the same time spirit children and ritual artifacts.

What has been thought, since then, to be a confusion concerning the nature of the *ibejis* has been reproduced in numerous studies and still survives today in many believers' minds. For example, in the 1940s, Edison Carneiro (1986: 71) wrote that the *ibejis* were "inferior spirits, *child*-orixás, collectively called *erês*." These spirits would include *erês* "of Cosmas and Damian, of Crispim and Crispiniam, of Doú and Alabá" (1986: 71). Carneiro also mentions the celebration of the *erês* in the Bahian *terreiro* of Flaviana, called "the rope of the *ibejis*," during which all the people in attendance would run toward the center of the room to catch fruits and coins hanging from a rope in a joyful and entertaining moment that represented a pause in the unfolding of the ritual celebrations.

However, this association of *ibejis* with *erês* has been criticized for several reasons. First of all, in most of the Nagô[5] houses of worship, the *ibejis* do not "come down," that is to say that they do not embody or possess anyone, since they do not have initiates who have been ritually prepared to "receive" them, i.e., to get possessed. In the Angola houses of worship, the *ibejis* are known under the name of *vunji*. We know of at least one initiate in the *vunji*

Table 14.1. "Childish" Spirits in Candomblé

Erês	Possession	Public ceremonies and initiation rituals—intermediary possession, following the *orixá* manifestation	Initiates display childish behavior
Ibejis	No possession	Annual celebration consecrated to Saints Cosmas and Damian—*caruru* of the *ibejis*	Ritual with seven children, who "represent" the twins and their "brothers"

worship in the *terreiro* of the famous *pai-de-santo* (religious leader) João-zinho da Goméia (Binon-Cossard 1970: 25). The relation between the *ibejis* (or *vunji*) and the *erês* is still strong in certain Angola *terreiros* where the *erês* are supposed to "represent" the *ibejis* (Serra 1978: 79).

For Bastide (1958: 199), this seems to prove the loss of African tradi-tions in the Bantu[6] houses of worship:

> It seems that the analogies between the twins who are children and the *erês* who are childish spirits played a role here. The [worshippers] tried to transform the celebration of the *ibejis*, which is an event without trances since the twins are not *orixás* and thus do not possess anybody in Bahia, into a celebration as that for the deities, that is to say punctuated by pos-sessions. They looked for a substitute in the childish possession by the *erês*, and that is why, little by little, an indissoluble association of ideas between the *erês* and the *ibejis* has been established in some minds.

Nevertheless, other Afro-Brazilian religious practices considered "tra-ditional" allow for possession by the sacred twins.[7] It is so in the case of the Batuque of the Rio Grande do Sul, where the *ibejis* are celebrated as though they are *orixás* with specific songs. The possessed person, no mat-ter their actual age, behaves like a small child. Before regaining his normal state of consciousness, and as happens with any other *orixá*, this person can go through an *erê* possession. According to Bastide (1958: 184), there are then two distinct kinds of childish trances in Batuque, those by the *ibejis* and those by the *erê*. *Erês* always follow the *orixás'* manifestation and are thought of as "childish" aspects of the deities.

Another Afro-Brazilian religion, the Tambor de Mina of Maranhão (northern Brazil), offers an example of the complex connections between the "oldest" deities and the "youngest" ones. In the Casa das Minas, the most traditional *terreiro* of São Luis do Maranhão, two types of spiritual entities are worshipped: the *voduns* and the *tobossis*. Bastide (1983: 320) linked the latter spirits with the *erês* and the *ibejis*. Later, in his work on Bahian Candomblé in 1958, he reconsidered that link, emphasizing the parallels between *tobossis* and *erês*. The *tobossis* of Casa das Minas, "young" deities, all female, provoke—as *erês* do in Bahian Candomblé—a childish state during which the female initiates speak in a ritual tongue and behave like small children. Following possession by the *voduns* (deities similar to the *orixas*, originally from Dahomey, now the Republic of Benin), the *tobossi* state represents what Parés (2001: 184) calls "a post-possession state." This state, which today has disappeared in the Tambor de Mina, was also characterized by a "moderate trance," by a childish language, and by doll play, reminding us of the possession by the *erês* that we will discuss in detail later. Like the *erês*, the *tobossis*—childish spirits—constitute "a second condition of the *vodun*," "different expressions of multiple facets of a same spiritual being" (Parés 2001: 189).

Yet the *tobossis'* characteristics are similar to the ones found in the worship of twins in Bahia, especially the tradition of begging for money before the celebration of Saints Cosmas and Damian. In Benin, the *tobossis* behave like *nübyodutò* or beggars (Parés 2001: 189). People possessed by these childish spirits stroll in the streets asking passers-by for money or food. This behavior was also once found among the *erês* of Candomblé, who, until the 1970s, would go to the market in small groups, accompanied by an elder of the *terreiro*. There, they would ask for charity, begging for money, bread, fruit. Sometimes, they would steal food (Parés 2001: 192).[8] Nowadays, the *erês*, once incorporated in the initiates' bodies, ask for money from those in attendance, who give them a few coins. In this way, the *tobossis* seem to be very similar to the childish spirits of Candomblé, especially the *erês*.

Likewise, in the Umbanda, the "children," *crianças*, are worshipped next to the other spirit guides: *caboclos* (Amerindian spirits), *pretos-velhos* (spirits of old African slaves), and *exus* and *pombagiras* (trickster spirits linked to the realm of magic). These childish spirits, also called *Ibejada* or *Dois-Dois*,[9] take possession of the Umbandist mediums. In esoteric Umbanda, one of the modes of worship in the Afro-Brazilian continuum (cf. Capone 2010), *crianças* constitute a "phalanx" of spirits, led by Saints Cosmas and Damian. These are spirits of children who behave as such during their manifestation and whose ritual dishes are made of okra, like the *caruru* of the *ibejis*.[10] They are often also called *erês*, a name used generally to refer to children in Brazilian *terreiros*.

Table 14.2. "Childish" Spirits in Afro-Brazilian Religions

Batuque	Tambor de Mina	Umbanda
Ibejis	*Tobossis*	*Crianças* (*Ibejada* or *Dois-Dois*)
Possession	Possession	Possession
Childish behavior	Childish behavior	Childish behavior
Erê possession, following the *ibejis'* manifestation	Like the *erês* in Candomblé, *tobossis'* trance follow the *vodun's* (god's) manifestation	"Phalanx" associated with *erês* of Candomblé and *ibejis* and led by Saints Cosmas and Damian

The link between the childish spirits—*ibejis, erês,* or *crianças*—seems to live on in most Afro-Brazilian modalities of worship. The different representations of these spirits in Brazil are all the product of elaborations and changes in customs, which seem to develop from West and Central African traditions about twins.

The *Erês:* The Mediators between Gods and Men

The *erê* spirits play a key role in the reinterpretation of the twins and other childish ritual figures in Afro-Brazilian religions. They are the mediators between the *orixás* and the initiates in Candomblé, as well as between the seclusion period during initiation, and everyday life, and are often interpreted as the "childish" facet of the *orixá.* The definitions and characteristics of these spirits have considerably changed since the beginning of the twentieth century. In the 1930s, Arthur Ramos (2001: 49) wrote that Erê was an *orixá* "of Jeje-Nagô origin," "the son of Xangô." This claim seems to reproduce the assimilation of *ibejis* to *erês,* who, however, are not generally thought of as *orixás* (gods) in Candomblé. The reference to the god Xangô strengthens the association between *erês* and *ibejis,* who are presented, in most of the myths related to them, as being the sons of Xangô and Oyá, the warrior goddess who rules over winds and tempests (she is better known in Brazil by the name of Yansan). Sometimes, they are associated with other female *orixás,* like Oxum or Yemanjá, who are thought to have raised them.

A few years later, Edison Carneiro (1937: 57) pointed out Ramos' "misunderstanding" by reminding us that *erê* is not an *orixá* but "an inferior spirit, a companion of the initiate." This caused Arthur Ramos (2001: 49) to add a note to the second edition of *O Negro brasileiro* in which he writes: "For certain blacks, Erê is not an *orixá; it* is only a kind of inferior spirit who accompanies the 'saint' or *orixá.*" In fact, the *erê* manifest themselves during public ceremonies, after the manifestation of the *orixá,* as a transitory possession state between the "state of saint" (*estado de santo*) and the "normal state" of consciousness.[11]

The first description of the *erês'* ritual behavior is the one given in the 1940s by Ruth Landes:

> For now the god had left, had been dispatched. In his place had come a mischievous imp called *erê.* The *erê* were always children, like the Saints Cosmas and Damian, and were supposed to be the offspring of Xangô and Yansan, the gods of thunder and lightning. This was really a second state of trance, lighter and happier than the first, and the women with *erê* could

do fairly normal things. They talked now, though it was a special language of baby talk and gestures, a mélange of pig [pidgin]-African and pig [pidgin]-Portuguese. They were fed the simple, tasteless starch dish called *acaçá*, their first food in long hours: it was fed to them dissolved in cold water. Then they remained playing on the mats like children. (1994: 55–56)

The link between the *erê*'s trance-like state and African customs has been discussed in further research. After a stay in Brazil, Melville J. Herskovits (1948: 9) wrote that the possession by the *erê*, which he had discovered in Bahia and in Trinidad, was "a major contribution of Afro-Americanist research to Africanist studies." For Herskovits, the term *erê* refers to the "small creatures" known in West Africa as *ijimeré, eré,* or *egberé* (1948: 9). Years later, Roger Bastide (1958: 199) revisited the *erê* ritual complex in Candomblé, questioning the interpretations of Herskovits, defined as "working hypotheses" which could not have been substantiated. Bastide referred to the writings of his friend Pierre Verger in order to find African antecedents of this trance-like state. In *Dieux d'Afrique* (1995, first published in 1954), Verger differentiated the states of stupor and of mental lethargy which follow "the ritual death" during the initiation into the *orixás*' worship in West Africa from the childish states experienced in Brazilian Candomblé. A West African initiate who has been through ritual death appears to have forgotten everything, does not know how to speak anymore and only expresses himself through inarticulate sounds. He is then called *obutun*: "It is in this state of *obutun* that the rhythms, the songs, the dances and the whole behavior of the god become familiar to the novice and settle in him" (Verger 1995: 134). According to Verger, this state should not be confused with the state of *erê*, which manifests itself once the *orixá* has left the body of an initiate of Candomblé:

During the ceremonies, when the god has left the body of the *iyawô* [initiate], the latter behaves like a very young child, by constantly laughing, by using childish words, by going alternatively through periods of childish cheerfulness and periods of sullen resignation. He remains like this for at least twenty-four hours. It is said in Bahia that the god leaves behind him *erê*, a sort of assistant who accompanies him. After the *soundidé* [a ritual sacrifice during initiation], the novices are in this same state and the Nagôs in Africa say that the novices are *omotun* (new children). The *omotun* will only regain consciousness of their human condition after the day when they receive from the gods their new name and after they proclaim their new name in a public ceremony. (1995: 136)

In Candomblé, the role played by the *erê* during the seclusion period in the initiation rituals is also extremely important. Throughout the manifestations of the new *orixá*, who "is born" during the initiation period just like the new initiate,[12] the deity is not yet "taught," she does not know how to behave. She, in her newly assumed human body, will have to be taught how to stand up, walk, dance, and behave in public. But this state, extremely tiring for the body, can last no more than a few hours: since swallowing is almost nonexistent, it is indeed impossible to feed the novice and other bodily functions are likewise suspended. It is then necessary to put the novice in a different state, called the "state of *erê*" (Binon-Cossard 1970: 163). This is a less violent trance-like state during which the ability to talk and stand are recovered as well as the ability to swallow, although the gustatory faculties are much diminished. In fact, the *erê* ingests anything, he can even swallow dirt or insects. The other bodily functions are also regained: "Diuresis is normal. Tactile sensitivity is not very acute. The memory of normal life survives, although no emotion is associated with it" (Binon-Cossard 1970: 165).

The *erê* partakes of the essence of the *orixá* to whom the novice is consecrated. The name expresses certain characteristics of the deity in question: the *erê* of a "daughter" (a female initiate) of Oxum will have a name relating to fresh water, a natural element over which this goddess reigns, whereas the *erê* of a "son" of Ogun, the god of iron and of war, will be called Captain, Little Sword (*Espadinha*), or General.[13] Unlike the *orixás*, the *erês* keep their eyes open while dancing and have the ability to talk, which is very rare during the manifestation of the *orixás* in Candomblé. Actually, the *erê* can be conceived of as an intermediary who enables the *orixá* to communicate during the initiation phase before the ritual of the "gift of speech" (*abrir a fala*), a ritual performed at the end of the initiation period after which the *orixá* will be able to "speak" the ritual name during the public ceremony of the *orunkó*.[14]

Although the *erê* is thought of as an independent entity, several aspects, besides his name, liken him to the deity who is "made" during initiation: the *erê* possesses the same gender and the same characteristics as those of the novice's *orixá*. Thus, the *erê* could be seen as a facet of the *orixá* "in his divine 'childhood'" (Serra 1978: 60). Like the *orixá*, he will have to be "taught" and to learn how to behave. This dependency on the *orixá* is explained by the fact that the *erê* calls the god of the person he possesses "my father" or "my mother." It is then in the course of the initiation phase that the *erê* seems to play his main role. The *erê*'s link to the initiation rites becomes even clearer when one knows that his favorite food, the *ekó* or *acaçá* (white corn dough), dissolved in water and sometimes mixed with honey, is the main food served to the novices throughout the initiation period. As time goes by and the initiate ages, manifestations of the *erê* will become so rare that it will eventually disappear.

The *erê* also plays a very important role during the two rituals that conclude the initiation period: the *panan* and the *quitanda*. The main goal of the *panan,* carried out the day following the "day of the name" (*orunkó*), is to enable the *iyawôs* (new initiates) to resume their daily activities. For this, they must repeat some gestures which will allow them to return safely to the profane world: such as cutting a piece of fabric and sewing it with a sewing machine, doing laundry, cooking, sweeping, ironing, etc. The *quitanda* (the market), during which the *erês* must sell fruits to those in attendance, occurs just after the *panan:*

> When the trays are almost empty, everybody tries to grab fruits without paying. The *erês* chase them and beat them with the *atori* [long sticks] that they hold in their hands. The confusion is extreme. The *ogans* start playing the drums, the [rhythm] *adarum,* in order to call the *orixás.* The *erês* go into a trance and the ceremony goes on like a Candomblé [public ritual]. Each *orixá* then dances to a series of three songs without being dressed in their specific costumes and insignia. Then, they are returned to the *ronkó* [the initiation chamber] and they are put again in an *erê* state. (Binon-Cossard 1970: 189)[15]

After this, the initiates pass from the unpredictable trance of the *erês* to the most controlled trance of the *orixás.* Finally, they are put into once more the intermediary trance-like state of *erê,* before returning to their houses at the end of the initiation. The ancient tradition of "selling"

FIGURE 14.2. *Erê* spirit with pacifier symbolizing his childish nature. *Photo: Stefania Capone.*

Table 14.3. Role Played by the "Childish" Trance-like States in the Initiation Rituals

West Africa—Orisha worship		Brazil—Candomblé
obotun	*omotun / erê*	*erê*
After the "ritual death" of the novice	Novice reborn as a "new child" (*omotun*)	"Childish" facet of the *orixá*
Lethargic mental state	Possession by *erê*	Lighter trance-like state
Inarticulate sounds	Childish speaking	Childish speaking and behavior
Ritual learning process	Ritual learning process	Ritual learning process
Mediation between the *orixá* and the novice	Mediation between the *orixá* manifestation and the normal state of consciousness	Mediation between the *orixá* manifestation and the normal state of consciousness, as well as between the seclusion period and everyday life, in *panan* and *quitanda* rituals

(Carneiro 1986: 97) the new initiate, according to which the *iyawô* was to be "bought back" by a member of his family or by a dignitary of the cult to which he owed allegiance for the rest of his life, has been relinquished in today's Candomblé as a mere memory of the slavery period.

"Childish" Trance and Ritual Inversion

If undoubtedly the *erê* plays a very important role during initiation, allowing the novices to survive this lengthy seclusion period, lying down on mats, playing like children, the relation between the "state of saint"— the possession by the *orixá*—and the "state of *erê*" cannot be reduced to a simple ritual sequence from "adult gods" to "child spirits." If it is true that, in some rituals, the *erê* is helpful in moderating the manifestation of the god, thus giving the initiate a moment's respite, it is also true that sometimes the possession by the *erê* can reach a climax that would lead the religious leader to trigger possession by the *orixá* in order to "calm" the manifestation of the divine child, as it happens during the *quitanda* (cf. also Serra 1978).

According to Bastide (1958: 201), there is in Candomblé a clear distinction between the "old gods who are moderate—adult gods who are
violent—and child spirits who are moderators." This hypothesis is put into
question by the unpredictable nature of the *erês,* who do not really make
a distinction between good and evil, often being able to lie or steal. A
parallel can be drawn between these behaviors that show a "rebellious"
nature and Exu/Eshu, the Yoruba trickster and his multiple avatars. Like
the *exus,* the *erês* are dangerous and not easily controllable. Yet, each *orixá*
is accompanied by an *erê* and an *exu,* which reminds us, as Bastide (1983)
suggested, of a spiritual triad of *orixá-exu-erê* which—along with the
eguns (ancestors)—makes up the mystical frame (*enredo*) of each initiate.

The followers of Candomblé have mixed reactions when face to face
with the *erês:* though their manifestation represents a pleasant and care-
free pause during the festivities, those present also show a certain apprehension, since the *erês* are considered dangerous creatures to which one
should never make a promise that cannot be kept. For some, the *erês*
express a state of madness, like the one triggered by the spirit of a dead
person who comes to haunt a living person (Lühning 1993: 94). The great
confusion and the unpredictable behavior of the *erês* seem to justify the
etymology proposed by Verger (1995: 138), for whom the term *erê* would
be the contraction of the word *ashiwere* which means "crazy" in Yoruba.
This "childish madness" would have given its name to these spiritual
entities. Ruth Landes (1994: 56) gives us the following description of the
uncontrollable conduct of the *erês* in the Bahia of the 1930s:

> Some of them would rush in the surrounding wood and climb trees, some
> tried to eat stinging nettle (this was considered a test of true possession),
> others tried to tear dogs to pieces. One might steal a pot of chicken and
> eat it all up, tough though it was from the temple style of ritual slaughter
> and cooking; she would go off with it in a corner, hiding it in her bosom.
> Women might drink whole bottles of oil or honey.

This unpredictability of the *erês* is also symbolized by the use of a language
which is both childish and full of double meanings: initiates in a state of
erê often pronounce words in such a way that they take on an obscene
or licentious meaning. Nonetheless, the *erês* also constitute a sort of religious superego, since they can tell, publicly and without shame, the very
intimate details of their "sons'" lives, while sometimes revealing secrets or
ritual mistakes made by the initiates. The *erê* knows everything about the
initiate's life, but he is psychologically detached from it, and can say the

FIGURE 14.3. *Erê* altar in Candomblé. *Photo: Stefania Capone.*

exact opposite of what the initiate would have said in his "normal" state of consciousness.

In reality, we can observe a true ritual inversion during the manifestation of the *erês,* marked by the modification of hierarchic roles (Serra 1978). Once possessed by these divine children, the *iyawôs* (the new initiates) abandon their traditional submissive attitude toward their elders and take on an attitude of defiance which is typical of spoiled children, even being at times aggressive. Moreover, the manifestation of the *erê* is very different from the one of the *orixá:* if the latter speaks only very rarely and in a low and deep voice while maintaining a hieratic posture and a solemn attitude, the *erê* is talkative and verbose, he speaks out loud in a high-pitched tone and gesticulates a lot like an ill-mannered child.

The role of the *erês* is equally very important in the ritual learning process of the new initiate. In the *terreiros,* the *erês* sometimes stage "fake Candomblés" (*Candomblés de mentira*), during which they imitate their respective *orixás* or pretend to be playing the sacred drums. As time goes by, the *erês* learn how to reproduce precisely the gestures and the attitudes of the *orixás,* reproducing what they did during the initiation process, when the *erês* start to learn the choreographies of the gods, their songs and their invocations. But the *erê* also functions as a challenge to the hierarchy within the cult since he enjoys a freedom of speech only comparable to that of the *exus* (cf. Capone 2010). During the manifestation of the *erês*, it seems that the "younger ones" actually have the upper hand in a world ruled by the principle of seniority. Since the manifestation of the *erê* becomes much rarer with advancing age, this ritual inversion will gradually diminish over time to eventually disappear.

In this chapter, we shifted from twins to childish spirits, exploring the relations between "older" deities and "younger" spiritual entities. The worship of African twins in Candomblé and Umbanda, the two most widespread Afro-Brazilian religions in Brazil, is nowadays limited to the annual celebration of Saints Cosmas and Damian. The association of *ibejis* with *erês*, the "childish" facet of the *orixás*, led us to question the role of "divine children" in Afro-Brazilian religions. *Erês* play a key role in initiation rituals in Candomblé. We saw how the *erê* precedes the "birth" of the novice's *orixá* during the initiation period. This childish spirit is then individualized before the god, who is supposed to be completely "made" only after the day of the name (*orunkó*), when he acquires his individuality by uttering the ritual name of the new initiate. The trance-like state of *erê* is also an intermediary state between the "state of the saint" and the "waking state" (the normal state of consciousness), enabling the return to normal life, as in the *panan* and *quitanda* ceremonies at the end of the initiation period.

Though the *erê*'s behavior is always unpredictable, this spiritual entity cannot be thought of as truly "crazy" (*ashiwere*), since it is in this particular state that the novice learns the foundation of the ritual conduct. Thus, he exhibits similarities with the *obutun*—the states of stupor and of mental lethargy which follow "the ritual death" during the initiation into the *orixás* worship in West Africa, making possible the learning of dances, songs, and ritual gestures (Verger 1995: 134). Nevertheless, the *erê* does not show the same states of stupor and of mental lethargy that characterize the *obutun*. His childish behavior and his mischievousness are actually closer to Verger's description (1995: 134) of the *omotun*, the West African initiate reborn as a "new child." The *erê* of Candomblé seems then to concentrate the ability to learn of the *obutun* and the childish behavior of the *omotun* in a process of ritual concentration which is the very basis of the creation of this kind of religion in Brazil.

If the worship of the *ibejis* is much less present in Candomblé today, its progressive fusion with the *erês* nonetheless allows us to shed light on other "childish" spirits who are incarnations of one of the facets of the *orixá* in the spiritual triad *orixá-exu-erê*. Like the *exus*, the trickster spirits, the *erês* play the role of mediators between gods and humans, enabling communication between these two realms of reality. This essay is a contribution to the understanding of this ritual configuration, in which the divine children play a central role in the constitution of the mystical frame (*enredo*) of each initiate.

NOTES

This article has been translated by Muriel Placet-Kouassi. I'd like to thank Philip Peek for his clarifying suggestions and critical support.

1. These twin saints, whose real names are thought to be Acta and Passio, were doctors in Syria and in Asia Minor before being persecuted under the reign of Emperor Diocletian and killed in 287 AD. They are the patron saints of doctors and surgeons.

2. The word *mabaça*, of Bantu origin, is generally used in Brazil to designate the sacred twins, notably the Yoruba *ibejis*.

3. Doú seems to come from Idowu, the Yoruba name given to the first child born after twins.

4. In Afro-Brazilian religions, the term "possession" is not commonly employed by worshippers, and it is substituted by the verbs "incorporate," "embody," "receive," or "manifest." Deities are said to "come down" into initiates' bodies, which "turn into the saints" (*virar no santo*), i.e., get possessed by the gods.

5. Candomblé is divided into ritual "nations": Nagô (Ketu, Efon, Nagô-Vodun), Jeje, Angola, Congo, Caboclo. The concept of nation lost its original ethnic meaning and is related nowadays to ritual specificities.

6. On the importance of the Yoruba model in the Candomblé, see Dantas (2009) and Capone (2010).

7. According to some old Candomblé initiates, possession by *ibejis* was also known in the Nagô Candomblé, but nowadays the rituals to initiate a novice into the worship of *ibejis* are almost forgotten.

8. This reminds us of the last ritual which concludes the initiation period in the Cuban *Regla de Ocha*, when the new initiate must go to the market in order to "steal" some fruit for his *orixás*. But, unlike the *erês*, he will not be in trance.

9. The term "*Dois-Dois*" refers to the intrinsic nature of these spirits, who are doubles, and the term "*Ibejada*" associates them with the *ibejis*.

10. Verger (1968) points out the link between *ibejis* and *abikús* (for the Yoruba, the children who are born to die). In Porto Novo they are given offerings of eight wooden statuettes representing six *abikús* and two *ibejis*, i.e., children whose birth is considered abnormal. The *obèlá* (a sauce made with okra) can also be found among these offerings. According to Verger, this ceremony is comparable to the *caruru* of Saints Cosmas and Damian in Bahia. Therefore, the *caruru* would correspond to the *obèlá* of the ceremony for the *abikús*.

11. In worshippers' discourses, the terms "*orixá*" and "saint" are interchangeable.

12. The *orixá* is indeed "made," just like the *iyawô*, the new initiate. It is said that "the saint is made" during initiation, just as "the initiate is made" by having him be reborn through the initiation rites.

13. This raises questions about the analysis of Rouget (1980), for whom the state of *erê* is a "trance (or state) of dispossession," since the *erê* is "a nameless child" who is not individualized.

14. Actually, during this ritual, the *orixá* only whispers the ritual name of his "son," which will then be repeated to the audience by a high-ranking initiate. In the public celebrations of Candomblé, it is very rare to see an *orixá* speaking— unlike in the Cuban *Regla de Ocha*—and it happens only in particularly serious situations when an urgent message needs to be transmitted to those in attendance.

15. On the *panan,* see also Herskovits (1953).

WORKS CITED

Bastide, Roger. 1958. *Le Candomblé de Bahia (Rite Nagô),* Paris: Mouton and Co.

———. 1983 [1973]. "Cavalos dos santos : um esboço de uma sociologia do transe místico." In *Estudos afro-brasileiros,* 293–323. Sao Paulo: Perspectiva.

Binon-Cossard, Giselle. 1970. *Contribution à l'étude des Candomblés au Brasil: Le Candomblé Angola.* Ph.D. Dissertation, Sorbonne, Paris.

Capone, Stefania. 2010. *Searching for Africa in Brazil: Power and Tradition in Candomblé.* Durham, N.C.: Duke University Press. First published as *La quête de l'Afrique dans le Candomblé: Pouvoir et tradition au Brésil.* Paris: Karthala, 1999.

Carneiro, Édison. 1937. *Negros bantus: Notas de ethnographia religiosa e de folklore.* Rio de Janeiro: Civilização Brasileira.

———. 1986 [1948]. *Candomblés da Bahia.* Rio de Janeiro: Civilização Brasileira.

Dantas, Beatriz Goias. 2009 [1988]. *Nagô Grandma and White Papa: Candomblé and the Creation of Afro-Brazilian Identity.* Chapel Hill, N.C.: University of North Carolina Press.

Herskovits, Melville J. 1948. "The Contribution of Afroamerican Studies to Africanist Research." *American Anthropologist* 50 (1): 1–10.

———. 1953. "The Panan: An Afrobahian Religious Rite of Transition." *Les Afro-Américains, Mémoire de l'Institut Français d'Afrique Noire* 27: 133–140.

Landes, Ruth. 1994 [1947]. *The City of Women.* Albuquerque: University of New Mexico Press.

Lühning, Angela. 1993. "O mundo fantástico dos erês." *Revista da USP* 18: 93–99.

Nina Rodrigues, Raymundo. 1988 [1906]. *Os africanos no Brasil.* Brasília: Universidade de Brasília.

Parés, Luis N. 2001. "O triângulo das *tobossi:* uma figura ritual no Benim, Maranhão e Bahia." *Afro-Ásia* 25–26: 177–213.

Ramos, Arthur. 2001 [1934]. *O Negro brasileiro.* Rio de Janeiro: Graphia.

Rouget, Gilbert. 1980. *La musique et la transe.* Paris: Gallimard.

Serra, Ordep J. Trindade. 1978. *Na trilha das crianças: os erês num terreiro Angola.* Master's Thesis, Universidade Federal de Brasília, Brasília.

Verger, Pierre. 1968. "La société egbé òrun des àbíkú, les enfants qui naissent pour mourir maintes fois." *Bulletin de l'IFAN* XXX, Série B (4) (Dakar): 1448–1487.

———. 1995 [1954]. *Dieux d'Afrique.* Paris: Editions Revue Noire.

CHAPTER FIFTEEN

The Ambiguous Ordinariness of Yoruba Twins

ELISHA P. RENNE

Of course, before I was born, she [my mother] suffered a lot, because her children always died. Her first lot of twins died after seven months, the second ones died when they were about a year old. The third ones died when they were about fifteen days or so. The fourth one[s] died, from what my mother says, at six or eight months. But in my own section, the last set of twins, my *Kehinde* died, when she was about five years old. She was a girl. So in order to remember her—that's why I plait my hair.

—TWINS SEVEN-SEVEN, *A DREAMING LIFE* (1999: 79)

Yoruba women living in southwestern Nigeria have one of the highest rates of twinning in the world (Creinin and Keith 1989; Nylander 1969). Histori-cally, their explanations for the birth of twins have been related to religious ideas about spiritual beings, cosmic disorder, and reincarnation, which had consequences for their treatment of twins. Because twins are more likely to die than singly born children, twins have been characterized as flighty and have sometimes been likened to *abiku*, children who are "born to die" and who torment their parents with repeated births and departures, as the Yoruba artist, Twins Seven-Seven, refers to in describing his own birth. *Abiku* children, of whom Azaro, the protagonist of Ben Okri's novel *The Famished Road* (1991), is a prime example, have spirit friends in heaven who are said to be continually calling them to leave the world, that is, to die, and parents of *abiku* must take special precautions to keep them. Similarly, par-ents feared that if a twin died, it would be calling for its surviving twin to join it—that is, to die as well. To placate the spirit of the deceased twin, *ere ibeji* twin sculptures (Chemeche 2003; Stoll 1980) might be made to represent the dead twin, with things done for the carved sculpture just as they were done for the living twin. However, the carving of *ibeji* statuettes to placate deceased twins has not historically always been the standard in southwestern Nigeria, nor is it done for many twins growing up in Yorubaland today. Indeed, oral historical evidence (Pemberton 2003) as well as nineteenth and twentieth century missionary reports (Hinderer 1873; Ijagbemi 1986) document widespread twin infanticide or abandonment of one or both twins in Yorubaland as a way of addressing their unnatural and extraordinarily inauspicious presence. The process of the symbolic inversion of twins from extraordinarily dangerous to auspicious is briefly considered as a way of foregrounding more recent assessments of Yoruba twins as ordinary beings who are perceived to be "like anyone else."

It would be tempting to characterize this recent reevaluation as a shift from religious representations of twins—as spiritual beings with extraordinary powers to cause harm or to bestow blessings—to a consideration of twins as secular beings associated with being modern. Indeed, the Yoruba concept of *olaju*, "enlightenment," literally "opening one's eyes" (Peel 1978), could be used to describe these most recent assessments of twins, which reflect changes in Yoruba women's and men's thinking as a result of increasing interactions with "things from outside," including Western education, biomedicine, and international travel.

Yet this teleological progression from spiritual to secular, which Asad (2003) and others have criticized, fails to acknowledge the role that religion, in particular conversion to Christianity and most recently Pentecostal Christianity, has played in constructing present-day attitudes toward twins. Furthermore, despite the reassessments of twins as conventional children, the character of twins often continues to be regarded as special in ways that have a particular moral cast. Thus, despite twins' apparent transition into secular beings, ordinary children—marked by the dwindling of religious cults served by traditional religious specialists, the decreasing frequency of special rituals, and the many twin babies who no longer receive traditional twin names—the images of twins continue to be represented in a range of popular media to invoke ideas about goodness, danger, Yoruba cultural identity, and the role of religion in constituting moral communities. How this ambiguous ordinariness of twins has come to be imagined and expressed is the subject of this chapter.

Precolonial and Colonial Yoruba Twins

In references to twin births in precolonial southwestern Nigeria, twins were considered to be abnormal and animal-like (Johnson 1921),

as excerpts from Ifa, the corpus of Yoruba divination teachings, cited by
Wande Abimbola (cited in Pemberton 2003: 31–32) suggest:

> When Eniyan delivered, she had twin babies,
> Aruwe shouted with great exclamation, that a monster was born. . . .
> Have you ever heard that anybody gave birth to two babies?
> You are advised to go quickly and throw them away.

People interpreted twin births as disordered nature and as ominous pre-
cursors of dangerous events, such as epidemics. In order to avoid this disorder, its source—twins—was eliminated in various ways. Solutions to
this problem of reproduction gone haywire included the abandonment of
a weaker twin, the secret fostering of one twin, and sometimes the killing
of one or both twins. For different reasons, and at different times in different parts of Yorubaland, this assessment of twins changed. The first reassessment of the dangers associated with twins is believed to have occurred
during the eighteenth century. According to the Yoruba historian Samuel
Johnson (1921: 25), when one of the wives of the Oyo king, Ajaka, gave
birth to twins, he decided, rather than having them killed, to exile them
"to a remote part of the kingdom and there to remain and be regarded as
dead." In another version of this story, it was said that an Oyo woman gave
birth to twins at Isokun (near Porto Novo in Dahomey [Benin]), where
"it was not the custom . . . to kill twins." When the Alafin of Oyo, Ajaka,
heard that the twins' parents had become rich, he ruled that twins should
no longer be killed in Oyo (Chappel 1974: 252). Twin births—previously
abhorred as an anomaly—came to be revered, which was expressed ritually in various ways (Awolalu 1979; Mobolade 1971; Oruene 1983, 1984;
Renne 2001; Thompson 1971; see also ch. 4.).

However, in other parts of Yorubaland, particularly in the eastern areas
which were not under Oyo rule and where the Oyo Yoruba were seen as
a hostile power (Oguntuyi 1979), this reassessment of twins did not take
place until the twentieth century. For example, in Ekiti and Bunu Yoruba
areas (Renne 2001), as well as in Ondo (Richards 1992: 175), twin infanticide continued well into the early part the twentieth century.[1] In eastern
Yorubaland, the shift from abandonment or killing of one or both twins
toward twin worship was probably related to conversion to Christianity.
The example of the Tommy Titcombe, a missionary with the Sudanese
Interior Mission cited by Ijagbemi (1986: 38) in the Yagba area just west
of Kabba, suggests that Christian missionary practices contributed to a
change in attitudes toward twins in Yoruba areas where this change had

not already taken place (see also Hinderer 1873: 179; cf. Livingstone, on Mary Slessor, 1916: 36). British colonial officials also contributed to this change through legal prohibitions of twin infanticide (Olomola 1984: 17).

With the reversal in the assessment of twins that turned them into extraordinary but beneficial beings in Yorubaland, they came to be associated with special rituals, objects, names, and practices which marked their special status. These included the carving of twin *ere ibeji* (twin sculptures), giving twins special names (Taiwo and Kehinde[2]), the performing of *ose ibeji* twin festivals, and the building of *ojubo ibeji* (twin) shrines. Some parents constructed shrines for twins (*ojubo ibeji*) within a corner of the main room of the house (Renne 2001: 76n5), consisting of mud structures, sometimes hidden by a white cloth, where offerings could be made. If one of the twins died, carved sculptures known as *ere ibeji* were commissioned to stand for the dead twin. Anything that was done for the living twin would be done for the dead twin-statue; otherwise, the jealous dead twin might call the living twin away, causing it to die (Houlberg 1973: 23; Renne 2001: 67). However, there have been various changes in Yoruba society which have affected these practices.

Changing Twin Worship Practices

When the Ekiti Yoruba carver, the late Omo Agbegileye of Itapa-Ekiti, was asked about new requests for the carving of *ere ibeji* in July 1999, he noted that "The demand for twin statues has reduced dramatically, unlike the past. . . ." Several people explained that since twins were more likely to survive in recent years, twin sculptures were less frequently requested. However, other changes in Yoruba society, particularly the proliferation of schools and churches, have affected thinking about twins, the carving of *ere ibeji*, and associated rituals. These shifts are exemplified by the comments of one 35-year-old Ekiti Yoruba man, interviewed in Itapa-Ekiti in August 1999. His wife had delivered two sets of twins, who were "growing normally and posing no problems in terms of their health," as he put it. He stressed that because he was a Catholic, he has rejected many traditional practices associated with twins (see Houlberg 1973: 20). However, he has adopted some practices considered appropriate by Western-educated Nigerians for the care of children in general, although he sometimes explained his behavior in terms of Christian practice. He noted that while everything he did for one twin, he did for the other with respect to food, clothing, and medical treatment, he did so to promote equity and prevent contagion. This man seemed to be making the point that his twins are ordinary, healthy children who, like others, do not have special spirits that needed to be worshipped or placated but rather are "in the care of the God who created them."

Making Twins into Ordinary Beings

This idea that twins do not need to be honored through special ritual practices such as the carving of *ibeji* twin sculptures or through sacrifice is not the result of a straightforward trajectory from traditional religious practices and ideas about twins to the rejection of twins' special status by Western-educated Christian converts who view twins as normal children, children whose birth and development are explained as the consequence of biological processes. Twins' anomalous status as two beings born as one has taken on other associations, reflecting new and sometimes contradictory aspects of Yoruba religious and cultural life. For even with the reduction in twin ritual practices and a decrease in the carving of twin sculpture, twinship continues to have special spiritual resonance for some religious leaders. Take, for example, Pastor Gbenga Oso (2006), whose monthly fertility revivals for women wanting children were advertised in Lagos as "2006 My Twins a Must." Even if twins do not have special spirits, their double birth still conveys ideas about the extra-ordinary—abundant blessings, special abilities, or troublesome excess—as may presently be seen in a range of contemporary cultural commodities, from photographs, to advertisements, children's books, adult fiction, music videos, and video films.

New Visions of Twinship and Technologies of Reproduction

While most people agree that the use of traditional ritual things for twins has diminished in recent years, new technologies of reproduction have allowed Yoruba women and men to represent and honor twins in other ways. Portrait photography, for example, a fixture of Yoruba town and village life since the 1930s (Sprague 1978: 52), is part of a constellation of practices and objects—e.g., radios, motor vehicles, and metal roofs—associated with *olaju,* "enlightenment," which those aspiring to modernity can approve. Rather than carving an *ere ibeji* sculpture associated with "uncivilized" traditional religious practices, Houlberg (1973), Sprague (1978), and more recently Schwartz (1996) and Picton (2003) have noted the use of photography by Yoruba Christian (and Muslim) parents in the 1960s to commemorate dead twins. By this means, twins may be memorialized with neither the religious complications of consulting a *babalawo* (traditional diviner) about sacrifices to be made for *ere ibeji,* nor the expenses associated with their carving. (For more on this practice, see chapter 7.)

These photographic images, which have come to replace *ere ibeji* for some parents, are produced through an imported Western technology, including the knowledge needed for using it, which parallels the rethinking of twins' supernatural extraordinariness as ordinary—based on knowledge of human biology and its processes. For some, twins are now considered to be merely genetic duplicates, if they are identical twins, or the product of multiple ovulation, if they are fraternal twins. These explanations of twin births, and the scientific and technological knowledge and practice which underlie understandings of how copies—from photographs to monozygotic twins—are produced, differ considerably from earlier ideas that attributed these events to spiritual beings or to animal or hypersexual couplings. Yet even the sorts of duplicate photographs made for dead twins in the 1960s and '70s are less common now, particularly as a wider range of technologies of reproduction are available to parents of twins, including digital cameras, video films, and desktop publishing and printing. These new technologies have contributed a plethora of what are seen as more "modern" representations of twins, which further disassociate these representations from traditional religious practice, yet express their special "ordinariness" in other ways. There is something anomalous about twin births which seems to require a particular cultural narrative.

Children's Books

A book by Ayotunde Opakunbi, *The Identical Twins and Other Stories* (2004), invokes the older genre of twin photography on its cover, along with a printed text that emphasizes both the ordinariness of twins and their specialness. The book's cover shows identical twins, much like the twins photographs described above, who only vary in the color of their shirts. Yet the story refers to a rather different conceptualization of twins from that expressed in earlier photographs made to honor dead twins. It recounts the life of a couple whose initial childlessness and various setbacks were overcome by Christian faith. After five years they gave birth to identical twin boys, Ted and Ked. (They are not given twin names, although the initial letters of those names—Taiwo and Kehinde—are retained.) They were treated as normal children, and "there was nothing abnormal in the growth of Ted and Ked" (Opakunbi 2004: 106). Indeed, their father

> Andrew also knew from Biology that there was nothing mysterious or abnormal in having twins. He therefore saw no reason why some people with twins were being deceived by fortune tellers and *marabouts* [i.e., *babalawo*, traditional diviners] into engaging in street begging or other primitive occupations. Some even believed that twins should be given special treatment and strange food! (Opakunbi 2004: 105)

Despite their unremarkable treatment and normal childhood, the twins together were able to perform a remarkable feat, rescuing a small girl from a burning house. "IDENTICAL TWINS SAVED GIRL" (Opakunbi 2004: 117) became front-page news. The twins were later rewarded for their actions with school scholarships, and at the story's end, their mother gives birth to triplet girls, fulfilling their father's belief that he and his wife would have five children.

The theme of twins being extraordinarily good or gifted is evident in another children's book, titled *The Twins I Know* (Olayiwola 1998). In this story, a pair of fraternal twins, Tayeolu, a boy, and Kehinde, a girl, are inseparable in school, and "the two of them are very brilliant" (Olayiwola 1998: 5). Indeed the narrator observes, "I have never seen these type of people" (Olayiwola 1998: 11), who surpass all other students in their exams. Thus even if these twins are children "like everyone else," they are especially good children who are blessed with exceptional talents. The promise of special benefits associated with twins is also suggested by advertisements that incorporate twin images.

Advertisements

For advertisements and branding to be successful, the images and messages portrayed must be associated with positive social values. By the 1940s, positive values—such as special blessings and abundance—associated with twins made them an attractive advertising device. The use of twins imagery in advertising began during the colonial period but expanded as the venues for advertising increased. Initially, advertisements that featured twins often took the form of trademarks used to identify specific products (Pedler 1974). In an example of a trademark registered for silk piece goods by the expatriate firm C. Zard and Company Ltd. (*Nigeria Gazette* 1949), twin heads are incorporated into the trademark (see

FIGURE 15.1a. "Twin Babies Brand—Ile Oni Ibeji" (House of Twins), for silk piece goods, registered by C. Zard and Company Ltd. on January 21, 1949. (*Nigeria Gazette 1949, p. 515*). FIGURE 15.1b. "Twins Special Bread," bread label, Ibadan, Nigeria (Ibadan: Twins House, 2002).

FIGURE 15.2. "The twins—our new baby," Knorr bouillon cube advertisement, Bodija, Ibadan, March 2006. *Photo: Josiah Olubowale.*

figure 15.1a). Contemporary printed paper bread labels have carried on this trademark tradition, with specific names associated with particular bread bakeries, such as "Twins Special Bread" (see figure 15.1b), sold in Ibadan in 2002. Other depictions may refer to twin owners of particular businesses, such as Twins Auto Ltd., in Lagos, whose chairman is the twin J. T. [Taiwo] Obembe (personal communication, Lagos, March 1, 2006). Advertisements may also emphasize an association of twins and doubling one's benefits, a common strategy in the West as well (Schwartz 1996: 38–41). Thus a recent advertisement for Knorr bouillon cubes featured identical twin girls, one holding a single wrapped cube, the other holding a single packet of two bouillon cubes, with the text "the twins—our new baby" (see figure 15.2).

Musical Videos

This idea of doubling, of getting twice as much or of getting two for one, is also a theme in the promotion of two twin singing groups popular in Nigeria today. One pair of identical twins, known as P-Square, referring to their first names, Peter and Paul Okoye, are described as follows: "Double acts are nothing new to the music industry in Nigeria, as other melodious twins like the Lijadu Sisters have made waves in their own time. Fast forward to the present day, and we have the duo of P-Square to fill-in the niche for crooning twin siblings" (Aminu 2006: 16). The song referred to here, "Bizzy Body," is danced along with other hip-hop-style songs on a music video (P-Square 2004) by the P-Square twins, who wear a range of identical outfits (soccer jackets, baggy pants, baseball caps, and sunglasses) and hairstyles reflecting the U.S. hip-hop image this group wants to portray. While their similar dress and synchronized song-and-dance numbers reinforce the idea of two bodies as one, they neither mention being twins in their songs' lyrics, nor do they go by the twin names of Taiwo and Kehinde. Indeed their songs, dress, and dance essentially distinguish them from traditional Yoruba musical performance.

Another singing twins group, A Jo Gba Jesu Twins (literally, one who dances and accepts Jesus), have also released a music video, called "Aluyọ," which portrays the (fraternal) twin brothers in a rather different way from the P-Square twins. While they wear identical outfits in Western styles (shirts and jeans), they sing songs in Yoruba which are reminiscent of earlier Christian songs recorded on records and cassettes. In their music video, the brothers sing on a stage, with microphones and other accoutrements of modernity. There is a congregation/audience, who after sitting and listening politely, eventually get up and dance to the twins' songs praising Jesus. As with the P-Square, the fact that they are twins is not mentioned in their songs' lyrics, although their name, A Jo Gba Jesu Twins, directly mentions their twin status. This name also possibly makes an oblique reference to the traditional connection between dance and twins' blessings, for as Thompson (1971: 79n31) has astutely noted, *ibeji* sculptures were made not only to be placed in shrines, but also to be carried and danced by their mothers.

In these examples of twins in music videos, as well as in children's books and advertisements, twins are depicted as especially gifted or good, as doubling goodness, and increasing enjoyment or blessings. With the exception of the singing group A Jo Gba Jesu Twins, religious belief does not play a prominent part in these depictions. Furthermore, all of these examples distance themselves from traditional Yoruba religious beliefs and practices pertaining to twins. Rather, ideas about the goodness and benefits of twins are largely harnessed in these cases for commercial use. In recent video films and fiction, however, twins are depicted in a somewhat different light, in order to explore ideas about what constitutes a moral Yoruba community.

The Dangers of Twins

The production of copies—whether of people (twins) or their photographs—and the new forms of knowledge and technologies with which they are associated may also be perceived as potentially dangerous (Schwartz 1996). Through infertility therapies using a range of hormonal medications and procedures such as in vitro fertilization, multiple births have become commonplace even outside of southwestern Nigeria. These multiple births—the products of reproductive technologies—are difficult to distinguish from "natural" twin births, and all may be lumped together as the results of modern practices or "progress," which may have

FIGURE 15.3. Cover of the DVD *Dangerous Twins,* part 3 (Ogidan 2004), showing the twins wearing Nigerian and Western dress, suggesting the transnational theme of this film. *Photo: Courtesy Elisha P. Renne.*

unintended, dangerous, or abnormal/antisocial consequences. In Nigeria today, these unintended consequences of modernity (of which these new technologies of reproduction are part) may take various forms—e.g., when elderly people lament the lack of respect paid to them by juniors or when wives refuse to attend village funerals for their husbands. As in the realization that progress has both positive and negative dimensions, the Yoruba video films *Dangerous Twins* (Ogidan 2004; see figure 15.3) and *Ibeji Orun* (Adedeji 2006), distributed on DVD, express an uncertainty about the modern reassessment of twins as ordinary beings.

Dangerous Twins

The story of *Dangerous Twins* is concerned with the social consequences of reproduction, transnationalism, and multiple cultural identities. In the film, identical twin brothers (Kehinde and Taiwo or Taiye) with identical genetic material represent trickster-copies who cannot be distinguished from one another. The popular Nigerian actor Ramsey Tokunbo Nouah plays both roles with the help of special camerawork and editing. The story begins with Kehinde bragging about his fast Lagos lifestyle, while his twin, Taiye, who has just arrived from England, goes to Kehinde's Lagos home. Taiye pretends to be Kehinde, fooling Kehinde's wife, Sola, and their three children, although the joke is soon revealed. However, Taiye has come to Nigeria to ask Kehinde to carry out a similar deception with his own wife in London, who has been unable to have a child. He begs his brother to temporarily fill in for him so that his wife can give birth, and afterwards they will go back to their original identities and lives. Kehinde initially objects but later agrees and the film shows him traveling to London. While Taiye's wife becomes pregnant according to plan, other aspects of the characters' lives spin out of control. Taiye, who has taken up Kehinde's job as a wheeling-dealing Lagos businessman, eventually destroys the business as he refuses to play the PR ("public relations"—i.e., bribery) game. Similarly, Kehinde ruins Taiye's London mortgage business and is sent to jail. Taiye finally manages to obtain a false passport and travels to London, where he rejoins his wife, while Kehinde is in prison. However, when Kehinde is released, the two brothers quarrel and one brother is killed. Eventually it becomes clear that the bad twin—Kehinde—has survived when he sells his wife's house and moves back to Nigeria. There, Kehinde is threatened with death by his businessman/gangster boss for stealing money. In a final scene in the businessman's posh house on Victoria Island, the businessman sees "Kehinde"— actually Taiye, who did not really die after all—on the street and has his henchmen bring him to the house, where the twins are reunited. When the police storm the house, the businessman shoots Kehinde and kills him. Taiye is later reunited with his British wife and son, although they stay in Nigeria, living "a quiet life in Abuja." The film ends with the statement, "None will forget the impact of totally identical twins."

The video incorporates a number of themes that underscore the association of moral ambiguity with seemingly ordinary twins. The theme of good twin–bad twin dominates the story, with Kehinde behaving badly by not returning to Nigeria as agreed, while Taiye, the good twin, begs for his passport so that he can return to London. The apparent ease of maintaining transnational statuses is problematized as the brothers' switching places causes both to ruin each other's lives in their respective transplanted locations, reinforced by the film's conclusion in which the surviving twin stays "at home" in Nigeria. The film suggests that the technological "miracle" of easy air travel—in Lagos one day, London the next—is not the panacea for the problems of Nigerian families but only brings about different ones. These dangerous twins and the modern transnational lifestyles they have embraced, rather than bringing beneficial good fortune to their respective families, have brought destruction.

Ibeji Orun

The film *Dangerous Twins* (2004) represents contemporary Lagos, replete with Hummers and Lincoln Navigators. While clearly about Yoruba families, the characters all speak English, dress in fashionable Western or Yoruba garments, and carry cell phones. In contrast, the more recently released video film, *Ibeji Orun* (*Twins of Heaven* [the Spirit World]; Adedeji 2006), was made with somewhat different intentions. The actors and actresses speak in Yoruba (without subtitles), and the story, while similar in its focus on the dangers of identical twins, makes reference to a range of traditional Yoruba religious practices associated with twins, which are entirely absent from *Dangerous Twins*.[3]

Ibeji Orun begins in a hospital, where a father has just been given his child's afterbirth to bury. It then switches to a scene showing the father insisting on buying things in twos for his only son Ekundayo, suggesting to the audience that the boy has a deceased twin sibling, despite his non-twin name. This idea is reinforced by the boy's mother visiting a *babalawo* (traditional healer-diviner) with "cloths and all sorts of things" for Ekundayo and presumably his twin, although the actual carving of an *ibeji* figure is not shown. It is only twenty years later, after Ekundayo—on earth—has become a successful accountant, that viewers see his twin's *ibeji,* which transmogrifies into his identical twin. The spirit-world form of Ekundayo complains bitterly to the *babalawo* who keeps his *ibeji* form that his family has forsaken him and broken their vow. After the *babalawo* begs him to be patient, the spirit Ekudayo changes back into an *ibeji.* However, a few days later the *babalawo* returns to his shrine to find the *ibeji* has disappeared, having changed back into its human form. The spirit Ekundayo then proceeds to destroy the life of his twin, earthly Ekundayo, who is mistakenly accused of stealing money. The film ends with the parents of the two Ekundayos agreeing to provide six cows to placate the deities; the spirit Ekundayo is shown returning to heaven.

Despite their differences, the two films share the theme of good twin–bad twin. In both, the fact that the protagonists are identical twin brothers allows the films' directors to play upon the confusion wreaked upon family and friends by people who cannot be visually distinguished (Schwartz 1996). This confusion is exemplified in both videos by sexual relations with spouses, by family relations, and in financial transactions where one twin uses his identical appearance to fool bank accountants, bosses, and sisters to claim his brother's money.

However, the local knowledge that the stories invoke and the tone of the films are quite different, which is indicated to viewers at the onset by language use. In *Ibeji Orun,* the characters only speak Yoruba. Furthermore, the portrayal of twins assumes knowledge of many traditional religious beliefs and practices pertaining to twins. These include materials given to a *babalawo* at the birth of twins, having an *ibeji* sculpture carved for a dead twin, and subsequently buying things in twos for twins, in this case for the living and dead twins. There are other examples of "insider" knowledge about a world (*aiye*) inhabited by spiritual beings more generally represented in the video—as in the scenes where armed robbers discuss the best *babalawo* who can help them with medicine (*juju*) for their work and where the spirit twin Ekundayo is approached by a small child who is begging for assistance. The spirit Ekundayo literally sees through the child, who is actually a spirit itself, saying, "I know you, even if you don't know me. You're an *orisa* (spirit, deity) and you were sent on an errand. I'm here for mine. So, go on your way." This scene reinforces the idea that there is a spiritual dimension to the world that only people with special vision can see, a power sometimes expressed as having "four eyes"—one set to see this world, another set to see the other—and associated with witches, sorcerers, and others spirit-beings (Renne 1995). The film's story revolves around the theme of the dead twin who has become dangerous because proper traditional ritual practices done for twins in the past have not been maintained. The setting of the film is Lagos, Nigeria—although in both its earthly and spiritual dimensions.

In *Dangerous Twins,* there is no mention of *ibeji* statues or *babalawo,* and no discussion of the use of *juju* to improve business. Rather, the twins live in a globalized world, where they travel internationally by jets and conduct cell phone conversions with global associates about various business transactions, including drug deals, money-laundering, and insurance fraud. While *Ibeji Orun* focuses on and even exaggerates the terrors of traditional Yoruba religious beliefs and practices, it also suggests the dangers of failing to acknowledge twin spirits and of forgetting one's cultural background and place in a moral Yoruba community. *Dangerous Twins* examines these questions of identity and moral place from a global perspective. It presents the dangers associated with uncritically aspiring to an ultramodern transnational lifestyle. While the film plays upon the good twin–bad twin trope with Nigerian ways associated with the bad twin, Kehinde, and English ways with the good twin, Taiye, it also suggests that it is a mistake to think that one can move seamlessly and identically—in either direction—between these two societies. Those who aspire to having homes both in Nigeria and outside risk being out of sync in both, a perspective similar in a way to the precolonial assessment of twins as polluting beings out of social place. Furthermore, identical twins' interchangeable identities are used to represent the ways that the multiple identities of dual citizens may upset the moral order associated with local kinship connections, proper cultural practice, and social obligations in Nigeria as well as with those overseas.

Two Novels about Twins

Twinship has also been used as a vehicle for examining questions concerning dual citizenship, Yoruba cultural identity, moral community, and kinship connections in literature exemplified by the Nigerian-British writers Buchi Emecheta and Helen Oyeyemi. In Buchi Emecheta's novel *Kehinde,* the protagonist, Kehinde, whose twin died *in utero* and whose mother died during childbirth, is brought to Lagos to be raised by a distant aunt. Because of her inauspicious beginning, she is not told of the circumstances of her birth and is given the non-twin name of Jacobina. Nonetheless, she intuits that she is a twin. When her aunt later confesses this fact, Kehinde becomes ill. "For me to get fully well, she [my aunt] asked a special *ibeji* carver to make me my Taiwo. They must have told her to start calling me my real name, Kehinde, and within a few years, I had forgotten that I had been called another name" (Emecheta 1994: 21). Later, Kehinde travels to London, where she works in a bank and marries a Nigerian man from her home village. When he returns to Nigeria, leaving her to sell the house before joining him, she experiences a series of conversations with her dead twin, Taiwo. When she goes to Lagos and finds that her husband has taken a second wife, she concludes that she is "unable to cope in this country." On returning to London, she enters the house and immediately, ". . . a voice inside her sang out, 'Home, sweet home!' Taiwo, who had not spoken to her since she had gone to Nigeria, was back" (Emecheta 1994: 108). Kehinde's return to London, her acceptance of her identity as a Nigerian-British citizen who is no longer "at home" in Nigeria and cannot return there, is comforted by the return of the voice of her twin sister. Indeed this homecoming also represents a coming together of her twin identities—"two become one"—at the novel's conclusion.

The themes of separation and unification are also explored in Helen Oyeyemi's (2005) novel *The Icarus Girl*. In this novel, the eight-year-old Jessamy, who is born in London of a British father and Yoruba-Nigerian mother, becomes inexplicably disturbed after the family's trip to Ibadan, where Jess encounters a girl-spirit-double, Titiola or TillyTilly, whom she befriends. It is through TillyTilly that she learns that she had a twin sister: "'Your twin's name was Fern. They didn't get to choose a proper name for her, a Yoruba name, because she was born already dead, just after you were born'" (Oyeyemi 2005: 176). When back in England, Jess's increasingly bizarre behavior causes her parents to take her to a psychologist. However, it is when she asks her parents about a twin sister that her mother discerns the root of the problem: "Three worlds! Jess lives in three worlds. She lives in this world, and she lives in the spirit world, and she lives in the Bush. She's *abiku,* she always would have known! The spirits tell her things. Fern tells her things. We should've . . . we should've d-d-done *ibeji* carving for her!" (Oyeyemi 2005: 181). Despite her parents' efforts, Jess's behavior becomes more and more destructive, although Jess attributes her actions to her spirit double, TillyTilly. It is only after they have returned to Nigeria and Jess is involved in a motor accident that her grandfather has an *ibeji* sculpture carved for her. In the final scene, Jess revives after becoming whole by encompassing her spirit double and twin, TillyTilly, back within herself.

As in *Dangerous Twins,* the authors of these two novels use the imagery of twins, of two beings as one, to examine transnational citizenship, specifically, the situation of Yoruba-Nigerians who live primarily in the West. For them, the question of where home is and the nature of one's cultural identity are particular concerns. Their lack of groundedness and their search for an understanding of what being "at home" means is represented by the authors—both Nigerian-born residents of England themselves—as twins who have been separated. It is only when the characters resolve their sense of being separated from a lost twin—when their missing twin is acknowledged and when their spirits are reunited—that they are "home" and that the troubles plaguing them are resolved.

This spiritual resolution of the problems of multicultural identities resonates with recent work on "vanishing twins," in which singletons seek to make connections with a missing twin, described by Schwartz: "The emergent legend of the vanishing twin makes of our selves our own kin. . . . In one body, at one and the same time, we may carry and confute our own nearest sister, closest brother. While vanished twinship assures us of a sempiternal human link, it affords us also the pathos of inexpressible loss" (1996: 21). It is perhaps appropriate, then, for those transnational individuals to recover their twins as a way of reclaiming a link with a situated social and geographical past, and with their Yoruba or Nigerian identities. At the same time, twins provide a way of acknowledging cultural loss. The carving of *ibeji* sculptures and knowledge about twins' special foods and songs serve as a way of regaining a version of a Yoruba past. Indeed, it is through this loss, reinforced through distance in space and time, that these practices can be disengaged from Yoruba traditional religion and reimagined as a Yoruba cultural identity that is acceptable to Yoruba Christians and Muslims.

Ambiguous Twinship

It seems entirely appropriate then, in the face of this sense of loss of a cultural past and reborn sense of identity, that an annual Festival for Twins was organized through the Nigerian Television Authority (NTA) in 2000, according to one of the station managers (personal communication, Lagos, 1 March 2006). The December 2005 Twins Festival held at NTA Channel 10, in Lagos, consisted of a range of activities including the marriage of sets of twins, twins' dress competitions, and "plenty of twins' foods, particularly beans and sugar cane" (Onochie 2005: 78). While avoiding, as educated Christians or Muslims, the stigma of being seen as practicing Yoruba traditional religion, this festival provides a way for Yoruba twins living in Lagos to address an anxiety over the loss of cultural identity—of having become too Westernized, too modern; of living in Lagos or overseas and forgetting about one's cultural background, family ties, about one's hometown or nation—as well as an occasion for

celebrating their special status as twins. They are doing this, even as the
past historical, sociocultural, and political-economic preoccupations of
Yoruba women and men with familial seniority and seemingly unnatural
fecundity are no longer pressing concerns.

Rather, for them, the need to maintain family ties and obligations, hometown associations, and a sense of Yoruba cultural identity and moral religious community, while also pursuing global linkages, constitute present-day
concerns. The polytheism of Yoruba traditional religious practice—which
includes the worship of localized deities through religious specialists associated with particular towns and villages, supporting social ties through
community sacrifice, prescribed ancestral sacrifices by families, and twin
cult rituals—is no longer an appropriate means for addressing these concerns, particularly for Yoruba Christians and Muslims. Thus, while conversion to Christianity during the nineteenth century was initially anathema
to many because it presented the social dilemma of choosing between one's
extended family and community or the church (Peel 2000), changes in the
economic, social, and political contexts of southwestern Nigeria during the
twentieth century—including British colonial rule for a period of time—supported conversion and the establishment of wider social networks. Although
Christian (as well as Muslim) religious practices have continued to sustain
extended family connections, the economic forces that encouraged ambi-
tious individuals to move from rural areas to the megacities of Lagos and Ibadan, as well as to the United Kingdom and the United States, have presented
new sorts of social problems. These include the pressing need for money—to
provide one's children with Western education, to buy land and build houses,
to attend hospitals and clinics, and to perform religious obligations—as well
as the desire to establish and maintain international connections. These are
concerns which the prosperity megachurches that have emerged in Nigeria
since the 1970s address. Converts to various forms of Pentecostal Christianity
share a "sense of belonging to a global movement and as having access, if not
immediately to financial or technological support, to resources such as literature and ideas" (Marshall-Fratani 1998: 284). These "born again" Christians
are mostly young, Western-educated aspiring members of the middle class
who, like the Ekiti father of twins cited earlier in this paper or like the author
of the children's book, *The Twins and Other Stories*, view twins as ordinary
beings and the performance of traditional religious rituals for them, other
than what would be done for other Christian children, as unnecessary.

As in the past, contemporary conceptualizations of twins—and the beliefs
that reinforce these reassessed conceptualizations—have occurred in

particular socioeconomic, political, and historical contexts, reflecting changing religious beliefs and practices in Nigeria (Bastian and Renne 2001). The shifts in the interpretations of twins—from extraordinarily bad, to extraordinarily good, and now to ordinary beings who nonetheless have special beneficial or dangerous qualities—reflect these changes. Unlike the Yoruba artist Twins Seven-Seven, who has unwaveringly maintained his traditional Yoruba religious beliefs and views twins as having special spiritual powers (Glassie 2010; Twins Seven-Seven 1999), for many Yoruba Christians or Muslims this special ordinariness of twins presents a certain ambiguity. While distancing themselves from traditional religious practices associated with twins, e.g., commissioning and keeping *ibeji,* twins *are* regarded as out of the ordinary—in advertisements, children's stories, and in music videos and films.

It is in the intertwined belief and disbelief in the specialness of twins and in their spiritual powers, represented in the exaggerated terrors of the vengeful dead twin depicted in the new technology of video films such as *Ibeji Orun,* that this ambiguity can best be understood. *Ibeji Orun* may be thought of as a Yoruba version of a particular film genre, the horror film (see Adesanya 2000: 39). As with horror films about supernatural ghost-like beings in the West, in Nigeria, churchgoing, educated viewers may both disbelieve the visions of terrifying dead spirits (such as *ibeji*) come to life as nonsensical superstition, and at the same time, fearfully acknowledge that such beings may exist. New technologies of reproduction—particularly the recent plethora of video films replete with a range of special effects that have been produced since the mid-1990s (Adesanya 2000)—are being used to depict this particular ambiguity.

John Picton (2003: 59) has observed the importance of attempting to understand how twin portrait photography came to take the place of carved *ibeji* statues during the twentieth century. One might suggest that these more recent technologies of reproduction—video films, digital photography, and desktop publishing—provide particularly appropriate media for representing the ambiguous ordinariness of twins in an era with changing moral and religious concerns.

NOTES

An earlier version of this essay was presented at the symposium "Twinning/ Splitting: Dualities in Africa and the Diaspora," held at Tulane University, New Orleans, January 2005. I would like to thank the organizer, Adeline Masquelier, as well as members of the Itapa-Ekiti community, including Pa Francis Adeyanju and the late Omo Agbegileye for their helpful discussions, and Kayode Owoeye and Josiah Olubowale for their excellent research assistance.

1. According to Peel (2000: 97), Charles Phillips, of the Church Missionary Society, considered the Ondo to be "'more violent and touchy' on the subject of twin-killing than on human sacrifice." Phillips noted this in a journal entry of August 31, 1880 regarding "the case of a Christian, converted at Leki, whose wife bore twins at his hometown, Ado (Ekiti), which was equally opposed to twins, who had to escape to Lagos" (cited in Peel 2000: 341n41).

2. "Taiwo means *Lo to aye wo,* 'go and taste the world,' and Kehinde means *Eni ti o kehin de,* 'one who comes last'. We believe that Kehinde who comes last is the senior of the twins because it was Kehinde who asks Taiwo to come first to the world.... The fact that Kehinde was [the one] to send Taiwo to the earth makes him the elder" (from Interview TI-6, June 1999, Ekiti, cited in Renne 2001: 68).

3. These two videos exemplify what Ogundele (2000: 108) has described as the two main forms of Yoruba video films, namely films that focus on "old traditional-metaphysical subjects" and those that focus on new social and secular situations, although he notes that these themes are often intertwined a single video film.

WORKS CITED

Primary Sources

A Jo A Gba Jesu Twins. n.d. "Aluyọ." Lagos: Bayowa Films and Record Ltd. (Purchased March 2006.)

Adedeji, Oluwole, director. 2006. *Ibeji Orun* [Twins of Heaven], Parts I, II. Lagos: Zanams Venture.

Knorr Foods. 2006. Knorr "Twins" advertisement. Ibadan.

Nigeria Gazette. 1949. Trademark notices. *Nigeria Gazette* no. 44 (1 September 1949), p. 515. Lagos: Government Printing Office.

Ogidan, Tade, director. 2004. *Dangerous Twins,* Parts I–III. Lagos: OGD Pictures.

Oso, Gbenga. 2006. Revival banner, Pastor G. Oso. Lagos.

P-Square. 2005. *P-Square Da Videos.* J. Okoye, dir. Lagos: (P) and © Tjoe Ent. Ltd.

Tijani, Adebayo. 2008. *Ibeji Orisa* [Twins of the Gods], Parts I–II. Lagos: Epasa-lumm Movies Productions Ltd.

Twins Auto Ltd. 2006. Business sign. J. T. Obembe, chairman. Lagos.

Twins House. 2002. Twins Special Bread, bread label. Ibadan.

Secondary Sources

Adesanya, Afolabi. 2000. "From Film to Video." In *Nigerian Video Film,* ed. Jonathan Haynes, 37–50. Athens, Ohio: Ohio University Center for International Studies.

Aminu, A. B. 2006. "P-Square: Twice the Talent." *Weekly Trust* 9 (25 Feb–3 March): 16.

Asad, Talal. 2003. *Formations of the Secular: Christianity, Islam, Modernity.* Stanford, Calif.: Stanford University Press.

Awolalu, J. O. 1979. *Yoruba Beliefs and Sacrificial Rites.* London: Longman.

Bastian, Misty, and Elisha Renne. 2001. "Re-Viewing Twinship in Africa." *Ethnology* 40 (1): 1–11.

Chappel, T. J. H. 1974. "The Yoruba Cult of Twins in Historical Perspective." *Africa* 44 (3): 250–265.

Chemeche, George. 2003. *Ibeji: The Cult of Yoruba Twins.* Milan: 5 Continents.

Creinin, Mitchell, and Louis G. Keith. 1989. "The Yoruba Contribution to Our Understanding of the Twinning Process." *Journal of Reproductive Medicine* 34 (6): 379–387.

Emecheta, Buchi. 1994. *Kehinde.* Oxford: Heinemann.

Glassie, Henry. 2010. *Prince Twins Seven-Seven: His Art, His Life in Nigeria, His Exile in America.* Bloomington: Indiana University Press.

Hinderer, Anna. 1873. *Seventeen Years in the Yoruba Country.* London: Religious Tract Society.

Houlberg, Marilyn. 1973. "Ibeji Images of the Yoruba." *African Arts* 7 (1): 20–27, 91–92.

Ijagbemi, Adeleye. 1986. *Christian Missionary Activity in Colonial Nigeria: The Work of the Sudan Interior Mission Among the Yoruba 1908–1967.* Lagos, Nigeria: Nigeria Magazine.

Johnson, Samuel. 1921. *The History of the Yorubas.* Lagos, Nigeria: CSS.

Livingstone, W. P. 1916. *Mary Slessor of Calabar: Pioneer Missionary.* London: Hodder and Stoughton.

Marshall-Fratani, Ruth. 1998. "Mediating the Global and Local in Nigerian Pentecostalism." *Journal of Religion in Africa* 28 (3): 278–315.

Mobolade, Timothy. 1971. "Ibeji Custom in Yorubaland." *African Arts* 4 (3): 14–15.

Nylander, P. P. S. 1969. "The Frequency of Twinning in a Rural Community in Western Nigeria." *Annals of Human Genetics* 33: 41–44.

Ogundele, Wole. 2000. "From Folk Opera to Soap Opera: Improvisations and Transformations in Yoruba Popular Theatre." In *Nigerian Video Film,* ed. Jonathan Haynes, 89–130. Athens, Ohio: Ohio University Center for International Studies.

Oguntuyi, Anthony. 1979. *History of Ekiti.* Ibadan, Nigeria: Bisi Books.

Okri, Ben. 1991. *The Famished Road.* London: Vintage Press.

Olayiwola, T. A. O. 1998. *The Twins I Know.* Ibadan, Nigeria: Rasmed Publications.

Olomola, Isola. 1984. *A Thousand Years of Ado History and Culture.* Ado-Ekiti, Nigeria: Omolayo Standard Press and Bookshops Co.

Onochie, Bridget. 2005. "Twins Festival Holds on Saturday." *The Guardian* (14 December), p. 78.

Opakunbi, Ayotunde. 2004. *The Identical Twins and Other Stories.* Ibadan, Nigeria: Positive Press.

Oruene, T. O. 1983. "Cultic Powers of Yoruba Twins: Manifestation of Traditional and Religious Beliefs of the Yoruba." *Acta Geneticae Medicae et Gemellologiae* 32 (3–4): 221–228.

———. 1984. "Magical Powers of Twins in the Socio-religious Beliefs of the Yoruba." *Folklore* 96: 208–216.

Oyeyemi, Helen. 2005. *The Icarus Girl.* New York: Doubleday.

Pedler, Frederick. 1974. *The Lion and the Unicorn in Africa: A History of the Origins of the United Africa Company 1787–1931.* London: Heinemann.

Peel, J. D. Y. 1978. "*Olaju:* A Yoruba concept of development." *Journal of Development Studies* 14 (2): 139–165.

———. 2000. *Religious Encounters and the Making of the Yoruba.* Bloomington: Indiana University Press.

Pemberton, John, III. 2003. "*Ere ibeji:* An affirmation of life in the face of death." In *Ibeji: The Cult of Yoruba Twins,* ed. George Chemeche, 31–49. Milan: 5 Continents.

Picton, John. 2003. "Seeing Double." In *Ibeji: The Cult of Yoruba Twins,* ed. George Chemeche, 50–59. Milan: 5 Continents.

Renne, Elisha. 1995. *Cloth That Does Not Die.* Seattle: University of Washington Press.

———. 2001. "Twinship in an Ekiti Yoruba Town." *Ethnology* 40 (1): 63–78.

Richards, Paul. 1992. "Landscapes of Dissent—Ikale and Ilaje Country 1870–1950." In *Peoples and Empires in African History: Essays in Memory of Michael Crowther,* ed. Jacob F. A. Ajayi and John D. Y. Peel, 161–183. London: Longman.

Schwartz, Hillel. 1996. *The Culture of the Copy: Striking Likenesses, Unreasonable Facsimiles.* New York: Zone Books.

Sprague, Stephen F. 1978. "How the Yoruba See Themselves." *African Arts* 12 (1): 52–59, 107.

Stoll, Mareidi, and Gert Stoll. 1980. *Ibeji: Twin Figures of the Yoruba.* Maunchen, Germany: self-published.

Thompson, Robert F. 1971. "Sons of Thunder: Twin Images among the Oyo and other Yoruba Groups." *African Arts* 4 (3): 8–13, 77–80.

Twins Seven-Seven. 1999. *A Dreaming Life: An Autobiography of Chief Twins Seven-Seven,* ed. Ulli Beier. Bayreuth, Germany: Bayreuth African Studies.

CHAPTER SIXTEEN

Twins, Albinos, and Vanishing Prisoners

A Mozambican Theory of Political Power

PAULO GRANJO

Some years ago, I paid a visit to Martins Matsolo, the hereditary chief of the region where the aluminum smelter Mozal was built, near Maputo, the capital of Mozambique. I wanted to question him about an idea which was becoming common among the workers that during the ceremony preceding the construction of the factory,[1] he had forbidden snakes to be killed inside the plant, saying otherwise accidents would happen.

He told me it was not true, and we debated for a while the reasons for that new rumor, which derived from the local belief that snakes can be possessed or owned by spirits (Granjo 2008a). But since those "special snakes" are supposed to live in places with special characteristics, our conversation led me to the unusual Matola cemetery, nearby the smelter. "That's a bad graveyard, isn't it?" I asked. "I mean, just near the river, which often overflows . . ."

He was silent for a while and, as often happens when one questions an older Mozambican person about a touchy matter, he did not answer me directly. Instead, he told me a story with no apparent connection to the subject from an outsider's point of view, although it would be easily understandable by somebody who knew the cultural references linking it to the question.

"Yes," he said, "in colonial times, PIDE[2] even used to hide the prisoners they killed there in their headquarters. Not really there, but just beside, even closer to the water."

It was the first time I heard about a symbolic connection between twins, albinos, and disappeared prisoners. Because, in short, twins must be buried in moist land or they will dry the country; albinos (who have the same cosmic origin) are not supposed to die, but to vanish; and vanishing prisoners were buried in the wettest land.

I knew that it is disrespectful to bury ordinary people in wet soil, since this corresponds to treating them as "people who dry the land," such as twins. And this was the reason for my question. By telling that story, Mr. Matsolo agreed with me and even emphasized the issue I raised. And, by responding as he did, he taught me something new. This new issue—the symbolic equivalence of the three categories I mentioned and its meaning—is the reason for this chapter.

There are, indeed, several ethnographic references to the social restrictions suffered by twins, albinos, and their mothers in Mozambique, and even some anthropological interpretations of them. If we compare those references and talk to people nowadays, it seems that such restrictions have not changed much during the last 100 years; similarly, there remain some geographical exceptions where twins have, on the contrary, a positive social valuation.

Nevertheless, those old resilient rules and their underlying concepts were pertinent enough to be selected as a way to talk and to think about disappeared political prisoners, both during colonialism and post-independence. But this is not, as we will see, a way to think about the many thousands of people expelled from the towns to the remote Niassa province in the early 1980s, accused of being "unproductive."

Was the twins/albino equivalence employed just because those prisoners vanished? For a while, I believed this explanation to be enough—at least, if we added to it the restrictions and stigma that political prisoners suffered. However, many more exiled people had vanished from Niassa, and they also suffered restrictions and stigma, yet the same equivalence is not used to talk about them.

I will, therefore, suggest that the symbolic equivalence between twins, albinos, and vanishing political prisoners is not only formal; it expresses a concept of the political power relations in which "subversive" prisoners, even if they were fighters for the independence, are considered negative and threatening social abnormalities—unlike the victims of domestic exile by State decision, who were understood to suffer from an unfair abuse of power.

Twins and Cosmic Order

According to the data provided by Henry Junod (1996: 266–272) on southern Mozambique, twins, the rain, and wet burials have a mutual interconnection that was already seen as ancient in the late nineteenth century,[3] and this was the object of complex rituals when drought threatened a region. When that happened, it was mostly ascribed to a previous burial in dry soil of twins, miscarriages, or babies who died before their presentation to the moon (which marks their social existence and integration in the community). Thus, the first step in order to get rain, besides performing purification rituals for the mothers (if they had hidden the dry burials), was to find the infant graves and to correct the situation. Their bones were exhumed and moved to mud or wet land, and their previous graves were soaked with water. These actions were performed by all the local women together, marching behind a mother of twins.

Junod also recounts how the birth of twins was treated. By the end of the nineteenth century (Junod 1996: 371–378), infanticide of the weakest twin was no longer practiced, "unlike in the old days," but they and their mothers were the object of special restrictions and social control. The day after a twin birth, nobody could farm or the crops would dry. All women in the village should depart in the four cardinal directions, singing "May the rain fall," and gather water that would be poured over the mother and the twins. Her hut would be burned and they would start living in a new one, outside the village, using objects that nobody else could touch and gathering water from an exclusive spot. The twins were not presented to the moon and would be fed with goat milk as soon as their mother menstruated again. They would only return to the village when the woman gave birth to a "normal" child. This could only happen after the woman had seduced four men who were not aware of her condition. After having sex with them, her impurity would be passed on, causing their deaths. Even then, twins were not allowed to play with other children, they were pointed out as examples of bad temper, and, like their mothers, were the object of special ritual protection during funerary ceremonies. According to Junod, many of these restrictions were parallel to those suffered by widows.

Basically, it was believed that the creation of twins results from a lightning bolt striking the mother, which kills the original child and turns it into twins. The cosmic significance of this event is signaled by calling the twins "storms without rain" and the mother "the sky" or creator. However, the threatening aspects which derived from this cosmic familiarity could become socially useful in moments of crisis: in the stronger rituals against drought, it was necessary to place a twins' mother inside a hole and cover her with water up to her neck. If frightening lightning bolts approached the village, only a twin could successfully ask the storm to go away.

As one would expect, Junod interpreted these practices and beliefs, which he heard about in a fragmentary way, according to the theoretical tools available to him—that is, using Frazer's typology of magic principles

(Frazer 1922). However, Feliciano (1998) was able to provide us more details and a broad interpretation of twins' position in southern Mozambique.

Besides the data already provided by his predecessor, Feliciano points out some other practices from the late 1970s, which, as I could verify, are still in use today. When a twin falls ill, it is forbidden to express sympathy, to give him/her medicines, or to ask if the person is getting better; on the contrary, the sick person should be insulted by sentences like "When will he die?" or "You will be eaten by the fishes anyway." At funerals, twins must keep a distance from the crowd. When one of them dies, the other one is forbidden to cry and ashes should be spread over his/her fontanel (the membrane connecting bones of the skull). Surviving twins are not allowed to attend their deceased sibling's funeral, in order to prevent their fainting and falling into the grave (Feliciano 1998: 334–336).

In addition to this, I observed that the surviving twin cannot react to the death of the other one. On the contrary, he/she must act as if the deceased just went somewhere faraway, and, if somebody who does not know about the death asks for news of the deceased, the surviving twin will lie, inventing some trip or saying that the deceased inhabits now in some other country or province. As often happens with such customary behavior, many people cannot present a clear reason for this and just say that it would be dangerous to do otherwise. Other people, though, explained to me that talking about the other twin's death would bring about the death of the survivor. Therefore, as the surviving twin cannot speak of such a death, it is as if, from his/her point of view, the deceased twin simply vanished.

Most relevant to the issue in hand is, however, the fact that twins must be buried in a wet environment or, like some other abnormal births and people (see Feliciano 1998: 326–352), they will dry the land. The reasons for this practice and the other restrictions imposed on twins in southern Mozambique became clearer after Feliciano's analysis (1998: 305–308) of the dominant local symbolic system. In short, the author states that all social and cosmic pertinent phenomena are "traditionally" conceived according to a set of different codes, with special reference to the sexual, thermal, and culinary ones. However, those codes are isomorphs and each one of them can be used in order to analogically represent (or even lead the representation of) phenomena belonging to another code's scope, as indeed happens regularly. In other words, those codes have the same number of elements, organized according to the same logical connections between them, and therefore sexuality and reproduction can be analogically explained trough the use of, for instance, the cosmic, the culinary, or the thermal code.

This is what happens in this case. The human reproduction is analogous to the interaction of an incubating pair: fire/water. The successful result, the living baby, is represented as water (which may or may not result from a storm, just like the baby may or may not result from an act of sexual intercourse), and, as water, normal babies propitiate global fertility. Initially, until the navel cicatrization and the end of the parturient bleeding, the baby and its mother are considered "hot." Thus, if a baby dies before that or is aborted, then it, still being hot, causes a global thermal imbalance which demands the burial of the corpse in a humid place lest the land dry. The analogies and mutual substitutions between different codes go further: "If the lightning bolt, fire that dries the land, is like an abortion, expelled blood that burns the baby, and the abortion dries the land, as a lightning bolt; then the lightning bolt burns the babies as if it was an abortion" (Feliciano 1998: 310).[4]

This point is crucial because, although other folk hypotheses do exist nowadays,[5] the birth of twins is most commonly still ascribed, like the birth of albinos, to a cosmic accident. They were both struck by lightning bolts inside their mother's uterus, with slightly different results: twins were split in two and albinos were burned. This is why twins are called "children of the sky" and are effective interlocutors with the storms. This is why albinos were mentioned in Ronga language as *qhlandlati,* meaning "charcoal from lightning bolt"—a word that most adult speakers still know but avoid due to its pejorative rudeness.

Meanwhile, the interaction between the sexual and the thermal codes clarifies another issue: due to their origin, twins (and albinos) are lightning bolts without rain. Unlike other babies, they never cease being hot, which has consequences. Besides the dangers to themselves that derive from such conditions, they propitiate dryness and infertility, social disharmony, and even illness—which is, in some cases, ascribed to an internal hot situation called *kuhisa* (often related to sex, as it is a condition which all are affected by immediately after sexual intercourse). In short, they are sociocosmic threats.

Now we have a set of benchmarks for understanding twins in southern Mozambique. In addition, Junod (1996: 272) mentions *en passant* a detail which shows that, more than a century ago, the characteristics ascribed to twins and other "land-dryers" could already be extrapolated to other groups of threatening people, and be connected with the disposal of their corpses. Indeed, it was said that it always rained when people gathered to catch the barbel fish in some lagoons when the dry season made them muddy. The rain came because, in the past, battles were fought nearby and the corpses of the deceased enemies were thrown to the lagoon.

But now let us ask: why assume, so many years later, that the modern vanishing political prisoners had also been thrown into water, or buried in wet land?

Albinos and Vanishing Prisoners

The missing link between twins and vanishing prisoners, both supposed to be buried in wet land, is in fact provided by albinos.

Concerning the local belief about albinos' vanishing, João Pina Cabral (2004) emphasized their interstitial status, neither "black" nor "white," suggesting that they "do not die" because they supposedly are not buried. In his point of view, such a refusal to connect them to the earth means a refusal of their belonging in a society in which to belong is primarily marked by the "black"/"white" racial divide.

We can indeed say that the current relevance of their "racial" ambiguity is a self-evident aspect both of albinos' situation and of people's interest in the representations about them. But it is only a small part of those representations and, most probably, not the key to understanding them. In a society like that of Mozambicans, where "race" is believed to be a biological reality and not a socioideological construction, and where skin color and detectable "race mixtures" are the basis for different behaviors toward people, one cannot ignore the issues of identity and hierarchy raised by a "black" person with "white" skin. But we should not ignore, either, that the hierarchic relevance of skin color is historically recent, and that current representations about albinos are far too complex to derive from "race" ambiguity alone—although they do refer to it as well.

We should, for instance, remember that as recently as the mid-nineteenth century the first emperor of Gaza, a huge state in southern and central Mozambique,[6] saw, in his own words, a "white-white" man (by contrast to the "white" Luso-Indians who used to trade in the Mozambican hinterland). But this man was only a guest taken to the royal *kraal* (compound) and not at all somebody with hierarchic precedence over local population and authorities (Neves 1987). Of course, "white" men were known long before, around the limited areas where they settled; but in most cases they did not play a dominant role, especially not in southern Mozambique. For instance, in 1833, the Governor of Lourenço Marques (now Maputo, the capital of the country, but back then just a presidium and a harbor surrounded by some houses, trade posts, and a palisade) was considered by the local king to be a lower chief who owed him tribute, and his insubordination was grounds to attack his fortress and to kill him (see Liesgang 1986a).

It is obvious that the social relevance of "whiteness" during the colonial period (1895–1975) and after is a much more recent phenomenon than the perceived abnormality of albinos as such. The social need to interpret and explain albinos' exception is much older, and would be pertinent even amongst people who thought that all humans had brown skin.

Curiously enough, Henry Junod does not mention albinos explicitly in his very detailed book, *The Life of a South African Tribe,* when he deals with the indigenous "Ideas concerning the different human races" (1996: 298–300). It seems that albinos were not, in those times, presented to him in terms of a "race" issue.

But I believe he indeed does talk about them, without noticing it, when he discusses the origin of the word *valungo* to designate "white men" (1996: 298–300). Junod denies that its etymology comes from a Zulu verb meaning "to be fair" and suggests instead the local word *valungwana,* which he translates by "inhabitants of the sky," speculating that such designation probably came from some forgotten mythologies about "white men." However, the ruling Portuguese were believed to come from the sea, not from the sky, while twins were (and still are) referred as "children of the sky."[7]

Although Junod never really decoded the meaning of this celestial designation, it was clear in the information collected by Feliciano in the 1970s, and I heard it myself some thirty years later. As I already mentioned, both twins and albinos are children of the sky because, independently of their earthly conception, they gained their exceptional condition while being struck by a lightning bolt inside their mothers' uterus. Twins were split in two, but albinos were not; they only got burned and therefore lost the color of their skin. Both achieved, via this incident, a close and privileged relation with the sky and the heavenly phenomena. This is a relation which, as I also mentioned, is threatening to the social order and fecundity because, in the symbolic framework where it is integrated, they are simultaneously "too hot" and "a storm without rain." Due to such characteristics, they carry the potential for disorder and illness, and to dry the sky and the land.

One of the consequences of twins' and albinos' common origin is that, if Junod was right about etymology, it is most probable that "white men" were metaphorically named after the albinos (in a sense of "pallid faces"), whose designation was based on previous beliefs about them. Thus, albinos were originally the reference to classify the "whites," and not the other way around.

But, more important to the issue in hand, albinos and twins are symbolically equivalent. Albinos are seen as incomplete twins that, still more than actual twins, carry in themselves the destructive power of the lightning bolt, which was not even able to split them apart—and, due to that fact, they also carry greater threatening consequences to the society and the cosmos than twins do.

I suggest that it is because of this superlative threatening condition that albinos are not supposed to be buried in special places and under special circumstances, as happens to twins; but are not to be buried at all. This is why, therefore, they are not supposed to die, but to vanish. Of course, albinos do die and are buried. A few of their closest kin take care of that duty in secrecy, following the same proceedings which are prescribed for twins as well as hiding the grave location. By so doing, they protect both the cosmic safety and the community beliefs:[8] albinos keep on vanishing, because no one can claim to have attended one's funeral.

Many political prisoners, both before and after independence, had also vanished from their communities and were no longer seen by the people who knew them. Most of them indeed died, although some just settled in the regions where they had been imprisoned when their detention came to an end. Also, many guerrilla fighters from the anticolonial movement (Frelimo) were killed by the Portuguese troops or political intelligence police (PIDE/DGS) after their capture and interrogation.

I already mentioned a tale about what happened to some of the vanished anticolonial partisans: their clandestine burial by PIDE/DGS, just beside the river water, near the present Matola cemetery. I say "tale" because, in fact, there is no evidence that such things ever happened in that place, and it would be a strange choice for secret burials.

Dalila Mateus (2004) provides another story about the hiding of partisans' corpses in wet places. She heard in Tofinho Beach, near the town of Inhambane, that PIDE/DGS used to throw the corpses of the people they killed into the sea so they would be eaten by the sharks. This local information is another significant tale because there are no man-eating sharks in that area. Also, the beach has suffered much erosion in the last decades, so what seems very easy to do nowadays would have been very difficult to do some thirty-five or forty-five years ago. Nevertheless, I heard, at the same beach, a variation of that story, now pointing to several big natural holes in the rocks that lead to underwater caverns. In this more plausible version, the analogy with the burial of twins is even more direct, since although the corpses were sent into the water, they were simultaneously thrown inside the earth.

There is still another current story about partisans' deaths and corpse disposal. It is said that, while transporting political prisoners by helicopter to Lourenço Marques (now Maputo), PIDE/DGS and Portuguese troops used to throw them into the sea, far away from the coast. While this might have happened occasionally, reliable reports from previous members of the Portuguese military, also horrifying, tell a significantly different story. Some military commanders and PIDE/DGS officials indeed used to throw guerrilla fighters out of helicopters when they believed they could not get more information from them; but this was done over the ground, and the victims' corpses were left unburied. One of the officials even used to shout sarcastically, on those occasions: "You say the land is yours, go get it!"[9]

So, in what seems to be a reinterpretation of actual practices which did not involve water, the folk accounts about the disposal of the corpses of vanished independence partisans systematically place them in wet environments. Those accounts can follow a direct analogy to twins' burials or they can even go a bit further (placing the corpses inside the water, instead of only in wet soil), just as albinos "go a bit further" than twins in the threat they represent and in the constraints imposed on their deaths.

This symbolic connection between vanishing prisoners, twins, and albinos continues after independence. Chronologically, the first case mentioned to me by common people concerns a rebellion of previous guerrilla fighters shortly after independence. According to those accounts, the rebels lost and were taken as prisoners to Xefina Island, near the shore in Maputo Bay, where they were fusilladed and thrown into the sea. The first part of this account is a well-known fact, but I could not get any confirmation about the corpses' disposal. The island was subsequently the location of a "reeducation camp" for people whom the regime considered "committed to colonialism," "reactionary," or ideologically heterodox. As to what happened during this phase, it is *vox populi* that the prisoners who died there were also thrown into the water. However, a previous prisoner of that camp denied the veracity of the story in a conversation with me, calling it a "myth."

Several other reeducation camps have been subsequently built, mostly in the hinterland and faraway from Maputo. About those, I heard several stories, told by people who never had been there, stating that the graves of dead prisoners were dug in the riverbanks. Although many camps were indeed built close to rivers, due to water supply necessities, I never heard any confirmation of such burial proceedings from somebody who had actually been there. Four previous prisoners, on the contrary, told me that they never saw that happen, and that riverbanks were used, in the camps where they had been imprisoned, to cultivate crops.

Folk stories do exist, also, about people who tried to escape from reeducation camps but did not succeed in returning home because they vanished on their way home. I heard six of those stories, and they all have a similar *leit motif*: the fugitive died trying to cross a river, where he drowned or was eaten by crocodiles—the iconic water predator of the hinterland.

So, in the case of the political prisoners who disappeared during the post-independence period, the folk stories systematically show them—as they showed vanishing anticolonial fighters—dying in the water, being eaten by water predators, or being buried in wet land or in the water itself. And notably, these stories are told quite independently of factual knowledge of actual events. The later characteristic reinforces the symbolic significance of such stories. But what is the meaning of the equivalence between vanishing prisoners, twins, and albinos which is so dramatically emphasized by these stories?

If we took consideration of only the data recounted so far, it would seem that the old beliefs about twins and albinos were used to discuss disappeared political prisoners in order to stress the fact that they had vanished. However, there was another conspicuous group of people who were also arrested, taken away from their communities and families, and detained in faraway lands from which many of them never came back. Yet, the same beliefs are not used to describe their situation.

Subversives and Victims

In May 1983, while informing the country about the results of the fourth Congress of Frelimo, President Samora Machel announced that one of the decisions was to "clear the towns of tramps, delinquents, prostitutes and all those who do not work." In the words of Gita Honwana (1984: 3):

> In this manner was started the grandiose operation for production, against hunger and unemployment, against marginality and criminality, for the dignity of Mozambican Man; an operation which is an integrant part of the economic battle we fight today; an operation which is being a school where also the Justice, through its Tribunals and through the action of its Judges, went to learn a lesson of legality.

To the common population, however, it was difficult to recognize the actual events they were living in this glorious rhetoric. What they remember and talk about are the constant roundups and roadblocks imposed by the police and the official militias near the bus stops and in residential areas. The people without an ID or work card in their pocket were taken away to Niassa before their families had the chance to intervene.

The unmarried mothers were deported as prostitutes and the unemployed people were treated as criminals by a state that owned the economy but was unable to provide them jobs. At this time also, many denounced others to the authorities in order to carry out personal revenge. People today recall the humiliation, the pain, the helplessness, and the sorrow. They stress in their tales the separated and destroyed families, the forced labor, the relatives vanished forever, the abuse of power over ordinary people, without any good results at all.

When we go back in time and look at the reality from the state's point of view through the official magazine *Justiça Popular,* both the apologetic *compte rendu* of the People's Judges (Honwana 1984) and the verdicts and appeals published as examples of jurisprudence (T.P.C.M. 1984) are consistent with the popular descriptions just mentioned.

No law was written on the subject of "Operation Production," but thirty-eight "verification posts" were created straight away in Maputo, holding the status of People's Courts but, unlike them, with the power to sentence the accused to prison or deportation to "production centers" or reeducation camps. In the first weeks, the roundups and arrests were so numerous that every appointed People's Judge often had to work forty-eight hours straight, deciding the fate of hundreds of people in a row nonstop. With the accumulation of accused people, the police forces started to send them directly to the evacuation centers—whence they were sent straight to Niassa. Later on, "sorting groups" were created in the verification posts, and only the "doubtful cases" were even presented to the People's Judges.

Many unfair decisions are reported in the magazine, even according to the draconian criteria of Operation Production. In the suburban areas, peasants were deported because, obviously, they did not have working cards from any employing company. The same happened to several employed workers, because many companies did not update their staff registers (Honwana 1984). According to a victim's personal communication, even amongst academics and other prominent professions, there were cases of people who were suddenly dismissed from their jobs and, arriving home, found police officers at the door, waiting in order to deport them as "unproductive." Other professions, like traditional healers and diviners and even handymen, were not recognized as such by the state, and, therefore, practicing these arts became a reason for deportation (T.P.C.M. 1984: 40).

An appeal mechanism was eventually implemented, in this case mostly based on judges with some actual juridical knowledge. The appeal criteria were often quite surprising. For instance, one of the jurisprudence examples is the confirmation of deportation to Niassa of an immigrant worker who was waiting in Maputo for the renewal of his passport because he did not have a Swazi work card—which did not exist. Also, because he did not, as the political police told him to do, make his inscription as someone who was looking for a job—which he was not, since he worked abroad—he was deported (T.P.C.M. 1984: 41). In fact, to appeal could worsen one's situation. The parents of a young woman asked for her liberation from a working camp near Maputo, claiming that because she was under 23 years old, she lived with them and helped them in agricultural work—so she was not "unproductive" according to the last guidelines transmitted to the verification posts. But the appeal judge decided that, since she was the unmarried mother of two children "faced with the total indifference of her parents," she was a "woman of bad behaviour" and should be judged again under that charge, and not as "unproductive" (T.P.C.M. 1984: 41). In this new situation, she was probably sent to Niassa.

The most arbitrary situations concerned, indeed, women and the accusation of prostitution. After six months of summary trials and deportations, a People's Judge timidly suggested that it was maybe time "to define clearly prostitution and to identify its punishment, according to our reality" (Honwana 1984: 9), while he mentions the case of a woman charged with prostitution because she put an end to a long unmarried cohabitation and, while living back with her parents, started dating another man before the "local structures"[10] ratified her previous separation. One of the appealed verdicts stressed that "a woman is not a prostitute just because she lived maritally with a Portuguese man" before independence (T.P.C.M. 1984: 42). And Stephanie Urdang (1989) heard, in a study trip through the deportation camps, systematic complaints of women who claimed to be there because they dated the "wrong men" or did not accept becoming lovers or concubines of the "right one," i.e., some member of their neighborhoods' local structures.

What happened to those thousands of people, so-called "unproductives," delinquents, or prostitutes? Initially, there were indeed some work camps in which to place them in order to perform hard labor, and there was space left in the reeducation camps. Soon, all those places were overcrowded and the state could not organize new ones, so people were just left faraway from their homes. First, they were left in distant villages; later (as happened to a recently deceased icon of Xipamanine neighborhood, a man who returned from Niassa by walking thousands of miles), they were left in the middle of the bush, in a province where lions were very common. In the end, most deportees were never provided with transportation

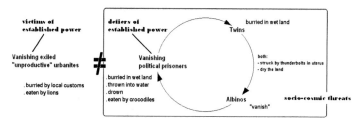

FIGURE 16.1. Symbolic relations between twins, albinos, prisoners, and "unproductive" deportees.

back to their towns. So, if they or their families could not arrange it, they died there or still live in the regions where the state left them. To their families and their original neighbors, they vanished.

Curiously enough, neither the common people nor the sympathetic international observers (Urdang 1989) ever pointed out the obvious similitude between the early colonialists' justifications for forced labor (Ennes 1946) and the speech about work which legitimated Operation Production, or the parallel between this one and the Pass Law and Bantustan policy of the South African apartheid. In the 1980s, all that either group pointed out was the huge number of people who were treated unjustly even according to the Operation Production principles. Only later, people say, were those principles seen as an abuse in themselves, but still without raising local historical analogies—although some previous officers with whom I managed to talk about this subject justified the Operation with another historical analogy, namely the limitations to the circulation and urban settlement of people inside the U.S.S.R.

Even so, deportees are seen, in general terms and in most individual cases, as ordinary people who simply became victims of an abusive utilization of political power. In the end, Operation Production endured as a collectively traumatic event, which only the subsequent horrors of the civil war[11] managed to minimize in people's memories.

While asking people from different areas of Maputo what happened to those deportees who never came back, I never received an answer that mentioned water, wet soil, or even crocodiles. In more than thirty interviews or informal conversations on this subject, there is also a common *leit motif* in what people said; but it is very different from the case of vanishing political prisoners. In these stories, deportees either kept on living in Niassa, or they were eaten by lions or died for some other reason and were buried according to the local custom over there.

Southern Mozambican people do not really know the characteristics of the Niassa funerary custom they mention, but they assume it would be in regular soil. Such an end is, nevertheless, seen as a reason for sorrow, because they expect the ritual to be different from their own and, therefore, strange to the dead deportees. It is also sad because the spirit of the deceased will stay alone there, without the company of his/her dead and living relatives.

I must underline that this recurrent account about corpses' disposal is most significant since when a stranger dies in your homeland you should bury that person in wet soil, "just in case" (Feliciano 1998). Local people can see that the deceased is not an albino, but they can never know if he/she is a twin, or in the case of a woman, if she is a mother of people who "dry the land." To assume that the people from Niassa did not take this usual precaution toward strangers who, after all, were in a stigmatizing position is, therefore, a strong statement (although probably not a conscious one) that they should not do it. It is, indeed, a claim that deportees did not deserve to be buried like threatening twins.

Also, the public accounts of the man from Xipamanine I mentioned above are doubly significant, because they were both statements of his personal experience and the reconfiguration of such experience under the light of audience expectations. While he crossed the country by foot, he had as well to wade through rivers in order to avoid possible roadblocks at the bridges. Those river crossings and the concomitant danger of crocodiles were impressive moments in his narrations, but he never ascribed the death of other deportees to crocodiles, although he often stressed their killing by lions and everybody's terror about the possibility of dying that way.

So, in complete opposition to the disappeared political prisoners (see figure 16.1), the vanishing deportees of Operation Production—who were also arrested and sent away by the state, under stigmatizing accusations and conditions—are systematically represented as being buried in dry soil or being eaten by land predators, even if we can expect that some of them actually drowned or were eaten by crocodiles.

In a rhetoric and a conceptual context where the political prisoners are equated with twins/albinos, the vanished deportees are, this way, vehemently presented as *not* twins or albinos. One of the consequences of this observation is that the image attached to the disappeared political prisoners cannot be, thus, just an affirmation of their vanishing. A second consequence is that we need to clarify the meanings ascribed to the differences between both groups of vanishing people in order to understand the meaning of that image.

A Folk Theory of Political Power

Since I already mentioned that the deportees of Operation Production are seen as *innocent* victims of the political power, it would be tempting to attach to the political prisoners who are treated differently the label of guilty. This would be, however, a simplistic assumption.

On one hand, it would be simplistic because two very different groups of vanishing political prisoners are merged, in people's accounts, under the same equation with twins and albinos: the heroes who died for the independence (which was soon presented as a synonym of the socializing revolution), and the people who, under stigmatizing charges, were accused of plotting against the independence, the Mozambican people, and the revolution.

Secondly, it would be simplistic because it is well known that to be arrested as a political prisoner was not necessarily the result of a censurable and guilty act. This benefit of the doubt is immediately assumed in the case of the anticolonial partisans. But most people will also agree that after independence, together with the "real" pro-colonialists, counter-revolutionaries, or ideologically heterodox, many prisoners were arrested just because they complained the most loudly about issues which also displeased their neighbors and colleagues, or because they took the "wrong" attitudes in the wrong moments, even if they were right in doing so—as in the particular case recounted in this the pungent account by a previous political prisoner:

> By then, I was not at all a counter-revolutionary. I was happy with the independence and I took it as it was, even in the things I didn't like
>
> For instance: if days of voluntary work were needed, why should I spend them with a hoe, cutting grass or making holes in the ground? I'm a mechanic, for God's sake! I didn't know how to use a hoe and most of the people around didn't know how to do anything else. I think I would be much more useful doing my job, for free in that day. Nevertheless, I never complained about such things. I didn't like it, but I did always my best and I accepted it—the same way as I accepted the rule of Frelimo, who brought us the independence.
>
> But I was sent to the reeducation camp as counter-revolutionary and saboteur! It was like that: an important piece of a machine got broken, and the director of the factory ordered me to make a new one. I told him this could not be done, that we needed to import it. I explained him that we didn't have the right steel and tools and, if we would try to

substitute it by some hand-made piece, other parts of the machine would collapse.

The director didn't know anything about mechanics or industry. He was just a "devoted comrade from the armed struggle,"[12] so I was arrested as saboteur. Eventually, it happened as I said it would. In fact, he was the real saboteur. But it was me who spent years in a *reeducation camp*.

So, the distinction common people make between deportees and political prisoners does not arise from the precise acts that they did (or did not) perform or from the guilt attached to those concrete acts, but from their position towards the power and from the public evaluation of that position. In other words, the object of people's evaluation, in this game of identification and differentiation, is not the guilt or innocence of concrete actors; but what is licit or illicit in the person's relationship with the established power, and in the way that power is performed.

As I mentioned before, one of the pertinent characteristics shared by twins and albinos in the southern Mozambican sociocultural context is that they both are sociocosmic threats who jeopardize the order of the world reproduction, in its natural and social aspects. Since vanishing is common to the disappeared deportees and political prisoners, the issue that is stressed in the opposed stories about their corpses' disposal is, indeed, the threatening character which is ascribed, or not, to each one of them. Thus, the simultaneous symbolic equivalence between vanishing political prisoners and twins/albinos, on one hand, and their differentiation from the vanishing deportees of Operation Production, on the other hand, expresses a concept—or should we say a theory—of political power relations that has interesting parallels with the suggestions of Harry West (2008) about northern Mozambique.

Being heroes of independence or people seen as opposing it, being people who were guilty or people who were simply considered subversive by the established power (it does not matter when or which), the political prisoners threaten global society, and not only those who occupy the position of power. Regular people who just happened to become victims of power abuse are not social threats; on the contrary, they are worthy of special public concern and consideration.[13]

In more general terms, according to this folk political theory, once an established power is recognized as such, it is illicit and socially threatening to jeopardize it, and those who do so become threatening social abnormalities. To jeopardize it is to jeopardize not only the powerful, but also the global social order and balance. Meanwhile, and of equal importance, it is also illicit for a legitimate and established power to make unfair decisions about the people under its responsibility, instead of take care of their basic welfare, as it should.

The resilient social representations about twins and albinos were, thus, manipulated in order to critically express a subtly balanced vision of power (or, to be more precise, an idealized and moral model of it), which can be very misleading if we focus our attention only on one of its poles. If we are not careful to take a broad view, all we will be able to see will be either a demanding and dependent attitude, or a resigned and almost automatic submission to power. When we take it in its whole, however, what we see is a local "social contract" (Rousseau 1974) which, in fact, is similar to many reports about "traditional" concepts of power in sub-Saharan Africa:[14] an established power can be considered legitimate due to several different reasons (in this context, genealogy, conquest, revolutionary legitimacy, or democratic elections); but the social recognition of the power's basic legitimacy, even if unquestioned, does not mean that all its decisions and practices are legitimate, even if they are performed under its established competences. The public recognition of the power's legitimacy imposes on the powerful responsibilities towards the protection and welfare of the people they rule. The concrete actions of the established power are publicly evaluated and, if it fails to fulfill or disregards its responsibilities in one of its actions, that action is illegitimate, even if the power itself is not.

Therefore, to focus on only one of the poles of this "social contract" as it is understood in Mozambique has broader consequences than the mere scientific or interpretative mistake. It can also restrict the ability to understand current political dynamics.

After eighty years of effective colonial domination and thirty-five years of independence with the same ruling party, which did not face explicit resistance in changing from a socializing paradigm to a neoliberal policy, it is quite understandable that Mozambican rulers focused on the pole of the social contract that involves people's resignation and submission to power. This is why, I believe, the local political elites were so surprised by the violent riots against rising prices that occurred in early February 2008 (Granjo 2008b), and claimed that there was an external "invisible hand" behind them.

But, if it seems now clear, from the data and interpretations I have presented, that the old representations about twins and albinos were selected to express systematically a folk vision of power and to classify recent actors of the political performance according to it, there is nonetheless nothing "natural" about that choice. The selection of this particular symbolic analogy, instead of the use of some locally widespread language to talk about power (like, for instance, sorcery), is on the contrary exceptional and surprising. Perhaps it all began with that disturbing act of vanishing that is common to both contexts and seems to have offered to albinos and twins an unsuspected symbolic pertinence to current political issues. Their selection for that purpose reveals how relevant the representations and beliefs about twins and albinos still are in contemporary urban Mozambique.

NOTES

The data for this article were collected during my fieldwork for two research projects financed by Fundação para a Ciência e Tecnologia.

I express my gratitude to João Pina Cabral, José Fialho Feliciano, Omar Ribeiro Thomaz, and Philip Peek for their critical reading of the manuscript.

1. It is the *kuphalha,* an invocation of the ancestors in which their leading descendant informs them about a plan of the living people and requests their authorization and protection for that plan (Granjo 2005).

2. Portuguese political police, who operated during the fascist-style dictatorship of 1926–1974; the force was renamed DGS in the last years of the regime.

3. Although his book *The Life of a South African Tribe* was first published in 1912, Junod started to write it in 1898, based on data collected between 1889 and 1895; some extra materials were collected in 1907 (Harries 2007), but these don't seem to have included his remarks about twins.

4. All translations from Portuguese language are my own responsibility.

5. I heard two of them in an urban context: (1) a woman will give birth to twins if her *xará* (the deceased person whom she was named after) had twins; (2) to become a mother of twins is hereditary. However, those new folk hypotheses avoid answering why twins exist in the first place, and actual cases of twin births in successive generations are, on the contrary, currently seen as very exceptional and demanding some further explanation.

6. Gaza was a nineteenth-century state that occupied most of southern and central Mozambique following the invasion of the region by a martial group of Zulu origin called the vaNguni, which had been pushed away from their previous territories by the conquest wars of King Shaka. Their defeat by the Portuguese in 1895 marks the start of the effective colonial occupation of the Mozambican hinterland (see, for instance, Clarence-Smith 1990; Pélissier 1994; Liesegang 1986b; Vilhena 1996; and Neves 1987). *Kraal* ("corral") was the local designation of the king's settlements and cattle.

7. See note 3; this data is from 1907, after the Portuguese had established their colonial domination.

8. Also in neighboring Tanzania, albinos are not supposed to die. But, paradoxically, parts of their bodies are sought for purposes of sorcery for personal

enrichment because personal enriching is seen as something that dries up all the wealth around the person. For that reason, at least nineteen albinos were killed in order to be mutilated *post mortem* during 2007; the number is derived partly because the deaths are known but the location of their graves is unknown, (Gettleman 2008). Also in Mozambique, the most powerful amulets and magical treatments to get and keep wealth and power require parts of human bodies but, as far as I know, not specifically from albinos. However, this might change soon, due to the Tanzanian events and the usually fast transnational interchange of magical techniques in the region.

The data on albinos' burial proceedings were provided by a personal communication of Danúbio Lihahe in 2005.

9. Personal communications of two Portuguese conscripts and one professional soldier, who all witnessed this proceeding and wanted to remain anonymous.

10. In a mono-party situation which merged the state and the ruling Frelimo Party, this expression was used for the appointed local Secretaries, the "Driving Groups" (*Grupos Dinamizadores*), and the local leadership of Frelimo "base organizations," like the women's and youth organizations. "Structures" eventually became the common people's designation for the state or Frelimo officers and leaders.

11. Soon after independence, in 1975, the white minority governments of Rhodesia and South Africa started supporting armed opposition groups operating in Mozambique whose actions eventually evolved into a large-scale and bloody civil war that only ended in 1992. About its horrors, see, for instance, Geffray (1991); Hall and Young (1997); and Granjo (2006).

12. The Mozambican independence in 1975 was preceded and shortly followed by a general exodus of people with European or Asiatic origin (Rita-Ferreira 1988). Since the access to school education and decision posts was highly race-based in the Portuguese colony, this created a dramatic shortage of qualified personnel in most areas and activities of the independent country. Therefore, voluntarism and political curricula were, often, the only criteria available for the appointments to leading posts in the economic or administrative institutions.

13. It would be interesting to check what kind of corpse disposal was ascribed to the people who died while performing forced labor during the colonial regime, but I could not find any references on that subject.

14. Besides the vast scientific bibliography on this subject, see, for instance, the fascinating South African novel *The Wrath of the Ancestors* (Jordan 2004).

WORKS CITED

Cabral, João Pina. 2004. "Os albinos não morrem: crença e etnicidade no Moçambique pós-colonial." In *O Processo da Crença,* ed. F. Gil, P. Livet and J. P. Cabral, 238–267. Lisboa, Mozambique: Gradiva.

Clarence-Smith, Gervase. 1990. *O Terceiro Impeério Portugueës (1825-1975)*. Lisboa, Portugal: Teorema.

Ennes, António. 1946 [1899]. *Moçambique, Relatório Apresentado ao Governo*. Lisboa: Agência Geral das Colónias.

Feliciano, José Fialho. 1998. *Antropologia Económica dos Thonga do Sul de Moçambique*. Maputo, Mozambique: Arquivo Histórico de Moçambique.

Frazer, James. 1922 [1890]. *The Golden Bough*. New York: Macmillan.

Geffray, Christian. 1991. *A causa das armas em Moçambique: antropologia da guerra contemporânea em Moçambique*. Porto, Portugal: Afrontamento.

Gettleman, Geffrey. 2008. "Albinos in Tanzania Face Deadly Threat." *International Herald Tribune*, http://www.iht.com/articles/2008/06/08/africa/tanzania. php.

Granjo, Paulo. 2005. *Lobolo em Maputo: um velho idioma para novas vivências conjugais*. Porto, Portugal: Campo das Letras.

———. 2006. "Back Home: Post-war Cleansing Rituals in Mozambique." In *Studies in Witchcraft, Magic, War and Peace in Africa (19th and 20th centuries)*, ed. B. Nicolini, 277–294. Lampeter, Pa.: E. Mellen Press.

———. 2008a. "Dragões, Régulos, e Fábricas—espíritos e racionalidade tecnológica na indústria moçambicana." *Análise Social* XLIII (187): 223–249.

———. 2008b. "Crónicas dos motins—Maputo, 5 de Fevereiro de 2008." http:// www.4shared.com/file/61860426/8ead98e0/Cronicas_dos_motins_Maputo _5_fevereiro_2008.html.

Hall, Margaret, and Tom Young. 1997. *Confronting Leviathan: Mozambique since Independence*. London: Hurts and Company.

Harries, Patrick. 2007. *Junod e as Sociedades Africanas—impacto dos missionários suíços na África austral*. Maputo, Mozambique: Paulinas.

Honwana, Gita. 1984. "Operação Produção—Actuação dos tribunais: consolidação da justiça popular." *Justiça Popular*, 8/9: 3–10.

Jordan, Archibald Campbell. 2004 [1940]. *The Wrath of the Ancestors*. Johannesburg: AD Donker.

Junod, Henry. 1996 [1912]. *Usos e Costumes dos Bantu*, vol. 2. Maputo, Mozambique: Arquivo Histórico de Moçambique.

Lieagang, Gerhard. 1986a. *A guerra dos reis Vátuas do cabo Natal, do Maxacane da Matola, do Macassane do Maputo e demais reinos vizinhos contra o presídio da baia de Lourenço Marques*. Maputo, Mozambique: Arquivo Histórico de Moçambique.

———. 1986b, *Vassalagem ou tratado de amizade? História do acto de vassalagem de Ngungunyane nas relações externas de Gaza*. Maputo, Mozambique: Arquivo Histórico de Moçambique.

Mateus, Dalila. 2004. *A PIDE/DGS na Guerra Colonial 1961–1974*. Lisboa, Portugal: Terramar.

Neves, Deocleciano Fernandes. 1987 [1878]. *Das Terras do Império Vátua às Praças da República Bóer*. Lisboa, Portugal: Dom Quixote.

Pélissier, René. 1994. *História de Moçambique: formação e oposição 1854–1918*, vol. 2. Lisboa, Portugal: Estampa.

Rita-Ferreira, António. 1988. "Moçambique *post*-25 de Abril: causas do êxodo da população de origem europeia e asiática." In *Moçambique: cultura e história de um país*, ed. M. V. Cabral, et al., 121–169. Coimbra, Portugal: Instituto de Antropologia.

Rousseau, Jean-Jacques. 1974 [1762]. *O Contrato Social*. Mem Martins, Portugal: Europa-América.

T.P.C.M. 1984. "Jurisprudência—Tribunal Popular da Cidade de Maputo: sentenças e recursos." *Justiça Popular* 8/9: 39–42.

Urdang, Stephanie. 1989. *And Still They Dance: Women, Destabilization, and the Struggle for Change in Mozambique*. London: Earthscan.

Vilhena, Maria da Conceição. 1996. *Gungunhana no seu Reino*. Lisboa, Portugal: Colibri.

West, Harry. 2008. "'Governem-se vocês mesmos!' Democracia e carnificina no norte de Moçambique." *Análise Social* 43 (187): 347–368.

Contributors

Stefania Capone is *Directrice de recherche* (Senior Researcher) at CNRS, the French National Center for Scientific Research. She is author of *Searching for Africa in Brazil: Power and Tradition in Candomblé* and *Les Yoruba du Nouveau Monde: religion, ethnicité, et nationalisme noir aux Etats-Unis.* She has edited special issues on Black cultures, religious transnationalism, and African American religions for several journals.

Susan Cooksey is Curator of African Art at the Harn Museum of Art, University of Florida. Her research has focused on art in southwestern Burkina Faso. She is author of *Iron Staffs in the Crossroads: Divination Arts in Toussiana, a Southwestern Burkina Faso Community,* and she has also published articles on the masquerades, ceramics, and spirit cults of Toussiana.

Ysamur Flores-Pena is Associate Professor at the Otis College of Art and Design. He is author of *Santería Garments and Altars: Speaking without a Voice* and has served as a consultant to museums and the movie industry on African-based religions in the Americas. He is also a twin and a Lucumí priest of Ochun and Olu Osanyin.

Paulo Granjo is Researcher of the Institute of Social Sciences, University of Lisbon, and Professor of Anthropology at the New University of Lisbon. He is author of *"We Work Over a Powder Barrel": Men and Danger at Sines Oil Refinery* and *Bridewealth in Maputo: An Old Language for New Marriages.* His work focuses on the social interpretations and management of uncertainty; traditional healer-diviners in Mozambique; climate change and coastal erosion in Portugal; and public violence.

Jan-Lodewijk Grootaers is Head of the Department of the Arts of Africa and the Americas at the Minneapolis Institute of Arts. He specializes in Zande history and art. In 2007, he curated a major exhibition on the region, "Ubangi: Art and Cultures from the African Heartland," and edited the accompanying catalog.

Marilyn Houlberg is Professor of Art and Anthropology at the School of the Art Institute of Chicago. Her research and publications focus on religion, art, and popular culture in Africa and the Diaspora, with special emphasis on Haiti. She also works on behalf of Haitian artists.

Gavin H. Imperato is a researcher in tumor immunology at Memorial Sloan-Kettering Cancer Center. He has also conducted research on twins and twinning in Mali.

Pascal James Imperato is Dean and Distinguished Service Professor of the School of Public Health at the State University of New York, Downstate Medical Center. He is co-editor of *Surfaces: Color, Substances, and Ritual Applications on African Sculpture* (Indiana University Press, 2009).

Frederick John Lamp is Frances and Benjamin Benenson Foundation Curator of African Art at the Yale University Art Gallery. He is author of *See the Music, Hear the Dance; Art of the Baga,* and many other books and articles.

Babatunde Lawal is Professor of Art History at Virginia Commonwealth University. He is author of *The Gelede Spectacle: Art, Gender, and Social Harmony in an African Culture* and *Embodying the Sacred in Yoruba Art.*

C. Angelo Micheli organizes exhibitions on African photographic portraits in France and works on the preservation of the photographic heritage of Africa. He specializes in West African images and portraits, and is interested in new forms of twinness in modern African cultures.

Philip M. Peek is Professor Emeritus of Anthropology at Drew University. He is editor of *African Divination Systems: Ways of Knowing* (Indiana University Press, 1991), and editor (with Martha Anderson) of *Ways of the River: Arts and Environment in the Niger Delta* and (with Kwesi Yankah) *African Folklore: An Encyclopedia.*

Elisha P. Renne is Professor in the Department of Anthropology and the Center for Afroamerican and African Studies at the University of Michigan. She is author of *The Politics of Polio in Northern Nigeria* (Indiana University Press, 2010). Her research focuses on religion and textiles, reproductive health, and the anthropology of development in Nigeria.

Allen F. Roberts is Professor of World Arts and Cultures at the University of California, Los Angeles. He is author of *The Rising of a New Moon: A Century of Tabwa Art; Animals in African Art;* and (with Mary Nooter Roberts) *A Saint in the City: Sufi Arts of Urban Senegal.*

Mary Nooter Roberts is Professor in the Department of World Arts and Cultures at the University of California, Los Angeles. She is author (with Susan Vogel) of *Secrecy: African Art that Conceals and Reveals; Exhibition-ism: Museums and African Art;* and (with Allen F. Roberts) *Memory: Luba Art and the Making of History* and *Visions of Africa: Luba.*

Walter E. A. Van Beek is Senior Researcher at the African Studies Centre at Leiden University and Chair of Anthropology of Religion at Tilburg University. He is author of *The Dancing Dead* and has performed extensive research among the Kapsiki/Higi of the Cameroon/Nigerian border and among the Dogon of Mali.

Steven Van Wolputte is Assistant Professor of Social Sciences and Program Director in the Department of Social and Cultural Anthropology at the Katholieke Universiteit, Leuven, and was awarded a Fellowship at the Internationales Kolleg Morphomata, University of Cologne, for the winter of 2010–2011. He has published in the fields of medical anthropology, political anthropology, and the anthropology of material culture. His research interests include the anthropology of borders and frontiers, and the anthropology of secondary cities in Africa.

Index